The Essential Guide to Computer Hardware

ISBN 013062013-0

90000

9 780130 620132

Essential Guide Series

The Essential Guide to Computer Hardware

JIM KEOGH

Prentice Hall PTR, Upper Saddle River, NJ 07458
www.phptr.com

Library of Congress Cataloging-in-Publication Data

CIP date available.

Editorial/Production Supervision: *Mary Sudul*
Composition: *FASTpages*
Acquisitions Editor: *Michael E. Meehan*
Editorial Assistant: *Linda Ramagnano*
Manufacturing manager: *Maura Zaldivar*
Art Director: *Gail Cocker-Bogusz*
Interior Series Design: *Meg Van Arsdale*
Cover Design: *Bruce Kenselaar*
Cover Design Direction: *Jerry Votta*

© 2002 by Prentice Hall PTR
Prentice-Hall, Inc.
Upper Saddle River, NJ 07458

Prentice Hall books are widely used by corporations and government agencies for training,
marketing, and resale.

The publisher offers discounts on this book when ordered in bulk quantities. For more information,
contact Corporate Sales Department, phone: 800-382-3419; fax: 201-236-7141; email: corpsales@prenhall.com
Or write Corporate Sales Department, Prentice Hall PTR, One Lake Street, Upper Saddle River, NJ 07458.

Product and company names mentioned herein are the trademarks or registered trademarks
of their respective owners. The Electronic Commerce Game™ is a trademark of Object Innovations. Inc.

Printed in the United States of America

10 9 8 7 6 5 4 3 2 1

ISBN 0-13-062013-0

Pearson Education LTD.
Pearson Education Australia PTY, Limited
Pearson Education Singapore, Pte. Ltd
Pearson Education North Asia Ltd
Pearson Education Canada, Ltd.
Pearson Educación de Mexico, S.A. de C.V.
Pearson Education — Japan
Pearson Education Malaysia, Pte. Ltd
Pearson Education, Upper Saddle River, New Jersey

This book is dedicated to Anne, Sandra, and Joanne,
without whose help it could not have been written.

Contents

Preface

Were you ever part of a conversation discussing digital cameras, cell phones, and computer hardware—and you didn't know what everyone else was talking about? Don't feel embarrassed, because you're in the majority, at least until you finish reading this book. Then you'll be in the minority of those who fully understand how computer hardware works and are able to translate technical jargon into English for the majority of your friends.

Computer hardware technology is a paradox in that the technology is build on chips, circuits, and other components that are difficult to appreciate unless you are an engineer. And yet all computer technology is based on performing simple arithmetic using two digits—zero and one.

I've written this book for anyone who has the drive to learn about computer hardware, but who seems to develop a mental block when it comes to understanding computer technology.

Let's say that someone asks you how a cell phone transmits your voice to another cell phone. Since you haven't yet read this book, I'm going to assume that you're baffled. Would you still be baffled if I told you that a cell phone uses basically the same technology as you use to make waves in a bathtub? Probably not, because you've jumped into the tub and seen waves form. For now I'll simply say that a cell phone also generates waves but at a much faster rate than waves in the tub.

I've taken the complexity of computer technology and translated it into plain, simple, and easy to read and understand language. And as you read through this book and develop your own understanding of how computer hardware works, I think that you'll find I've met my goal.

I begin with basic science that you learned in grammar school that illustrates how an electronic signal is generated. Don't worry. I purposely left out any math problems. If you can turn a light switch on and off, then you'll do fine.

From there you'll follow a clear, straight path that leads you through the technology behind cell phones, ADPs, mobile devices, digital cameras, CD-ROM, hard disks, speech recognition, WebCams, networks, computer audio, computer video, workstations, and a rare look inside your computer. Your journey will be peppered with a few humorous stories that I picked up while I was writing this book.

The last few chapters are devoted to the business side of computer hardware, where I take you on a tour of the movers and shakers who decide how networks operate. You'll recognize a few of the companies as being those which are the pride of tech stock traders. However, many are not household names, yet have a dramatic role in computer hardware technologies. I'm sure anyone who has remotely followed tech stocks will enjoy this look at the computer hardware industry.

If you're a nontechnical person interested in learning more about computer hardware, then buy this book because it's the best way to learn about computer hardware without having to sift through technical stuff you don't need to know.

This book is perfect for anyone who is responsible for the administration of computer hardware for their organization or sales people, law firms, research organizations, marketing personnel, human resources professionals, project managers, networking managers, and high-level administrators.

Part 1

Technological Fundamentals

No doubt you've heard all the hype about the latest computer technology and listened to reports from Wall Street analysts on how tech stocks are hot—then not so hot. Probably you also realize that tech companies and analysts only provide you with information that they want you to have—and sometimes leave out information you need to know to become productive.

Throughout this book I'll provide you with information that helps blow away the advertising clutter to reveal technological details that will help you do your job. I've painstakingly avoided technology clutter that is likely to confuse and intimidate you because you don't need to explore the nerdy level of technology unless you want to become an engineer. And if that's the case you are probably reading the wrong book.

However, before learning about the latest computer features on the market and deciding whether or not they are right for you and your company, it is important to have a good grasp of basic concepts that are used in computer technology.

In Part 1, you'll begin building your knowledge of computer hardware from the ground up. We'll start with a brief history of computers. If the word *history* brought a yawn, then I'm sure that will be the last yawn you'll have until bedtime. The history that you'll stroll through in Chapter 1 has a mixture of "how did they do that?" and the competitive reasons that drove computer technology to where it is today.

In Chapter 2, you'll be given a cook's tour of a computer beginning with a cursory walk about the computer case. From there you'll be presented with an executive walk-through of how a computer works. You'll learn enough about a computer's operation that will enable you to appreciate the new technology features that I discuss throughout the book.

1 A Look Back

In this chapter...

- Nonelectronic Computers

- Electronic Computers

- Personal Computers

- Workstation Computers

- Graphical User Interface

- The Central Processor Revolution

"Pausing to look back helps one appreciate today's bounty."

Anonymous

Would you spend $1,000 for a computer with 8K of random access memory (RAM), a black-and-white monitor, and a keyboard? No, there aren't any typographical errors in my question. And, no, I didn't leave out any equipment. I rushed out and bought one and so did thousands of other computer nerds.

Back in the late 1970s, Tandy's TRS-80, affectionately known as the trash 80, was the hot computer of the day. (Tandy is the parent company of Radio Shack.) The computer itself was in the keyboard and the only permanent storage device was an audio-tape recorder—and that was unreliable.

Today no one, including a collector of historical computers, would pay $1,000 for such an underperforming computer that couldn't run even Windows 2.0. Yet, in its day, the TRS-80 was arguably using the leading PC technology.

We tend to take computer technology for granted. And those of us who lived through and participated in a small way in the computer revolution probably forgot what it was like to crank up the PC and spend the next several minutes trying to load a simple game program from an audio tape into the computer.

In this chapter, I'll jar a few memories of those who remember the not-so-good old days of early computers and for everyone else provide an entertaining and informative trip that will serve as a foundation to begin to learn about the inner workings of today's computer hardware. You'll learn the origins of:

- Mechanical computers

- Mainframe computers

- Minicomputers

- Personal computers

- Workstation computers

- Microprocessors

REALITY CHECK ....

Computers can be intimidating, as I discovered when my oldest daughter received her first high school English assignment. This was a time when computer training wasn't part of the daily routine in grammar schools.

Although computers have been in my home since before the IBM personal computer was introduced, my family considered computers a daddy thing. They probably referred to the computer as daddy's toy when I was out of earshot.

However, the English assignment quickly changed my family's attitude. My daughter needed an electric typewriter to write her English assignment. My arguments to use the word processor in my computer fell on deaf ears.

So we spent a couple of hundred dollars for an electronic typewriter and the necessary supplies—correction fluid, messy typewriter ribbons, and a dictionary for checking misspelled words. In fact the typewriter still exists today in my attic, nearly brand new and used for one English assignment.

The reality of using a typewriter soon became apparent to my daughter when she produced her first error-free page. It took her nearly an hour to do so. Then she inadvertently ripped the page when pulling it from the typewriter. From that day on the entire family used daddy's toy whenever they had to write a letter, do a report for school, or play a game. They simply cannot live a day without using a computer. It is safe to say that none of us ever want to go back to a time without computers.

NONELECTRONIC COMPUTERS ....

Now for a brief test: Define the term *computer*. Don't go racking your brain trying to compose an academic definition of a computer because I'm sure you know what a computer is . . . or should I say you can picture a computer in your mind.

For most of us a computer is the box that sits on our desk or on the floor or something we lug around on trips. Beyond that we probably haven't a notion of how a computer works and the meaning behind the advertising buzzwords that bombard us by those trying to sell us a computer. By the end of this book you'll be able to cut through the hype and know how modern computer hardware works—and be able to give computer sales representatives a run for their money.

For now think of a computer as a counting machine, a machine that can add, subtract, multiply, and divide numbers—and nothing more. Computers don't seem intimidating when you realize all a computer does is simple math that you learned in elementary school. Even acts performed by computers that seem to appear as near human intelligence are nothing more than grammar school math.

One of the functions of a computer that baffled me when I first began learning about computers in the TRS-80 days is how a computer knows when two things are the same or are different. You've seen this function performed when you enter an ID and password into a computer to access your corporation's network.

At first I thought comparisons involved some abstract scientific formula that was electronically embedded into a chip inside the computer. Then I learned how computers compared two things—by using subtraction.

Here is how this works. Information such as an ID and password are represented as numbers. I'll show you how this is done in the next chapter. The computer, following instructions from a programmer, subtracts the information entered into the keyboard from known information stored inside the computer.

Let's say my ID is 12345. This ID is stored in a database that contains my ID and other employees' IDs. The network administrator, the person responsible for the network, assigns IDs to all employees and enters them into the database. After I enter my ID when I log on to my company's computer network, the computer compares my ID against each ID stored in the database.

In this example, the first ID the computer comes across is 00001. The computer subtracts 12345 from 00001. The result is –12344. However, the computer cares only if the result is zero or not zero because a zero means the ID entered at the keyboard is the same as the ID in the database. A nonzero result means they are different.

In this case, the result is not zero. The ID I entered is different than the first ID in the database. When the computer tries the second ID in the database, which is 12345, the result of subtraction is zero (12345 – 12345 = 0). The IDs match.

Computers Are Not Electronic

I will bet that when I asked you to define a computer you envisioned some type of box filled with electronic components. If so, then you are in the majority of people who associate computers with electronic devices. Actually a computer is anything that can help us count.

Fingers and toes are the computers I (and probably you) used when I taught my daughters how to count. At first glance, these digits may not seem sophisticated since the maximum value that can be counted using your hands is ten. Yet that is not entirely true because it depends on how you represent numbers with those digits.

Time for another quiz. What is the maximum number that you can count with your fingers? You don't need to use any of your lifelines because I'll give you the answer. The answer is 30. Puzzled? Here's how this is done.

Each time you finish counting digits on your right hand, hold up a digit on your left hand. Begin counting again on your right hand. Each digit on your left hand represents five for a total of 25. You still have five fingers on your right hand extended when you finish counting. This gives you a combined total of 30.

This is more than a dinner table trick because it demonstrates the basic concept of number places that was used in the original mechanical computing device called the abacus. The abacus consists of rows of 10 beads each. Each row represents a number place (see Figure 1-1).

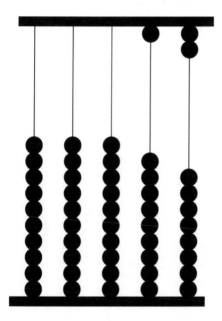

Figure 1-1
An abacus is an ancient mechanical computer that used beads to represent digits of a number

Tech Talk
Abacus: The first computer that used rows of beads to assist in adding and subtracting numbers.

In 3000 B.C., the abacus was used as a way of extending the use of fingers as a counting tool. The first row in the abacus is similar to our right hand and the second row takes the place of our left hand in our example. However, instead of five digits the abacus uses ten beads. And instead of two hands, the abacus has many rows.

Fundamentally the process is the same. The count begins by moving each bead from one end of the row to the other end. When all the beads are at the other end of the row, one bead in the next row is moved to the other end of the second row. All the beads in the first row are returned to their original starting position and the beads are counted again. Subtraction is also possible with an abacus by moving the beads in the opposite direction that you moved them when adding numbers together.

A merchant who is proficient using the abacus can be stiff competition for anyone who is using an electronic calculator. The merchant can zip through moving the beads long before the calculator is powered up and the first numbers entered into the keyboard.

The Illusive Dream

While the abacus was an improvement over the fingers, it still left much to be desired, especially when there was a need to perform complex calculations in science and business. A more efficient machine was required.

Leonardo da Vinci was one of the first to recognize this need. In the 16th century, da Vinci drew the first plans for a mechanical calculator that could perform addition and subtraction. However, he never lived long enough to see those plans become reality.

It wasn't until the 17th century that a mechanical adding machine was developed. And we can thank the tax collector for this marvel. Actually, it was the tax collector's son, Blaise Pascal, a French mathematician who designed and built the first working adding machine called the Pascaline. Pascal built the Pascaline (see Figure 1-2) to help his father collect taxes.

Although the French taxpayers may not have been pleased by the efficiency the Pascaline gave to collecting taxes, the Pascaline did prove to the world that a machine could add and subtract faster and more accurately than people.

The Pascaline used a similar concept as the abacus. However, instead of beads, the Pascaline used a series of wheels interlocked with gears. Each wheel had 10 digits (0 through 9) displayed on the wheel. When the first wheel reached past nine and returned to zero, the second wheel moved to one. A similar effect occurred for each wheel.

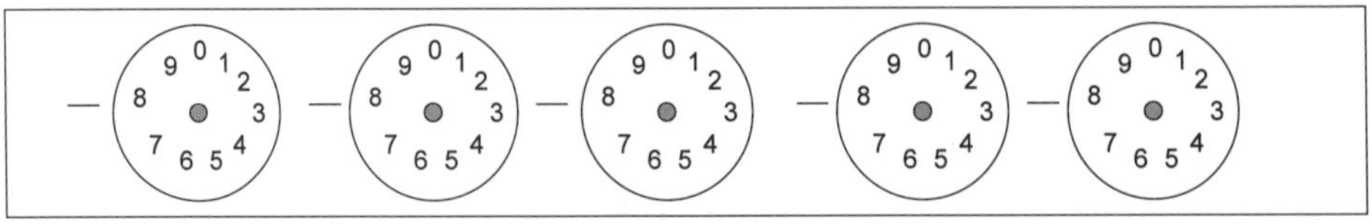

Figure 1-2
The Pascaline used interlocking gears to reproduce the basic functionality used in the abacus

Tech Talk

Pascaline: The first working mechanical computer that could add and subtract. It was designed by Blaise Pascal.

Pascal surely impressed his father, but the Pascaline couldn't overcome a major hurdle that still faces the computing industry. That is, the early versions of any computer are very costly and are not seen as cost-effective.

The Pascaline was hand built and not durable for the daily ordeal of tax collecting. In fact only the inventor himself could keep the Pascaline running when it broke down. The cost of building and maintaining the Pascaline adding machine was dramatically more costly than hiring additional clerks to perform math by hand.

The Pascaline may not have been a business success but it paved the way for the success of computing. The concepts developed by Pascal were used in every mechanical computing device until the middle of the 1960s.

With improvements in manufacturing, the Pascaline gave birth to assorted mechanical adding machines that were widely used in universities, business, and government in the 18th century. However, these machines were limited to addition and subtraction and were unable to handle the sophisticated calculations that were needed to drive the Industrial Revolution in the 19th century.

These calculations required several steps and involved addition and subtraction as well as multiplication and division of very large and very small numbers such as required by bankers when creating a repayment schedule.

In those days, mathematicians created calculation tables that reduced the number of calculations a banker or scientist had to perform by hand. For example, a calculation table (see Figure 1-3) might have the interest payments for a series of interest rates based on one dollar of principal. A banker looked up the table for the appropriate interest paid for a specific interest rate, then manually multiplied the interest payment by the number of dollars in principal of the loan.

Figure 1-3 This table contains the interest payment for a dollar at various interest rates and was used as a way to speed calculations

Years	6%	8%
1	1.060000	1.080000
2	1.123600	1.166400
3	1.191016	1.259712
4	1.262477	1.360489

Calculation tables increase the efficiency of bankers, but calculation tables were not without errors. Calculation tables were created by hand and were error prone. There was still a need for a machine that could perform complex calculations without errors.

Charles Babbage expanded Pascal's concept of wheels and gears and designed a mechanical computer that could also multiply and divide as well as add and subtract. The machine was called the Difference Engine and the Analytical Engine.

Tech Talk

Difference Engine and the Analytical Engine: The first mechanical computer that was designed to add, subtract, multiply, and divide, but was never commercially built. Principles used in this computer are still found in modern electronic computers.

As with the Pascaline, Babbage's design never got off the ground because of cost and the lack of technology to build the engine. The design called for thousands of wheels and gears powered by a railroad engine. Babbage's mechanical computer would have been the size of a football field—and could perform 60 addition calculations per second. Babbage's design, however, did become the foundation of today's general computer.

Can You Repeat That?

Pascal and Babbage gave birth to mechanical computers that could perform calculations, but that's only part of the historic development of computing. People had to perform each calculation themselves rather than having the computer automatically perform repeating calculations.

Let's say that you wanted to create an identification code that used 10 letters (A through J). How many individual codes can you create using 10 letters? You can answer this question by multiplying 9 times. Here's how it's done.

Multiply 10 × 10, then multiply the product by 9. Multiply that product by 8 and continue the process until you multiply the final product by 1. Mathematicians call this factorial. The answer is there are 3,628,800 combinations that can be made using 10 letters.

Tech Talk

Factorial: A mathematical formula used to determine the number of unique combinations of a set of objects such as letters of the alphabet.

You'd need to perform nine separate calculations if you used a mechanical calculator based on Babbage's concept. This wasn't efficient because the mechanical calculator could not repeatedly multiply results on its own.

In this example, it would be nice to enter the number of letters in the identification code (10), then press a button that instructs the calculator to automatically determine the number of combinations.

Today's computers and calculators perform factorial calculations and other similar repeating calculations nearly automatically because those devices store instructions. One of the many challenges facing 19th century inventors was to devise a way for a mechanical calculator to repeat instructions automatically.

The answer loomed in the loom. Joseph-Marie Jacquard, a French weaver at the turn of the 19th century, inadvertently solved this computing problem. Jacquard developed a loom that used holes in cards to control the operation of the loom. Holes punched into a card directed the loom to create a specific design. Each new design required a new card with holes punched according to the design requirements.

The loom could re-create any design automatically as long as Jacquard inserted the corresponding punch card. Although Jacquard's objective was to run the loom longer hours and employ workers with less skill—and less pay—than weavers could work and get paid, Jacquard inadvertently found the solution to having a mechanical calculator repeat instructions automatically.

It wasn't until later in the 19th century that Jacquard's invention was considered applicable to mechanical calculators. Lady Ada Lovelance, a mentor to Babbage, was the first to put forward the idea of using punch cards to instruct a mechanical calculator. Although Babbage's computer never became fully operational, the idea of using punch cards to instruct mechanical—and later electronic—computers was later a success.

Lovelance's place in computer history was firmly established when the U.S. Department of Defense named one of its first programming languages—Ada—after her. Many consider Lovelance the first programmer.

Tech Talk

Programming language: A set of words recognized by a computer and used to instruct a computer to perform specific tasks.

It wasn't until almost the turn of the 20th century that punch cards took center stage—but it was the railroad and not Lovelance that provided the inspiration. However, punch cards were first used to store information, not instructions.

Tech Talk

Information: One or more words that are used to describe something.

The U.S. Bureau of the Census needed an efficient way to count people. Herman Hollerith decided punch cards and a punch card reading machine was the answer and won a bid to count the population.

Hollerith invented the punched card tabulating machine based partly on the way tickets were punched by railroad conductors. The railroad devised a clever system to catch would-be fare cheats. A railroad ticket was preprinted with characteristics of their customers such as gender, hair color, eye color, etc. Railroad conductors punched out on the ticket the characteristics that described the customer before giving the customer the ticket. The tickets were called a punched photograph.

Census takers punched specially designed punch cards for the Bureau of the Census that described a person. Hollerith created an electrically (not electronically) operated machine that read and sorted the punch cards and tabulating dials that summarized the count based on characteristics of each person.

If Only I Invested in TMC

Hollerith founded one of the first successful computer manufacturing and servicing companies, the Tabulating Machine Company (TMC). TMC was built on Hollerith's success with the census and gradually branched out to service the business community.

TMC later evolved into the Computer-Tabulating-Recording Company with the merger of TMC and complimentary businesses a decade into the 20th century. By 1924 the company again had a makeover. This time the Computer-Tabulating-Recording Company was renamed the International Business Machines Corporation (IBM).

The first half of the 20th century is the era of the electro-mechanical accounting machine, which was the improved version of Hollerith's original tabulating computer. The electro-mechanical accounting machine built by IBM consisted of eight separate components: an accounting machine, card punch, collator, interpreter, reproducer, sorter, summary punch, and verifier.

Each component was a separate machine that performed specific instructions using data that was recorded on thousands of punch cards. Instructions used to control the electro-mechanical accounting machine were programmed by inserting prewired control panels into each component.

Programmers in that era didn't learn computer languages as they do today. Instead, they plugged wires called patch wires into holes on each component's control panel based on the task that the programmer wanted the machine to perform.

There were no disk drives, tape drives, floppy disks, or computer networks in those days. Instead a machine room operator had to carry thousands of punch cards encoded with data from component to component. And the whole process came crashing down if the pile of punch cards was dropped.

ELECTRONIC COMPUTERS ....

As IBM was providing computing services to governments and businesses using its electro-mechanical accounting machine, a professor and his graduate student at Iowa State University took a unique approach to computing. Instead of using an electro-mechanical technology, they used the new electronic technology.

Dr. John Atanasoff and his student Clifford Berry spent seven years developing an electronic computer to aid students in performing complex physics calculations. They hit many roadblocks along the way. It wasn't until the winter of 1937 that the plan came together over a late night drink in an Illinois tavern.

Atanasoff and Berry figured out how to use vacuum tubes (see "Inside Vacuum Tubes and Transistors") and other electronic components to form logic circuits (equivalent to the central processing unit [CPU] in today's computer) and memory (see Figure 1-4). They also figured out how to use the binary numbering system (see "Computers Count to Two") to represent data and instructions.

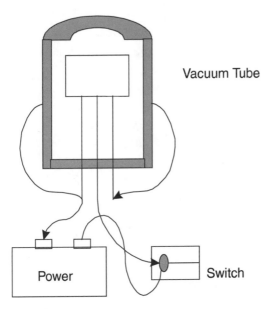

Figure 1-4
A vacuum tube is an electronic switch that redirects the flow of electricity using a charged plate

Tech Talk

Vacuum Tube: An electronic switch that uses a charged plate to change the flow of electricity in a circuit.

By 1942, they had a working prototype called the Atanasoff Berry Computer (ABC), which was the first automatic electronic digital computer and the beginning of the electronic computer revolution.

There were two major blunders. First, neither Iowa State University nor Atanasoff and Berry patented the ABC computer. This not only had obvious financial repercussions, it failed to document Atanasoff and Berry's discovery. Decades of legal battles over who is credited with inventing the electronic computer finally culminated in 1973 when the courts ruled that Atanasoff invented the automatic electronic digital computer.

IBM made the second blunder. Atanasoff tried in vain to interest IBM in ABC computing technology. IBM's response: "IBM will never be interested in an electronic computing machine." I guess you can never say never.

COMPUTERS COUNT TO TWO

You've probably heard the term binary used whenever anyone talks about the zeros and ones used to represent data inside a computer. Binary refers to a mathematical system used to count and perform math functions very similar to the method we use to balance our checking account.

Let's take the mystery out of binary math by first reviewing our common system of mathematics called the decimal system. Our system contains 10 digits—zero through nine—which is referred to as base 10 because there are 10 digits before we must carry over a value.

When we reach the ninth digit, we carry over one value, which gives us 10. Notice the right-most digit is 0, the digit we started with. We count sequentially and when we reach 19—notice the right-most digit is 9—we carry over another value to give us 20.

A similar process occurs within the binary system except it contains only two digits—zero and one. Counting begins with 0 just like in the decimal system, but a value is carried over when the value reaches two because there isn't a digit 2 in the binary system.

Let's say we wanted to write the value two in decimal. We simply use the digit 2. However, we'd write 10 to represent the same value in binary. No, this is not 10, although it resembles the value 10 in decimal.

Here's how it works. We begin counting with 0. Remember, this is binary so we must stop counting when the right-most digit reaches 1, then carry over a value and reset the right digit to 0.

COMPUTERS COUNT TO TWO (CONTINUED)

Don't feel embarrassed if you are confused by binary math. This baffles even computer science majors until they become use to dealing with the concept of using two digits instead of 10. However, there is a reason computer scientist settled on binary math when dealing with computers.

Computers manipulate information by performing addition and subtraction on data stored inside the computer. Remember, data is represented by a setting of eight switches and each switch can be on or off. Sometimes more than eight switches are used, but don't concern yourself with that right now.

Binary math lends itself to representing the state of a switch and enables standard mathematical operations to be performed on those values. You can perform the same math using binary values that can be performed using our decimal values.

First Generation of Computers

Atanasoff and Berry's work became the foundation for Dr. John Mauchly's efforts in 1946 to solve a perplexing problem for the military—the creation of accurate trajectory tables. Errors in trajectory tables caused bombing mistakes during World War II. Eighty percent of the bombs came outside of 1,000 feet of their targets.

Mauchly and his associates at the University of Pennsylvania developed a vacuum tube-based computer called the Electronic Numerical Integrator and Computer (ENIAC) that dramatically increased the accuracy of trajectory tables.

ENIAC was the fastest computer available and performed 500 multiplication calculations and 5,000 addition calculations per minute using 18,000 vacuum tubes. The ENIAC weighed 30 tons and took up almost an entire floor of an office building. Lights in Philadelphia dimmed whenever the ENIAC was working.

Although the ENIAC advanced computer technology appreciably, some computer technology historians believe Mauchly made one blunder. Instead of using the base-2 binary numbering system as Atanasoff and Berry did, Mauchly used the base-10 decimal numbering system.

Tech Talk

Base-10 numbering system: A system of numbers that uses 10 digits from zero to nine. This is commonly called the decimal system and is the prevalent system used in everyday counting.

The base-10 numbering system didn't compromise the accuracy of the ENIAC results. It did, however, require the use of more vacuum tubes to represent numeric values. For example, 10 vacuum tubes were required to represent the number one in the ENIAC. One vacuum tube represented the same value in the ABC computer using the base-2 (binary) numbering system.

Neither the ABC nor the ENIAC computer was designed for commerce. The ABC computer was used to help students at Iowa State University with complex physics problems, and ENIAC created computerized trajectory tables for the military.

It wasn't until 1951 that the first commercially available electronic digital computer was introduced and formally began the first generation of computers. Mauchly and his associates at the University of Pennsylvania were enlisted by the Remington-Rand Corporation to develop the Universal Automatic Computer, better known as the UNIVAC 1.

UNIVAC 1 was quickly put to work counting the 1951 census, but was more widely known projecting results of the Presidential election early on election night. With only 5 percent of the votes counted, UNIVAC 1 awarded the election to Dwight Eisenhower. The projection was broadcast by CBS News, which was the first media outlet to introduce computer technology into the average home four years after Chuck Yeager broke the sound barrier.

The UNIVAC 1 was also a wake-up call for IBM. Electronic computer technology proved to be a commercial success with many a high-profile business demanding to have its own UNIVAC 1. IBM saw the handwriting on the wall—and the profits to be made in the commercial electronic computer market.

In 1954, fewer than 50 large corporations and government agencies employed IBM's punch card–based computers to help manage their operations. This was the size of the commercial computer market. IBM sought to capitalize on its existing customer base by designing an electronic computer that became a natural upgrade for its customers. The computer was called the IBM 650.

IBM expected 50 sales of the IBM 650. IBM made 1,000 sales and the first wave of the commercial computer revolution had begun.

Saving Grace

The first-generation computers were the first to use electronic instructions that didn't involve prewired panels. You'll recognize these electronic instructions as programs. Prewired panel programming was on its way out and a more convenient punch card program took its place.

Tech Talk

Program: A set of instructions that tells a computer how to process information.

Programmers encoded their instructions for the computer onto punch cards that could be read by the computer. A common problem of the day was that there wasn't a standard programming language that could be used across various models of computers. This meant that programmers needed to specialize in writing programs for a particular make and possibly model of computer.

This didn't make sense to Grace Hopper, who was involved with computer systems for the Department of the Navy. She set out to streamline the task of writing a program and became the catalyst that created the first standard programming language called Common Business-Oriented Language (COBOL).

Here's how her idea worked. Consider that each computer is like a country that has its own language. The language is used to instruct the computer on how to process information such as what numbers to add together.

Let's say one computer understood instructions written in French and another computer understood instructions in German. Of course French and German are not computer languages, but I'll pretend that they are so you can easily understand the problem and Hopper's solution.

If you were to have both computers add two numbers, you would need to write instructions in French and rewrite instructions in German. Hopper and most of the computer industry at that time thought this wasted the programmer's time.

Hopper's solution was to create a third language that every programmer would learn. She called it COBOL. No computer understood the COBOL language, which was fine. However, Hopper and her associates created a special program called a compiler that translated the COBOL language into a language understood by each computer.

Tech Talk

Compiler: A program that translates an English-like programming language into the unique language of each model computer.

A programmer who wanted to instruct a computer to add two numbers needed only to write these instructions in COBOL, then have a compiler translate COBOL instructions into the computer's language, the results of which could be run on the appropriate computer.

Hopper's idea revolutionized the way computer instructions were written. COBOL later gave way to other programming languages such as FORTRAN, C, C++, and Java, all of which use the same basic principle: Translate a standardize set of instructions into a set of computer specific instructions.

Hopper has another claim to fame in computer history. She was the first person to coin the term "bug" to describe a computer malfunction. One of her computers was producing questionable results. She investigated and discovered a moth in a relay in the computer. Hopper removed the "bug" and the computer worked fine from then on.

Relay: A switch that is turned on and off electrically.

Second Generation of Computers

A new generation of computers was ushered in as the ball dropped in Times Square to welcome 1960. The monster size computers of the first generation that used energy-hungry vacuum tubes and required enormous cooling systems gave way to trimmer, more efficient, and less expensive second-generation computers.

This was all made possible by the invention of the transistor at Bell Laboratories in New Jersey. Transistors replaced vacuum tubes as the electronic switches (see Figure 1-5) used to store and process data (see "Inside Vacuum Tubes and Transistors").

Transistor: A silicon-based device that performs as an electronic switch.

Transistors were tiny compared to vacuum tubes and could be manufactured faster with higher quality control because, among other reasons, they had fewer parts than a vacuum tube. The slim size of a transistor enabled more electronic switches to be placed inside a second-generation computer than the number of vacuum tubes that could fit into a first-generation computer. This meant more processing power.

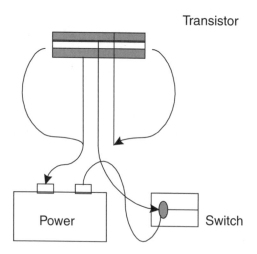

Figure 1-5
A transistor uses the properties of silicon to become an electronic switch

Computers were still pricey, ranging from a few hundred thousand to upward of a million dollars in 1960 dollars. Although the price still placed computers out of reach for most medium and small businesses, an increasing number of larger businesses found computers affordable.

The market for computers was expanding and so was competition. IBM now faced challenges from Honeywell, UNIVAC, Burroughs, and NCR, among others. Each was staking claim to a piece of the computer market.

First- and second-generation computers were mainframe computers. But that began to change in 1963, just around the time when the Beatles were taking over the American music industry. That was when a smaller version of the mainframe computer called the minicomputer was introduced.

As the name implies, a minicomputer was to some degree a scaled-down version of a mainframe computer in size, power, and price. For around $20,000 in 1963 dollars a business could harness the power of a computer to run a portion of its operation.

Digital Equipment Corporation was the first computer maker to successfully claim a major piece of the growing demand for minicomputers with the introduction of the PDP-8 minicomputer. Data General and 20 or so other manufacturers soon joined the revolution by the early 1970s.

INSIDE VACUUM TUBES AND TRANSISTORS

A computer is a box of electronic switches that are connected to form logical circuits. Information is stored in a computer by setting one or a series of switches a certain way, very similar to a two-way light switch.

You can set the light switch on or off and each of these settings can have a different meaning. For example, in my household we turn on the outside light by the front door until everyone arrives home for the evening, at which time we turn off the light. Anyone knowing this rule can determine if the entire family is home or if at least one member of the family is not home by seeing if the light is on or off.

Each setting of a switch inside a computer is associated with a binary value. A switch in the off state represents a zero and in the on state represents a one. And by grouping switches a computer can store information such as numbers, letters, data, and instructions, which you'll learn more about in the next chapter.

INSIDE VACUUM TUBES AND TRANSISTORS (CONTINUED)

First-generation computers used vacuum tubes as electronic switches. Second-generation computers and their successors used transistor technology for the same purpose. A transistor looks like a three-legged spider. Conceptually transistors were miniaturized and placed on integrated and large integrated circuits.

A vacuum tube and a transistor work very similarly. Each has at least three wires. Let's called them A, B, and C. When the switch is closed (on), electricity flows from wire A to wire C. When the switch is open (off), no electricity flows between these wires.

When electricity flows through wire B, the connection between wire A and wire C is broken. That is, the switch is open. However, the switch is closed when electricity doesn't flow through wire B.

Engineers are able to connect wires from other electronic switches to form a logic circuit that uses the setting of one switch to change the setting of one or more other switches.

There are vast numbers of logic circuits built into various chips inside a computer, and designing those circuits has gotten so complex as to require a computer to design the circuits. You could say that computers are now designing and building computers with engineers becoming involved in the higher design level.

Third and Fourth Generation of Computers

Computer technology doesn't stand still for very long. It seems that every five years or less advances in technology quickly antiquate existing technology. Case in point occurred in the mid-1960s when second-generation computer technology based on transistors became outdated with the invention of integrated circuits. Hundreds of transistors that populated second-generation computer circuit boards, making them look like little cities, were now reduced to a circuit the size of a pin head.

Tech Talk

Integrated circuit: A computer chip that contains many microscopic transistors connected together with the wires etched into the chip.

Integrated circuits enabled computer manufacturers to build smaller, more powerful, and less expensive computers. The power of many ABC computers that once filled a floor of an office building was now available on the head of a pin in the form of an integrated circuit.

IBM became one of the major computer manufacturers that was quick to incorporate integrated circuits into its computers, the first of which was the IBM System 360. The IBM System 360 was a family of computers that set a high standard for commercial computers.

Integrated circuits and a strategic plan enabled IBM to offer customers computer power that made it uneconomical to continue using second-generation computers. IBM's plan centered on the expectation that advances in computer technology will continue to make existing computers out of date.

IBM introduced the concept of upward compatibility, something that wasn't heard of in the computer industry until then. Today we call this backward compatibility. Customers simply didn't have the time or finances to re-create their programs and data each time computer technology changed and made their existing computers obsolete.

Engineers at IBM assured customers that beginning with the IBM System 360 all new IBM computers would use the same programs and data with little or no modification. This promise plus the vast leap integrated circuits gave to computer technology encouraged many IBM customers to abandon their existing computers for the IBM System 360.

In 1971, two years after Apollo 11 landed on the moon, another evolution of computer technology was born with the onset of large-scale integrated circuits. Engineers were now able to increase the number of transistors that could be placed on an integrated circuit.

Tech Talk

Large-scale integrated circuits: A chip that contains many integrated circuits.

Large-scale integrated circuits technology enabled an entire computer circuitry to be placed on one computer chip. This followed the trend set by previous generations, making computers ever more powerful and smaller at very affordable prices.

PERSONAL COMPUTERS ....

It's hard for most of us to fathom a time when there weren't personal computers. However, personal computers didn't join the computer evolution until 1975 with the introduction of the Altair 8800 personal computer on the cover of *Popular Electronics*.

The Altair hardly resembled today's personal computers. It didn't have a disk drive or any of the other features that we expect to find on a personal computer. In fact, the Altair wasn't designed for consumers. Electronic hobbyists, people who enjoyed building radios and other electronic gizmos, were the target audience.

The Altair was a diamond in the rough, and four young men set out in the same year to cut that diamond into their own design. They were Bill Gates, Paul Allen, Steven Jobs, and Steve Wozniak. Gates and Allen formed Microsoft while Jobs and Wozniak launched Apple Computer.

Although Gates, Allen, Jobs, and Wozniak are the names most recognized as pioneers of personal computers, there were many others, such as Tandy Corporation's TRS-80, which I spoke about at the beginning of this chapter; the Atari Commodore; and the Osborne Computer, which became the first all-in-one transportable personal computer.

Early PCs suffered from a problem similar to those of early mainframe computers: Each PC understood instructions written in its own language. Simply stated, a program written for the TRS-80 couldn't run on an Apple computer and vice versa.

As you'll learn in the next chapter, a computer is nothing more than a box of electronic switches. A special set of programs called an operating system such as Windows brings the computer to life by turning switches on and off based on a set of instructions by programmers who wrote the operating system.

Tech Talk

Operating system: A set of programs that operate the computer hardware and interfaces between the computer user and the computer hardware.

The TRS-80 and the Osborne Computer used a variation of an operating system called CP/M, and Apple Computer used the Applesoft operating system. Notice that I didn't mention DOS because DOS arrived in 1981. More about this in a minute.

Personal computers needed to adopt Grace Hopper's concept of a standardized programming language. Two professors at Dartmouth College, Dr. Thomas Kurtz and Dr. John Kemeny, developed the BASIC programming language.

BASIC enables programmers to write instructions in a standard language that could be translated into specific machine languages for each type of computer. Gates built on Kurtz's and Kemeny's work and developed a version of BASIC that ran on personal computers.

Although commercial programs of the day such as word processing and very simple games were still written in machine specific language, other more customizable programs were written in BASIC.

About 800,000 computers were sold by 1981 with Tandy and Apple Computer taking the lion's share of the market. Then the market changed. IBM decided to join the fray—and made one of the biggest blunders in the history of computers.

The IBM Gambit

IBM again saw the handwriting on the wall. Personal computers were small and relatively powerful computing devices that were slowly finding their way on the desktops of corporations. Actually, very few corporations purchased personal computers because there were few business-oriented programs and even fewer employees who knew how to use a personal computer.

In the late 1970s, I worked for Volkswagen of America, the North American arm of the German car manufacturer. I also owned one of the first TRS-80s. At that time, my attic was more computerized in terms of personal computers than Volkswagen of America. I created a pricing model on the TRS-80 that was used by Volkswagen of America to determine optimum pricing. Paper, pencils, and a calculator were used for pricing until that time. Spreadsheets hadn't been developed yet.

In 1981, IBM handed Gates and Allen the multibillion dollar lottery ticket. IBM needed an operating system for the new IBM personal computer. After failed attempts to acquire the CP/M operating system, they visited Gates, who was already known in this fledging industry because of his development of BASIC for personal computers, and asked if he had an operating system.

Gates and his associates said yes when in reality the answer was no. Gates knew someone who created an enhanced version of the CP/M operating system and called it DOS. Gates quickly purchased DOS for $50,000, then cut a deal that IBM has been kicking itself ever since.

Instead of selling DOS to IBM, Gates licensed DOS to IBM. The license gave IBM the rights to install DOS on its personal computers in exchange for a per-unit charge. Furthermore, the license was nonexclusive. This meant that Gates and his company received a piece of every personal computer sold by IBM and retained the right to license DOS to other competing computer manufacturers—which they did.

IBM's management thought this was a good deal because they considered personal computers ancillary to their existing mainframe business. In keeping with that idea IBM dug itself deeper into a financial hole by changing their design philosophy.

Computers made by IBM, until the IBM personal computer was introduced, were considered closed systems. That is, no manufacturer except IBM made components for IBM computers. Customers could have any feature they wanted for their IBM computer as long as they purchased it from IBM.

This gave IBM a near-monopoly on the mainframe computer industry because of their market share and the closed-system design philosophy. It was commonly said among corporate computer managers that no one every got fired for buying IBM computers.

IBM moved to an open-system philosophy when it came to the IBM personal computer. IBM freely shared specifications for their IBM personal computer with component manufacturers in hopes of minimizing their investment and risk by encouraging other manufacturers to enhance the features of the IBM personal computer.

Customers who purchased an IBM personal computer had the option of upgrading by buying additional hardware from IBM or from a third party. Third-party computer component manufacturers were quick to rise to the occasion in anticipation that IBM personal computers would become the industry standard.

What IBM Didn't Anticipate

When IBM release the technical specifications for the IBM personal computer to the industry, they practically gave away the design for their personal computer. Many third-party component manufacturers stopped making IBM personal computer compatible components. They made computers that were practically the same as the IBM personal computer. We know these today as IBM PC clones.

Manufacturers were able to modify the IBM's personal computer design sufficiently to avoid patent violations and still enable the computers to use IBM or third-party components.

IBM soon realized that the deal with Microsoft wasn't a smart move. Clone manufacturers rushed to Microsoft and licensed the DOS operating system for use in their computers. Technically IBM used Microsoft's PC-DOS and the clone manufacturers used Microsoft's MS-DOS. Although the name implies two different operating systems, PC-DOS and MS-DOS were basically the same.

This meant that IBM PC clones looked and acted just like an IBM personal computer and could run any program that could be run on an IBM PC. One of the main differences between the IBM personal computer and a clone was the price. Clones were sold at a much lower price than the IBM product, yet delivered the same quality and computing power.

And I can't leave out the fact that now Microsoft received compensation for every personal computer sold except for Apple computers. This didn't matter much because Apple's market share never reached beyond 10 percent of the personal computer market.

Corporations gradually became convinced that personal computers had a place in the business community; they were no longer just a hobby. IBM's endorsement of personal computer technology was a major catalyst in adopting PCs for business use.

Likewise, IBM defined the standard for personal computers. Soon computers such as the TRS-80 and the Osborne fell to the pressure of IBM. Apple Computer felt the pressure, too, but was and remains able to hold on to a share of the market.

Software: The Key to Success

Even IBM realized that there wouldn't be much of a market for personal computers in business unless there was software that could streamline business operations. There was a need for a killer application, an application that businesses couldn't live without. And the killer application for the personal computer was Lotus 1-2-3.

In the same year IBM launched the IBM personal computer, Mitchell Kapor created an enhanced version of the first spreadsheet program called VisiCalc. Kapor called his spreadsheet Lotus 1-2-3, which was designed to run on an IBM PC. Lotus 1-2-3 was just what IBM needed to entice businesses to purchase its product.

Personal computer programming was in its infancy. Corporations immediately found Lotus 1-2-3 a revolutionary business tool. Around the same time word processing software such as Word Star expanded the use of a personal computer and practically replaced the office typewriter.

Just as the IBM PC was gaining a foothold in the business community, I had the opportunity to help introduce personal computer programming to the technology community in my Programmer's Notebook column that appeared in *Popular Electronics*, the same publication that introduced the Altair (see "Personal Computers").

Soon the business community realized the personal computer was more than a computerized typewriter and electronic spreadsheet. With the right software, PCs could handle many of the routine, small computation and data processing jobs that were processed by mainframe computer systems.

WORKSTATION COMPUTERS ....

IBM, Digital Equipment Corporation, and other established computer manufacturers didn't see personal computers as a threat to their central line of business—mainframe computers and minicomputers. Personal computers at that time were simply underpowered and lacked connectivity to each other to make an impact in the mainframe and minicomputer market. In those days, there weren't any computer networks, as we know them today.

This would change in 1982, Sun Microsystems introduced the first workstation. Today the term *workstation* has many meanings from any computing device such as a personal computer that is used to perform your primary work to a particular class of computers.

However, the term *workstation* back in 1982 was used for a new kind of computer, a computer that was based on the reduced instruction set computer (RISC) technology developed by John Cocke in 1980. Sun Microsystems positioned the workstation to capture the market segment held by minicomputers and low-end mainframe computers.

RISC requires fewer instructions to process the same amount of information as non-RISC computers. Personal computers did not use RISC. Workstations were capable of processing information more efficiently than minicomputers and at less cost.

The industry began to feel the pressure of this new wave of computers with the introduction of the SPARCstation™ 1 in 1989. The SPARCstation™ 1 was the size of a pizza box and was quickly adopted by major Wall Street firms such as Salomon, Inc., as its computer of choice for running mission-critical database applications. IBM and other computer manufactures soon followed with their own entries into the workstation market.

Tech Talk

Mission-critical database applications: Computer programs that manage data that is important to a business. The business would stop running if a mission-critical database application stopped running.

UNIX: A computer operating system that can manage multiple users and multiple applications using the computer at the same time.

Proprietary operating system: A computer OS that was specifically designed for a particular computer and not made available for use with other computers.

Various versions of UNIX were developed at universities and research labs but it never gained a wide commercial acceptance until Sun Microsystems adopted the UNIX operating system as the OS for its workstations.

Sun Microsystems created its own version of UNIX called Solaris. IBM followed suit calling its UNIX version AIX. Except for workstations and PCs, other computers such as mainframe computers used a proprietary operating system.

Sun Microsystems workstations later became a computer of choice for specialty applications such as computer animation for Hollywood. In 1995, Sun Microsystems workstations were used to create Disney's *Toy Story*, which is the first all computer–generated feature film. This was the same year that Sun Microsystems introduced the Java programming language.

Tech Talk

Java: The first universal software language designed for use on the Internet and corporate intranets that enables programmers to write an application once that can be run without modification on any computer.

GRAPHICAL USER INTERFACE ....

Until the mid-1980s personal computers were not user friendly. Anyone who used a PC needed to learn special commands since the personal computer presented only a prompt (c:>) on the screen.

This became imposing for many people who soon believed that special skills were required to put the personal computer through its paces. Gates, Allen, Jobs, and Wozniak realized this problem early on and began looking for a solution. The solution resided at the Xerox research center.

Xerox engineers designed a primitive graphical user interface (GUI) that used a mouse in addition to a keyboard, enabling a person to interact with the computer's operating system. No longer was the user presented with a prompt and had to learn special commands.

Tech Talk

Graphical user interface: A method of enabling users to interact with the computer using small graphic images called icons rather than typing commands at a prompt.

In the face of objections from a number of Xerox engineers, the company invited Gates, Allen, Jobs, and Wozniak, among other technologists, to see a demonstration of their user interface. This group was more than casual observers. They took notes, asked questions, and learned how the GUI worked.

Jobs and Wozniak saw the GUI as a way to make their personal computers compete against the IBM PC. In 1984, Jobs and Wozniak introduced their new Apple computer that was designed to take advantage of their own GUI, which was based on technology observed at Xerox. The computer was called the Macintosh, and it was a hit.

IBM depended on Microsoft for DOS and DOS was not a graphical user interface. Microsoft rushed to create its own GUI and introduced Microsoft Windows in 1985. However, the early version of Windows wasn't everything customers expected. Windows wasn't fully integrated into the operating system.

Windows was simply another program running in DOS, a program that required more personal computer resources than other programs. Windows required a faster PC with much more memory than was available on the average IBM personal computer. Windows was ahead of its time and had to wait until hardware improvements caught up.

Apple didn't have this problem because of several unique situations. First, Apple's GUI ran on a new computer. The company didn't try to retrofit the existing Apple II computers to run the GUI.

Also, Apple Computer controlled both the GUI and the design and manufacturing of the Macintosh. Microsoft had to build around the existing IBM personal computer limitations. Furthermore, the GUI was fully integrated into the Macintosh operating system, something Microsoft didn't do. These factors gave Apple the edge.

Another problem that faced Microsoft and IBM was complications involved in writing a Windows program. Many more lines of instructions are needed to create a Windows program than is required to create a similar DOS program.

This meant that Windows programs cost more to create than DOS programs. Therefore, software manufacturers and corporations that built their own software were not rushing to write Windows programs. In addition, programmers had to be retrained to acquire the necessary skills to write Windows programs.

In 1985, two years after CDs were introduced by the recording industry, Microsoft took its Windows roadshow to Wall Street with Windows on Wall Street where Gates and his crew highlighted Windows applications built for internal use by Wall Street firms. I was on a Windows development team at Merrill Lynch, whose Windows application was featured at the show. At that time Gates had just entered the billionaire club.

While Gates's PR people caused much excitement about Windows in the press and among those who attended the roadshow, Windows got off to a very slow start. It was another five years before Windows was widely adopted. By that time the IBM PC became more powerful and the tools to make it easier to develop Windows applications became more prevalent. Microsoft had trained an extensive number of Windows programmers, and Microsoft itself sold many of the key Windows applications, such as Word and Excel, under its own brand name.

THE CENTRAL PROCESSOR REVOLUTION..............

The brain of a computer is the central processor, commonly known as the CPU or the microprocessor, such as the Pentium III. This is a chip inside the computer that executes instructions written by a programmer. The CPU is the major component that defines a computer, as you've probably realized looking at advertisements for personal computers. You'll learn more about the functions of a CPU in the next chapter.

Companies, such as Intel, which design and manufacture processors determine the power that can be packed into a computer. More robust processors mean computer manufacturers can offer more powerful computers—and software manufacturers can create dazzling programs.

It's hard to believe with all the hype about Intel that there were other processor-manufacturers that designed CPUs for the early personal computers. These included

Motorola Zilog. Zilog manufactured the Z80 processor, which was the most desirable processor for computers that used the CP/M operating system. The TRS-80 computer was one of the first computers to use the Z80 processor as the name implies (T is for Tandy; RS is for Radio Shack; 80 is for the Z80 processor).

However the processor industry was in for a radical shake-up in late 1981 when IBM made its choice of processor for the IBM personal computer. The winner was Intel's 8088 processor. IBM had made the 8088 processor the defacto industry standard.

An interesting point is that the 8088 processor was not the best processor Intel had to offer. In 1979, Intel designed the more powerful 8086 processor. IBM decided to choose second best for its personal computer because IBM wanted to save time and money.

Here's why. An important characteristic of a processor is the amount of information it can accept for processing at the same time. This is analogous to a highway toll plaza where information is the number of cars and processing is the number of cars that can pass through the toll plaza at the same time.

In computer terms, the processor is the toll plaza, and a bit (i.e., one or zero) represents data. Wires etched into the computer's motherboard are similar to lanes of a highway except instead of cars the wires provide a path for data to reach the processor.

The 8086 processor accepted 16 bits (16 cars) at the same time and the 8088 processor accepted 8 bits (8 cars) at a time. Therefore, the 8086 processor could receive more information per second than the 8088 processor.

The problem IBM experienced was with the data path (lanes of the highway) that had to be etched onto the IBM personal computer's motherboard. It was faster and less costly to build a motherboard with 8 data lines (an 8-lane highway) than it was to build one with 16 data lines (a 16-lane highway).

Keep in mind that IBM was under pressure to make a presence in the fledging personal computer market as quickly as possible. And the strategy was to use the personal computer as an ancillary product to the mainframe product line.

The Processor Race Was On

Computers could become more powerful only if improvements were made in the design of the processor. A key characteristic of power in the early days of personal computers was the amount of random access memory (RAM) installed in the computer.

Tech Talk

RAM: The place inside the computer where programs and data are stored.

Simply stated, the more RAM a computer had, the more instructions and data could be stored inside it and the less time it spent reading data from an alternative storage location such as a floppy disk.

A computer that used the 8088 processor was limited to 64 KB of memory. The storage area inside the processor that is used to hold a memory address mathematically established the limit.

Each memory location is identified by an address, which is very similar to how each house in your town is identified by an address. A memory address is a number that is represented as a series of binary numbers such as 10011011 (see "Computers Count to Two").

Inside the processor there is a place called a register that holds the memory address of the next instruction to process. The processor looks at the memory address stored in the register, then goes out to that memory location and retrieves the instruction for processing.

The register in the 8088 processor could hold 8 bits, which meant that 64 KB was the largest number that could be held in the register. Therefore, computer manufacturers could include more than 64 KB of memory in their computers, but the processor couldn't access that memory.

Microsoft and computer manufacturers initially worked around this problem by implementing a technique called page switching. Page switching required the operating system to exchange the contents of a block of memory called a page with a similar size block on a disk. Page switching increased access time (not a good thing) whenever a switch from disk to memory was made, however this enabled the processor to handle 128 KB of memory, which was a good thing.

The first IBM personal computer gave the business community a taste of the computing power that can be placed on the desktop. Business leaders knew that the personal computer could revolutionize the way to do business. They also knew the job they wanted the personal computer to perform, but the early PCs were underpowered to meet their needs.

Intel's response was to increase the size of the address register from 8 bits to 16 bits, which set the upper memory address limit to 1 MB. This is a far cry from today's 4-gigabyte (GB) memory addresses, but was revolutionary at the time.

Intel, Meet the Competition

Although Intel was chosen to be the processor for the first IBM personal computers, Intel management realized that IBM could easily use a processor built by a different manufacturer in future models. Intel strategy to maintain the IBM contract was to aggressively incorporate new features into its processor while maintaining backward compatibility with existing processors. Simply said, programs running on existing processors would work without modification on new additions to the Intel line of processors.

Intel identified its line of processors as the x86 family with 80286 becoming the first member of the family to appear in the IBM personal computer. The x86 family began in force when the 80286 replaced the 8088 processor. From then on new processors were given similar family names such as the 80386 and the 80486 although advertising copy typically dropped the 80 and referred to them as the 286, 386, and 486.

A frequent computer trivia question is why did Intel begin with 80286 rather than the 80186? There was an 80186, but because of the rapid development in processor technology the 80186 never found its way into the IBM personal computer.

Using numbers as the name for a family of processors seemed a good idea. The name implied that the higher numbered processor was a greater value than a lower numbered one. While this is true, using numbers almost proved to be disastrous.

Numbers could not be protected under the trademark laws. This meant a competitor could reverse engineer the technology used in the Intel processor and use it to create a functionally compatible processor—and give it the same numbered name as the Intel processor.

This is similar to an automobile manufacturer calling a model a 4X4. The expression 4X4 can be used freely by any carmaker. Intel's problem was that it had already established the processor name as a functional trademark. Now competitors could capitalize on the established processor name.

Intel discontinued using numbers as product names with the onset of what would have been the 80586. Names such as the Pentium were used rather than numbers because names could be legally protected by a trademark.

Improvements Along the Way

New features that increase performance are incorporated in the processor each time the name of the processor changes. The 8088 processor read information in 8-bit chunks. The 80286 doubled this capacity by reading information in 16-bit chunks.

The 80286 also introduced the concept of protected mode. Protected mode placed restrictions on memory access to programs and enabled the computer to access 16 MB of memory. You'll learn more about protected mode in the next chapter.

In 1985, Intel introduced the 80386 processor. The 80386 enhanced memory access by using a feature called paging, which used a combination of real memory (chips inside the computer) and disk space to create 4 GB of virtual memory. The 80386 also read 32-bit chunks of information at a time, doubling that of the 80286. This dramatically increased the speed of processing many programs.

Tech Talk

Virtual memory: Memory that appears to exist to the computer, but doesn't physically exists.

Four years after the introduction of the 80386, Intel came out with the next generation processor called the 80486. The 80486 included a math coprocessor and special memory called a level 1 cache built into the processor.

Computer programs were gradually becoming graphical, which involves the calculation of very large and very small numbers quickly. Earlier processors required many steps to perform these calculations and that caused a noticeable delay in the presentation of the graphic on the computer screen.

Not every customer required sophisticated graphics. Those that did purchased an additional processor that could perform these calculations using fewer steps than the main processor. The additional processor was called a math coprocessor. Any time the CPU was required to perform sophisticated calculations it turned over processing to the math coprocessor.

Intel realized that PCs were moving to a GUI, which would require every personal computer to perform these sophisticated calculations. Therefore, the math coprocessor was fully integrated into the CPU with the introduction of the 80486.

The level 1 cache also introduced with the 80486 reduced the time necessary for the processor to read information from memory by storing the most frequently used information inside the processor. I'll explain more about this in the next chapter.

Tech Talk

Cache: Computer memory set aside for a special purpose such as storing frequently used data.

The next generation of Intel processors came in 1993 with the introduction of the Pentium. The Pentium processed 64 bits of information at a time; it also included two onboard caches of memory.

Intel followed the Pentium with the Pentium Pro and the Pentium MMX. The Pentium Pro incorporated a level 2 cache memory while the Pentium MMX contains features for multimedia. And in 1996 the Pentium II made its debut, which among other design enhancers combined the features of the Pentium Pro and the Pentium MMX into one processor.

Marketing managers at Intel soon realized that the computer market was dividing into five segments: low-price computers for home use, desktop computers for general use, mobile computers for business use, servers for computer networks, and workstations for general business use.

Each segment had its own special needs and price point. Intel's competitors such as Motorola, Digital Equipment Corporation, and Advanced Micro Devices, among others, saw an opportunity to design comparable processors and sell them below Intel's prices. They could do this because their chips removed features not required for specific market segments.

Intel introduced new processors to meet this competitive strategy. The Pentium II Xeon and the Pentium III Xeon provided the high processing speed that is required for servers. The Pentium III is targeted for desktop and workstations. And the Celeron processor is designed for the home market.

SUMMARY ....

Although most of us take for granted how well computers help us in everyday chores, computer technology followed a long road to get us where we are today. Regardless of its power, a computer is a counting machine that can add two numbers and subtract two numbers. And that is where the first computer began.

The first successful computer began in 3000 B.C. It was called the abacus. The abacus was a mechanical computer that used rows of beads to represent numbers. Moving a bead in one direction facilitated addition and, in the other direction, subtraction.

It wasn't until the 17th century that Blaise Pascal, a French mathematician, developed a mechanical adding machine. The machine was called the Pascaline and used wheels and gears to perform addition and subtraction based on the same principle used in the abacus.

Charles Babbage expanded Pascal's concept and designed the Difference Engine and the Analytical Engine that could multiply and divide as well as perform addition and subtraction. However, the Difference Engine and the Analytical Engine was never built because it simply cost too much.

It wasn't until almost the turn of the 20th century that Herman Hollerith created the first electrical computer that used punch cards to read data and later instructions. His company was called Tabulating Machine Company, which later changed its name to the International Business Machines Corporation, more commonly known as IBM.

In 1937, Dr. John Atanasoff and Clifford Berry, a professor and his graduate student at Iowa State University, created the first electronic computer that used vacuum tubes to store information and perform mathematical calculations. The computer was called the ABC computer. They were also the first people to apply the binary numbers system to store and manipulate information.

In 1946, Dr. John Mauchly of the University of Pennsylvania used technology developed by Atanasoff and Berry to build the first generation of computers called the

Electronic Numerical Integrator and Computer (ENIAC). The ENIAC had one purpose—to create accurate trajectory tables for the Department of Defense.

Five years later, Mauchly built the Universal Automatic Computer, better known as the UNIVAC 1, for the Remington-Rand Corporation, which became the first well-known commerce electronic computer.

The second generation of computers was ushered in when scientists at Bell Laboratories in New Jersey developed the transistor. The transistor provided the same electronic switching capabilities as a vacuum tube but at lower power, a reduced size, and lower cost.

The third generation of computers was launched in the mid-1960s with the discovery of integrated circuits. Hundreds of transistors that populated second-generation computer circuit boards, making the circuit board look like a little city were now reduced to a circuit the size of a pin head. Computer manufacturers were then able to build smaller, more powerful, and less expensive computers than second-generation computers.

The year 1963 saw the first challenge to mainframe computers. Digital Equipment Corporation introduced the first minicomputer called the PDP-8. A minicomputer was to some degree a scaled-down version of a mainframe computer in size, power, and price. For around $20,000 in 1963 dollars a business could harness the power of a computer to run a portion of its operation.

Fourth-generation computers were born in 1971 with the introduction of large-scale integrated circuits. Large-scale integrated circuits technology enabled an entire computer circuitry to be placed on one computer chip.

Four years into the fourth-generation computers, the first personal computer was introduced, called the Altair 8800. The Altair was design for the hobbyist. However, a few short years later more refined personal computers entered the market. These included the TRS-80 and, of course, the Apple computer.

It wasn't until 1981 that personal computers were taken seriously by the business community. It was that year when IBM launched its own personal computer with the aid of Microsoft and Intel. IBM set the standard for personal computers.

The year 1984 was another turning point in the history of computers. The first commercial graphical user interface was introduced for the Macintosh line of Apple computers. Microsoft followed the next year with the introduction of Windows. Computers became easier to use because users clicked icons rather than typed commands at a prompt.

Around the same time, Sun Microsystems began developing its first workstation. Sun Microsystems incorporate the reduced instruction set computer technology developed by John Cocke in 1980. Workstations became widely adopted in 1989 with the introduction of the SPARCstation™ 1. Workstations became a more desirable alternative to minicomputers and low-end mainframe computers.

Summary Questions

1. Why are transistors important to computer technology?

2. How did IBM freeze out competitors?

3. What blunders did IBM make when signing the operating system contract with Microsoft?

4. What is the difference between a minicomputer and a workstation?

5. Why were early versions of Microsoft Windows not widely accepted?

6. Why is there an advantage of using the base-2 numbering system over the base-10 numbering system?

7. Why were mechanical computers that performed multiplication and division not widely accepted?

8. What technique did competitors use to obtain technology employed in Intel processors?

9. What is the difference between integrated circuits and large-scale integrated circuits?

10. Why did IBM select an inferior processor from Intel for the first IBM personal computer?

2 An Inside Look at How a Computer Works

In this chapter...

They Said It...

"Intimidation disappears once the facts are revealed."

Anonymous

It's baffling how a box of switches that we call a computer can perform feats beyond the capabilities of mortal men, to paraphrase the Superman comic strip. Although computers may lack the power of a locomotive and cannot leap tall buildings, computers are nearly faster than the speed of sound. And it is this speed that sets computers apart from other tools.

Computers are counting machines that can also store numbers. Engineers and programmers are able to harness these two simple features and create computers that can manage complex corporations, control sophisticated machinery, and even help us calculate our taxes. I'm still hoping for the day when computers will pay my taxes, but I don't see that happening any time soon.

How can a box of switches that can only count and store numbers be able to take the drudgery out of everyday mundane chores? How can a computer sift through hundreds of thousands of possibilities and arrive at the best choice all within a few seconds?

I'll answer these questions and let you see for yourself the inner workings of a computer in this chapter. There are many categories of computers including mainframe, workstations, servers, and personal computers. Although each has its own design, all computers contain the same basic components and operate using very similar principles, which is the topic of this chapter. Here's what you'll learn in this chapter:

- How information is identified inside a computer

- Parts of a computer

- How a processor works

- How computer memory works

- How information flows inside the computer

REALITY CHECK ....

About 10 years ago, I was given the assignment to automate the process of clearing security trades in the Pacific Rim countries for the Wall Street firm Salomon, Inc.

Each day, customers of Salomon, Inc., issued instructions to either sell or buy securities of companies that were on various stock markets in the Pacific Rim, such as the Tokyo stock market.

Salomon, Inc.'s clearance clerks had to review the client's account to be sure that the client had the stock or cash necessary to complete the trade, then fill out various forms that were telexed to the proper international bank. The international bank's local branch handled the transaction in the local stock market.

These steps had to be performed faultlessly and within a prescribed deadline. As trading volume increased, clearance clerks found it more and more difficult to achieve these goals. Errors crept into the process, which exposed Salomon, Inc., to additional cost. The handwriting was on the wall. The international clearance process for the Pacific Rim had to be automated.

Most of Salomon, Inc.'s customers were major financial institutions such as insurance companies. This meant that customers were able to enter trades into their own computers and send the data pertaining to the trade to Salomon, Inc.

As trade data arrived, Salomon, Inc.'s new computer system verified that the customer had the necessary balance in the account. Information that the international bank required to complete the transaction was copied from the trade data and electronically sent to the international bank for processing.

All of this took place within seconds after the trade was received from the client. The human factor was nearly removed from the process except for the clerk at the client's end who entered to the trade data into the client's system.

Trades no longer missed deadlines and Salomon, Inc., was able to reduce to zero financial losses that stemmed from clearance clerks.

A TOUR OF THE OUTSIDE ....

Most of the components of a computer are contained inside the computer box, which is called the computer case. Some components, however, are visible from outside the computer (see Figure 2-1). The most obvious components that you can see are the floppy disk drive and the CD drive. The CD drive comes in various flavors including CD-ROM, CD-R, and DVD. I'll go into details on how CD drives work in Chapter 5. For now all you need to know is that both the floppy disk drive and the CD drive are used to store information.

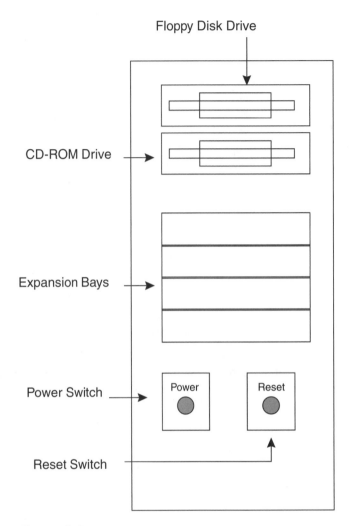

Figure 2-1
Components visible from outside the computer

You'll also notice various lights. The lights are not miniature light bulbs. Instead they are light-emitting diodes (LED). As electricity flows through the circuits that contain the LED, the LED glows, giving off visible light. The light isn't sufficient to read a book, but it is sufficient light to indicate that something is—or is not—working.

Tech Talk

Light-emitting diodes: An electronic component that generates light when electricity flows through the component. Also known as LED.

For example, an LED is commonly used to indicate that a disk drive or CD is operating. LEDs are also used to indicate the communication status of a modem, if the modem is external to the computer (see Chapter 7 for more information about modems).

There are a number of switches that are located on the computer case. The most important switch is the one that turns on the power. Another important one is the reset switch.

A computer goes through various preparation steps before components are ready to run a program. This is called the startup and occurs whenever you turn on the power switch. The startup procedure can take anywhere from less than a minute to over five minutes depending on the kind of computer.

Tech Talk

Reset switch: A switch on the computer case that refreshes the computer hardware without going through the full startup procedure.

Startup procedure: A process that occurs when a computer is powered up that prepares the computer for operation. Also called booting the computer.

Sometimes a computer hangs whenever a program goes astray. Windows is noted for doing this, leaving you without control of your computer. Both the mouse and keyboard are dead and don't respond to your commands. The only recourse is to re-boot by turning the power switch off and on, then wait for the computer to complete the startup procedure. However, you can shorten this delay by using the restart button instead of using the power switch. The computer then performs a shorter procedure before giving control back to you.

Laptop computers have a sleep button. The sleep button is a power savings technique that shuts down all nonessential devices without turning off the computer. Be sure to use the sleep button whenever you pause for a substantial length of time, for example, while you're having a telephone conversation.

Computers also have several silver strips of metal usually on the back of the computer. The strips cover predrilled, elongated holes that cover the expansion section of the computer. The expansion section is the place where you can expand the features of the computer by inserting circuit boards into expansion slots inside the computer. More about this later in the chapter.

Some expansion circuit boards connect to external devices such as an internal modem that connects to the telephone line. The internal modem is on the expansion circuit board and the telephone line is the external device connected to the modem. In this case, a metal strip in the expansion section is removed and replaced with the side of the circuit board. This is where the telephone line connects to the modem.

In addition to devices that connect directly to a circuit board, there are other receptacles that are used to plug devices directly into the computer's main circuit board, called the motherboard.

These devices include the monitor, mouse, keyboard, printer, speakers, microphones, and joystick. Receptacles for these devices are called ports. There are three common ports—serial, parallel, and USB—integrated into the motherboard. Apple computers have a FireWire port, which is comparable to the USB port. You'll learn more about the motherboard and ports later in this chapter and throughout the book.

Tech Talk

Motherboard: The main circuit board inside the computer that contains components such as the central processing unit, the clock, and computer memory.

Port: An integrated circuit on the motherboard that enables external devices to be connected to the motherboard's circuitry.

Electricity flowing through components inside the computer generates heat. While this temperature isn't sufficient to boil an egg, the heat could eventually destroy one or more components.

Engineers address this problem in various ways. One of these methods is to use heat sinks. A heat sink is a metallic component connected to the circuit board that can absorb and temporarily store heat similar to how a kitchen sink stores water.

Heat is removed from the area around the motherboard by air currents that flow through air vents that you see cut into the computer case. A fan is used inside the computer to increase the airflow, thereby cooling components faster.

HOW INFORMATION IS IDENTIFIED......................

Before I take you on a tour inside the computer, we need to explore the way information is encoded for use by the computer. Once you have a grasp on the zeros and ones, bits and bytes that you always hear about, then you'll find it easier to understand how components on the motherboard use information to perform near miracles.

Information can be a person's name, a production identifier such as a bar code, or the number of the winning lottery ticket. We identify written information by using various lines to form letters and numbers.

For example, a specific arrangement of line forms a letter and a letter placed in a specific sequence forms a word that we associate with a thing or an idea. The specific arrangement of lines to form letters and numbers and the sequence of letters to form words are dependent upon local culture commonly referred to as a native language.

Computers don't understand the way letters and numbers are written in any language, yet they are able to take and manipulate our information, such as searching a database for particular information.

Engineers had to devise a way to bridge the gap between the method we use to identify information and the way computers identify information. The solution is with two numbers, zero and one, and the binary numbering system.

As I mentioned in the first chapter, a numbering system is a method used to count. Nearly all of us use the decimal numbering system that consists of 10 digits, zero through nine. Once the count reaches nine, we carry over one value to the left of the original digit and begin counting over again starting with zero.

The binary numbering system consists of two digits, zero and one. However, the same carryover process (see Figure 2-2) occurs when the count reaches one. The next value, three, requires us to carry over one value to the left of the original digit and begin counting with zero.

While the binary numbering system is more than a bit (pardon the pun) confusing for most of us to understand than the decimal system, the binary number system is ideal for use by computers. Computers contain millions of switches in the form of transistors embedded into large-scale integrated circuits (see Chapter 1).

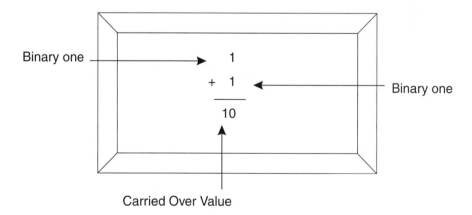

Figure 2-2
The carryover process is the same in binary math as it is in decimal math. Once the digit one is reached, the next increment causes a value to be carried over

Each switch has two states. I like to think of these states as off and on although this infers the absence or present of the flow of electricity. Switches inside the computer actually redirect the flow of electricity from one circuit to another. A binary value can be associated with the state of a switch. The off state can be represented by a zero and the on state by a one.

A binary value is more than a symbol used to identify the position of a switch. A binary value is a number that can be used in calculations identically to how you and I use decimal values in calculations.

This is an important factor to understand because switches are arranged into logic circuits that are activated or deactivated based on the results of a calculation. In the previous chapter, I showed you how computers use subtraction to determine if two values are the same or different. A logic circuit is designed to flip switches a certain way based on subtracting two binary numbers. The resulting switch settings are "read" by other logic circuits to determine if the difference is zero or not zero. That is, to determine if the numbers are the same or different.

Exploring how engineers create these logic circuits requires a detailed discussion on circuit design theory, which is beyond the scope of this book. You don't need to know this information to gain a good understanding of the inner workings of a computer.

From BITS to Numbers

A binary digit is called a bit. You and I identify information as numbers, words, or a combination of both. Our decimal numbers are easily translated into a binary number because both are numbers. This means that information that we identify as a number, such as a person's age, is also identified as a number inside the computer using binary instead of decimal numbers.

Let's say that a person's age is 21 and you want to store that information in a computer's memory. Memory consists of a set of switches, the settings of which are represented by a binary digit. This means that the decimal value 21 must be converted to the binary number 10101, which is 21 in the binary numbering system.

A program automatically performs this conversion. However, you can convert from decimal to binary and back by using the calculator that comes with Windows. You'll find the calculator by selecting:

1. Start
2. Programs
3. Accessories
4. Calculator

5. View from the menu

6. Scientific from the pull-down menu

Enter the decimal value (21) then click Bin. The calculator converts the decimal value and displays the equivalent binary number on the screen. Clicking Dec reverses the conversion back to decimal numbers.

Each binary value is a switch. Therefore, five switches are necessary to store the number 21 inside the computer. Another way to say this is 5 bits of memory is required to hold the number 21.

Five bits of memory? That sounds strange because we hear memory spoken in bytes not bits of memory. Computer scientists group memory into sets of eight switches commonly referred to as a byte.

Tech Talk

Bit: A binary digit that has the value of zero or one.

Byte: A set of 8 binary digits.

The largest number that can be represented in a byte is 255 or in binary 11111111. Obviously we need to store numbers larger than 255 and we do so by combining bytes. For example, 2 bytes can hold up to the value 65,535, and 4 bytes, 4,294,967,295.

Notice that all the numbers that I've mentioned are whole numbers. None of them have fractional values. That's because numbers that contain a fractional value are referred to as floating-point numbers. A floating-point number has two components. The first consists of all the digits in the numbers, both the whole and fractional amounts. The second component is a number that implies the position of the separator.

Tech Talk

Floating-point: A method used to represent the separator (i.e., decimal point) between the whole number and the fraction.

Let's say that we wanted to store our monthly salary of $8,543.23 in computer memory. Since there is a fractional component to the number, we must use the floating-point method. The two parts of the floating-point value are 854323 and 2. All the digits in the number 854323 and the value 2 indicate that the separator is in the second position from the right. That is, between 8543 and 23.

Fortunately, you are not concerned with floating-point numbers because computer programs handle all the details for you.

In some situations, the computer must store the sign of a number. A signed number is a number that has a plus or minus sign such as –100 indicating that this is a negative number. A bit is used to store the sign of a signed number.

A programmer can write a program that reads the bits of a signed number, then translates the sign bit to a plus or minus symbol and the rest of the bits to the appropriate number.

From BITS to Letters

Textual information is the most common form of information used in a computer. Textual information consists of words and numbers that are not used in calculations such as a house number in an address. Punctuation marks, dollar signs, and other symbols are also considered textual information.

Engineers devised a coding method that translates letters and symbols into binary numbers that can be stored in computer memory. A standard was formed called the American Standard Code for Information Interchange (ASCII) that assigned one of up to 255 values to letters and symbols. Remember that 255 is the largest number that can be stored in a byte of memory. Table 2-1 contains a sample of the ASCII code.

Table 2-1   A sample of the ASCII code

ASCII value	Character	ASCII value	Character	ASCII value	Character
32	SPACE	64	@	96	`
33	!	65	A	97	a
34	"	66	B	98	b
35	#	67	C	99	c
36	$	68	D	100	d
37	%	69	E	101	e
38	&	70	F	102	f
39	'	71	G	103	g
40	(	72	H	104	h
41	)	73	I	105	i
42	*	74	J	106	j
43	+	75	K	107	k
44	,	76	L	108	l
45	-	77	M	109	m

Table 2-1   A sample of the ASCII code (continued)

ASCII value	Character	ASCII value	Character	ASCII value	Character
46	.	78	N	110	n
47	/	79	O	111	o
48	0	80	P	112	p
49	1	81	Q	113	q
50	2	82	R	114	r
51	3	83	S	115	s
52	4	84	T	116	t
53	5	85	U	117	u
54	6	86	V	118	v
55	7	87	W	119	w
56	8	88	X	120	x
57	9	89	Y	121	y
58	:	90	Z	122	z
59	;	91	[	123	{
60	<	92	\	124	|
61	=	93	]	125	}
62	>	94	^	126	~
63	?	95	_		

The original ASCII standard used 7 bits that identified 128 symbols. This was later expanded by IBM to accommodate primitive graphical images such as lines and corners at a time before the graphical user interface (GUI) such as Windows became widely accepted.

Each letter of the alphabet is represented twice in the ASCII code. Once in uppercase and the other lowercase. Let's say I wanted to convert "Jim" into ASCII code. I look up in the ASCII table the decimal number for an uppercase J, which is 74. Using the same procedure I locate the lowercase ASCII numbers for "im," 105 and 109 respectively.

Although I converted "Jim" to the equivalent decimal number, I can easily convert the decimal number to a binary number which can be easily stored in computer memory. Table 2-2 shows the conversation process.

Table 2-2   Converting "Jim" to the equivalent binary value

Letters	ASCII decimal value	Equivalent binary value
Jim	74 105 109	01001010 01101001 01101101

The binary equivalent of the number 74 is stored in computer memory, however the computer doesn't differentiate between the ASCII number 74 and the number 74. That is, the computer sees the number 74 and has no idea whether the number represents the letter J or the number 74.

The only way for the number 74 to be converted back to the letter J is by a computer program such as a word processor. A programmer who writes a program tells the computer to treat the number (i.e., 74) as an ASCII value and not as a pure number. The computer then looks up the ASCII symbol that corresponds to the number and displays the related symbol on the screen.

A similar type of table is called EBSDIC. EBSDIC is commonly used on mainframe computers, although this is changing as ASCII becomes the standard of choice.

There is an inherent problem with the ASCII code. There aren't sufficient numbers available to accommodate symbols used in every language such as Asian languages that use ideographs. This problem was solved with the introduction of Unicode.

Here's how Unicode works. Unicode contains two distinct blocks of code. One is called Unicode-2 and the other Unicode-4. Unicode-2 uses a 16-bit (2 bytes) number to represent symbols. This means 65,536 distinct symbols can be assigned a Unicode-2 value.

If a language contains more than 65,536 symbols, Unicode-4 is used. Unicode-4 uses a 32-bit (4 bytes) number, which can handle about a million symbols.

The most commonly used symbols in every language are assigned a Unicode-2 number. Therefore, most of the textual information is stored using 2 bytes per symbol. Unicode-4 symbols are inserted into the information where necessary.

Engineers stayed away from using only Unicode-4 because they found nearly all textual information can be represented with 2 bytes. Using 4 bytes would require more storage space, most of which would be wasted.

Although Unicode accommodates every language, it has a major drawback when used to represent English. Unicode requires nearly double the storage space when compared to the same English text represented by ASCII code.

Not all symbols used in Unicode or ASCII code are visible. Some symbols, such as tab, linefeed, and carriage return, are nonprintable symbols. This means you can include these symbols in the textual information, but you cannot see them on the screen or when the text is printed.

Nonprintable symbols are commonly called control characters. For example, two characters are entered in the text whenever you press Enter. These are the linefeed and carriage return characters.

Tech Talk

Control character: A character embedded in a document that has special meaning to a device, such as indicating that a page must be ejected from a printer.

The linefeed character tells the video adapter or printer to move the cursor to the next line. The carriage-return character instructs the device to move the cursor to the beginning of the line. The device recognizes a control character then translates the character into the appropriate action.

A TOUR OF THE INSIDE ....

Until now I've been referring to a computer as a counting machine that contains a bunch of electronic switches. While this is generally true, a computer consists of more than switches, some of which you recognize because you've read about them and others that are less publicized.

An electronic switch is a component. One of the most important components inside a computer is the larger circuit board that connects all components. This is called the motherboard. The motherboard looks like a miniature city with various chips dotting the landscape and connected together by strips of exposed wires etched into the motherboard. These strips are collectively called a bus.

Tech Talk

Bus: Two or more wires that are usually etched into a circuit board over which information travels to components.

Components have various functions and collectively they make the computer work. The most important component on the motherboard is the central processor (CPU), also known as the processor. This is the brain of the computer where all the computations occur. The processor slips into either a slot or a socket on the motherboard depending on the type of processor that the computer uses (see Chapter 3 for details on the available processors).

Computers used as servers and for other high-performance purposes sometimes use two or more processors that enable the computer to process multiple instructions at the same time. I'll talk more about this in the next chapter.

Tech Talk
Memory chip: A large-scale integrated circuit used to store information.

Another important component are memory chips. There are two general kinds of memory chips. These are read-only memory (ROM) and random access memory (RAM). ROM contains instructions and data that are etched into the chip when the chip was manufactured. These instructions are typically used to tell the processor how to load other programs such as the operating system as in the case of ROM-BIOS (read-only memory basic input output system). The processor can only read information from ROM and cannot write or change information contained in ROM. Instructions contained in ROM are called firmware.

In contrast, RAM does not contain any etched programs. Instead, RAM contains nothing until the processor places either instructions (a program) or information (data) into RAM by setting the state of each bit of RAM.

I'll go into much more detail about RAM in the next chapter. For now simply understand that ROM and RAM are chips used to store instructions or data and are either permanently affixed to the motherboard or are placed in a slot on the motherboard.

Other components on the motherboard are used for various features that are integrated into the motherboard. These include video display cards, sound cards, modems, keyboards, and external ports such as the serial and parallel ports.

A port is a receptacle that enables an external device to be connected to the motherboard. For example, information that flows to a printer travels along the wires etched into the motherboard from the processor to a port (usually either the serial or parallel port) that is connected by a cable to a printer.

The motherboard also contains expansion slots. An expansion slot is a receptacle that enables circuit boards to be connected directly to the motherboard. For example, a modem can be built into a circuit board that is inserted into an expansion slot. This has a similar effect as if the modem were fully integrated into the motherboard.

Wires etched into a side of the circuit board match connectors in the expansion slot, which in turn connects directly to the wires etched into the motherboard. Information flows from the processor to the circuit board in the expansion slot just as if the circuit board were fully integrated into the motherboard.

Another important component attached to the motherboard is the power supply/voltage regulator. The power supply/voltage regulator consists of a group of circuits that receives alternating current from the power cord and converts the alternating current to direct current used to power the motherboard.

Components on the motherboard require specific voltage to properly interpret the signal that contains the binary number. The binary digits are represented as adjustments to the voltage that flows throughout the motherboard. You'll learn more about this later in the chapter.

Besides converting power from AC to DC and reducing incoming voltage from 120 volts to under 5 volts, the power supply/voltage regulator also maintains one or multiple steady voltages as required by components on the motherboard.

The clock is the heart of the computer. It is the clock circuitry that pushes information between the processor and other components such as memory and ports.

You can think of the clock as sending a pulsating wave. Each wave sends an instruction or data along wires etched into the motherboard. This pulse is called a clock cycle. A clock cycle is measured in megahertz (MHz). A hertz is one cycle of an electronic wave per second. A megahertz is a million cycles per second. Therefore, the higher the megahertz value, the faster instructions and data will move within the computer.

Be careful not to relate the clock cycle with processor throughput. Processor throughput is a measurement of the number of instructions that can be processed by the processor per second. This processing involves more than the clock speed, as you'll learn later in this chapter.

The purpose of a clock, which is located outside of the processor, is to organize the movement of information inside the computer so that each component has time to work.

Some components such as the processor work very fast while others such as the main memory require more time to react. Since components work at different speeds, the clock is used to set a pace at which all components can operate efficiently. This is called a synchronous computer because all components work at the same pace regardless of their internal working speed.

The clock sets the speed outside of each component such as the processor. Typically, a component runs internally at a faster speed than the clock speed. Let's say that the clock speed is 300 MHz and the processor runs internally twice as fast as the clock's speed, meaning the processor runs at 600 MHz, which is the speed you see quoted in advertisements.

Some devices such as the ISA input-output bus operate at a slower speed than the clock. This is because these devices must adhere to industry standards that specify transmission speed. For example, the ISA input-output bus runs at 8.33 MHz. ISA devices are designed to send and receive information at this speed. A faster speed might cause some ISA devices to fail.

Devices such as a floppy disk drive, hard disk drive, and CD-ROM drive are found usually inside the computer case, but external to the motherboard. These devices are connected to a component on the motherboard or to a circuit board in an expansion slot by a cable. The cable enables the device to communicate with components on the motherboard through a bus.

Sometimes these drives are placed externally to the computer case and are connected to the motherboard by a cable and expansion circuit board. In this case, these devices receive power externally from the computer as compared to inside devices that get their power from the computer's power supply.

HOW A COMPUTER WORKS ....

Once a computer completes the startup process, it seems to wait for someone to give a command. The computer is already running a program called the operating system such as Windows or UNIX, which is placed into memory during the startup process.

The operating system consists of more than one program, although usually only one of those programs is running while the computer waits for a command. The other programs perform unique utility routines such as moving a command entered at the keyboard to the processor for processing. These utility programs are copied from the startup hard disk or floppy disk and stored in memory ready to be called upon by the processor at any time.

Each device that can request the CPU to process information is assigned to an interrupt request line when the device is installed in the computer. These devices include the keyboard, mouse, disk drives, modems, and devices connected to ports.

An interrupt request line is one of the etched wires on the motherboard that is used to transmit an interrupt message from a device to the processor. An interrupt is a message telling the processor to stop the current processing and run the program that is associated with the interrupt message.

Programs associated with an interrupt message are called interrupt service routines. The address of each interrupt service routine is contained in the interrupt vector table, which is loaded into memory as part of the startup process.

The interrupt vector table is similar to a two-column spreadsheet. The first column contains the number of the interrupt, which is called the interrupt type. The interrupt type is the value of the interrupt message that is sent to the processor by a device. The other column contains the memory address of the interrupt service routine that is associated with the interrupt type.

Let's say that you press CTRL + ALT + DEL while a program is running. These three keys are your panic keys on a computer running Windows. When all else fails, CTRL + ALT + DEL enables you to shut down a wayward program or restart the computer.

CTRL + ALT + DEL causes the keyboard to send an interrupt type value along the interrupt line to the processor. For this example, I'll call the interrupt type Type 8. (Type 8 may not be the proper interrupt type for this process. The actual interrupt type will vary depending on the type of computer in use).

The CPU might be processing another program at this time such as the wayward program, but realize the interrupt type has higher priority than continuing to process the program. The CPU places the address of the last instruction executed and relevant data into temporary memory before responding to the interrupt.

The CPU then references the row in the interrupt vector table (see Figure 2-3) that contains interrupt Type 8. The second column in that row, called a slot, contains the memory address of the first instruction of the interrupt service routine that displays the Close Program dialog box.

Each instruction is read into the CPU and processed in the order prescribed by the programmer who wrote the interrupt service routine. When the last instruction finishes processing, the CPU resumes the program that was in progress when the interrupt message was received.

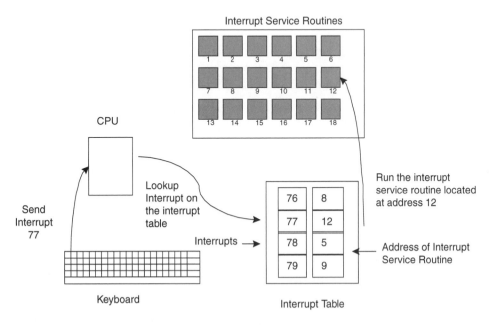

Figure 2-3
The interrupt vector table contains interrupt message types and the addresses of corresponding interrupt service routines

INTERRUPTS: ISA VS. PCI

Interrupt requests are sent along an interrupt request line. There are several interrupt request lines etched into the motherboard. Each device that can make an interrupt request is assigned to an interrupt request line.

Assigning a device to an interrupt request line can at times be tricky depending on the type of bus used in the computer. The ISA bus, which is used in many older and in some new PCs, requires that the interrupt request line be manually assigned to each device, usually by changing a configuration setting using a program. Sometimes the assignment is made by manually resetting a jumper switch on the device itself.

Many times the device manufacturer preconfigures the interrupt request line setting. Hopefully this line is not already in use by another device. Two devices can use the same interrupt request line at the same time, however this can cause the computer to go a little haywire. Both devices can send an interrupt request, but the processor won't know which device sent the request. This can be confusing. The only way to fix the problem is to manually reassign the device to an unused interrupt request line.

The newer personal computers use the PCI bus. PCI bus devices avoid conflict in two ways. First, interrupt request lines are assigned dynamically. There is no default interrupt request line assigned by the manufacturer as with ISA bus devices.

Second, each device uses a different voltage to send an interrupt request. This means the processor won't be confused as to which device sent the interrupt request even if two devices are assigned to the same line.

INTERRUPTS AND VIRUSES

The purpose of the interrupt vector table is to add flexibility to the operating system. A clever programmer can create her own interrupt service request by substituting the address of her program in the interrupt vector table for that of the regular interrupt service routine. In this case, the processor runs the new interrupt service request in place of the existing interrupt service routine without raising any questions.

This flexibility enables programmers to write sophisticated routines that enhance features available from the operating system. Let's say that you want to be emailed each time particular files on a hard disk were accessed.

The interrupt service routine that is run to access a file doesn't provide this feature. However, a programmer can write a program to handle this functionality, then load the program into memory. The address of this program is then inserted into the appropriate place in the interrupt vector table in place of the address of the interrupt service routine that accesses a file.

The last instruction of the new interrupt service routine tells the processor to run the original interrupt service routine. When a user requests a file, the processor runs the new interrupt service routine, then runs the original interrupt service routine. The user never realized that the email was sent.

This is exactly the same method used to run a computer virus. A computer virus is a program that is out to do harm to a computer. When the virus first enters the computer, it copies the virus program and a launch program to the hard disk. It then modifies the startup file such as autoexec.bat on a computer running Windows so that the launch program is run whenever the computer starts up.

When the computer runs the launch program, the launch program places the virus into memory and modifies the interrupt vector table by substituting the memory address of an interrupt service routine with that of the virus program.

The first time the processor receives the corresponding interrupt type, the processor runs the virus program rather than the original interrupt service routine. Even restarting the computer won't get rid of the virus because the launch program is automatically run as part of the startup procedure.

Moving Instructions and Data Inside the Computer

There are at least three sets of wires etched into the motherboard that are used to transport information to components inside the computer. Collectively these are called buses. For example, an interrupt line discussed in the previous section is a bus, as is the data bus used to transmit data within the computer.

Computers have a variety of bus types. These include the IDE bus that connects disk drives to the motherboard and the serial port, parallel port, universal serial bus (USB), and the FireWire bus. These will be discussed in more detail later in this book.

You can consider a bus a multilane highway over which information travels. Information in this case are binary numbers that are encoded into the small amount of electricity that flows inside the computer.

Electricity flows from the power cord at 120 volts of alternating current, which is too strong to safely operate the computer. Engineers designed computer components to operate on fewer than 15 volts of direct current. Therefore the computer's power supply converts 120 volts AC to the necessary DC voltage.

The DC voltage is used as the transport mechanism to distribute information throughout the computer. DC voltage is illustrated as a square wave. A square wave (see Figure 2-4) consists of a base line and a height where the height of the wave represents a voltage.

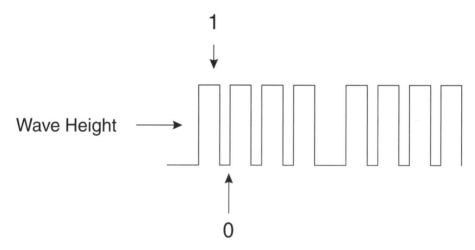

Figure 2-4
Information is transported as a binary value that is encoded as a voltage inside the computer. The height of the wave indicates the voltage

Binary values are encoded into the wave by changing the voltage. Two voltages—a high and a low—are used to accomplish this. A high voltage represents a binary number of one and a low voltage represents a binary number of zero. For example, 3 volts might represent a one and 2 volts represent a zero. Special circuits on the motherboard called voltage regulators are responsible for maintaining specific voltages.

The clock provides the push needed to fluctuate the DC voltage at a specific number of cycles as described previously in this chapter. With each clock cycle, one bit of information flows over each etched wire of the bus. The more clock cycles that occur per second, the faster information flows over the bus.

Older PCs used an 8-bit bus to transport data within the computer. An 8-bit bus has 8 etched wires (an 8-lane highway). One byte could be transported over the bus for each clock cycle. In those days many personal computers used the Intel 8088 processor (see Chapter 1), which could receive 8 bits at a time to process information.

Some processors can process 2 bytes or more at a time such as the Intel 8086 processor. This means that if such a processor was used on a motherboard that had an 8-bit bus, then the processor needed to wait two clock cycles before the processor could begin processing. The first clock cycle is used to read the first byte and the second clock cycle used to read the second byte.

A few older computers used a mismatch between the processor's input capabilities and the bus to provide low-cost personal computers. For example, advertisements would offer a computer with 386 processor at an attractive price. The 386 read and processed 2 bytes at a time. However, the motherboard used an 8-bit bus. The processor had to make two reads from the bus. This made the computer relatively inefficient.

An efficient computer architecture style is to match the number of bits on the bus with the number of bits the processor can read and process at one time. This is like having a multilane highway with each lane having its own tollbooth. Information can be processed as fast as information is moved along the bus.

Computer efficiency is measured as throughput. The number of clock cycles, the size of the bus, the number of bits the processor can read at one time, and the internal processing power of the process collectively determine a computer's throughput.

Tech Talk

Throughput: A measurement of the number of instructions that can be processed by the processor per second.

As you'll learn in the next section, the processor is similar to a small computer in that the processor has an internal clock and an internal bus. The internal clock might be faster or slower than the external clock. Likewise, the internal bus could handle more or less bits than is handled by the external bus.

THE BUS DEFINITION

You can imagine the complexity of designing and manufacturing a computer when you consider that different manufacturers probably create every component on the motherboard. The only way to assure that components can send or receive information over a bus is by creating a bus definition.

A bus definition specifies the number of pins that are used to connect components to the motherboard, the purpose of each pin, the voltage level each pin requires, and a timing factor. The timing factor indicates that a signal remains on the pin for a specific time and that voltage will fluctuate at a specific rate.

Bus definitions are created by standards committees within the industry or by a lead manufacturer putting forth a specification and asking other manufacturers in the industry to recommend modifications—and later adopt those specifications as their own.

A major manufacturer sometimes dictates electronic standards, as was the case in the early 1980s when IBM created and adopted the ISA I/0 bus standard for personal computers. Everyone in the personal computer industry had to adopt the standard to remain competitive.

Moving Data from the Outside

Each component inside the computer is assigned an address along the bus. For example, each byte of memory has a unique address, which is used by the processor to copy information from memory or send information to memory.

Likewise each expansion slot and port has a unique address. An expansion slot is used to expand the motherboard with expansion circuit boards, such as a modem, that are not built into the motherboard.

Each expansion circuit board has its own set of components and bus, which is used to transmit information around the expansion circuit board. The expansion circuit board's bus also extends to metallic fingerlike strips on the edge of the expansion circuit board that are inserted into the expansion slot on the motherboard (see Figure 2-5). These strips connect the bus on the motherboard to the bus on the expansion circuit board, thereby enabling a clear pathway used to exchange information.

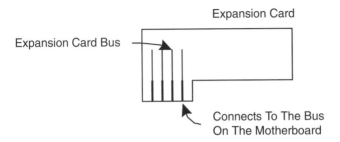

Figure 2-5
Expansion circuit boards have a bus that is connected to the bus on the motherboard using fingerlike strips on the edge of the expansion circuit board

Ports are also an extension of the bus on the motherboard. However, ports are also considered a bus unto themselves because each port contains its own set of wires.

Two of the most common are the serial and parallel ports. The serial port is used to connect serial devices such as an external modem to the motherboard through the use of a cable. You've probably seen a cable connected to your computer. A cable seems to be one thick wire; however, that wire actually contains several other wires. Each of these wires carries 1 bit of information between the computer and the external device.

A serial port carries bits of information sequentially over one wire. This is different than the way bits are carried over the bus on the motherboard. The bus carries bits of information in parallel. That is, 8 bits that travel over the bus at the same time.

Here's how a serial port works. Let's say that a modem is connected to the serial port of the computer. The processor is instructed by a program to send a byte (8 bits) of information to the modem. The byte flows from the processor over the bus to the address of the serial port. Once the byte arrives, the serial port temporarily stores each bit of the byte in memory, then sends 1 bit at a time over the serial cable to the modem.

The serial cable is the bus of the serial port because wires within the cable are used to communicate between the serial device and the computer. One of those wires is used to send information to the device. Another wire is used to receive information from the device. The other wires are used for utility purposes such as coordinating the status of the modem.

The parallel port is similar to the bus on the motherboard and similar to a serial port. A parallel port has a unique address on the motherboard's bus. And the parallel port is used to connect devices outside of the computer to the motherboard through the use of a cable called a parallel cable.

The parallel cable contains several wires, eight of which are used to transfer a byte of information at the same time. In contrast to a serial port that carries 1 bit at a time, the parallel port carries 8 bits at a time similar to the bus on the motherboard.

Improvements have been made to serial ports since the introduction of PCs. Initially, serial ports were seen as inefficient, which gave way to the introduction of parallel ports. As technology evolved, the efficiency of serial ports was improved, and although a serial port carries a bit of information at a time, a serial port throughput rate has surpassed that of the parallel port. Furthermore, serial port technology can carry information over a longer distance than parallel port technology.

The latest improvement in serial port technology is the USB and the FireWire bus. Both offer greater throughput than the traditional serial port and are used to transfer large amounts of information such as from a digital camera. These buses are also used to connect a variety of devices such as printers and monitors to the computer.

As I mentioned, a bus is a pathway used to transport information. Besides the serial and parallel ports, other buses are used to connect external devices to the motherboard. These include the mouse port, the keyboard port, and the video adapter card port (assuming the video adapter card is integrated in the motherboard).

Each one of these ports connects a device to the motherboard using a cable over which bits of information are sent and sometimes received.

INSIDE THE PROCESSOR ....

The processor is the large-scale integrated circuit that executes instructions written by programmers to process information. Three kinds of information are received by the processor: interrupt messages, instructions, and data. Interrupt messages were discussed previously in this chapter.

> **Tech Talk**
>
> **Instructions: Statements of a program written by a programmer that tell the processor to perform a specific task.**
>
> **Data: Information that is necessary to complete the task.**

For example, the programmer can write a statement that tells the processor to add two numbers and display the sum on the screen. There are several discrete tasks to fulfill this statement (see List 2-1). Each of the numbered steps in this list is an instruction. Memory addresses that hold numbers used in the calculation and numbers themselves are data that is necessary to perform these instructions.

List 2-1 Discrete tasks to add two numbers and display the sum on the screen.

1. Go to a specified memory address where the first number is stored and bring the first number to the processor.
2. Store the first number in a memory location inside the processor called a register.
3. Go to a specified memory address where the second number is stored and bring the second number to the processor.
4. Store the second number in another register.
5. Copy both numbers from the registers to the arithmetic logic unit, which is placed within the processor where the calculation occurs.
6. Perform addition using those numbers.
7. Move the sum to another register.
8. Move the sum from the register to the video display adapter.

When a person runs a program, such as when you click OK on an icon on the Windows desktop, the operating system copies the program from the disk into memory.

Actually, the processor receives an interrupt request when you click OK. The interrupt request contains a specific interrupt type, which the processor uses to run the corresponding interrupt service routine as described earlier in this chapter.

The interrupt service routine locates the beginning of the file that corresponds to the file name, then copies the file into memory. The last task of this interrupt service routine is to give the processor the memory address of the first instruction of the program.

The address of the first instruction is placed in a register inside the processor. The processor then copies the instruction into another register before the instruction is executed. Once the instruction is executed, the processor increments the address in the register, which is the memory address of the next instruction. This process continues until the last instruction is executed, at which time the program ends and the processor is free to perform other tasks.

Tech Talk

Register: A small amount of memory located in the processor and used to store instructions and data temporarily.

Instruction Processing

The processor recognizes a limited number of commands that are integrated into the circuitry of the processor. These commands are called an instruction set and each processor type has a unique instruction set.

Most programmers don't use a processor's instruction set directly. Instead, they use a computer language that contains English-like commands. These are C, C++, Visual Basic, and Java to mention a few.

Programs written in one of these programming languages are converted into a language that the processor understands called machine language. A program called a compiler performs the conversion.

The converted program can run on a specific kind of processor because the instructions the programmer originally wrote are now in a form that the processor can understand. Commands in a machine language are the same as those found in the processor's instruction set.

The processor's instruction handler is the circuitry responsible for getting an instruction and interpreting the instruction. The instruction handler also controls execution of the instruction. That is, to make sure instructions are received in the proper order.

The instruction handler contains subcircuits, called units, which manage each phase of processing the instruction. These are the prefetch, the instruction decoder, and the control units.

The prefetch unit examines the first information read from the bus and determines whether or not the information is a complete instruction. If the information is part of an instruction, the prefetch unit requests the missing piece from memory.

Once the prefetch unit is satisfied that a complete instruction is received, an assessment is made as to what data, if any, is necessary to execute the instruction. Data can be found in one of three places. These are within the instruction itself, which is called an immediate data item; in a processor register, which occurs if the data was used in a recent process; or in computer memory, which requires the processor to copy the data from memory into a register.

Once the processor receives the necessary data, the next step is for the instruction decoder to evaluate the instruction and decide the proper circuitry in the processor to use to execute the instruction.

Let's say that the instruction contains several steps, one that requires the processor to perform a floating-point calculation. Instead of using the main processor, the instruction decoder is likely to give this instruction to the integrated math coprocessor, which is specifically designed to efficiently perform float-point calculations.

A list of these special circuits is contained in the microstore, which is a library stored inside the processor. The portion of the instruction that is sent to a special circuit is called a microinstruction. Features such as those used for multimedia and 3D graphics are made possible by microinstructions.

CISC vs. RISC

There are two general styles of instruction sets. These are the complex instruction set computing (CISC) and the reduced instruction set computing (RISC). The main difference between CISC and RISC is the size of the instruction. Computers using CISC, such as PCs, use variable length instructions while computers using RISC, such as workstations, (see Chapter 1) use fixed length instructions.

The difference becomes noticeable when a computer must process many instructions within a short time period, such as processing trades on Wall Street. As mentioned earlier in this chapter, the size of the bus and the number of bytes the processor can read from the bus are a set size and number. If an instruction is larger than either the size of the bus or the number of bytes a processor can read in one clock cycle, then more than one clock cycle is required to read the instruction.

Therefore, a computer using CISC might use more than one clock cycle to read an instruction depending on the size of the instruction. A computer that uses RISC avoids this problem because all instructions are the same size and can be transported and read by the processor in one clock cycle.

The difference in efficiency between a computer using CISC and a computer using RISC is irrelevant for most PC applications because personal computers don't usually process a lot of instructions.

However, this difference becomes material when a computer is called upon to perform heavy data processing. This is one of the reasons why many Wall Street firms employ workstation category computers to handle demanding processing.

Bus Interface Unit

Pins on the processor connect the processor to the bus on the motherboard. This is called the processor's bus interface unit, which monitors information flowing into and out of the processor.

It is also the job of the bus interface unit to transmit a strong enough signal so that information sent by the processor is able to be received by the furthest component connected to the bus. Likewise, the bus interface unit reduces the strength of the signal it receives to a strength that is acceptable for processing information inside the processor. Signal strength is measured in voltage.

The bus interface unit also has the job of synchronizing the internal and external clocks. Some processors run internally faster than the clock cycles used to move information over the bus, which is called the bus frequency. Synchronization assures that information flows smoothly in and out of the processor.

Registers: Memory Inside the Processor

The processor must store information temporarily while an instruction is processed. The place where information is stored is called a register, which is very similar to computer memory that exists outside of the processor.

The number and size of registers inside a processor vary according to the type of processor. The Intel 8088 processor that practically started the PC revolution has 14 registers, each of which can hold a 16-bit number. Today's processors holds 64-bit numbers and have a relatively larger number of registers compared with the 8088. The additional registers are used to support complex features that weren't available on earlier computers.

The processor is able to use registers efficiently. Although a register can store a 64-bit number, the register can also be logically split into smaller units. Two letters usually identify a register. The first letter is the name of the register. The second letter indicates the portion of the register that is to be accessed.

Let's say a register that holds a 64-bit number is called Register A. The processor can store one 64-bit number in the register or two 32-bit numbers. The letters *AX* might be used to reference all 64 bits while the letters *AL* represent the lower 32 bits and *AH* the higher 32 bits. The actual letters that represent registers are dependent on the instruction set.

Registers are also identified by the role they play in processing instructions. Most processors have an accumulator register, which is used to store the results of calculations. The instruction pointer register is used to store the memory address of the current instruction. This is sometimes called the program counter and the address value stored in the instruction pointer is incremented by the processor once the instruction is completed.

Memory Cache

Typically the processor can execute instructions faster than the processor can read information from the bus. This situation provides less throughput than is possible because once the processor completes an instruction, the processor waits for a fraction of a second for the rest of the computer to catch up. Those fractions add up over time and can have a dramatic impact on programs that perform high volume of data processing such as database applications or multimedia applications.

Most delays occur because the processor is waiting for either an instruction or data to be copied from memory. Engineers were able to rectify the situation by placing memory inside the processor. This memory is called a memory cache.

A memory cache is similar yet different from registers that I spoke about previously in this chapter. A register is memory used to temporarily store small amounts of information such as the results of a calculation.

In contrast, memory cache is used as a stopping point for instructions and data between the main memory and the processor. When an instruction or data is required, the processor has the memory cache control circuit copy the information from main memory and place the information in the memory cache. The processor then copies the information from the memory cache into the appropriate registers. Likewise, processed information is sent to the memory cache from registers after the memory cache control circuit sends the information to main memory.

Although a memory cache seems to be a time-consuming intermediate step between the processor and main memory, this step reduces the delay of moving information to and from main memory and the processor.

Chips used for memory caching can operate at a faster speed than that of main memory chips. This means memory caching chips can keep pace with the processor. Once information is placed in the memory cache by the processor, the processor is free to perform another task. The memory cache control circuit handles the transfer of data to main memory while the processor moves on to the next instruction.

Probably the most important way memory caching increases throughput of a processor is by retaining copies of the most recent data used by the processor. Let's say that the processor is asked to calculate a raise in salary. List 2-2 contains the steps required to do this.

List 2-2 *Steps used to calculate a salary increase.*

1. Copy the instruction from main memory.
2. Determine the data required to complete the instruction.
3. Copy the percentage increase from main memory.
4. Copy the salary from main memory.
5. Multiply the dollar value of the salary increase by the percentage increase.
6. Copy the value of the salary increase into main memory.
7. Copy the salary from main memory.
8. Copy the value of the salary increase from main memory.
9. Add the value of the salary increase to the salary.
10. Copy the sum, which is the new salary, to main memory.

Notice that steps 4 and 7 are the same. Both copy the salary data from main memory. However, this data is retained in the memory cache until the data is overwritten. The memory cache is overwritten whenever the memory cache is full and new data must be placed into the memory cache.

Until that time, data used by step 4 remains in the cache. In step 7 the processor doesn't have to wait until data is retrieved from main memory because the data is already in the memory cache. The memory cache control circuits do not need to copy the data from main memory again.

Some processors are manufactured with one or two memory caches, which are called level 1 (L1) memory cache and level 2 (L2) memory cache. A memory cache is valuable for applications that use the same instructions and/or data repeatedly. However, the size of a memory cache is extremely small when compared with main memory.

Therefore, a limited number of instructions and/or data are retained in the memory cache, which can lower the effectiveness of using it. This is because there is a low probability that an instruction or data required by the processor is stored in the memory cache due to the size of the cache.

Engineers attempt to minimize this problem by including a second level cache with the processor, which practically doubles the amount of memory cache available. The additional memory cache becomes a price consideration for the consumer because fast memory chips that are appreciably more expensive than main memory chips are used in a memory cache. It would be cost prohibitive to use fast memory chips as main memory.

Computer and processor manufacturers tout the inclusion of one or more memory caches in their products as a come-on to buy their computer. Sometimes advertisements refer to caches as an instruction cache, data cache, read cache, and direct mapped cache among a variety of other terms.

It is important not to be caught up in the hype. A memory cache is advantageous only if the programs you frequently use require fast processing and use repeated instructions and data, such as a game program. You are unlikely to notice an improved performance by using memory cache if you only use office products such as a word processing and a spreadsheet program.

INSIDE COMPUTER MEMORY ....

By now you understand that computer memory, sometimes called main memory, consists of integrated circuits that are used to hold information. Information is stored as a setting of a series of switches that are logically grouped in sets of eight. Each switch can store a bit and the set stores a byte.

Every byte of memory has a unique address, although not every address contains a memory chip. The maximum number of memory addresses that can be referenced by the processor is determined by the size of the address register inside the processor (see Chapter 1).

An address register of 32 bits can address 4 gigabytes (GB) of memory. However, many of these addresses won't be associated with real memory chips. This is because most applications don't require that much memory.

There are two general categories of memory: ROM and RAM. ROM chips contain information that can't be changed such as instructions used by the video adapter to display information on the computer display. Special nonvolatile RAM (NVRAM) is also used for this purpose. The nonvolatile feature of this RAM enables information to be retained in memory even after the power to the computer is turned off.

Direct Memory Access

The processor is the device inside the computer that accesses memory whenever an instruction or data is needed. However, there can be more than one type of processor inside the computer such as is the case with a network adapter card.

Tech Talk

Network adapter card: A device either integrated on the motherboard or inserted into an expansion slot that connects the motherboard to a local area network.

Local area network: Circuits, cables, and software that link together computers, servers, printers, and other devices. Commonly known as LAN.

When information from the LAN (read *The Essential Guide to Network* for a full discussion about networking) arrives at the network adapter card, the network adapter card must place this information into main memory. There are two ways this is accomplished.

The first method is for the network adapter card's processor to send an interrupt message to the CPU. The interrupt basically tells the CPU to stop processing and to copy the information received by the network adapter card to a place in main memory.

In the second method, the network adapter card's processor has direct access to main memory and can independently copy incoming information to memory without requiring help from the CPU.

This method is called direct memory access (DMA). There are two forms of DMA—standard and bus mastering. Standard DMA gives devices such as the network adapter card direct access to the main memory. This lessens the load on the CPU because the CPU can be doing other things while the device interacts with main memory.

Bus mastering DMA gives all devices access to main memory and the ability to communicate with other devices that are connected to the computer's bus. The computer's bus is called the DMA channel. This means a device such as the network adapter card can save information to a hard disk if so programmed without requiring the services of the CPU.

While direct memory access increases the throughput of the CPU and the overall performance of the device using DMA, there is a major drawback. As mentioned previously, many CPUs have memory cache that contains some previously used data.

Data in the memory cache is a copy of data that also appears in main memory. Devices that use direct memory access have the ability to change the main memory copy of the data. This might result in the same data having two values: one in main memory and one in the memory cache.

Therefore the device's processor notifies the memory cache control circuit any time a value in main memory is changed by the device's processor. The memory cache control circuit then either deletes the data from the memory cache or updates the data with the new value.

Memory Addressing

Computer designers can use various methods to address main memory depending on the memory mapping used with the computer. Memory mapping is the way in which memory locations are identified inside the computer.

Each memory location has a physical address. This is the address on the bus that is associated with the pins of the memory chip. Some computers such as personal computers don't use the physical memory address. Instead these computers use the virtual memory address, which is sometimes called the logical memory address. Each virtual memory address is directly associated with a physical memory address.

Memory can be organized in segments of 65,536 virtual addresses. The combination of the segment value and the virtual address identifies a physical memory address. Processors such as those used in personal computers store the memory segment in a segment register and the virtual address in another address register. Typically the value in the segment register remains unchanged as the processor increments the address register when running a program. The virtual address is an offset of the segment value.

Here's how it works (see Figure 2-6). Let's say the computer has 30 bytes of physical memory divided logically into three segments each representing 10 bytes. The first physical memory address is referenced as segment 1 virtual address 0. The 11th physical memory address is referenced as segment 2 virtual address 0. Therefore, the 11th physical memory address is said to be one offset of segment 2.

Before the physical memory address can be referenced using a segment value and a virtual address, the computer must be running in real mode. Real mode is one of three modes in which a personal computer can operate. The other modes are protected and Virtual 86.

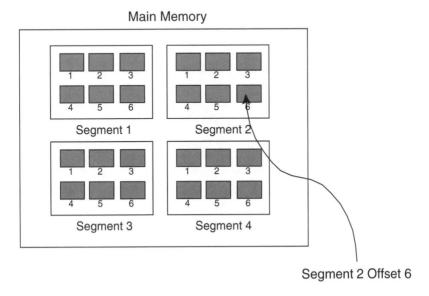

Figure 2-6
Memory is organized in segments. Within each segment a virtual memory address is identified by a value that is offset from the segment

In real mode, the computer runs one program at a time. This means each program has access to all available memory locations, which is the mode of older personal computers. Today's personal computers start up in real mode but quickly move into protected mode.

Protected mode enables the computer to run multiple programs at the same time. Each program assigns region of memory (see Figure 2-7). This prevents one program from interfering with another program's memory.

The memory addressing method used in protected mode is dramatically different than that used in real mode. Each region of memory is identified by a row in a descriptor table. Each row has three columns of information about the region. These are the physical memory address that begins the region, the size of the region, and access rights information. Access rights identify the programs that can use the region.

The processor identifies a region using a selector value and a virtual address. The selector value is similar to the segment value in real mode except the selector value points to one row in the descriptor table. The virtual address is a specific address within the region. This is the same offset concept used in the real mode.

Protected mode offers two important advantages over real mode. First, a program isn't restricted to the size of a segment. Instead, the region of memory in which the program operates can be adjusted according to available memory (i.e., memory that is not being used by a program that is currently running in the computer).

The other advantage of protected mode is that access to a region is restricted. Programs that attempt to address a physical memory address outside of its region are stopped by the operating system and an error message is displayed. Typically the mes-

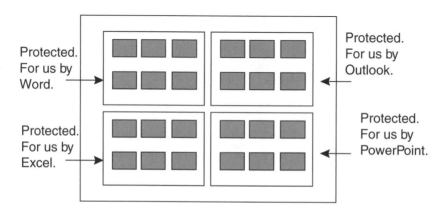

Figure 2-7
Memory is organized in regions when a personal computer operates in protected mode. Each program is restricted to a memory region

sage says something about a "Page Fault" or a "General Protection Fault," which you've probable seen more than once if you use Windows.

The Virtual 86 mode is used to run old MS-DOS programs on new computers. The computer runs in protected mode and then simulates running an 8086 processor in real mode. I won't go into how memory is addressed in Virtual 86 mode because this mode is rarely used today.

Another concept used in memory management is called paging. Paging enables the operating system to use more memory addresses than the physical memory addresses by off-loading memory to a hard disk.

Here's how it works (see Figure 2-8). Let's say there are only 30 bytes of main memory that are divided into three 10-byte regions. Two programs are already running, each having its own region. The third program requires 15 bytes of memory, but there is only a 10-byte region available.

Rather than the operating system displaying a message that there is insufficient memory to run the program, the operating system creates virtual memory on the hard disk. Virtual memory is memory that seems to exist but doesn't physically exist.

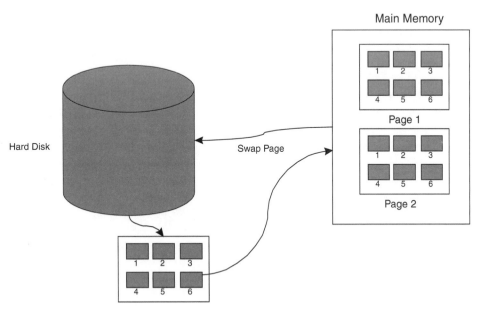

Figure 2-8
Paging expands the physical memory by using part of a hard disk as memory, then swapping contents between physical memory and a hard disk

In this case, instructions and data (5 bytes) that don't fit in the 10-byte region are stored on the hard disk and organized as if they were stored in memory. This enables the operating system to swap those 5 bytes of virtual memory with the contents of real memory whenever the processor needs to use those 5 bytes.

SUMMARY ....

Although computers vary in size, power, and cost, they tend to function similarly. Computers have the same general components and have the same objective. That is, to process information.

Engineers devised a way of using the binary number system to represented data inside a computer. The binary number system has two digits—zero and one. The state of electronic switches is indicated by binary digits. A zero implies an off state and a one implies an on state.

Several binary digits are used to store a number, such as a person's salary in a computer. Decimal digits, which are used in everyday life, can be mathematically converted to binary digits. Binary digits can be directly used in calculations.

Engineers developed the ASCII and other similar standards to associate letters and symbols used in languages to a numeric value. A program such as a word processor is used to convert letter and symbols you see on the screen into corresponding numbers in the ASCII table. Likewise, a program translates numbers into the associated ASCII letter or symbol, which is displayed on the computer screen.

There are three kinds of information used inside a computer. These are instructions, data, and interrupt messages. Instructions are programs written to direct the computer to perform a specific task. Data is information the computer needs to perform an instruction. An interrupt message is a signal to the central processor to stop whatever the processor is doing and to do something else.

The CPU, also known as the processor, is the brain of the computer. It is this component that performs all the calculations and processing. The clock is the heart of the computer and moves information along etched wires, called a bus, on the motherboard, which is the main circuit board inside the computer. Information is stored in memory chips. A memory chip is a circuit that contains many electronic switches. Each of these switches can store one binary digit called a bit.

Whenever devices such as the keyboard want the processor to do something, for example, rebooting the computer, the device sends the processor an interrupt message that contains an interrupt type.

The processor stops what it is doing, then looks up the interrupt type on the interrupt vector table. The interrupt vector table contains the memory address of the interrupt service routine. An interrupt service routine is a program the processor runs whenever an interrupt message is received.

A common request made by the keyboard or mouse is for the processor to run a program. The name of the program is either entered in the Run dialog box or is associated with an icon on the desktop.

Once a person selects the program, an interrupt is sent to the processor to run the interrupt service routine that loads the requested program into memory. Once in memory, the processor receives the memory address of the first instruction of the program.

The processor examines the contents of this address and determines if the whole or partial instruction is received. If the instruction is incomplete, the processor looks at the next address in sequence, which usually contains the other portion of the instruction.

Next, the processor determines if any data is required to complete the instruction. If so, then the data is retrieved from the relative memory address before the CPU processes the instructions.

The result of the process is temporarily stored in memory called a register inside the processor until the instruction is fully processed, at which time the result is either stored in main memory or sent to the video display adapter where the result is displayed on the screen. This depends on another instruction from the program.

Once the last instruction is processed, the processor waits for the next request to arrive from a device that is integrated into the motherboard or is connected to the motherboard via a port or expansion slot.

A port such as a serial port is a circuit on the motherboard that is used to connect an external device such as a printer to the bus on the motherboard. An expansion slot is an opening on the motherboard where compatible circuit boards such as a modem can be placed, expanding the features of the computer. An expansion slot also connects the circuit board to the bus on the motherboard.

Summary Questions

1. **What is the function of a memory cache?**

2. **What is the difference between an ASCII number and a binary number?**

3. **How does paging work?**

4. **What is the difference between real mode and protected mode?**

5. **Why is a clock used in a computer?**

6. How can a virus use an interrupt vector table to attack a computer?

7. How are binary values represented in signal within the computer?

8. What role does segment play in determining a memory address?

9. What is meant by the error message "General Protection Fault"?

10. Why is a descriptor table used in a computer?

PUTTING IT ALL TOGETHER ....

Here's a challenge. Break into my computer network. I'll give you a start by telling you that my ID is JK1234 and that the password consists of 10 digits. Each digit can be from zero to nine. Your job is to uncover the correct password.

You might wonder how to approach this problem. I'll give you a hint. First determine the number of combinations of 10 digits. That is the same as calculating the number of possible passwords. You do this by using a factorial calculation, which is simply multiplying 10 by 9, then the product by 8, then by 7, and continue until you multiply the final product by zero.

Until the 20th century, mathematicians had to perform this multiplication by hand. And it wasn't until the early 1950s when a commercial computer the size of an office floor was built that you could perform the same calculations using electronic components.

I'll admit that performing nine multiplication problems does not require a mechanical or electronic computer, but the next part of your challenge does. There are 3,628,800 possible passwords. Your job is to try each one until you gain access to the network.

I'll agree that this is an impossible task to perform by hand, yet a computer could do this in a few minutes thanks to the introduction of large-scale integrated circuits in 1971 and the 19th century concepts of using repeated code developed by Ada Lovelace.

A programmer can write a few lines of instructions to have a computer try each password, then stop when the correct password is entered. Programmers write instructions using a high-level programming language such as C++ or Java, which is compiled into machine language. Machine language contains a set of commands called an instruction set that is understood by the computer's processor.

The programmer executes the program by entering the name of the program into the computer. This causes a signal called an interrupt message to be sent to the processor telling the processor to stop whatever it is doing and run the interrupt service routine that is associated with the interrupt message.

In this case, the processor runs the interrupt service routine that copies the program from the disk into memory, then provides the processor with the first instruction of the program. The processor evaluates the program and decides if data is required before the instruction can be executed. If so, then the processor finds the data in memory. The data required for this program is the user ID and the number of digits in the password.

Data is stored in registers inside the processor and is used to process the instructions. First, the processor calculates the number of possible passwords and stores this result in memory. Next the processor assembles the first set of user ID and password and sends a login message with this information to the port that contains the network adapter card, which tries to log on to the network.

If the network adapter card reports an error message such as an invalid login ID or password, the processor executes the next instruction. This increments the value of the password and then has the processor make another attempt to log on to the network.

Today's computers can execute these instructions quickly because information moves around components inside the computer at a very fast rate, which is measured in megahertz clock cycles. The higher the megahertz rating, the faster the computer can process instructions—and the faster the computer will learn the correct password.

Memory cache is another feature that is important to cracking the password. Memory cache retains frequently requested instructions and data. In this program, memory cache will probably retain the instructions to send the ID and password to the network adapter card and the instructions to calculate the next password.

Likewise, the user ID and the last password attempted will too be retained in the memory cache. This means that no time is wasted retrieving these instructions and data from memory each time the processor attempts using another password.

Of course, memory cache, a fast clock, and an efficient program is still no guarantee that the computer will break the password code quickly. Other factors can slow down progress. These include an inefficient network adapter card, a slow network connection, and a poor response from the computer running the login program.

Not much can be done about a slow network connection or a poor response from the remote computer, however the performance of the network adapter card might be improved. Some network adapter cards use a technique called direct memory access. This enables the network adapter card's onboard processor to directly access the computer main memory, which frees the processor to continue processing.

Without DMA, the network adapter card must send an interrupt to the computer's processor asking it to copy the information received from the network and store that information into the computer's main memory.

Regardless of whether or not you are trying to uncover my password, the same basic functionality is performed millions of time each day by your computer when you run a program.

Part 2

Computer Hardware Components

Computer technology is like the weather because both are forever changing. As my mom always said, there's nothing you can do about the weather. However, there is something you can do to keep up with changing computer technology. You can read Part 2.

Part 2 explores all the components of computer technology in a down-to-earth way. You'll learn the basic science used in each component and then you'll learn how components work.

Chapter 3 looks at the nuts and bolts of every computer. These are the motherboard, memory, and processors. You'll move on to monitors and video cards in Chapter 4 and storage devices in Chapter 5. Storage includes disk drives, CD drives, and other devices used to save information.

Chapter 6 explores printing technology, where you'll learn about inkjet printers, laser printers, and nontraditional printers. In Chapter 7 you'll get an insider's view of modems and networking devices.

Chapter 8 looks at input devices such as keyboards, game controllers, and speech recognition. Chapter 9 focuses on audio

devices such as sound cards, speakers, and headphones. Chapter 10 examines digital cameras and scanners. You'll also be shown how to create your own webcam.

Chapter 11 explores the latest in cell phones, PDAs, and other wireless and mobile devices.

3 Motherboards, Memory, and Processors

In this chapter...

- The Inside Story of Motherboards
- The Inside Story of Memory
- The Inside Story on Processors

They Said It...

"Anyone can understand technology once they're shown the ropes."

Anonymous

For many of us a computer is defined by the shape of the box that sits on our desk—and possibly the brand name on the box. However, there is more to a computer than this. Just as you cannot judge a book by its cover, you cannot judge a computer by a fancy metal box.

All computers function in a similar way, which you learned in the previous chapter. Yet all computers are remarkably different. These differences lie with the components inside the computer.

You'll notice that there are many components inside a computer if you pop off the cover of the computer. In the midst of the many chips, diodes, wires, and circuit boards are three components that give a computer its recognizable characteristics. These components are the motherboard, memory, and the processor.

The right mixture of these components makes any computer hum along without a hiccup. The wrong blend and the computer will operate as if it was speeding along a pothole-filled highway. It is your job to select the right assortment of components so that the computer can tackle any job effectively and cost efficiently.

In this chapter, you will learn about the motherboards, memory, and processors on the marketplace. You will also explore:

- Chipsets
- Power supplies
- Ports
- Memory-access methods
- Details of the latest processors

REALITY CHECK ....

Among my favorite movies is *Apollo 13*. This was the ill-fated moon-landing attempt in April 1970, as you might remember. An explosion onboard the spacecraft following the launch left three astronauts practically floating in space with little electrical power.

The flight was one of NASA's notable failures and successes when the astronauts were recovered a bit worn for wear but essentially unharmed. What startled me was the scene when engineers in mission control calculated the amount of fuel required to bring the astronauts home. They didn't use computers or calculators. They used slide rules.

It dawned on me during that scene that astronauts successfully landed on the moon in 1969 and engineers brought the Apollo 13 mission to a relatively safe ending with less computer power than that used in today's handheld computers.

Arguably the most popular computer in that day was the IBM System 360, which was a mainframe computer housed on a floor of an office building. And it was another four or five years before the Altair 8800 personal computer was introduced to the world.

Circuitry and components that we'll be discussing in this chapter dwarf the technology used to send the first astronauts to the moon. This is amazing when you stop to think of how we take for granted the power in our desktop.

THE INSIDE STORY OF MOTHERBOARDS...............

The motherboard is the focal point of any computer for this is the circuit board that contains tiny wires and nearly all the other components of the computer. This is the place where key components come together to process information.

It is difficult to imagine that the motherboard grew out of the photographic process, but this is a fact. An image such as a picture of your dog is transferred to film when you expose the film to light (except for a digital camera, which you'll learn about in Chapter 10).

The image takes the form of a negative image where components such as your dog's nose are reversed from what you see in the camera's viewfinder. The negative image is made into a positive image in the photo lab by placing the negative over photographic paper, then shining light through the negative. Chemicals are used to make the positive image appear on the photographic paper.

This same basic process is used to create the motherboard—and other circuit boards—except the motherboard replaces the photographic paper in the process. The motherboard is a sandwich. Two outer pieces—the bread—consist of a nonconductive material. The inside piece—the meat—is a conductive material. Wires are etched into the motherboard by removing a portion of the outer piece, causing the conductive material to be exposed. The exposed conductive material is the etched wire.

Tech Talk

Nonconductive material: Material that resists the flow of electricity.

Conductive material: Material that has little or no resistance to the flow of electricity.

Etch: The technique of removing the nonconductive material outer coating and exposing the inner conductive material.

Before this process begins, engineers decide where they want the etched wires to appear on the motherboard. They make the decision based on electrical engineering principles and the needs of components that will be used on the circuit board. Most of this technique is beyond the scope of this book and you probably won't find it very interesting unless you want to learn about electrical engineering.

Lines that represent the length and width of the etched wires are drawn into position using a computer program. The computer transforms those lines onto the motherboard through either a chemical process similar to the one used for photographs or by using a laser.

In either case the results are the same. Wherever the lines appear on the computer image of the motherboard, the corresponding outer portions of the real motherboard are removed exposing strips of the second layer's conductive material.

Once the design is etched onto the motherboard, holes are drilled into the motherboard wherever chips or other components are to be connected. A robot inserts the chips and other components into those holes, which are soldered into position.

Tech Talk

Soldered: The technique of using heated metal to connect two pieces of conductive material such as pins on a chip and etched wires on a circuit board.

Components on a Motherboard

The motherboard, sometimes called the planar, desktop board, and system board, contains diodes, capacitors, resistors, jumpers, connector receptacles, power supply, voltage regulators, and an assortment of chips. Only a few of these components are important for you to understand because these are the components that make each computer different.

Components that we'll focus on are chips, connector receptacles, and power supply and how they come together to transform the motherboard into a computer. A chip refers to a large-scale integrated circuit that contains the logic to store, retrieve, transmit, and process information.

One of the most important chips on the motherboard is the central processing unit (CPU), also known as a microprocessor and simply the processor. This is the brain of all the chips as you learned in the previous chapter. You'll learn the specific characteristics of today's popular processors later in this section.

The clock (see Chapter 2) is another important chip and its job is to synchronize information flow on the motherboard. I like to think of the clock as the heart of the motherboard because the clock provides the pulsating wave that pushes information at a specific rate over the etched wires on the motherboard to the other chips.

Memory chips dot the landscape of the motherboard and are used to store information. There are two categories of memory chips. These are read-only memory (ROM) and random access memory (RAM), variations of which are discussed in detail later in this chapter.

As you learned in the previous chapter, memory chips are tiny electronic switches that store information, permanently in the case of ROM, and temporarily for RAM. The most important memory chip on the motherboard is the ROM chip that contains the main basic input/output system (BIOS).

There are a number of BIOS chips in a computer. Some are found on the motherboard and others on circuit boards that are connected to an expansion slot. For example, the video adapter typically contains a ROM chip with the instructions to operate the video adapter. The video adapter circuitry might be integrated into the motherboard circuits or on a video adapter card circuitry. Disk drive controller circuitry and network adapter circuitry are other common features that have their own BIOS.

Main BIOS stores the first set of instructions that is read when a computer is powered on. These instructions bring the motherboard and peripherals such as the keyboard, mouse, and monitor alive. And this is the BIOS that loads the operating system from the disk.

Expansion Slots

A motherboard is usually designed with expansion receptacles commonly called expansion slots, although some manufacturers don't offer any as a way to lower the price of the motherboard. Expansion slots are used to enhance features of a motherboard. A feature that is not built into the motherboard can be added by inserting a circuit board that contains the feature into an expansion slot, as is discussed in the previous chapter. This circuit board is called an expansion circuit board.

Fingerlike pieces of an expansion circuit board touch connectors inside the expansion slot on the motherboard enabling information to flow to and from the motherboard and the expansion circuit board. The number of fingerlike pieces on an expansion circuit board depends on the type of expansion slot built into the motherboard.

There are various kinds of expansion slots on the motherboard. Typically motherboards manufactured by Intel—and competitors—have three types of expansion slots. These are the Industry Standard Architecture (ISA), the Peripheral Component Interconnect (PCI), and the Accelerated Graphics Port (AGP).

The ISA expansion slot is found on older computers and on some new computers that want to maintain backward capability with existing expansion circuit boards. However, the PCI expansion slot is gradually replacing ISA. The PCI expansion slot is found on most personal computers and on Apple's Macintosh.

The important difference between the ISA and PCI expansion slots is speed. A PCI expansion slot can transfer information quicker than ISA, which is why most expansion devices for computers use a PCI expansion slot.

AGP expansion slots are used on motherboards for expansion circuit boards designed to process video information. Video requires much more information to be transported onto a motherboard than most other kinds of information such as that used in a database application.

The AGP expansion slot along with the appropriate expansion circuit board must be used to maintain a level of processing that produces acceptable video reproduction on the computer screen. You'll learn more about video in the next chapter.

Ports

In addition to chips and expansion slots, the motherboard has ports that are used to link the motherboard to external devices such as printers and modems. I like to think of a port as a hole in the computer where I plug in the keyboard, mouse, speakers, video, and joystick.

Some ports are dedicated for a particular device such as the keyboard and mouse. Other ports are used to connect a variety of devices such as printers and modems. There are five popular ports found on a motherboard. These are the serial port, parallel port, universal serial bus (USB), Small Computer System Interface (SCSI) port, and the A-D port.

The serial port, sometimes called the RS-232 or COM port, sends and receives information between the motherboard and an external device one bit of information at a time. In contrast, a parallel port transports information 8 bits (1 byte) at a time. I talked about both ports in the previous chapter.

Devices plugged into the small USB port work instantaneously without the need to restart the computer. This is a sharp improvement over other ports where the computer must be restarted before the operating system recognizes the device connected to the port.

With ports other than the USB, the operating system assumes that all devices connected to the computer when it started remain connected while the computer is running. Likewise, the operating system assumes that no new devices were connected to the computer.

Of course, that may not be the case if you decide to connect a device such as a printer to a port while the computer is powered up. The USB port notifies the operating system when the status of the port changes such as when a device is removed from or inserted into a port.

In addition to being a smart port, there are two other features the USB port offers that makes it the choice of both device manufacturers and computer buyers. These are the fact that the USB port can provide power to devices that are external to the computer and the USB port can be used by multiple devices through the use of a USB hub.

Let's say that a computer uses an external modem. The modem must be connected to a serial port and plugged into a power source. However, a modem designed for use with the USB port can get power from the USB port. This lowers the cost of manufacturing and the hassle for the user to find enough power outlets for add-on computer devices.

The other feature is the ability to create a USB port hub (see Figure 3-1). A USB port hub makes one USB port expandable to handle up to 127 devices as long as these devices are within 3 meters of the hub. The hub connects directly to the USB port and USB port devices connect directly to the USB hub. As with any USB device, the hub can be powered by the USB port or by an external power source. Additional USB hubs can be connected to the USB hub that is directly connected to the USB port. This means that you can have an almost endless number of USB devices connected to a computer.

The USB port is not only replacing the serial and parallel ports but also dedicated ports such as those used for the keyboard, mouse, and video displays. However, the USB port suffers from two important problems.

First, it does not provide a fast enough connection for some devices such as a hard disk. USB 1.1 has a 1.5 MB per second transfer rate. USB 2.0 is an improved version of USB and has a transfer rate of 60 MB per second. Therefore the USB port is not the candidate of choice for all devices. The other problem is with the operating system. The operating system must be able to respond to the signal that a device has been plugged into—or removed from—the USB port while the computer is running. Windows 98 is such an operating system, but not Windows 95.

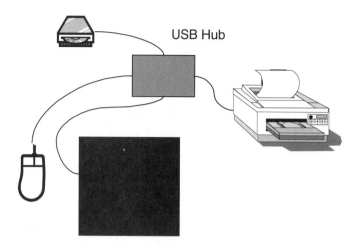

Figure 3-1
A USB hub enables multiple devices to connect to one USB port

The SCSI (pronounced "scuzzy") port is another type of port found in some computers. SCSI is primarily used to link together many devices to the motherboard using one port. This technique is called daisy chaining and uses some of the general concepts found in computer networks (see Figure 3-2).

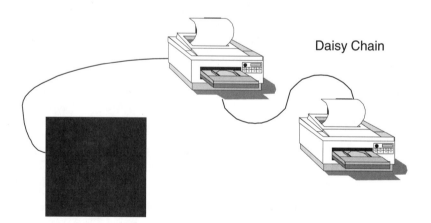

Figure 3-2
SCSI devices are daisy-chained and pass along information between devices

SCSI ports may not be integrated into the motherboard as the other ports I mentioned in this section. This is because SCSI devices, which are devices that plug into the SCSI port, are not as commonplace as devices designed for use with other ports.

Here's how SCSI works. Each SCSI device has two SCSI ports of its own. One is used to connect the device to the SCSI port on the motherboard. The other is used to connect to the SCSI port on another SCSI device. This configuration is called daisy chaining.

Each SCSI device has an address that uniquely identifies it along the daisy chain. As described in the previous chapter, each port has a unique address inside the computer. All devices connected to the SCSI daisy chain are accessed by using the SCSI port address.

The SCSI controller, which is the name given the SCSI port circuitry, is able to know which SCSI device is to receive the information through the use of logic built into the circuitry. Computers that don't have a SCSI port—or a USB port—integrated into the motherboard use a SCSI (or USB) expansion card.

There are several flavors of SCSI: asynchronous, synchronous, Fast SCSI, Ultra SCSI, Ultra2 SCSI, and Wide SCSI. The primary difference among these variations is transmission speed. Asynchronous SCSI is the slowest because there is a waiting period from the time a command is sent to a SCSI device to the time a response is received. This delay doesn't exist in synchronous SCSI. Synchronous SCSI uses a coordinated communication approach that increases throughput across the SCSI cable.

The standard transmission speed for SCSI is 5 MHz. Fast SCSI doubles this rate of speed and Ultra SCSI doubles the Fast SCSI speed to 20 MHz. Ultra2 SCSI can bring transmission speeds up to 40 MHz. And Wide SCSI uses a 68-pin cable to further speeds.

The A-D port, sometimes called a game port, is integrated into many motherboards. The A-D port converts an analog signal generated by an analog device such as a joystick to a digital signal. An analog signal is similar to the signal generated by your voice in that the signal contains various values. For example, your voice produces various values called frequencies as you speak or sing. In contrast, a digital signal has only two values represented by a zero or one.

A joystick generates many values as the stick is moved. Unfortunately the computer won't understand these values unless they are simplified into zeros and ones—and that's the job of the A-D port. This port is also used for more purposeful jobs than playing a game. It is also used to record signals from measurement instrumentation such as those used hospitals.

Power Supply

None of the components on the motherboard operate without sufficient electrical power, which is supplied by the power supply. The power supply receives 110 AC volts from the wall socket and converts the power into DC voltage, which is required for all components and devices connected to the motherboard. The power supply also contains the fan that maintains airflow inside the computer.

Power supplies are measured in watts. Common wattage is 150, 200, 220, and 250 watts. Computers come with a power supply sufficiently rated to handle all the features that are built into the motherboard and to power most expansion circuits.

However, there may not be enough power from the standard power supply to address increasing demands from external devices that draw power from the computer. For example, many devices can connect to a USB port, especially if a USB hub is in use. The USB port can supply power to these devices, which might be over and above the watts available from the power supply. In these situations, the power supply can be replaced with a higher rate power supply.

Other Connections

Devices such as disk drives are typically enclosed within the computer and connected to the motherboard by a controller circuit. The controller circuit can be integrated on the motherboard itself or can be on an expansion card.

Integrated controller circuits contain either exposed pins or a receptacle similar to that used by expansion slots. In either case, one end of a cable is inserted into the motherboard and the other plugged into the device. These connections are commonly used for floppy disk drives, hard disk drives, various flavors of CD drives, and DVD drives.

Characteristics of a Motherboard

A motherboard defines a computer. Whenever you choose a computer you are actually making the decision based on the characteristics of the motherboard unless your choice is based on the color of the box.

Knowing a motherboard's characteristics helps you reach an intelligent decision to purchase a new computer or upgrade the motherboard in an existing computer. The most prominent characteristic of any motherboard is its form, which is called the form factor.

The form factor is defined as the size and shape of the motherboard as well as the port types that are integrated into the motherboard. The form factor also includes the power supply connector type, which defines the type of power supply that can be used to power the motherboard.

The form factor is less important when buying a new computer than it is when upgrading because the form factor and the computer case must be compatible. That is, size and position of the motherboard must fit properly inside the computer case.

There are five types of form factors. These are AT, AT (BAT), ATX, LPX, and proprietary. The AT, AT (BAT), and LPX are older style motherboards that are of limited availability because they don't include the latest technology.

The ATX motherboard is the latest motherboard form factor and comes in three styles—miniATX, flexATI, and NLX, each having a slightly different form factor definition. Some computers use a proprietary motherboard, which is a motherboard that is specifically designed for a computer and is not available from third-party vendors. Workstations and specialty computers use proprietary motherboards. Most personal computers use nonproprietary motherboards such as ATX.

Although motherboards are manufactured without a processor and other chips, they are designed to support a particular processor and group of chips. Collectively these are called the chipset, which is discussed in detail in the next section.

Engineers design motherboards with a specific socket or slot that accepts a particular type of processor. A word of caution: Support for a processor involves more than having the proper socket or slot to accept the processor. Although the processor fits on a motherboard it doesn't mean that the motherboard supports the processor.

There are six common designs. These are socket 7, socket 8, socket 370, socket A, slot 1, and slot A. The Pentium/MMX uses socket 7 and the Pentium Pro uses socket 8. The coppermine-core Pentium III and the PPGA Celeron processor use socket 370. The AMD Athlon K75 thunderbird core processor uses socket A.

Slot 1 is designed to accept the Pentium II, Pentium III, and the Celeron. In addition, processors that use a socket 370 can be used in a slot 1 with the aid of a conversion adapter. Slot A is designed for the AMD Athlon processor.

Tech Talk

Socket: A receptacle attached to the motherboard that contains several holes, each of which is designed to match a pin in the processor.

Slot: A receptacle attached to the motherboard that accepts the edge of the circuit board that contains the processor very similar to an expansion slot.

Other factors that define the characteristics of a motherboard are the bus and power supply, which are discussed in detail later in this chapter.

Chipsets

A chipset is the group of computer chips that makes the motherboard come alive. I like to think of a motherboard as a town and a chipset as town services such as police, fire, and government. Without these services the town ceases to function.

A chipset consists of anywhere from one to three chips depending on the manufacturer's design. These are usually the large chips that you'll find on the motherboard and are labeled with the manufacturer's name and possibly the chipset code symbol. The chipset code symbol typically consists of numbers and/or letters such as the VIA used on Intel's chipset. Many times you can identify the chipset by visiting the motherboard manufacturer's web site and use either the make and model of the motherboard or the chipset code symbol to look up the chipset information.

Although you might at first think of the processor as the only important chip on the motherboard, there are other chips that are necessary to support features of a processor. For example, one or more chips in the chipset are responsible for transferring information over the bus to the processor and memory.

As discussed in the previous chapter, some processors use memory cache that stores a copy of previously used instructions and data for later use. It is the chipset that determines if an instruction or data is to be retrieved from main memory or from the memory cache. Therefore, a motherboard must have a chipset capable of handling memory cache, otherwise the motherboard will not be able to use a processor that uses a memory cache.

The chipset must be designed to manage the transfer of information at various speeds on the motherboard. Some components work faster than others (see Chapter 2) and it is the job of the chipset to efficiently maintain several transfer speeds at the same time.

This is accomplished by using buffers to store the information temporarily as a way to accommodate the needs of components on the motherboard. As with memory cache, the chipset must be designed with sufficient buffers to effectively handle transfer required by features found on the motherboard.

A chipset is designed to work with one family of processors. However, some chipsets will also work with compatible processors. A family of processors usually consists of a generation of processors made by the same manufacturer. For example, the Pentium is the sixth generation of processors produced by Intel. A chipset on a motherboard that uses the Pentium must be able to support the features the Pentium offers.

Information travels among components on the motherboard over a bus. The bus speed at which information is transported between memory and the processor is dependent on the capabilities of the chipset. Intel's chipset can handle a speed of 66

MHz although other manufacturers produce chipsets that can handle a 100 MHz speed. This is called the bus system speed.

The chipset determines if the speed of buses on the motherboard (see "The Bus" following this section) is coordinated or works independent of the memory bus. A chipset synchronizes buses on a motherboard.

For example, the speed of the PCI bus is typically half the speed of the memory bus. Therefore, the chipset uses a factor of two to adjust the speed of the PCI bus. This is commonly referred to as a synchronous motherboard. A motherboard is referred to as asynchronous if speeds of each bus are set independently of other buses.

Likewise, the chipset must be able to handle the speeds required by the processor. Processing is performed within the processor at a faster rate than the speed information moves along the memory bus. The processor rate is specified as a factor of the bus rate, such as two times the bus speed.

Some processors such as those manufactured by Intel use multiplier locks. This means the speed of the processor is determined by the bus speed. As the bus speed increases, the processor speed will increase proportionately. Other processors such as those made by AMD do not use a multiplier lock. That is, the processor's speed is independent of the bus speed. The chipset must be able to handle the speed of the processor otherwise the processor will not be operating at peak capacity.

There are a variety of other features that need the support of a chipset. These include direct memory access controller, Plug and Play support, AGP support, USB or FireWire support, and multiple processor support.

The Bus

A bus is the set of etched wires on the motherboard that are used to transport information among components and is a characteristic of a motherboard. Components connect to the bus through pins that are either inserted directly into the motherboard or into a receptacle attached to the motherboard such as an expansion slot.

Information can flow in both directions along a bus such as to and from the processor and memory. There are multiple buses on a motherboard and components may be connected to more than one bus. This enables components to become multifaceted in that information can flow using more than one pathway on the motherboard.

The term *bus* is sometimes used to describe a port such as one that connects the motherboard to the video adapter. A port is a bus in that a port provides an electronic path between components on the motherboard and an external device over which information flows. However, a port is considered a special type of bus because a port connects one external device with the motherboard. In contrast, a bus connects multiple components.

There are six types of buses commonly used in computers: AGP, cache, local input/output, memory, processor, and standard input/output.

The AGP is a dedicated bus designed to transport display information quickly between the processor and the video adapter card. This is particularly useful in graphics-intense applications such as games.

The cache bus carries information between the processor and cache memory, which consists of instructions and data that were recently used by the processor. Information can travel along the cache bus at speeds equal to the internal processing speed of the processor.

The local input/output bus handles communication between the processor and input devices and input/output devices. These include disk drives, CD drives, network adapters, and video adapters.

Some motherboards have a special local input/output bus called the PCI. The PCI bus is designed to connect many external connections called PCI slots that are integrated on the motherboard.

The memory bus connects main memory with the processor although some motherboards combine the functionality of the memory bus with that of the processor bus. The processor bus, sometimes called the host bus, transfers information between the processor and the chipset.

The standard input/output bus is the bus used on the original personal computers. This is sometimes known as the ISA or the AT bus. The standard input/output bus is similar to the local input/output bus except it connects to expansion slots integrated on the motherboard.

A bus is defined by width and speed. A bus is divided into two segments (see Figure 3-3). One segment is used to transport addresses of components such as a memory address and the other is used to transport data.

The width of a bus is the number of etched wires that are used for the transmission of information. Although there are several buses on the motherboard, the width of these buses is the same and different depending on the bus segment. The address segment of each bus is the same width because all addresses on the motherboard are the same size. However, the data segment can have different widths.

Keep in mind that etched wires of a bus are like lanes of a highway. The more highway lanes, the faster traffic will flow. The same principle holds true with the width of a bus. The more etched wires a data segment has, the more data will flow across the bus.

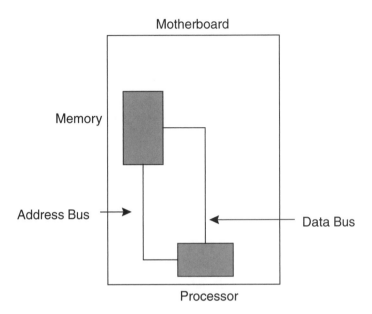

Figure 3-3
A bus is divided into the address segment and the data segment

The width of a bus is measured in bits that can be transported at one time. Each bit is carried over one etched wire on the data segment of the bus. Older computers such as the first IBM personal computer used an 8-bit wide bus, but soon moved to a 16-bit bus with the introduction of the IBM AT and the ISA bus. Today's computers use 32-bit and 64-bit buses. For example, the PCI bus found in new personal computers is 32 bits wide.

The width of the data segment of the bus should equal the data pins of the processor. This provides the best throughput between data flowing over the bus and into the processor. As was discussed in the previous chapter, a processor with double the data input capacity of the data segment of the bus would require at least two clock cycles before it can begin processing data.

Although the address segment of the bus is the size of an address, the width of this segment determines the amount of addresses that can be used on the motherboard. For example, a 16-bit wide address segment can address up to 65,536 addresses compared with 4,294,967,296 addresses if a 32-bit wide address segment is used. These are the largest values that can be represented by either 16 bits or 32 bits.

The bus speed is determined by the bus clock speed, which is measured in MHz. This is the number of clock cycles per second. One set of bits travels over the bus in one clock cycle and the number of bits in a set is equal to the width of the bus.

The product of multiplying the number of clock cycles by the width of the bus is the maximum number of bits of information that can be carried across the bus per second (see Table 3-1). This is called the bus throughput and shouldn't be confused with the computer's throughput, which is the amount of information that can be processed per second.

Remember the bus only delivers information to the processor. The processor's internal bus, instruction set, and internal clock cycles among other factors—including the bus throughput—determine the computer's throughput (see Chapter 2).

Table 3-1   Common bus types, widths, and speeds

Bus type	Width (bits)	Speed (MHz)
ISA	16	8.33
PCI	32	33.33
AGP	32	66.66

You might have heard about other types of buses such as the Micro Channel Architecture (MCA), Extended Industry Standard Architecture (EISA), and the VESA local bus (VLB). These were used on older computers and are not found on today's motherboards.

Power Supplies

The power supply provides the motherboard and its components with the electricity to distribute and process information. Although 110 volts AC is supplied from the power cord, the motherboard requires a much lower DC voltage of 12 volts or less. It is the power supply and related circuitry that steps down the voltage and converts power from alternating current to direct current. For example, disk drives require 12 volts, the processor and memory use 3.3 volts, and other components use 5 volts.

The trend among component manufacturers is to design components that require a minimum voltage to operate. The purpose of this energy conservation is to make the computer energy efficient and reduce the heat generated by electricity, which extends the life of components. In addition, reduced power consumption enables designers to build more powerful components because of the reduction in heat.

For example, progress in the design of the Pentium processor has managed to reduce the voltage requirement from 5 volts to just under 3 volts. Although this reduction might seem an irrelevant change in design, it has reduced the heat generated by the processor sufficiently to enable Intel to give the Pentium more processing power.

As component design improves, motherboard manufacturers must be prepared to supply various voltages. Voltage regulating circuits called a voltage regulator module (VRM) are integrated into the power supply and related circuits. VRM adjusts the voltages supplied to a component based on the component manufacturer's specifications.

There are a variety of power supplies on the market, each conforming to standard specifications. There are a number of characteristics used to define a power supply. These range from elementary considerations such as the power supplies' form factor to electrical ratings. The *form factor* is the term used to describe the dimensions of the power supply. Simply said, the form factor determines if the power supply can fit into the computer case.

There are a number of important electrical ratings that define a power supply. The one that you hear about the most is the voltage, sometimes called the nominal voltage. This is the voltage that is received from the power cord.

There are two common nominal voltages: 110 and 220. You probably recognize this as household current. Many power supplies can be adjusted to accept either of these because power supplies are designed for the global market. That is, the same power supply sold in the United States where 110 volts is common is also sold in Europe where 220 volts is used.

Typically a switch on the power supply enables you to go from 110 volts to 220 volts and back. A few power supplies are not manually switchable. Instead the power supply senses the incoming voltage and then automatically makes the adjustment. This is called an autosensing power supply.

A word of caution: The motherboard will be damaged if nominal voltage is 220 volts and the power supply is set to 110 volts. No damage will be caused if the power cord supplies 110 volts and the power supply is set for 220 volts, although it is likely that the computer will not work properly.

The motherboard and its components are made to strict tolerance and expect a rather steady stream of electricity. Although the voltage regulator module keeps voltage within an acceptable range for each component, the voltage regulator module requires voltage from the power cord to be within a steady range called the operating voltage range.

The utility company supplies electrical power to a facility such as an office within a specified operating voltage, which is usually between 90 volts and 135 volts. This means that on the average there will be 110 volts of electricity available from the outlet. However, at any point the voltage might drop as low as 90 volts or reach as high as 135 volts.

The computer's power supply has an operating voltage rating, a voltage range within which the power supply can provide a steady stream of electricity to the voltage regulator module.

Power utilities can experience situations when it is unable to provide power within the specified voltage range. For example, in times of heavy electrical demands, there isn't sufficient electrical power to go around. Electricity is reduced and a brownout occurs. This means power drops below the minimum voltage.

In contrast, a power line might be hit with lightning or a power line transformer malfunctions. Both of these situations typically result in a short burst of voltage beyond the range of normal operations. This is called a spike or surge and can provide too much energy to the computer resulting in damage to components.

It is important that the power supply operating voltage rating is compatible with the range of voltages supplied by the power company, otherwise power to the motherboard will not be reliable.

Additional equipment might be required if the power utility is unable to provide continuous, reliable power. Two of these are a line conditioner and an uninterruptible power supply (UPS). A line conditioner assures that the voltage supply remains close to the 110 volts or 220 volts required for optimal operation. The UPS provides power for a limited time should the power supply from the utility be cut off. You'll learn more about the UPS later in this chapter.

The power supply is expected to provide the motherboard with various voltages at a specified rating measured in watts. Power supplies can be compared by wattage rating with the most desirable power supply having the highest wattage at the voltage rating required by the motherboard and related components.

Tech Talk

Volt: The amount of electricity flowing over a wire.

Watt: The multiplication of volts and ampere, a measurement of current, to define a measurement of electrical work.

Current: The speed of electricity flowing over a wire.

The efficiency of a power supply is an indication of how much power is lost during the conversion of power from electricity coming from the power cord to the electricity being delivered to the motherboard. Watts are the electrical measurement used to measure the efficiency of a power supply.

There are two watt ratings that are important to consider when evaluating a power supply. These are the input watts and the total output watts. The ratings are the same in an ideal world where there is no loss of energy from the electrical conversions performed by the power supply. However, the real world is much different.

A power supply's efficiency is reported as the percentage the output wattage is of the input wattage. Let's say a power supply has an input wattage of 400 watts and provides the motherboard with 300 watts. The efficiency rating of the power supply is 75 percent.

The objective is to use a power supply that has the highest efficiency rating because this assures that electricity is not wasted. Efficiency may not be top priority when making a purchasing decision for a home computer. However, efficiency is material when purchasing computers for business because the cumulative savings from an efficient power supply results in relevant cost savings.

In addition to watt and efficiency ratings, the quality of a power supply is determined by several other criteria. The more important criteria are circuit protection, emissions, hold up time, line and load regulation, mean time between failures (MTBF), and ripple.

Circuit protection is a feature that cuts power to the motherboard if voltage and current exceeds the maximum value that can be handled by the motherboard. In the worst case, the computer will lose power, but circuitry on the motherboard will be safe.

All power supplies generate electronic waves similar to radio waves, which can cause interference with other devices connected to the same power line or devices within the area close to the power supply. The Federal Communications Commission assigns a power supply to a specific emission classification based on the emissions generated by the power supply. These are either class A or class B, with class B given to power supplies that generate a low amount of emissions.

Hold up time is a characteristic of how well a power supply maintains power during a power failure. There is a time lapse between the time electricity from the power cord enters the power supply to the time electricity reaches the motherboard. This delay is the hold up time and is measured in milliseconds.

There are occasions when power to the power supply drops off for a fraction of a second due to a sudden demand for electricity by one or more devices that are connected to the same power line. Sometimes this is so sudden that there isn't time for the lights to flicker. Other times there is a complete power failure and it takes a split second for the backup power unit to kick in.

In either case, the hold up time becomes vital to the continual operation of the computer. A long hold up time means that the motherboard will continue to operate without being affected by the sudden loss of power. That is, there is sufficient electricity stored in the power supply to keep power flowing to the motherboard until incoming power stabilizes.

Line and load regulation is a feature that uses circuitry to assure that stable voltage continues to flow throughout the motherboard. Line regulation monitors and adjusts if necessary voltage coming from the power cord while load regulation performs the same function within the computer.

For example, there could be a sudden demand for power when several devices such as a CD and disk drive start up at the same time. This tends to drop voltage levels within the motherboard and could cause a disruption running the computer. Load regulation circuits in the power supply prevent any disruption from occurring.

MTBF is a rating that indicates when the power supply is expected to fail. The rating is stated in hours of operation. Let's say that a power supply has an MTBF of 50,000 hours. This means that the power supply should work fine for nearly six years of constant running.

The ripple characteristic of a power supply defines how well the power supply converts alternating current to direct current. Components on the motherboard expect to receive a steady stream of direct current. On the other hand, electricity from the power cord is alternating current. Typically the conversion process isn't perfect and there is an amount of alternating current that seeps through to the motherboard.

Here's what happens. Alternating current forms a wave while direct current forms a straight line. The conversion process may result in a tiny wave forming in the direct current instead of a perfectly straight line. This tiny wave is called a ripple and is rated as a percentage such as 1 percent ripple. Simply stated, the lower the percentage of ripple, the better performance you will received from the power supply.

BACKUP POWER SUPPLY

It goes without saying that a computer's power supply can provide the motherboard with electricity only if power is available to the power cord. However, steps can be taken to continue power to the computer in the event of a power failure. There are two commonly used methods. These are standby power and a backup power supply.

Standby power requires an electrical generator to kick in during a power outage, which supplies electrical power until the electrical utility restores power. Typically only large businesses can afford standby power.

A backup power supply is a battery-powered device that automatically provides power to a computer for a short time period during a power failure. The purpose of a backup power supply is to provide power to properly shut down a computer.

Not all backup power supplies are alike, so you need to find one that best fits your needs. Look for a backup power supply that automatically activates within 4 milliseconds from the time power is lost. This is usually with the hold up time of the computer's power supply. The computer will lose power if the activation time of the backup power supply exceeds the computer power supply's hold up time.

Backup Power Supply (continued)

Ideally, the backup power supply will automatically run the computer's shut down program whenever the backup power supply is activated. This ensures that the computer is properly shut down should a power outage occur when the computer is unattended.

Backup power supplies must be maintained. For example, the battery must be replaced regularly. It is best to select a backup power supply that has a user-replaceable battery rather than one that requires a manufacturer's service center to replace the battery.

Likewise, choose a backup power supply that uses a circuit breaker rather than a fuse. If power exceeds an acceptable level, the circuit breaker or fuse will disable the backup power supply. However, while you can reset the circuit breaker by pressing a reset button, the fuse might need to be replaced by the manufacturer's service center.

The backup power supply you select should display a battery status light that indicates whether or not the battery is fully charged. The manufacturer's documentation will state how long the battery will provide power to the computer, after which the battery needs to be recharged or replaced.

The Practical Side to the Motherboard

Learning about the motherboard is interesting and at times might be confusing especially when you try to apply your knowledge in the real world. There are things about a motherboard that will help you and other things that don't matter much unless you are an engineer. For now I'll focus on those characteristics of a motherboard that you can use to make an intelligent purchase.

Purchase a computer that has a motherboard with a wide bus. A 32-bit bus is fine for most computers although a 64-bit bus is necessary for computers that perform heavy processing such as real-time transaction processing applications.

There should be sufficient expansion slots on the motherboard to accommodate future enhancements. Although many features are integrated into the motherboard, some may become outdated. You cannot upgrade features integrated into the motherboard directly. However, you can insert expansion circuit boards to enhance features on the motherboard if there are sufficient expansion slots available.

The voltage supply is a component that is given little thought when evaluating a purchase. The power supply of most computers is adequate for components that come with the computer. It is important to consider, however, components that you will add to the computer such as a compact disc-recordable (CD-R) drive, digital video disk (DVD), multiple hard disk drives, and multiple processors.

A 450-watt power supply is sufficient for a typical desktop computer. Servers, especially those with multiple processors and multiple hard disks, should be powered by a 650-watt power supply. As a general rule, don't replace the power supply that comes with a computer. Instead, assess your needs and purchase a computer that has specifications that meet your needs.

For example, if the computer is to be used as a server, then make sure it has at least a 650-watt power supply. This will reassure you that the power supply will meet your requirements and is compatible with the motherboard.

An alternative to purchasing a computer is to upgrade an existing computer by replacing the motherboard, power supply, and related chips and chipset. Although upgrading a computer is challenging, it may not be economical. The cost of the motherboard and components purchased at retail price is usually more expensive—and definitely more risky—than buying a new computer.

THE INSIDE STORY OF MEMORY...........................

Computer memory is a series of logic circuits that function as switches. As discussed in the previous chapter, each logic circuit can be set to one of two states, which you can consider as on and off.

Although it is easy to understand logic circuits by using the metaphor of a switch, a logic circuit actually directs the flow of electricity down one path or the other depending on the state of the circuit rather than turning electricity on or off. There can be millions of logic circuits in computer memory, all of which are interconnected with the bus.

I have some bad news and some good news for you. The bad news is that you need to learn about various types of computer memory if you are to have a thorough understanding of computer hardware. The good news is that you don't have to learn about the logic circuits. All you need to know are the characteristics of memory.

Memory Characteristics

Computer memory is contained on a chip and these chips are typically physically grouped together, sometimes called a memory row, to form a memory package. Memory is also logically grouped into banks.

You purchase computer memory in a memory package rather than individual memory chips. A memory package is typically a small circuit board that contains at least one bank of memory chips and can be easily connected to a receptacle on the motherboard or on an expansion card.

There are six common forms of memory packaging. These are dual in-line memory module (DIMM), dual in-line package (DIP), Rambus RDRAM module (RIMM), single in-line memory module (SIMM), single in-line pinned package (SIPP), and small outline DIMM (SODIMM).

DIMM has from 100 to 168 pins and uses connectors on both sides of the circuit board to connect to the motherboard. DIP is one of the original memory packages and resembles what most of us know as a chip, that is, a black rectangle that has a series of pins protruding from two sides of the chip. This packaging is no longer used in new computers.

RIMM is nearly identical in shape to the DIMM memory package. The only outward distinguishing characteristic is a notch on the top of the chip, which is used as a reference point when installing the chip on the motherboard.

SIMM is a very small circuit board that contains several DIP chips. One edge of a SIMM slips into a socket on the motherboard making connection to the bus. Although SIMM was replaced by the newer DIMM, SIMM is still used in some older computers and is frequently used in other devices such as printers.

SIPP memory packaging is an early design to place more memory into a smaller area on the motherboard, but is rarely used today. SODIMM is a form of DIMM memory packaging that is found on notebook computers and video adapter cards.

The amount of memory contained in a memory package is defined in rounded bytes. For example, it is common to refer to a quantity of memory as a megabyte (MB). In reality that is 1,048,576 bytes. Table 3-2 lists common terminology to describe a quantity of memory and the corresponding actual amount of memory.

Table 3-2   Measuring the real quantity of memory

Expression	Common throughput	Real quantity
Byte	1 byte	1 byte
Kilobyte (KB)	A thousand bytes	1,024 bytes
Megabyte (MB)	A million bytes	1,048,576 bytes
Gigabyte (GB)	A thousand million bytes	1,073,741,824 bytes
Terabyte (TB)	A million million bytes	1,099,511,627,776 bytes

Types of Memory

There are two general categories of memory: RAM and ROM. RAM stores information temporarily as long as power is supplied to the memory chip. A program can change the contents of RAM. In contrast ROM retains information when the computer is powered down and a program cannot change information stored on ROM.

There are two types of RAM: dynamic RAM known as DRAM and static RAM also called SRAM. Performance and cost separate the two. Performance is measured by the time it takes to access the contents of memory, which is measured in nanoseconds.

DRAM has a 60-nanosecond access time as compared with 6 nanoseconds for SRAM. The primary reason for the difference is in the way information is stored. DRAM retains information for a fraction of a second even when the computer is powered up. This means that the processor must continually refresh the information stored in DRAM, otherwise the information is forever lost. SRAM does not require refreshing.

Although DRAM does not have the best access time, it uses less power than SRAM and is less expensive. Therefore, DRAM is primarily used for main memory and SRAM is used for cache memory.

There is a special kind of memory called flash memory that has the characteristics of both RAM and ROM. Flash memory retains its contents when the computer is powered down. A program can change information stored in flash memory.

This is possible because a small battery that can last many years powers flash memory. Flash memory is primarily used to store BIOS such as those used to start the boot process on your computer.

The primary advantage of flash memory is that the BIOS can easily be upgraded by using a program to change the content of the BIOS's flash memory. This is a more efficient method than replacing the entire BIOS chip, which was the way upgrades were handled before the advent of flash memory.

International Business Machines introduced a new type of RAM called magnetic random access memory (MRAM). MRAM uses magnetic settings rather than electrical charges to store information on the chip. This technique has a dramatic impact on power consumption because MRAM chips don't use electricity to store information.

MRAM also provides an instant-on feature where computers and computer-based devices such as cell phones don't need time to boot. Instead, the computer will respond as quickly as a radio responds when power is turned on.

MRAM consists of magnetic material that is sandwiched between two metal layers. As electricity is passed through the outside layer, the magnetic material changes its polarization, which represents a zero or one depending on the polarity of material. Some engineers believe MRAM will replace flash memory as soon as MRAM becomes cost effective. Each MRAM chip holds 256 MB of information.

Information is stored in a ROM chip as etched electronic circuits. The etching occurs through a photo-electronic process described earlier in this chapter.

The Workings of Memory

The way in which the processor transfers information to and from memory is called the memory access method. There are two commonly used memory access methods. These are asynchronous and synchronous.

The asynchronous memory access method requires the processor to follow a data transfer schedule called a window. The window specifies the length of time within which the processor can access memory.

The major disadvantage is that the processor must wait until the transfer time limit expires before the processor can perform another task. Although the window is a small fraction of a second long, it is longer than a clock cycle. This leads to reduce throughput because the processor is idle waiting for time to expire once the transfer is completed.

Fast page mode DRAM, extended data out DRAM, and burst extended data out DRAM are types of asynchronous DRAM, but are not commonly used in new computers.

The synchronous memory access method does not use a window and instead places the processor and memory in lock step. That is, the processor and memory use the same clock cycle to transfer information, thereby not inhibiting throughput. This is the memory access method used on new computers.

JEDEC synchronous DRAM (SDRAM), PC100 SDRAM, and double data rate SDRAM are common synchronous memory.

There are two important factors that influence the performance of memory. These are error checking and whether or not memory is protocol based. Error checking is a process used to assure that information sent from the processor arrived intact and without errors.

Although the circuitry used to transport information between the processor and memory is fairly stable, there are times when erroneous fluctuations could infer the wrong information. That is a zero instead of a one or vice versa.

There are two techniques used to attempt to trap those errors. These are parity memory and error checking and correcting. These techniques are typically used for network servers that are involved in a very high level of processing. Rarely are these techniques used on standard desktop computers.

Parity memory uses parity to determine if all bits were received. Here's how this works. An additional bit is placed at the end of the information. The value of the bit—

zero or one—depends on two things: if parity is odd or even and the number of ones used to represent the information.

Odd parity means that there is an odd number of ones in the information and even parity means there is an even number of ones. Before the information is sent, the ones are counted and the parity bit is set.

If parity is odd and there is an odd number of ones in the information, then the parity bit is set to zero. If parity is even and the number of ones is odd, then the parity bit is set to one, which gives the information an even number of ones without affecting the actual information.

The number of ones is counted when the information is received and compared to the parity setting (odd or even). If the parity setting is odd and the number of ones is even, then a transmission error is suspected. Likewise if parity is set to even and an odd number of ones is received, then, too, an error is suspected.

Parity checking is encoded into parity memory chips. Not all memory chips are parity memory chips; therefore, you must be careful not to mix the two types of chips.

Another method of error checking is called error checking and correcting (ECC). This is a more advanced method of error checking than is offered with parity memory. It uses more than one bit to check for errors.

The number of error checking bits used by ECC depends on the size of the information. One byte of information requires 5 additional bits. Two bytes requires 6 ECC bits. Seven are used for 4 bytes and 8 bits for 8 bytes. As you can imagine, these additional bits lower the performance of accessing memory.

Protocol-based memory is a method used to increase the access to memory by reducing the number of buses used during the transfer of information between the processor and memory. Some computers use three buses to connect memory and the processor. One bus is used to reference a memory address, another to transport the data, and a third to control the transfer process.

The function of these buses is consolidated into one narrow bus that is designed to transfer information faster than that of a nonprotocol-based memory. There are two standards for protocol-based memory. These are Rambus DRAM and synchronous link DRAM.

Rambus and Intel developed Rambus DRAM as a proprietary standard, which is licensed to other manufactures. Synchronous link DRAM is a royalty-free standard.

The Practical Side to Memory

While understanding how memory works inside a computer is interesting, the real question is, what information is important to remember? Computer memory has practical implications when it comes to running applications.

Generally speaking, the more RAM and cache memory that is available in a computer, the faster an application can run and process information. The computer manufacturer determines the type of RAM used inside the computer. The question you must answer is, how much RAM do you need?

The easy answer to this question is, as much as you can afford to pay. The proper answer is, it depends on the operating system and the job that you want the computer to perform. For example, the text-based version of Linux requires less memory than the graphical user interface version of Linux. Table 3-3 contains what I consider the ideal amount of memory for various configurations.

Another practical consideration regarding memory comes into play whenever you upgrade memory. First, you must use compatible memory chips and memory packaging, otherwise conflicts could occur on the motherboard.

You must also upgrade memory in fixed sizes, which are 4 MB, 8 MB, and 16 MB. Additional memory beyond 16 MB comes in 16-MB increments. However, you may find yourself discarding existing memory because there is insufficient room on the motherboard to insert the new memory (i.e., replacing two memory packages that in total contain 48 MB with one 64 MB memory package).

Table 3-3   Ideal memory configurations

Operating system	Variation	Ideal memory size
Windows 95		64 MB
Windows 98		64 MB
Windows NT	Workstation	128 MB
Windows NT	Server	256 MB
Windows 2000 (Professional)	Workstation	128 MB
Windows 2000	Server	256 MB
Linux	Workstation	128 MB
Linux	Server	96 MB

THE INSIDE STORY ON PROCESSORS ....

After reading the previous chapter, you probably have a good idea of the processor's role in the computer. It simply moves information around the motherboard and devices connected to the motherboard according to instructions written by a programmer.

Although it seems that this important chip can perform all sorts of feats, a processor has three basic functions: follow instructions, move information such as instructions and data among components, and perform arithmetic.

All processors perform these three jobs, yet each type of processor performs them in its own way based on the processor's characteristics. You'll explore those characteristics in the next section, then learn about the various kinds of processors on the market.

Characteristics of a Processor

The critical characteristics of a processor are the processing speed, instruction set, memory cache, and the size of information the processor can read or send at the same time.

Processing speed is measured in megahertz (MHz), which is the number commonly advertised by computer manufacturers. This measurement is the internal clock speed. That is, the speed at which information is processed once the information is read by the processor from the bus. Typically the internal clock rate is faster than the external clock rate because of the access times required by other components on the motherboard.

The instruction set, as discussed in the previous chapter, consists of the commands that are recognized by the processor. There are two kinds of instruction sets. These are the complex instruction set computing (CICS) and the reduced instruction set computing (RISC).

CICS instructions are variable in length and can require multiple clock cycles to read one instruction. In comparison, RISC instructions are fixed in length and can be read on one clock cycle.

Memory cache is a segment of memory that is either within the processor or on the motherboard. The most recent instructions and data are retained in the memory cache so they can be recalled faster than if the request were made to main memory. Processors can use multiple memory caches if available.

The size of information that can be read in one clock cycle greatly influences the throughput of the processor. Throughput as you'll recall is measured as the amount of information that can be processed per second. The processor should read the same number of bytes that is carried over the bus in one clock cycle.

Another important characteristic found on new processors is called pipelining. Pipelining enables the processor to give each processing step its own path. As discussed previously in this chapter, the processor must load an instruction, decode the instruction, and load data before the instruction is actually executed. Older processors used the same path for each step, which is not as efficient as if each had its own path.

The pipelining style of processor architecture is enhanced with the superscalar architecture, which provides multiple pipelining. This means that multiple instructions can be processed at the same time.

Types of Processors

There are various kinds of processors available for devices that include computers and things not normally thought of as computers such as appliances. New appliances usually have a small computer controlling the operation of the appliance. These are called imbedded processors. I'll concentrate on processors that are used for traditional computers.

I like to categorize processors in two ways. Those that are manufactured by Intel and those manufactured by other companies. The reason why I approach processors in this way is because of Intel's strength in the market. As you learned in Chapter 1, IBM's adoption of Intel's 8088 processor for IBM's first personal computer established Intel's technology as a de facto standard.

Over the years Intel has managed to manufacture enhanced versions of their processor. And although other processor manufacturers might develop an Intel compatible processor that includes an advanced feature, Intel is quick to incorporate that feature into its own product line, making that standard (such as MMX) a component of future processors.

The star of the Intel line is the Pentium 4 processor, which is the first time in recent years that Intel has redesigned its processor from the ground up. The result is a processor that dramatically increases processing throughput.

The Pentium 4 uses NetBurst micro-architecture that include features that reduce the number of instructions necessary to execute a program and reduces the processor's idle time. The Pentium 4 is ideal for applications that require heavy processing such as 3D displays, speech, video, and games.

As mentioned earlier in this chapter, a processor typically must wait for instructions or data to be retrieved from memory. The NetBurst micro-architecture employs several interesting methods to dramatically reduce this wait time.

These methods include the rapid execution engine, the 400 MHz bus system, advanced transfer cache, and a reduced instruction set. The rapid execution engine enables the arithmetic logic unit to run twice as fast as the processor's clock. The 400

MHz bus system delivers 3.2 GB of data per second. This is nearly three times the amount of data that is delivered by the Pentium III's 133 MHz bus.

Cache is critical to the effective operation of the processor because cache contains the latest instructions and data that might be reused by the processor. The advanced transfer cache method speeds the transfer of information from cache to the processor. A Pentium 4 running at 1.4 GHz clock speed has a 44.8 GB per second data transfer rate, which is a far cry from the 16 GB per second data transfer rate on the 1 GHz Pentium III.

Intel built on the single instruction multiple data (SIMD) instruction set that was introduced with its MMX enabled processors. SIMD enables the processor to work with more instructions at the same time. The Pentium 4 uses streaming SIMD Extension 2, which added 144 more instructions. One of these instructions combines several of the SIMD instructions.

The Pentium III is the forerunner of the Pentium 4. The first version of the Pentium III used a Katmai core and a 100 MHz bus system. This was later replaced with a coppermine core version that used a 133 MHz bus system and an advanced transfer cache technology.

Tech Talk

Coppermine core: A design that uses copper-interconnect technology, where copper instead of aluminum is used to connect together components.

The Pentium III uses a modification of the RISC. The Pentium is a CISC-based processor, but is able to translate CISC instructions into RISC instructions, which are then processed by the processor. The translation improves throughput on a 32-bit operating system although a slight reduction in throughput is seen in a 16-bit operating system.

The competition for home computers has driven down computer prices. Intel is competing in the home market by selling an inexpensive version of the Pentium III called the Celeron, with a clock speed of up to 800 MHz. Celeron includes features like streaming SIMD extension, dynamic execution technology, a 100 MHz bus system, and two levels of cache.

Types of Non-Intel Processors

There are two major competitors of Intel all vying for a segment of the processor market. These are Advanced Micro Devices (AMD) and Cyrix. There were three until 1999 when Integrated Device Technology (IDT) sold its processor group to Cyrix.

AMD manufactures the Athlon line of processors. The Athlon processor is in the Pentium III class and has a larger memory cache and bus system than the Pentium.

The Pentium III uses a 32 KB level 1 memory cache while the Athlon has a 128 KB level 1 memory cache. The Athlon has a 266 MHz bus system compared with the Pentium III's 133 MHz bus system. However the Athlon lacks the chipset and motherboard support that is found with the Pentium III.

AMD also produces the Duron line of processors. With a clock speed of 800 MHz, the Duron is in head-to-head competition with the Pentium III and the Celeron. The Duron offers a larger level 1 cache than its Intel counterparts and has double the bus system speed of the Pentium III.

Cyrix manufactures the VIA Cyrix III processor that runs at 700 MHz and is designed for very low-end personal computer market. I like to position the VIA Cyrix III as a competitor to the Celeron.

The Apple G4 Processor

Apple Computer, Motorola, and IBM developed a G4 processor for use in the Power-PC and other computers in Apple's product line (Power Mac and PowerBook). The G4 processor is specifically design to process the many complex calculations that are found in graphical applications.

Some graphical applications can require a billion floating-point calculations per second. This is commonly referred to as a gigaflop. The G4 is designed to perform over a gigaflop, a capability that was found only in computers selling for $50,000 a few years ago.

At the center of G4's design is the velocity engine that accelerates data-intensive processing, which is necessary for using large data set for real-time simulations. The G4 with the velocity engine can read 128 bits of information at a time at a speed of 533 MHz.

The Practical Side to Processors

Who could image back in the 1980s that the day would come when the average consumer would want to know about the processor used in a computer? Until computer manufacturers began advertising to consumers, only engineers who designed computers worried about the type of processor to use. This still holds true with computers other than personal computers.

There are two important questions to answer to help you decide what processor you should purchase—I should say, what computer you purchase: How much processing power do you require? How much are you willing to spend?

The Celeron, Pentium III, and Athlon will suffice for typical business applications. The Pentium 4 or the G4 are my choices for servers and applications that re-

quire heavy processing such as 3D imaging, video, and speech. The Celeron and
Cyrix III are a good bet for inexpensive computers.

SUMMARY ....

The motherboard, memory, and processor define a computer. The motherboard is the
largest circuit board inside the computer that contains many components, two of
which are memory chips and the processor. Memory chips store instructions and data.
Those instructions tell the processor how to process the data.

Each motherboard has characteristics that distinguish it from other motherboards. The most prominent of these are the form factor, which is the shape of the
motherboard, the chipset, the bus, and the power supply.

A chipset consists of from one to three large-scale integrated circuits that make
the motherboard come alive by coordinating the activities of the circuits and components that are integrated into the motherboard.

A bus is the electronic pathway etched into the motherboard over which instructions and data flow to components. Typically there are six buses on a motherboard and
components may be connected to more than one bus. These are the AGP, cache bus,
local input/output bus, memory bus, processor bus, and the standard input/output bus.

A bus is defined by two critical measurements. These are width (number of
wires) and speed (clock speed). A bus is divided into two segments. One segment is
used to transport addresses of components such as a memory address and the other is
used to transport data.

The power supply converts alternating current from the power cord to direct current, which is passed along to the motherboard to power components. The power supply contains voltage-regulating circuits called a voltage regulator module (VRM),
which is used to adjust the voltage supplied to a component integrated or connected to
the motherboard.

Computer memory comes in six different forms called memory packaging.
These are dual in-line memory module (DIMM), dual in-line package (DIP), Rambus
RDRAM module (RIMM), single in-line memory module (SIMM), single in-line
pinned package (SIPP), and small outline DIMM (SODIMM).

The ideal amount of memory to install in the computer depends on the type of
work you want the computer to perform. Computers that perform heavy data processing or use a graphical user interface require more memory then computers that are
used for typical office applications or are text based.

The processor is the keystone component on the motherboard. There are four
important features used to define a processor: processing speed, instruction set, memory cache, and the size of information the processor can read or send at the same time.

The processing speed is the clock speed commonly used in advertisement. This indicates the speed at which the processor performs calculations and moves information inside the processor.

The instruction set is the group of commands that the processor understands. There are two kinds of instruction sets: CICS and RISC. CICS instructions are variable length and can require multiple clock cycles to read one instruction. In comparison, RISC instructions are fixed in length and can be read on one clock cycle.

The choice of processor depends on the tasks the computer will perform and the budget. The Pentium 4 and the G4 processors are good candidates for computation intense applications such as for video, speech, and mathematical modeling. These processors are also good for servers. The Pentium III, Celeron, Duron, and Athlon work well for typical business desktop application. And the Celeron, Athlon, and VIA Cyrix III are suitable for home computers.

Summary Questions

1. **What factors are involved in determining the throughput of a computer?**

2. **What are the roles of the various buses found on a motherboard?**

3. **Why is the hold up time of a power supply important?**

4. **What is the difference between DRAM and SRAM?**

5. **What is the relationship between the processor clock speed and the bus system speed?**

6. **How does MRAM work?**

7. **What is the difference between a bus and a port?**

8. **Why is it important to match the wattage rating of a power supply with the needs of a computer?**

9. **What is the benefit of the superscalar architecture?**

10. **How is a gigaflop used to measure the performance of a processor?**

4 Monitors and Video Cards

In this chapter...

- Inside Monitors
- Inside Video Adapters

*"A good first impression requires
a good appearance."*

Anonymous

Today, when someone asks you what you have on your desktop they are probably not talking about your desk. Instead they are referring to applications that are on your computer's desktop, images on the display that represent applications.

Most of us take for granted the quality of these images and other images generated by computer applications, yet it wasn't too long ago when any image, regardless of quality, made an application outstanding—and drew a wow from everyone.

The barons of technology have issued a challenge to the engineering community—blend computer technology with television and film technology to produce a multimedia device that will become the information and entertainment center for homes and businesses.

Engineers have accepted the challenge and devised a multiphase strategy that initially focuses on enhancing the way computers generate images. And over the past few years their efforts have produced the dramatic results that you see today.

You'll explore these advances in this chapter and learn:

- How computer monitors draw images on the screen

- How the video display adapter card works

- The different kinds of video memory

- How to choose the best monitor and video display adapter card

REALITY CHECK ....

Like many of my age, I grew up watching cartoons on television, so I couldn't wait to relive a sliver of my childhood when the movie *Toy Story* reached the theaters. *Toy Story* gave kid-wanna-bes like me the right to see a feature film cartoon in the movies without feeling embarrassed.

A few weeks after seeing the movie I watched a documentary on television that showed how they made *Toy Story*. It was amazing to say the least. By now you probably know that computers generated the entire film. These computers weren't personal computers (PCs) but a more powerful workstation computer made by Silicon Graphics.

The documentary showed how focusing on details was the ingredient that made *Toy Story* come alive. For example, an important detail is lighting. Lighting does more than illuminate objects. It gives objects depth, which is a key element that helps us distinguish whether or not an object is real.

Sun and lamps produce lighting for most movies. Lights are repositioned whenever the director wants more depth in the scene. This is not the way it works in a computer-animated film such as *Toy Story*. There are no lights.

Instead, engineers use the physics of light as the basis for manipulating tiny pieces of the computer monitor to make an image appear to be lighted on the screen. The director needs only to tell the computer animation artist the position of the light and the type of light to be used in the scene.

The computer animation artist uses a program to tell the computer hardware how images must appear on the screen to make them look real. The result is a nearly perfectly lit scene. As the animated actors move around the scene, the animation program automatically directs the hardware on how to adjust the lighting to make the actors and other things in the scene appear real.

Lighting details and other aspects of a computer-animated film are dependent on the computer hardware's ability to quickly change the settings of millions of tiny pieces of the monitor that form the image on the monitor screen. Simply said, the higher degree of detail in the movie requires the computer to store and process more information quickly.

The research at companies like Silicon Graphics that produced sophisticated video display adapter cards, monitors, and more efficient ways to display images on the screen has lead to improved graphical displays that are used in computers that you and I can afford.

INSIDE MONITORS..

Even before you began reading this chapter you probably had a good idea what a monitor is. Yet what you don't know about a monitor will likely surprise you. A monitor is the face of your computer in that the monitor is the device that displays information in the form of text and images. And it is the monitor that prompts you to do things such as telling you when the computer is ready for you to run a program.

The monitor is one of a three-member team that presents information. The other members are the video display adapter and the video cable that connects the monitor to the video display adapter.

The video display adapter receives information from the processor such as elements of an image and translates that information into a form that can be displayed on the monitor. You'll learn more about the video display adapter later in this chapter.

The video cable transports translated information from the video display adapter to the monitor where circuitry within the monitor generates the image in tiny pieces onto the monitor screen.

Components of a Monitor

Most computer monitors use the same technology to display an image as is used to produce a television image. Others kinds of monitors such as those used in a laptop computer employ different technology, which is discussed later in this chapter.

The monitor screen is the front of a cathode ray tube (CRT), which is sometimes called a picture tube. If you looked inside the monitor case you'd see the CRT as a sealed large funnel-shaped device.

At the narrow end of the CRT is one or more electron guns that shoot a stream of electrons to the wider end of the CRT, which is the back of the glass that you recognize as the computer screen (see Figure 4-1). The back of the computer screen is covered with tiny dots of a chemical called phosphor. Phosphor used in the CRT is a mixture of chemicals called a compound.

The phosphor has a unique feature. When an electron shot from the electron gun hits phosphor, the phosphor glows The glow is seen as a very small dot on the screen. The dot is so small that it probably looks like a speck of dust, if you can see the dot at all. However, by shooting every phosphor dot across a screen, the electron gun produces an image that is easily recognizable. The image is a thin line.

Tech Talk
Electron: An element of an atom that surrounds the atom's nucleus.

The phosphor has three segments sometimes called subpels, each of which glows in one of three colors—red, green, or blue. When an electron strikes the red subpel, the tiny dot is displayed in red. When the green subpel is struck, a green dot appears and the same holds true for the blue subpel.

Each phosphor dot is an element of a picture, which is called a pixel or pel. A pixel and pel both refer to the smallest piece of a picture. However, I like to use the term *pixel* whenever I speak about a graphical image such as one you create with a graphics program, and I use the term *pel* whenever I talk about a dot on a monitor.

Images that appear on the computer display are composed of millions of picture elements, each of which is represented by a pel. Although each pel is separated from

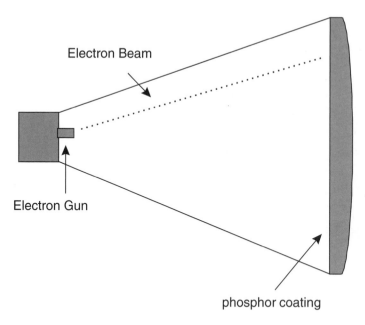

Electron Beam

Electron Gun

phosphor coating

Figure 4-1
The electron gun shoots a beam of electrons to illuminate the phosphor coating on the back of the screen

other pels, the space between pels is so small that your eyes blend pels into a continuous image.

This is the same technique used to print pictures on paper (see Figure 4-2). Here's an interesting task. Hold up a magnifying glass to a picture in the newspaper. You'll see for yourself the pixels that comprise the picture. Pels appear as tiny dots of black—or red, green, or blue for colored pictures.

The distance between the same color subpel of two pels determines the resolution of a monitor. This is called the dot pitch. A high-resolution monitor, one with a small dot pitch, produces a sharper image on the screen.

Colors and the Electron Gun

The electron gun zigzags the screen, called scanning the screen. The video display adapter inside the computer directs the electron gun to either fire or not to fire. This sequence of events places elements of an image on the screen as glowing pel.

There are actually three electron guns in most monitors although some monitors such as Sony Trinitron CRTs use one gun. Each electron gun aims at a segment of the

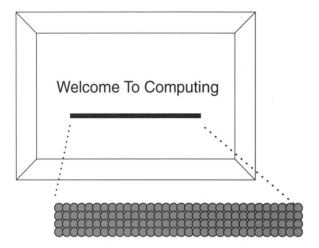

Figure 4-2
*A picture in a newspaper is composed of tiny dots very similar to
the pels used to display an image on the computer screen*

pel that generates a specific color, called a subpel. For example, one electron gun targets the red subpel of the pel. Another electron gun shoots the green subpel and another the blue subpel.

Red, green, and blue are mixed to produces millions of colors similar to how pigments of the same colors are mixed in a paint can to arrive at a particular color. Pels are similar to paint pigments.

The blend of these colors creates other colors. For example, the absence of these colors in all three subpels produces the color black. Using only the blue subpel generates a dark blue color. As more green is added, the display turns to a lighter shade of blue.

Here's how it works with an image. Let's say that you displayed your picture in a graphics program such as PhotoShop. And let's say you want to change the shade of blue in your eyes. Your picture is made up of millions of pixels. The group of pixels that comprises one of your eyes is a blend of colors, although you probably don't see it that way. Instead, you probably view the image of your eye as you see your eye in a mirror.

The zoom feature of the graphic program enables you to examine a representation of nearly the pixel level of your eye. When you zoom in, you'll see the various colors. When you zoom out, these colors blend with each other to give the impression of a different color.

You can change the color of your eyes by modifying the color values of some of these pixels. The modification is changed into instructions by the graphics program. Those instructions tell the processor to change the setting of pels in video memory and to instruct the proper electron gun to hit the desired pel segment. This results in the change of color on the screen.

The number of pels that can be controlled by the video display adapter is dependent on a number of factors, which is discussed later in this chapter. One of these factors is number of bits in memory used to store video information. If 8-bits are used to represent video information, 16.7 million colors are possible.

Parts of the Electron Gun

The electron gun sounds like something out of a science fiction move, but the concepts used to generate the beam of electrons is easy to understand. As you'll remember from your high school science courses, electrons are elements of an atom that surround the nucleus of the atom. These are the same electrons that are shot from the electron gun.

Electricity flows to the CRT and heats the cathode, which is an element in the CRT. Some electrons are freed from atoms as the cathode is heated. These electrons are formed into a thin beam by the circuitry of the CRT.

The electron beam is sent across the deflection yoke inside the CRT. The deflection yoke uses electromagnetism to alter the path of the beam (see Figure 4-3). The deflection yoke aims the electron-beam across and down the screen, striking pels as directed by the video display adapter circuit.

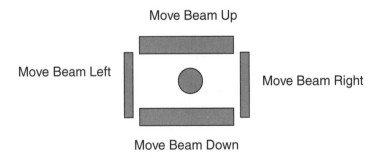

Figure 4-3
The deflection yoke controlled by the video display adapter directs
the path of the electron beam

An electron beam has a circular shape that is similar to the shape of a subpel. This ensures that the complete subpel is hit and gives off a consistent glow. However, an inherent problem exists with the CRT. Some subpels are hit in the center and others at an angle as the electron beam is deflected across the screen.

The angle at which the subpel is hit by the electron beam determines sharpness of the image that appears on the screen. A subpel hit squarely produces a sharp image. A subpel hit at an angle produces a distorted image. The amount of distortion depends on the angle of attack. The further away the electron beam is from the center of the subpel the blurrier the subpel appears. Better-quality monitors contain circuitry that adjusts the electron beam to compensate for the angle of attack. The result is a sharp image across the entire screen.

Engineers enhance the sharpness of the image further by using a mask between the electron gun and the rear of the screen. The mask physically defines a pel using a grid of metal much like a stencil is used to make a street sign. Some masks divide the screen into dots, each representing a pel, while other masks create a vertical stripe.

In both cases, holes in the mask allow electrons to pass through to the phosphor while the metal frame around the holes absorbs electrons. Using a mask has two drawbacks. First, images on monitors that use a mask appear dimmer than on monitors that don't use a mask. This is because the metal grid absorbs electron beams that would normally have caused pels to glow.

The other problem is with the metal grid itself. The metal grid becomes hot as the metal absorbs electrons. Metal tends to expand whenever it is heated and the expansion distorts the shape of the metal grid, losing the definition of some pixels.

Engineers have minimized the dimming effect by keeping the width of metal grid lines to a minimum. This means fewer electrons are being absorbed. The grid is also made from metal alloy such as Invar that retains its shape under extreme heat.

UNMASKING THE MASK

The concept of masking didn't begin with computers, but instead with television. The original type of masking, called a shadow mask, holds the shape of a triangle with each corner handling a color segment of a pixel. The shape of the hole produced jagged edge lines although you had to look very close to the screen to see the jagged edge.

In the 1960s, Sony introduced the aperture grill in the company's Trinitron television sets. The aperture grill uses thin vertical strips rather than triangular holes. This means pels were abutting each pel to its top and to its bottom. The aperture grill separated the sides of the pel from neighboring pels. The aperture grill produced brighter images than those found on shadow-mask monitors. However, the aperture grill could easily come ajar if the CRT was bumped.

NEC took the best features of the shadow mask and the aperture grill and created a new mask called the slotted mask. The slotted mask uses large rectangular slots, each over a color segment of a pel. The slotted mask exposes more of the phosphor than the shadow mask, making the image brighter, and the slotted mask is not vulnerable to bumps.

Hitachi also made an effort to improve the shadow mask by changing the size and shape of the holes in the grid. Hitachi increased the size of the hole and changed the shape to an isosceles triangle. This produces an image that contains finer details than the shadow mask.

Scanning Images onto the Screen

As you'll learn in more detail later in this chapter, information that is displayed on the screen resides in video image RAM on the video display adapter. Video image RAM is organized into frame buffers. A frame buffer is a portion of video image RAM that holds one screen of information.

Circuits in the video display adapter read and send bits of information in synchronization with the movement of the electron gun. That is, the first few bits of a frame buffer contain information on how to display the pixel in the upper left corner of the screen. The actual number of bits used to represent a pixel is determined by the colors used to display the image. I'll explain this concept in more detail in the "Inside Video Adapters" section of this chapter.

Personal computers use raster scan to create an image on the screen. Raster scan directs the electron gun to zigzag down the screen. Some computers such as those used in laser shows use vector scan, which directs the electron gun to draw the lines and curves of an image rather than zigzagging down the screen.

The electron gun moves left to right then back to the left before moving down to the next row of pels. Once the electron gun reaches the bottom right corner of the screen, the electron gun is repositioned to the upper left corner before starting the process over again.

Every microsecond electrons from the electron gun strike a subpel at a particular strength determined by the number of electrons that strike the subpel. A stronger flow of electrons produces a brighter glow from the subpel and a weaker flow produces a dimmer glow.

At full strength a subpel glows for a specific time period before turning dark. This time period is called the decay factor. Each pel must be refreshed for an image to remain on the screen. The amount of time a subpel must be refreshed to maintain a steady image is called the refresh rate.

The refresh rate is the time taken for the electron gun to return to a subpel. An acceptable refresh rate is 60 times per second. You'll notice image flicker whenever the refresh rate falls below 60 times per second. This is because some subpels have already darkened before they can be recharged by the electron gun.

Years ago when I was an editor for the now defunct *Personal Computing* magazine, our photographers had a difficult time photographing images that appeared on the computer screen. It seemed that every shot captured only a portion of the image. The rest of the image was black.

The reason was the refresh rate of the monitor. The exposure speed used to take the picture was faster than the refresh rate. Eventually, the photographer adjusted the exposure speed to 1/60 of a second to capture the full screen. Today there are special devices used to transfer screen images to film.

Monitor Cable

The monitor cable connects the video display adapter to the monitor. As you learned in Chapter 2, a cable contains two or more wires. The monitor cable used in most computers has 15 wires that are connected to a 15-pin connector that inserts into the video display adapter.

Two wires of the monitor cable send a digital signal used to drive the movement of the electron gun across and down the screen. The same wire is also used in some computers to control the sleep-state of the monitor.

New computers have a power saving feature that temporarily shuts down power-hungry devices when they are not needed. One of these devices is the monitor. The power management circuits integrated on the motherboard send a signal to the video display adapter to tell the monitor to turn off power to the CRT. Other circuits in the monitor remain powered on. When the user moves the mouse or presses a key, another signal is sent to the monitor to restore power to the CRT.

Three other wires are used to control the strength of the flow of electrons to the subpel. Each of these wires focuses on one subpel of the pel. This enables information regarding the strength of each color to be sent at the same time to the monitor, thereby eliminating the inherent delay if these signals were sent one at a time.

A LOOK AT VIDEO GLASSES

Surfing the television channels you no doubt come across a story about a guy who has a video monitor in his glasses. The guy is avoiding passersby with one eye as he walks down the street and the other eye is checking the stock ticker scrolling across the lens of his glasses.

Yes, those glasses are real and you can buy a pair for yourself. The glasses are called video glasses. The lens contains liquid crystal displays with a resolution of typically 800 x 225. You can see the image up close or from a distance of a little over 6 feet.

Most of them work on a 9-volt battery and come with earphones. The sticker price is around $600. The more popular models are the Sony Glasstron, the Olympus Eye-Trek, and i-O Display i-Glasses.

Although video glasses are more an expensive toy than a practical monitor, one thing puzzles me. Most of the manufacturers offer an AC adapter for their video glasses. One would think that if you had an AC adapter available that you would use a more traditional monitor.

Characteristics of a Monitor

Computer monitors comes in various shapes and sizes and all perform basically the same function, that is, to set pels on and off according to the signal received from the video display adapter. Although monitors fundamentally do the same thing, they have characteristics that make each monitor different from other monitors.

One of the most noted characteristics is the monitor's resolution. There are two common definitions of resolution of a monitor.

The first is the distance between subpels of the same color. The second is the number of pels per line and the number of lines that can be produced on a monitor. For example, a typical monitor has 1,024 pels per line across the screen and 768 lines down the screen. The resolution of the monitor is given as 1024 x 768.

The resolution of a monitor is different from the resolution of an image although both have similar measurements. The monitor's resolution defines the best resolution that can be used to display an image.

Here's what happens. The manufacturer fixes the maximum resolution that can be displayed by a monitor. You are unable to change this resolution because of the physical characteristics of the monitor. Simply said, the manufacturer has determined the number of pels that are used on the monitor.

The person who created the image determined the number of pixels that are used to display the image. The resolution of the image can be increased to the maximum resolution of the monitor by using a graphics program such as PhotoShop.

Likewise, the resolution of the image can also be increased beyond the monitor's resolution. However, the video display adapter changes the image's resolution by averaging pixels before sending the image to the monitor. This results in the image appearing at the maximum resolution of the monitor rather than at the image's resolution.

The monitor's resolution is based on the diameter of the electron beam, which is called the spot size. The space between dots must be as large or larger than the spot size for the monitor to display a clear and bright image.

The distance between the subpels of the same color is called the dot pitch and is measured as a fraction of a millimeter (i.e., 0.22-mm). Having the dot pitch and the spot size the same value produces the brightest image.

Some monitors use stripes instead of dots because of the type of mask used to shield the phosphor from the electron beam. However, the same measurement is used to determine the resolution of a monitor that uses stripes. That is, the distance between the stripes is called the stripe pitch.

Caution: You must adjust the dot pitch whenever you compare a monitor with dots instead of stripes because these are not directly comparable. Multiply the dot pitch by 90 percent (0.9). This will give you a value equivalent to a stripe pitch.

Color Model

A color model defines the way in which a monitor generates colors. So far in this chapter I spoke about how red, green, and blue are mixed to form many other colors. This is called the RGB color model that is used on many personal computers. However, there are two other kinds of color models. These are the subtractive color model, also called the CMYK model, and the HSB color model.

The RGB color model is called an additive color model based on the way the color is produced. Each primitive color (red, green, and blue) has 256 degrees of intensity. You'll see this if you ever set the color for an image using a graphics program. Each color can be set to a value from 0 to 255. Increasing the value from 0 is said to add more of a primitive color to the image. Therefore, combining a particular intensity of red, green, and blue produces the final color.

The CMYK color model is called a subtractive color model because some colors of the primitive colors are absorbed and others are displayed. The absorption is a way of subtracting colors. The primitive colors used in the CMYK model are cyan, magenta, yellow, and black. The letter K is used to represent the color black (the letter B usually refers to blue).

LCD panels such as those found on laptop computers use the CMYK model as do inkjet printers. In an LCD panel, light passes through three layers of liquid crystals. Each layer contains a primitive color. The layer is adjusted to allow a certain amount of light to pass through the layer, thereby forming the color image.

The HSB color model is used to produce color in television images. It adjusts the hue, saturation, and brightness of the image rather than adding or subtracting color.

Size and Shape

A monitor's size and shape must be adequate to view images on the screen. Applications such as video editing programs require a large monitor so that various elements of the video can be placed on the desktop.

The size of a monitor can be misleading because there are two size measurements. The first is the diagonal measurement, which is similar to the measurement used to define the size of a television. The diagonal measurement measures the distance from opposite corners of the monitor and is typically measured in inches.

However, if you look closely at your monitor you will see that a portion of the CRT is hidden by the monitor case. This means that you might have purchased a 17-inch monitor only to find that about 15 inches of the monitor is used to display the image.

Therefore, it is important to judge a monitor by the viewable size instead of the diagonal size because the viewable size defines the actual portion of the CRT that is used to display images.

The shape of the monitor, called the tube geometry, is an important consideration because it determines if there will be any distortion over any portion of the viewable area of the monitor.

Most monitors today use a cylindrical tube, which gives a flat appearance vertically and a rounded appearance horizontally. This provides less distortion around the edges of the tube as compared to the spherical tubes used in older models. Spherical tubes are rounded both vertically and horizontally.

The latest CRT technology is the flat square tube (FST) which minimizes distortion by using a large sphere that gives the appearance of a flat screen. However, additional hardware cost to produce the flat square tube has made it a pricey alternative to a cylindrical tube monitor.

Synchronization and Controls

The synchronization range is a characteristic of a monitor that represents a combination of other characteristics. The synchronization range is a measurement of bandwidth, which reflects the color, refresh rate, and resolution of the monitor.

The synchronization range is divided into two values. These are vertical and horizontal scanning frequencies. Vertical scanning frequency is the same as the refresh rate and states the number of times each second the screen is redrawn. The minimum vertical scanning frequency is 60 Hz although higher frequencies produce a more stable image. Horizontal scanning frequency is the length of time required to display one line across the monitor.

Controls are the buttons and switches that let you change the brightness, contrast, and other features of the monitor. There are common controls found on most monitors. These enable you to adjust the horizontal and vertical position of the monitor to ensure that the image is centered. More sophisticated monitors have additional controls used to fine tune the image.

Types of Monitors

The CRT monitor that I've been speaking about throughout this chapter is one type of monitor. There are also flat screen displays, touch screen displays, and liquid crystal displays that are used with computers.

The flat screen monitor is a CRT although the monitor resembles a liquid crystal display in width and height. This is why the flat screen monitor is sometimes called a thin CRT or short neck CRT. Both names refer to the shorter distance between the electron gun and the screen than found in a standard CRT. Special circuitry is used to adjust the electron beam to prevent any distortion caused by the shorter distance.

A touch screen monitor lets the user point to images on the screen rather than using the mouse or keyboard to interact with the computer. There are several variations. Some use a transparent membrane that sits over the screen. A signal is sent to the computer whenever someone touches the membrane. Segments of the membrane generate a unique signal similar to the signal sent when you press a key on the keyboard.

Another variation uses a grid of infrared light beams around the parameter of the monitor. When a segment of the grid is touched by a person's finger, the light beam is broken, sending the corresponding coordinates to the computer. The computer program associates the coordinates with whatever appears on the screen, such as a menu.

Still another type of touch screen monitor requires a person to use a pointing device such as a light pen to select a portion of the screen. The light pen uses a photocell to detect the glow of the pel at the location pointed to by the light pen.

The circuitry in the light pen and in the light pen's control card relates the position of the light pen to specific coordinates on the screen. The coordinates are associated with particular images displayed on the screen by a computer program.

Liquid Crystal Displays (LCD)

Liquid crystal display (LCD) is the monitor used on laptop computers. There are two variations, based on the way images are displayed. These are passive LCD and active-matrix display, also called TFT.

Passive LCD creates an image similar to that of the CRT. That is, each pel is activated by the horizontal and vertical scan. However, there isn't a time decay since the passive LCD uses electrodes instead of phosphor to generate the pel glow. The pel is turned on to a specific brightness and remains static until the pel is reset.

A passive LCD monitor has a container of three layers of liquid crystal fluid that has a grid-like arrangement of electrodes. Each layer contains a primitive color. Light is shined through the back end of the container and is prevented from shining through the front of the container by properties of each of the polarized liquid crystal fluid layers.

This is similar to how polarized sunglasses block some light from hitting your eyes. I like to think of this as thin horizontal blinds. Sunlight is prevented from entering the room when the blinds are closed and freely enters the room when the blinds are opened.

The grid of electrodes is similar to sets of blinds, where each intersect in the grid is one set of blinds. When electrodes at a particular grid intersect are energized by electricity, the "blinds" are opened, causing the pel to glow.

A major drawback of a passive LCD monitor is the inability for the pels to be reset quickly. The refresh rate is appreciably slower than that in a CRT although sufficient for most office applications. However, the refresh rate is too slow for video and sophisticated animated graphics.

The active matrix LCD monitor uses thin file transistors (TFT) memory circuits instead of using electrodes to change the setting of pels. There are three memory circuits for each pel, one for each subpel. Memory circuits provide a much quicker response than electrodes. Therefore, an active matrix LCD is capable of displaying video and animated graphics.

Practical Side to Monitors

The best monitor to purchase is one that fits your needs. Let's say that the monitor is primarily used with programs that create high-resolution graphics such as video editing. You need a monitor that produces a stable image, one with a refresh rate of 90 Hz and above. However, a monitor with a 60 Hz to 70 Hz refresh rate is adequate for most office applications.

Find a monitor that has a resolution compatible with images that you'll typically display on the monitor. If you're going to display very high-resolution images on a regular basis, then you'll find it worth the additional expense to purchase a monitor that also has that resolution.

If you don't, then the video display adapter will reduce the resolution of the image to meet the highest resolution that can be displayed on the monitor. You lose the finer details that are contained in the image.

Be sure that you purchase a monitor where the dot pitch and the dot size are the same value because this assures you that the image will be displayed as bright as possible. Generally, the smaller the dot pitch and dot size, the finer the image will appear on the screen.

Make sure that you adjust the dot pitch value whenever you compare a monitor with a dot pitch to a monitor with a stripe pitch. You must multiply the stripe pitch value by 0.90 to arrive at a comparative value to the dot pitch.

Don't get fooled by the diagonal size of a monitor. The diagonal size is not the same as the viewable size. The viewable size is less than the diagonal size. This becomes an important consideration if the monitor will be used for graphical applications where you require a large desktop to be displayed on the monitor.

Generally, stay away from touch screen monitors unless you have a special purpose in mind. Grids used on touch screen monitors don't provide as many contact points as you normally find using other pointing devices such as a mouse. A contact point is the point on the screen that is identified when you touch the screen.

I also suggest choosing a cylindrical tube screen over a flat screen primarily because I don't believe that most of us can justify the extra expense for the flat screen.

However, I'm sure the price of flat screens will someday be comparable to cylindrical tubes.

Stick with active matrix LCD laptops. You'll find the quality of the image much better than passive LCD screens and you'll be able to watch your favorite movie if you purchase a laptop with a DVD player. You'll learn more about DVD players in Chapter 5.

Once you've settled on specifications for a monitor, then you need to hunt for the best buy. I'd limit my search to brand name monitors, then look at models within your budget.

Although I surf the net for prices, I also get a bid from my local computer stores. In fact, I usually end up buying from my local store because by the time I add shipping and handling charges for an online purchase, the price is about the same. However, I have the advantage of returning the monitor to the local store without any hassles. I also get a chance to see the monitor in action at the store.

INSIDE VIDEO ADAPTERS ....

The video display adapter is the brain behind how information is displayed on the screen. A program such as Microsoft PowerPoint provides instructions to the processor for displaying information on the screen.

Display instructions are automatically sent to the video display adapter for processing. The video display adapter translates these instructions into a signal to drive the electron gun, which produces the image on the screen.

Many names are used to describe the video display adapter, including the video graphics adapter card and simply the video adapter. The term *card* was frequently used when talking about a video display adapter because the video display adapter was contained on an expansion card inserted into the expansion slot on the motherboard. Some video adapters in use today are also on expansion cards, although many of the video adapters have been integrated into the motherboard.

The term *graphics* is sometimes used to describe a video display adapter as a holdover from the early days of computers where there were two modes of display: character and graphics. A character display is where the screen is logically divided into character blocks, each consisting of a 5 × 9 matrix of pels (see Figure 4-4). Any displayable ASCII character can be created by turning on and off a combination of pixels within the character block.

A program to display characters on the screen sent instructions to the processor to place a certain character in a particular character block. The processor knew the location of the character block and the set of pels to activate to display the character.

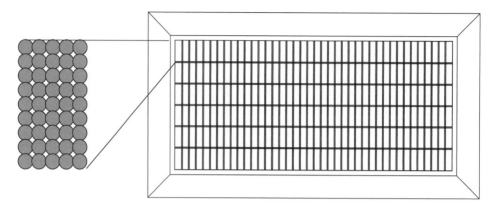

Figure 4-4
Character mode divides the screen into character blocks, each consisting of a set of pels

Most programs in those days were character-based. That is, they did not address each pel as is done today. The computer needed to be set into graphics mode before a program could address each pel to display a graphic.

Engineers realized that the integrated video display adapter in the original personal computers couldn't effectively handle the growing need for graphics. Therefore, engineers built video graphic expansion cards to process graphical display instructions.

All video display adapters are video graphic adapters and incorporate a graphic accelerator to efficiently process video information.

Tech Talk

Graphic accelerator: A coprocessor specifically designed to display graphical information quickly on the screen.

A program sends video instructions to the main processor, which resends them to the graphic accelerator, freeing the main processor to execute nonvideo instructions. The graphic accelerator contains a special instruction set to handle the transfer of video information from memory to the monitor.

On new computers, graphic information is sent from the main processor to the video display adapter over the Accelerated Graphics Port (AGP).

Tech Talk

Accelerated Graphics Port: A special bus on the motherboard that transfers information only to the video display adapter at a faster speed than information flows over the PCI bus.

How a Video Display Adapter Works

A computer's video circuitry consists of two major components: the video display adapter and video memory. The video display adapter is a small computer that processes video information using the video display adapter's own processor, clock, and bus.

A graphics program instructs the main processor to display an image and provides the main processor with information that describes the images in the form of zeros and ones. Although the main processor can process video information, it does so inefficiently.

In contrast, the processor on the video display adapter is optimized to process video information. Therefore, the main processor passes video instructions and data directly to the video adapter.

Video information consisting of instructions and data are stored in video image RAM, which is located near or on the video display adapter to provide a quick access time to instruction and data. Some computers utilize all of main memory to store video information, as is the case with the Silicon Graphics Inc. visual workstation. Other computers such as personal computers limit video information to video image RAM.

A portion of the video image RAM is designated a frame buffer. In a sense, a frame buffer is the memory version of the video display screen. A video display adapter can use more than one frame buffer. The purpose of multiple frame buffers is to improve the time necessary to build an image in memory and display the image on the screen.

Tech Talk
Frame buffer: Video image RAM that contains one screen of information.

Here's how this works. The setting for each pel on the screen is represented by multiple bits of information stored in a frame buffer. The video display adapter's output circuit reads each bit in the frame beginning with the bit that represents the upper left corner of the screen. The value of the bit is translated into a horizontal and vertical signal that directs the movement of the electron gun (see Figure 4-5).

The output circuit scans a frame buffer at the same rate the electron gun scans the display screen. This is called synchronized sweeping because both the output circuit and the electron gun are synchronized.

A slight delay can occur whenever the video display adapter updates information in the frame buffer. This delay is rarely noticeable unless a lot of information is updated frequently such as when you view animation. The time it takes the video display adapter to update the frame buffer could cause the animated movements to appear jumpy.

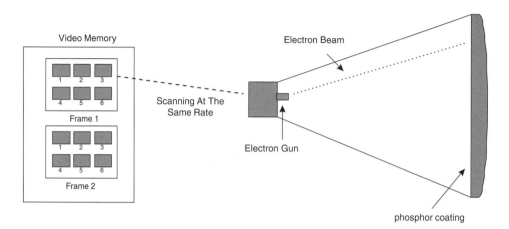

Figure 4-5
The frame buffer is scanned at the same rate the electron gun scans the screen

Engineers solved this problem by employing more than one frame buffer. For example, as the output circuit scans a frame buffer, the video display adapter coprocessor is filling another frame buffer with information for the next frame that is to appear on the screen.

The output circuit is then using the second frame buffer whenever the program tells the processor that it is time to change the image. The video display adapter coprocessor continues the sequence by updating the first frame buffer with the next image.

One of the key elements that differentiate the main processor from the video display adapter coprocessor is the way in which each addresses pels. The main processor's instruction set contains low-level instructions used to set each pel individually. In contrast, the video display adapter coprocessor's instruction set uses a high-level approach to setting pels.

Let's say that you want to have a line drawn on the screen. The main processor interprets the instruction as a set of color values for a group of pels. However, the video display adapter coprocessor interprets the instruction as a request to draw a line of a particular width and color at a particular location on the screen. Video instructions are contained in the video display adapter coprocessor's display list and one of those instructions is to draw a line.

This means that the video display adapter requires fewer instructions to process drawing a line than the main processor requires for the same line. Fewer instructions translates into fast processing, which is required to produce snappy graphical images on the screen.

Video Image RAM

The move from character-based displays to graphical displays improved the image quality shown on the screen and also increased the amount of memory required to display the image. Character-based display used character blocks and required 2 bytes of information: 1 byte to represent the ASCII character and the other to represent the display characteristics such as color, blinking, and underline.

Graphical displays dramatically increased the amount of memory required to display an image because each bit must be addressed individually, and graphical designers want to use more than the limited colors that were available in character-based displays.

The number of possible colors that can be used for each pel is called the color depth and is directly influenced by the amount of video image RAM used to represent a color for a pel. Each color has its own bit value and the larger number of bits, the more color choices are available for a pel.

You can determine the number of colors a set of bits can represent by raising two to the power equal to the number of bits. For example, 4 bits has a maximum of 16 colors. This is 2^4 or $2 \times 2 \times 2 \times 2$. Eight bits can represent 256 colors. Many video adapters, especially those used in personal computers, use 24 bits to represent the color of a pel. This means there are 16,777,216 available.

Some video adapters used 32 bits to represent colors; however, 8 bits are used to represent information other than color such as the degree of transparency of the image. This means how much of the underlying image is displayed, which is called alpha channel information.

A video display adapter processes colors differently if 24-bit values are used rather than 4- or 8-bit values to represent colors. The video display adapter directly sets the colors of pels when colors are represented by 24-bit values and indirectly if 4 bits or 8 bits are used.

The indirect method employs a lookup list of colors called a palette. A palette is used to expand the color offering from 16 colors or 256 colors, which are the limits of 4- and 8-bit representation of color. By switching colors in a palette, an image can be displayed in various sets of 16 colors or 256 colors. The palette is typically contained within the image and is loaded into memory when the image is copied into memory. The palette lists all colors used by the image.

Components of a Video Adapter

The video display adapter contains a graphics processor also known as a graphics co-processor. This processor dramatically improves the throughput of video images to the screen by using a special instruction set. The instruction set focuses on creating standard image components such as lines, ovals, arcs, and squares rather than repeating instructions to set each pel in the image.

Video image RAM is RAM stored close to the video display adapter and exclusively used for processing images. Both the main processor and the graphics coprocessor have access to video RAM, which enables each processor to work independently transferring and processing video information.

Engineers continue to improve upon the types of memory chips used for video image RAM. The latest is Synchronous Graphics RAM (SGRAM), which has a 6 nanosecond access time. You'll find SGRAM used in more expensive video display adapters.

SGRAM is an improvement on its predecessor, the synchronous DRAM (SDRAM). SDRAM has an 8-nanosecond access time and can be found on low to medium priced video display adapters. SDRAM succeeded Windows RAM (WRAM), video RAM (VRAM), and extended data out DRAM (EDO DRAM) memory chips, all of which are outdated.

Another component of the video display adapter is the random access memory digital-to-analog converter (RAMDAC). As mentioned earlier in this chapter, computers process images using digital information (zeros and ones). The CRT displays information using analog information.

Therefore, the video display adapter must translate digital information into analog information so the monitor can properly display the image. The RAMDAC circuit performs this translation.

Video display instructions that are sent to the main processor by a graphic application are not designed for the optimal use of the video coprocessor. For example, the application may send several instructions to set a series of pels to form a line. The video coprocessor needs to know only that a line is to be drawn at specific coordinates with a specific width and color.

A special program called a driver converts the application's video display instruction into the optimized instructions required by the video coprocessor. This ensures that the image is displayed in the most efficient way on the screen.

Video display adapters also contain a bus used to transfer information between the video coprocessor and the main processor. One of two buses is used for this purpose: the PCI bus (discussed in Chapter 3), or the AGP. The AGP is called a port because it connects only two devices. Technically a bus connects more than two devices, although both a bus and port function the same way to transfer information.

The AGP is more advantageous than the PCI bus primarily because the AGP has a much higher throughput than the 133-MB-per-second speed available from the PCI bus. In addition, the PCI bus carries more than video information, whereas the AGP carries only video information. This becomes a critical factor with newer video adapters that support the demanding 3D graphics.

Characteristics of a Video Adapter

Video adapters are rated based on five features: color depth, refresh frequency, resolution, throughput, and whether or not the video display adapter is designed to handle 3D images.

Color depth is the maximum number of individual colors that can be used to display a pel, sometimes referred to as the amount of data needed to display each pel. Most video display adapters are backward compatible in that a video display adapter that uses a 24-bit color model can automatically switch to 4-bit, 8-bit, and 16-bit models depending on the colors used to create the graphic.

The refresh frequency, sometimes called the refresh rate, is the number of times per second that the video display adapter replaces the image on the monitor. A refresh frequency of 60 Hz or 70 Hz is acceptable for most business applications. A higher frequency is required for specialty applications such as video editing that requires a more stable image be displayed.

Resolution is the number of pels per frame buffer that can be addressed by the video display adapter. Typically a video display adapter can be set to one of a group of standard resolutions, which is adjustable using operating system software such as Windows.

Throughput is a measurement of how much video information can be processed by the video adapter. Just as with the main processor's throughput (see Chapter 3), the video adapter's throughput is dependent on a number of factors. These factors include the width of the video bus, the internal speed of the video coprocessor, the external speed of the video bus, whether or not the AGP is used, and the amount of data that must be processed.

The number of bits used to represent a pel (color depth), the number of pels in a frame buffer (resolution), and whether or not the video display adapter is in 3D mode determine the amount of data processed by the graphics coprocessor.

Newer video display adapters have 2D and 3D models. As the name implies, the 3D model adds depth to flat images produced by the more common 2D model.

Video display adapters that use the 3D model are capable of producing realistic images because of two features. First, they can easily incorporate details of an image such as textures and reflections. They also adjust the image based upon the user's view of objects on the screen. For example, lighting of objects in an image is adjusted based on the movement of the object, such as when an airplane flies overhead.

Practical Side to Video Adapters

When you get down to it, the best video display adapter is the one that is right for your application. It doesn't make sense to purchase a high-end video display adapter to display the output of business applications. Likewise, video editing, medical imaging, computer-aided design and game applications require more than the average video display adapter to produce desired results.

Don't pay extra for a video display adapter that uses the 3D model unless you use applications that display 3D graphics. Remember that the application program generates the image. The video display adapter and monitor reproduce—not enhance—the image.

Applications that display 3D graphics and millions of colors require a video display adapter with a substantial amount of video memory usually in the 16-MB range. However, 8 MB of video memory is adequate for most business applications.

Features of video adapters continue to improve as applications produce more complex and realistic images. Therefore, you need to make sure that you can upgrade the video display adapter in the future.

Video display adapter cards don't pose a problem because you can also replace the existing card. However, video adapters that are integrated into the motherboard could pose a problem. You need to make sure that you can disable the video display adapter so it doesn't conflict with an enhanced video display adapter card inserted into an expansion slot that will provide you with the latest features.

As a general rule, I make sure that an AGP is available in any computer I purchase. This enables me to use a compatible video display adapter that gives me greater video throughput.

And the last, but probably the most important, feature of a video display adapter is a driver compatible with the operating system running on your computer. Make sure there is a driver available, otherwise your operating system will not recognize the video display adapter.

SUMMARY ....

Information is displayed on the computer monitor by using three video components: monitor, video cable, and video adapter. An application program sends instructions to the main processor whenever the application wants to display information on the screen.

The main processor immediately sends the instruction to the video adapter. The video display adapter is like a little computer in that the video processor contains a video coprocessor, a bus, a clock, and video memory.

The instruction to display information is sent to video RAM by the main processor, which then sends an interrupt to the video coprocessor telling it that new information has arrived and must be displayed.

The video driver translates the main processor instructions into instructions that the video coprocessor understands. The video coprocessor uses a special instruction set that contains instructions specifically designed to draw pieces of images on the screen.

Bits that are used to represent the image are copied into a frame buffer. A frame buffer is the video memory image of the monitor's screen. Several bits in the frame buffer represent each pel on the screen. The actual number of bits used to define a pel is dependent on the color depth, that is, the number bits used to define the color of a pel.

The video display adapter output circuit scans the frame buffer at the same speed as the electron gun in the monitor scans the screen. The movement of the electron gun is controlled by the horizontal and vertical signals generated by the video display adapter output circuit.

Electrons are given off as the CRT in the monitor is heated by electricity. An electromagnetic mechanism called a yoke directs the electron beam from the electron gun to the phosphor coating on the back of the screen.

A glow is emitted from the portion of the phosphor that is hit by the electron beam. The brightness of the glow is determined by the strength of the beam. The more electrons that hit the phosphor, the brighter the glow.

The phosphor glows for a short time, called the decay time, after which the phosphor turns dark. The electron gun must continue to refresh the phosphor to maintain a stable image on the screen. The length of time it takes the electron gun to reach every pel of the screen is called the refresh rate. The higher the refresh rate, the more stable the image on the screen.

Some monitors such as those used on laptops don't use an electron gun. Instead they use other technology. Laptops display images using a liquid crystal display that is embedded with a grid. Either an electrode (passive matrix) or a small circuit that contains transistors (active matrix) controls each cell in the grid. Pels are displayed by changing the state of a cell.

Summary Questions

1. **What advantages does the AGP have over the PCI bus?**

2. **What is the advantage of having more than one frame buffer in a video adapter?**

3. **What impact does the color model have on video RAM?**

4. What are the advantages and disadvantages of using a touch screen monitor?

5. What signals flow over the wires in a video cable?

6. What is the difference between character mode and graphic mode?

7. What is the difference between dot pitch and stripe pitch?

8. What impact if any does the diameter of the electron beam have on the image displayed on the screen?

9. What is the purpose of a mask?

10. What is the relationship between a pel and a subpel?

5 Storage Devices

In this chapter...

"A safe place assures a quick recovery."

Anonymous

Who would have thought that a grammar school science experiment would have an impact on computer technology? You probably remember back to the time when your science teacher placed iron shavings on a piece of paper, then made them stand on end with a magnet. It looked like magic, yet it proved a natural phenomenon that is the basis of storage technology.

Magnetism changes the state of iron, and when carefully applied can be used to store information on a disk or tape. It still seems a bit magical how thousands of words, sound clips, and pictures are placed on a thin sheet of plasticlike material and are able to be recalled in a millisecond.

However, what I just described is becoming old hat with the onset of laser technology. Energy from a laser is used to burn information into CDs using the same method used to create music and movie CDs. Lasers have revolutionized the storage technology industry. The amount of information that can be stored on a CD and the speed at which information can be retrieved dwarfs a similar size disk.

In this chapter you'll learn everything you need to know about storage technology and how to apply that knowledge when purchasing computer equipment. You'll learn about:

- Floppy disk drives

- Hard disk drives

- Removable disks drives

- Microdrives

- RAM drives

- Tape drives

- CD drives

- DVD drives

- Magneto-optic discs

REALITY CHECK

Over the years I've written more than 50 books and while that might have killed a social life, it did make me realize how the way we store information has changed over that period. The information I'm talking about are the words I write.

My first few books were written using a typewriter. A typewriter is that rather clunky machine that used characters die-cut into metal to strike through an inked ribbon to display the character onto paper. And the paper wasn't the only thing getting inked whenever I wrote a book. So did my hands and anything I touched after changing the typewriter ribbon. I felt that I had to define the term *typewriter* because of my readers who may never have seen a typewriter except in old movies.

Before I started to write a book I placed two reams of paper—500 sheets each—next to the typewriter. This was the way I measured my progress. As the stack of empty paper slowly shrank—and the stack of completed manuscript paper grew taller—I knew I was on target to hit my deadline.

Today I measure progress by the size of the Word file that contains manuscript pages. Actually, there are no real pages anymore. Instead, there is a line count, about 55 lines to a printed page. Word places a marker in the file indicating a page break.

I just continue writing until I've exhausted the topic and I save the manuscript to a file stored on a hard disk, a floppy disk, and a disk on a network server. I have many copies of the same manuscript just in case something happens to the original file.

In the not-so-good old days, it was a major job to make additional copies of a manuscript. I would use something called a carbon packet. A carbon packet consisted of sheets of paper and carbon paper sandwiched into one thick sheet. I could make three copies of the manuscript as I typed the original page. Later I switched to using a copy machine. But nothing beats storing a manuscript on a disk.

INSIDE COMPUTER STORAGE

The challenge that faced engineers was how to store the zeros and ones that represent characters, sound, and video in a way for these binary values to be permanently stored and accessed and modified in a few milliseconds.

Magnetism and iron provided the solution to this storage problem. Engineers used the ability of an electrically powered magnet to change the polarity of tiny iron particles so that each polarity represents a binary value.

Tech Talk
Polarity: A positively or negatively charged particle of iron.

Engineers used a compound of iron oxide to coat a plasticlike material that was formed into the shape of a disk. You know this as a floppy disk. A strong magnet powered by electricity is then moved over a tiny portion of the disk. As electricity flows through the magnet, the polarity of the iron oxide is changed. This is how a bit is written to the disk. I'll go into more detail on how this is done later in the chapter.

Today's floppy disks can hold about 265 typewritten pages, which is 1.4 MB of data. Floppy disk technology led the way to hard disk storage, where multiple disks called platters are used to hold bits of data using the same basic method as is used to store information on a floppy disk. Hard disks can hold upward of 25 gigabytes (GB), or 25 billion bytes of data.

You'll hear the terms *disk* and *disk drives* used interchangeably although each is different: A disk is the component on which data is stored. A disk drive is a device that accesses data stored on a disk.

This is obvious whenever you use a floppy disk. The floppy disk is the disk, and the place where you insert the disk into your computer is the disk drive. However, this is less obvious when talking about a hard disk.

A hard disk is something inside your computer that you don't notice other than maybe a flashing light on the console and the whinny noise that sounds whenever you save a file. Yet a hard disk has the same basic components as a floppy disk except the disks and the disk drive are all in one box inside the computer. You'll learn more about how hard disks operate later in this chapter.

No disk drive is infallible. A drive can come crashing down making it impossible for you to access data stored on the drive. There's little you can do but cry and say a few words that shouldn't be said in mixed company.

You cannot prevent a disk drive from crashing, but you can take precautions to minimize the loss of information once a crash occurs by frequently backing up data stored on a disk. If a crash occurs, you can replace the disk drive, then copy data from a backup disk and you're up and running in no time.

The volume of data stored on a typical hard disk is well beyond the capacity of a floppy disk. You would use hundreds of floppy disks to back up a typical hard disk. There are three other storage devices commonly used to back up data from a hard disk: a removable disk drive, a CD drive, and a tape drive.

A removable disk drive such as the Iomega Zip drive can write up to 250 MB of data on one disk. And when one removable disk fills up, you can quickly slip in another and continue to back up the hard disk.

A CD drive is similar to the CD drive used in your stereo and used to load programs onto your computer. You can use a compact disc-recordable (CD-R) drive or a compact disc-rewritable (CD-RW) drive to make a copy of data stored on your hard disk. I'll tell you more about CD drives later in this chapter.

A tape drive uses a variation of the cassette tapes used years ago for music. Musical cassette tapes stored analog information. Tapes used for computers store digital data. This enhances the accuracy of the transfer.

Tech Talk

Analog: Representing information as a series of values.

Digital: Representing information as one of two discrete values (zero or one).

A tape drive consists of a tape player/recorder and tapes. A tape is a filmlike material coated with iron oxide just like the tape used in your VCR. An electromagnet in the tape player/recorder polarizes the iron oxide elements similar to the polarization used in a disk drive to represent the zeros and ones that represent data on the disk.

Tech Talk

Electromagnet: A piece of metal that is magnetized when electricity is passed around the metal.

However, a tape drive differs from a disk drive in the way the data is organized on the tape. As you'll learn in later sections of this chapter, data is stored randomly on a disk. This may appear chaotic, but it is a fast way to find information.

A tape drive stores data sequentially. The first bit goes first, then the next bit second, and so on. The difficulty comes when you need to find a piece of data located somewhere toward the center of the tape. That's when the tape drive must read all the bits from the beginning of the tape before it can locate the data you require.

Engineers have made strides to speed the search for data on a tape, but they haven't reached the level of performance as that found with disk drives. That's fine because typically you'll wait the extra few minutes to copy data from a tape to a new disk since the alternative is not to recover data at all.

Some nerds believe the days of floppy disk drives, hard disk drives, removable disk drives, and tape drives are numbered because the CD drive is coming on strong. A CD drive uses CDs that can store 650 MB of data.

There are two kinds of CD drives. These are a CD-ROM drive that can read data stored on a CD and a CD writable drive that can read and write—and erase—data on a CD. You are probably familiar with the CD-ROM drive if you've purchased a new computer recently. Most computers come equipped with a CD-ROM drive.

Prices of CD-R drives are dropping, making them an economical alternative to a tape drive and removable disk drive. As you'll read about later in this chapter, the speed of a CD drive hasn't yet reached the performance of the average hard disk.

OPERATING SYSTEMS AND DISK DRIVES ....

The way in which data is stored on a disk drive is directly related to the operating system running on the computer that contains the disk drive. The operating system consists of many programs, one of which is responsible for reading and writing information to a disk. However, before any data can be exchanged between a hard disk drive and the computer, the operating system needs to know how data is organized on the disk so it can write and read data quickly.

The most widely used computer operating system is Windows, which has its roots in the early operating system (OS) called Disk Operating System (DOS). We'll look at how Windows organizes information on a disk. There are other operating systems such as Linux that use a different approach, which you'll learn about later in this chapter.

The program within an operating system that interfaces with a disk drive is called the file system. The file system is responsible for making sure a disk is organized properly to store data. The file system also has the job to read and write data to a disk drive.

Each disk has a physical structure and a logical structure. The physical structure of a disk consists of one or more platters each having one or more surface areas arranged in concentric tracks.

Tech Talk

Concentric tracks: Circular tracks that don't touch each other.

A platter is what you recognize as a floppy disk. The surface areas of a platter are the top and bottom of a disk. Both sides of these surfaces are coated with iron oxide. The disk manufacturer specifies whether or not both sides meet the quality standard necessary to store data on both surfaces. Most floppy disks are double-sided, meaning that data can be written to the top and bottom surfaces.

Hard disks have two or more layers of platters that are organized so that tracks in each platter are aligned (see Figure 5-1). Tracks that are in the same position on each platter are called a cylinder. You'll learn more on how a hard disk works later in this chapter.

Tracks are evenly divided into sectors. A sector is the physical place on a disk where data is stored. The number of sectors on a disk varies based on the capacity of the disk. The more sectors available, the higher the capacity the disk has to store data.

Each sector can store 571 bytes although some operating systems use larger sectors. Fifty-nine bytes in a sector are used for administrative purposes such as to identify the sector and the remaining 512 bytes are used to store data.

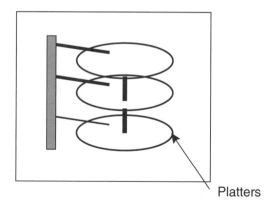

Platters

Figure 5-1
Platters are stacked on top of each other in a hard disk

Disk Formatting

Every disk must be prepared before a disk drive is able to write information to the disk. This preparation is called formatting. The initial step is for the operating system to physically format the disk by placing data into each sector on the disk. Data includes sector numbering stored in the sector's header, meaningless data in the sector body, and error correcting data in the sector trailer.

> **Tech Talk**
>
> **Header: The first few bytes of a sector.**
>
> **Trailer: The last few bytes of a sector.**

The next step in the formatting process is dependent on the type of disk that is being formatted. In the case of a hard disk, it must be partitioned. Partitioning divides the hard disk into one or multiple logical disks.

> **Tech Talk**
>
> **Logical disk: The operating system treats divisions of a physical disk as individual disks.**

Each partition is assigned a drive designator such as D: and E:, which gives you the appearance that two or more hard drives exists in the computer when there is really only one hard drive. You probably don't need to partition a hard disk because many computers come with hard disks fully operational—and loaded with bundled software. The manufacturer wouldn't be able to bundle software with the computer unless the hard disk was partitioned and formatted.

Floppy disks do not need to be partitioned, so the next step in the formatting process for a floppy disk and for a partitioned hard disk is to logically format the disk. During logical formatting, the operating system may place the boot record on the disk if you want to use the disk to start up your computer.

Tech Talk
Boot record: The first bytes of data read by the basic input/output system (BIOS) when a computer is started.

The boot record contains a program that loads the operating system into memory. Most if not all hard disks are formatted with a boot record. A floppy disk may or may not have a boot record depending on the options selected when the disk is formatted.

You've probably seen the error message "nonsystem disk or disk error" whenever you inadvertently left a floppy disk in the disk drive and you started your computer. This means that the BIOS on the motherboard (see Chapter 4) tried to load the boot record from the floppy disk but couldn't find the boot record because it wasn't placed on the floppy disk when the disk was formatted.

If no floppy disk is in the floppy disk drive when the computer starts up, the BIOS automatically looks for the boot record on the first hard disk, which usually has the boot record. The BIOS then uses the boot record to load the full operating system into memory.

Logical formatting also creates a file allocation table (FAT). A FAT is a directory of all clusters on the disk, where they are located, and if they already contain data. In addition, a file allocation table indicates whether or not a cluster is damaged. I'll tell you more about clusters later in this chapter.

Tech Talk
Cluster: A group of sectors on a disk where data is stored.

One of the last tasks performed during the logical formatting is the creation of the root directory. The root directory is a table that associates filenames and related data with the beginning cluster that contains the first byte of the file.

Avoiding Bad Sectors

Although disk-manufacturing techniques have dramatically increased the quality of production from that experienced in the early years of computing, there hasn't been a perfect disk built. This means that a portion of the surface area is not able to accurately store data. In other words, some clusters on a disk are bad.

You and I aren't concerned about bad clusters until our data is stored in one. However, the operating system takes great pains to avoid placing data in a bad cluster. The OS notes which clusters did not respond properly during the formatting process. These are considered bad clusters and are marked as such in the FAT, which also reduces the capacity of the disk.

You may never realize a reduction in the reported capacity of a hard disk because the capacity of a hard disk is typically unreported. Let's say that a disk is reported to have a capacity of 2 GB. Actually, the disk has more capacity that the manufacturer hasn't told you about and it is this extra, unreported capacity that is used to make up for bad clusters.

Tech Talk

Reported capacity: The number that appears on the screen indicating the maximum number of bytes that can be stored on a disk.

A cluster that is unreported logically replaces the bad cluster. The bad cluster is still physically on the disk. The reserve group of clusters is usually found at the end of each track.

Clusters and Fragmentation

The OS reads and writes information to a disk in a group of bytes called a cluster. A cluster consists of more than one sector. The number of sectors within a cluster is dependent on the OS.

A cluster has a fixed number of bytes, a factor that can lead to wasted disk capacity. This is because regardless of the size of the data being written to a disk, the entire cluster is dedicated to that data.

Here's how it works. Let's say that the operating system uses a cluster size of 4K and the data contains 100 bytes. The operating system allocates 4K—one cluster—for the data, leaving 3,900 bytes of the cluster practically empty. The empty space is called the slack space.

Slack space is filled with data should additional data be written to the file. However, until then sectors that comprise the cluster are unavailable for use by another file.

A file of a larger size can also waste sectors in the same way. For example a file that contains 10K is stored in three consecutive clusters on the disk. This means that all the sectors that make up the cluster are next to each other on the disk. This produces 2K of slack space because the last cluster of the file contains 2K of information.

The location of sectors that comprise clusters of the same file is critical to the efficiency of retrieving data from the disk. Let's say that the 10K file was saved to disk and placed in consecutive sectors. Then more data is added to the file before the file is once again saved. Now the file is 16K.

Previously the file used three clusters. Four clusters are needed to store the new file. However, the cluster next to the third cluster may already contain another file. This means that the OS must have used a cluster located somewhere else on the disk. The file is said to be fragmented (see Figure 5-2).

A hard disk uses a read/write head to read and write data to the disk. The disk drive must move the read/write head over the first sector of the first cluster used to store a file. Each sector is then read sequentially, then the read/write head moves to the next cluster and the pattern continues until all the clusters of the file are read.

A factor that affects the quickness with which a file is read is the amount of time necessary for the read/write head to position itself over each sector of a cluster. A minimum amount of time is expended if clusters of the same file are next to each other on the disk. Additional time is necessary if some of the clusters are located in other places on the disk.

As available storage space on a disk is taken up by files, the disk becomes more fragmented, resulting in slower response time. You'll notice the impact fragmentation whenever you run programs that use video and music.

Video and music files are very large as compared with a word processing document or a spreadsheet file. In addition, the contents of these files must be read quickly in an uninterrupted stream, otherwise the music won't sound proper and the video will look jerky. Any fragmentation of the files interrupts this steady stream.

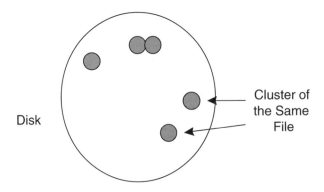

Figure 5-2
Disks can easily become fragmented where clusters of the same file
are spread across the disk

You can rectify this problem by using a defragger program such as the one that comes with Windows. A defragger program defragments the disk, meaning the defragger program recopies all the clusters of a file into an area of consecutive clusters on the disk.

A Closer Look at a File Allocation Table

The file allocation table is similar to a roadmap where roads are clusters on the disk. Information contained in the file allocation table relates a file name to the cluster that contains the first bytes of the file. Information at the end of each cluster points the operating system to the next cluster associated with the file (see Figure 5-3).

Two copies of the file allocation table are stored on a disk. One copy is the active file allocation table and the other a backup.

If the operating system is unable to read both the active and backup file allocation, the file allocation becomes inaccessible. This means that the operating system is not able to read any files from the disk. Clusters that contain the file are likely to be intact, but they are useless unless the operating system knows the location of the first cluster.

Each cluster contains a reference number to the next cluster on the disk. In this way, a file can use many clusters, but the file allocation table need only record one cluster for each file.

Three values are stored in a file allocation table: the reference number area of a cluster, a value that indicates if the cluster is available or is bad, the address of the next cluster indicating the end-of-file (EOF) marker.

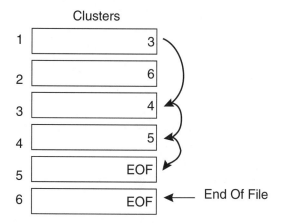

Figure 5-3
The first cluster tells the operating system the location of the next cluster of the same file

Tech Talk

End-of-file marker: A value that tells the OS that there are no more clusters for the file.

There are three file allocation standards: FAT12, FAT16, and FAT32. The number implies the number of bits used to represent the address of a cluster. FAT12 uses a 12-bit cluster address; FAT16, a 16-bit cluster address; and FAT32, a 32-bit cluster address.

The number of bits used to represent a cluster address determines the number of clusters that can be placed on a disk. The highest number that can be represented by 12 bits is 4,095; 16 bits, 65,535; and 32 bits, 4,294,967,295.

FAT12 is the file allocation standard used on all floppy disks and hard disks that are not more than 16 MB in size. This is because 16 MB is the largest amount of bytes that can be stored in 4,095 clusters.

FAT16 is used with a hard disk that has a capacity greater than 16 MB and less than 2 GB, which is the largest capacity that can be stored in 65,535 clusters. FAT16 is the default file allocation standard used in Windows for hard disks. FAT32 is used for a hard disk with a capacity at least 512 MB but is typically used for a hard disk that has a greater than 2 GB capacity.

A file allocation standard is one factor that establishes the amount of data that can be stored on a disk. Another limiting factor is the capability of BIOS on the motherboard. A typical BIOS on a personal computer can work with a disk not greater than 137 GB. While this may seem like an unattainable value because most of us use a small fraction of that amount, the capacity limitation of BIOS can impact certain applications such as video editing applications. Minimize the effects of the BIOS capacity limitation by partitioning a hard disk into partitions that are less than 137 GB.

Other File Systems

The UNIX operating system is another operating system similar to MS-DOS and Windows that is used on all categories of computers including personal computers. Unlike Windows, UNIX comes in variations commonly called flavors such as ext3 Linux and SunOS. Each flavor has features not found in the standard UNIX operating system.

Most UNIX flavors use a file operating system that reads and writes a block of data at a time to the disk rather than using the cluster technique used in Windows. Each block is 8K in length. The block-at-a-time scheme is used because most files are written and read sequentially in their entirety.

The block-at-a-time allocation method is wasteful. Sun Microsystems developed a file-clustering file allocation method for its SunOS system. The clustering system uses a smart algorithm that allocates contiguous blocks to a file by anticipating further allocation requests. This results in increased performance without altering the on-disk file structure.

Microsoft enhanced the FAT standard with VFAT and New Technology File System (NTFS) to compensate for features that FAT lacked. VFAT is used in Windows 95 and Windows 98 to extend the filename limit of FAT.

The FAT standard has a limit of 8 characters and a 3-character file extension (this is after the period). And the characters used for the filename are limited, for example, spaces and periods cannot be used in the file name.

Filenames under the VFAT standard can contain up to 255 characters and include some characters prohibited from being used in FAT such as spaces and periods. VFAT also preserves the case of the filename, but as with FAT these filenames are not case sensitive.

NTFS is used in Windows NT to greatly improve VFAT and FAT. Both VFAT and FAT can be used on a disk no larger than 2 GB. Before VFAT or FAT can handle a larger capacity disk, the disk must be divided into partitions no larger than 2 GB. However, NTFS can handle a disk as large as 1,024 terabytes (TB), also known as 16 exabytes (EB).

NTFS also increased VFAT and FAT fault tolerance and security. Fault tolerance means that the file system can recover from a disk error or power failure. VFAT and FAT don't offer any fault tolerance.

Fault tolerance is offered by NTFS by recording into a log file every change made to the disk. In this way the log file can be used to recover from a disk failure. This also enables NTFS to automatically repair a hard disk without displaying an error message on the screen.

Another feature of NTFS is the ability to secure directories and files on your computer. VFAT and FAT enable you to password protect files on your computer that are shared with others across a network. However, no such protection is offered to files that are not shared. This means someone could use your computer and access any file. NTFS enables you to password protect any directory or file, shared or not.

HARD DISKS ....

A hard disk is a disk concealed inside your computer. Although we use the term *hard disk*, we are really talking about the hard disk drive that contains one or more hard disks.

The hard disk drive is a sealed box that prevents even air from entering. This protects the mechanism and the hard disks from dust and other fine debris that can easily slip between the read/write head and the hard disk. The read/write head is the portion of the hard disk drive mechanism that reads and writes information to the hard disk.

A hard disk is similar to a floppy disk in the way information is copied and written to the disk. However, a hard disk is harder than a floppy as you surmised by the name because a hard disk is made of either aluminum or glass.

Aluminum and glass aren't as sensitive to temperature as the Mylar used for floppy disks. This means that hard disks don't expand and retract as temperature rises and falls. This enables that hard disk drive mechanism to squeeze more information in the same space on a hard disk than a floppy disk.

Here's how this works. The area on the disk where information is stored must always be in the same position, otherwise, the disk drive mechanism won't be able to find it. The size of this area must compensate for the expansion and retraction of the disk material. Since aluminum and glass have little expansion or contraction, the area used to write information could be smaller than the same space used in a floppy disk.

How Hard Disks Work

Inside the sealed case that we recognize as a hard disk is the mechanism that writes information to the disk and reads information from it. Most hard disk drives contain more than one disk, which is called a platter. Platters sit on top of each other, connected to a center spindle.

This is very similar to some CD drives where the CD is the platter and the hole in the center of the CD is placed on the spindle of the CD drive. Hard disk drives are different than a CD drive in many ways, one of which is that CDs are not stacked on a spindle.

The read/write mechanism contains several read/write heads: one for each platter and each attached to an arm. As data is read or written to the hard disk, the spindle rotates the platters as the arm assembly moves across all the platters at the same time toward the cluster specified by the operating system (see Figure 5-4).

Each read/write head floats a millionth of an inch above the platter on a cushion of air caused by the rotation of the platters. This is about the thickness of a hair, so you can imagine how even the tiniest dust particle can interfere with reading or writing data.

Whenever a disk stops working, commonly referred to as a crash, there is a slight possibility of retrieving data stored on the disk. The entire hard disk drive must be sent to a company that has a clean room where the sealed hard disk drive can be opened and fixed. A clean room is a room where every particle is removed from the air.

Read/Write Heads

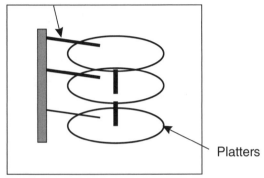

Platters

Figure 5-4
The read/write mechanism moves the read/write heads of clusters
on each platter in a hard disk

Finding the right spot on the platter that contains the cluster requested by the operating system is tricky and requires two steps. First, a voice coil actuator is used to move the arm into the general area of where the cluster is located. Next, a servomotor moves the arm to the exact location on the platter.

Tech Talk

Servomotor: A motor whose rotation can be controlled incrementally.

The Connection

The hard disk drive is attached to a rack inside the computer and is connected to the motherboard using a cable and a disk drive controller. A disk drive controller is the circuit that handles communication between the motherboard and the disk drive (both the hard and floppy disk drives). The disk drive controller circuit might be imbedded into the motherboard or on an expansion card.

In some cases, the disk drive controller circuit is contained in the hard disk drive assembly and a host adapter circuit is used to connect the disk drive controller circuit to the motherboard.

This happens when a SCSI controller is used to interface the hard disk drive and the motherboard. A SCSI controller is used to daisy-chain devices to a computer, one of which can be a hard disk drive.

When the OS needs to access the hard disk drive, a request is sent to the disk drive controller. The disk drive controller translates the command into one or more commands the disk drive understands and sends those to the disk drive mechanism.

New hard disk drives are built with a monitor system similar in function to the system check that occurs whenever you start your computer. The monitor system is called self-monitoring analysis and reporting technology (SMART).

Whenever the computer is powered up, the hard disk drive continually examines hard disk drive components in an effort to detect a potential problem. An error flag is signaled if a potential problem is detected. The computer's BIOS or another program must be able to read the error flag and react to the condition, otherwise the hard disk drive will crash.

For example, the time between the potential problem is uncovered and the time the hard disk drive crashes might be sufficient time for you to save a file to another disk.

REMOVABLE DISKS..

While hard disks have a high storage capacity, they are limited in that you cannot re-move the disk. Instead, you must remove the entire hard disk drive. This is not conve-nient whenever you want to share a large amount of data stored on the hard disk with a friend.

An alternative is a removable disk drive. A removable disk drive enables you to remove the disk itself without removing the disk drive. A floppy disk is an example of a removable disk, although most of think of Jaz or Zip drives whenever we hear the term removable disk drive being used.

A floppy disk is 3½ inches in size and typically holds about 1.44 MB of infor-mation. This is sufficient to store a word document or spreadsheet file, but is probably too small to store a typical commercial program. Years ago floppy disks were used to distribute programs, but today most software manufacturers have settled on using CD-ROM disks because of the larger storage capacity as you'll learn later in this chapter.

Floppy disks are classified by storage capacity. The common classifications are double density, high density, and extra density. Double-density floppy disks can hold 720K of information and are rarely used today. High-density floppy disks are the most commonly used and hold 1.44 MB of information. The extra-density floppy disk can store 2.88 MB.

The amount of information that can be held is directly related to the mechanism used in a floppy disk drive to read and write to the disk. Unlike a hard disk drive that has several disks, a floppy disk drive has one disk. And unlike a hard disk drive which uses a two-phase process to position the read/write head to the requested cluster, a floppy disk drive does this in one phase.

A floppy disk drive uses a stepper motor to position the read/write head over a disk. The area over which the read/write head is positioned is larger than a similar area used on a hard disk. This means that a hard disk drive can pack more data into the same area than the typical floppy disk drive.

Another important difference is with the read/write heads. Read/write heads on a hard disk float on a cushion of air and never touch the disk.

In contrast, the read/write heads on a floppy disk drive touch the head as the floppy disk rotates. This eventually wears down the surface of the floppy disk. However, engineers reduce the likelihood of damage by slowing the rotation speed of the disk, which also results in a reduced capacity of the floppy disk.

A new kind of floppy disk drive called a super floppy disk drive overcomes these limitations. A super floppy disk drive uses the same technique as is used by a hard disk drive to read and write information to the disk.

However, even the super floppy disk drive is unable to overcome one of the basic limitations found on a floppy disk—the capacity. A viable alternative to a floppy disk is a removable hard disk.

A removable hard disk such as Jaz and Zip drives uses a hard disk that is contained within a cartridge that is slipped into the docking bay of the removable hard disk drive. Once in the docking bay, the removable hard disk drive operates nearly identical to that of a hard disk drive.

A removable hard disk drive can be either installed within the computer or connected to the computer using a USB port, FireWire port (see Chapter 3), or a SCSI host adapter. The actual connection depends on the make and model of the removable hard disk drive.

The two most popular removable hard disk drives are Iomega's Zip and Jaz. The Zip drive can use either 100 MB or 250 MB removable disks. The Jaz drive uses 1 GB or 2 GB removable disks.

More About Connecting Disk Drives

Hard disk drives are connected to the motherboard using either the Integrated Device Electronics (IDE) controller or a SCSI controller as I mentioned previously in this chapter. IDE, which is sometimes called the AT Attachment (ATA) interface, is the more commonly used and is also used to connect CD-ROM drives to the motherboard.

The way in which data moves between the motherboard and the hard disk is called a data transfer mode and greatly influences the performance of the hard disk drive. There are two types of data transfer mode that is supported by IDE: direct memory access (DMA) and programmed input/output (PIO). Each has submodes.

The choice of data transfer mode is determined by the BIOS on the motherboard. Some BIOS do not support the more efficient mode. In that case the OS determines which is the best data transfer mode for the BIOS.

As discussed in Chapter 2, DMA gives devices connected to the IDE controller direct access to memory without first sending an interrupt to the processor asking that it transfer data from the IDE controller to memory.

PIO requires that the IDE controller send an interrupt to the processor. This tends to slow throughput and reduces the amount of data that is transferred between the motherboard and the hard disk drive.

THE PRACTICAL SIDE TO HARD DISKS ....

I discovered that hard disk drive manufacturers load their advertisements with numerous measurements and ratings. While I'm sure that all this information has meaning to an engineer, I find only a few measurements important to me whenever I buy a hard disk drive.

These are data transfer rate, rotation rate, average access time, and wattage. I also consider more practical things: if the disk drive will fit inside my computer, the capacity of the disk drive that I require, and if the disk drive is compatible with my disk drive controller.

The data transfer rate is the amount of information that can be moved between the motherboard and the hard disk each second. Data transfer reflects other measurements such as cache size and rotation speed.

Manufacturers report various types of data transfer, therefore you must be careful whenever you compare competing hard disk drives. I compare the sustained data transfer rate because this truly measures data transfer that is important to you and me. Other types of data transfer rates are burst, internal, and external. The sustained data transfer rate is quoted as MB/seconds and the higher the sustained data transfer rate, the better the hard disk drive.

The rotation rate is the speed at which the hard disk drive mechanism spins platters around the spindle. The rotation rate is measured in revolutions per minute (RPM) and the higher the rotation rate, the more data flows under the read/write head.

The average access time is a measurement of how fast the read/write head moves to a specific sector on a track on a platter. This measurement is based on the average seek time and the average latency. The average seek time is the time required for the read/write head to move over a track. Average latency is the time required for the hard disk drive mechanism to rotate a desired sector beneath the read/write head.

You don't need to worry about average seek time and average latency. All you need to be concerned about is the average access time, which is measured in milliseconds. The lower the average access time, the better the hard disk drive.

Wattage is a measurement that is sometimes overlooked when evaluating a hard disk drive—or any device. As you learned in Chapter 3, wattage is a measurement of electrical current. Internal hard disk drives are powered by the same power supply that is used to power the motherboard.

Therefore, you must make sure that there is sufficient power to run all the devices inside your computer and the new hard disk drive. Failure to do this might result in a lower performance of the drive.

Once you understand the important measurement of a hard disk drive, you can turn your attention to the other practical considerations. First, make sure that you have space inside the computer to place the hard disk drive.

If you're replacing an existing hard disk drive, you can do what I call a "give me." That is, you remove the drive from the computer, go to your local computer shop, show the technician the drive and say, "Give me one this size, but . . ." and include your new specifications.

If you're adding another hard disk drive to your computer, the "give me" won't work for you. Instead, copy down the make and model number of the current hard disk drive and give it to the technician. The technician will look up your hard disk drive in a catalog to learn exactly what shape you need.

Make sure you see if there is room for another hard disk drive. Disk drives usually fit into a shelf inside the computer called a bay. If there isn't a bay opened, then you'll need to purchase a new bay. If you don't, you'll have the computer opened, the new hard disk drive in your hand, and wonder where you're going to put the new hard disk drive inside the computer.

Of course, the safest way to be sure that you get the right fit is to bring the computer to your local store and let a technician worry about getting the proper size hard disk drive. You'll pay a little more than doing it yourself, but you avoid all the aggravation brought on by the finer details of installing a hard disk drive.

You'll still need to determine the capacity of the hard disk drive and if the drive is compatible with your disk drive controller. I normally choose a brand-name hard disk drive that has a capacity of at least 8 GB. However, I balance the capacity size with the performance measurements that I spoke about previously in this section. This is because I have found that high-capacity drives have relatively slow performance measurements although most are adequate for normal office applications.

INSIDE CD DRIVES ....

Computer software has become sophisticated and large—too large, in fact, to be stored on a few floppy disks. This became evident with the release of office applications that required five or more floppy disks to distribute the application.

A better way for distributing software needed to be found and engineers turned to the music industry for the solution. The music industry had already migrated from phonograph records and eight-track and standard cassette tapes to CDs as a means of distributing musical performances in the mid-1990s. These are called CD-DA (digital audio).

By the late 1990s, Hollywood discovered an improved version of the CD called the digital video disk, then called digital versatile disk (DVD). This new type of CD could be used to distribute films. Similar to CDs, the DVD offered easy manufacturing, distribution, and better quality than its tape counterpart.

The software industry adopted the CD as the primary means of distributing applications because unlike a floppy disk that holds 1.44 MB of information, a CD holds 600 MB, which far exceeds the space requirements of even the most advanced software. In comparison a DVD holds 4 GB of information.

CDs and DVDs have another advantage: They last longer. Disks and tapes use an iron oxide coating to store information. Over the years this coating can wear and lose its magnetic strength. CDs and DVDs don't use magnetism to store information and nothing touches the CD or DVD, so there is little if any wear.

How CDs Work

You can say that CD technology uses a bit of smoke and mirrors traditionally employed by magicians. Actually, the technology uses mirrors—no smoke—and a laser to store and read information.

A laser is a device that produces a steady stream of light waves of a particular frequency. Light waves are very similar to the waves that are made when you drop a dish in a dishpan filled with water, except the light waves go much faster. The energy of the dropped dish pushes the water molecules so fast that some cannot move fast enough so they get pushed up, causing the wave. The same kind of reaction happens when a light source such as a laser generates photons.

Tech Talk
Photon: A molecule that generates light.

This is similar to a crowd queued to enter a movie theater. If people at the back of the line move faster than people in the front of the line, then some people will be temporarily pushed out of the line, causing a bulge in the line. As soon as the front of the line speeds up, the people move back in the queue.

A new CD that hasn't been used to store information has a smooth reflective surface much like a mirror. Only one side of the CD is available for storing data. The other side is used for the CD label. Data is stored on the CD by creating pits strategically along the surface of the CD, after which a clear plastic coating is placed over the CD as protection against dust and scratches.

A powerful laser beam is used to create the pit. This process is called burning a CD because a layer of the CD surface is burned away creating the pit (see Figure 5-5). Therefore the size of the pit is the same size as the light beam generated by the laser.

Some laser beams can burn because sufficient power has been applied to the laser to force the photons to move very rapidly. It is this energy stored in the photons that causes the burning to occur. A lower powered laser also generates photons, but those photons don't have the energy to burn.

This is very similar to how you can sit beneath a light bulb for hours without the light burning your skin, yet sit in sunlight for the same amount of time and the ultraviolet light generated gives you a sunburn. Ultraviolet light generates more energy than a typical light bulb.

Bits that represent information are translated into pits and no pits. No pit is equivalent to a zero and a pit is a one. Therefore, any data that is stored on a disk can easily be stored on a CD. Instead of polarizing the iron oxide on the disk, pits are used on a CD.

A laser is also used to read data from a CD. In this case, a low-powered laser shines a beam on the CD at specific locations along a single spiraling track similar to sectors on a disk. A pitted area reflects light at a specific frequency and the nonpitted area reflects light at a different frequency (see Figure 5-6). Circuits in the CD drive, which translate reflections into zeros and ones, detect the reflection.

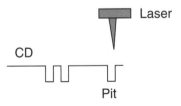

Figure 5-5
A powerful beam of light from a laser creates a pit on the surface of the CD

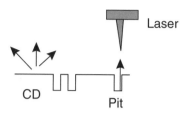

Figure 5-6
A pit reflects light differently than a nonpitted surface of a CD

Unlike disks that have concentric tracks, a CD has one track that spirals into the center of the CD. This means that the CD-ROM drive must increase the rotation of the CD as the laser moves closer to the center of the CD. This concept is called constant linear velocity (CLV).

Engineers developed the CLV CD-ROM driver for audio CDs, which typically reads one large file at a time. CDs that contain programs, however, read shorter files randomly. That is, some files might be toward the outside of the CD and the next more near the center. Therefore, the additional work is necessary to move the laser through various parts of the CD, which limits the maximum data transfer rate (see the next section).

A new method, called the constant angular velocity (CAV) method, was introduced. The CD is rotated at one speed regardless of where the data is located. The CAV method produces a variable data transfer rate as opposed to a consistent data transfer rate generated by the CLV method.

The primary benefit of using the CAV method is cost and power savings. CLV CD-ROM drives require expensive motors that consume a relatively high amount of power when compared to motors used in CD-ROMs that use the CAV method.

Another method that some CD-ROMs use to read data from a CD is called the partial CAV (P-CAV) method. The CD-ROM drive spins the CD at two constant speeds depending on where the laser points. This provides a consistent data transfer rate.

For example, the CD spins slower when the laser moves close to the center of the CD and faster when it moves to the outer area of the CD. The boundary of these areas varies according to manufacturer specifications.

A recent development in the way information is read from a CD occurred with the introduction of the TrueX drive, which uses several laser beams to read multiple areas of the CD at the same time.

As you can imagine, the data transfer rate for a TrueX drive is appreciably higher than traditional CD-ROM drives. However, this comes at a price. TrueX drives are expensive, generate more heat than traditional CD drives, are noisy, and have a low performance when accessing files randomly.

CD-ROM

The most common CD drive is the CD-ROM drive, which is read-only. CD drives used to read and write data to a CD are discussed in detail later in this chapter.

CD-ROM drives are measured by several ratings. The most important are the average access rate and the data transfer rate. The average access is the amount of time necessary for the CD-ROM drive to read a bit from the CD. The data transfer rate is the amount of data that can be transferred from the CD-ROM drive to the motherboard per second.

Although the average access time is an important measurement of a CD-ROM drive, this is an often misleading measurement because manufacturers do not use the same testing specifications. This leads you to comparing apples to oranges although both have the same name.

Average access time is measured in milliseconds and the lower the rating, the better the CD-ROM. However, I'm always suspicious when an off-brand claims a better average access time for a lower price than a brand name CD-ROM.

The data transfer rate specifies the amount of data that can be read from a CD in one second. Each sector on a CD holds 2,353 bytes. Sectors are grouped into logical tracks. All but one track is numbered. The unnumbered track contains the table of contents.

All 2,353 bytes are used to store music on an audio CD; 2,048 bytes are used to store data on a CD. The additional bytes are used for error checking. Error checking isn't required in an audio CD because you probably don't notice a few lost bits when listening to music.

A CD-ROM running at the same speed as the CD-ROM used to play an audio CD transfers data at a rate of 150K/second. This is an important number to remember because the data transfer rate of all CD-ROM drives is measured by this value. 150K/second is referred to as 1X.

You probably recognize the X rating used in advertisements for CD-ROM drives. The X rating indicates the multiple of the 150K/second rating. This means a 12X CD-ROM has 12 times the data transfer rate as a 1X CD-ROM drive.

However, the X rating is typically used for CLV CD-ROM drives. CAV and P-CAV CD-ROM drives are measured as X MAX such as 30X MAX. This means that the maximum possible data transfer rate is 30X or whatever the value is. The actual data transfer rate is likely to be less than the quoted rate.

DVD

DVD technology is similar to CD technology in that data is encoded onto a CD in the form of pits—or the absence of pits. However, DVD technology employs other features that enable more information to be stored.

First, pits are smaller, making it possible to squeeze more pits in the same area size as used in a CD. This is because a DVD drive uses a laser that generates a visible red light that has a shorter wavelength (is smaller) than the lasers used in a CD.

Next, a DVD has four surface areas that can be used to record information, two on each side. Each side has two layers, each of which can be read by basically focusing the laser to the proper depth. This makes it possible to store more than 16 GB of information on both sides of the DVD. Another reason for the high capacity is that the DVD information is compressed into a small size by using the MPEG2 compression algorithm.

DVD is divided into two types: DVD-Video and DVD-ROM. DVD-Video is used to store video data such as a film. DVD-ROM is used to store anything but video games and backup data from a hard disk. DVD drives that read DVD-Video can also read DVD-ROM, but the opposite is not true.

There are three ratings that are important regarding DVD: the number of recordable sides, the number of layers, and the data transfer rate. A DVD is either single-sided (SS) or double-sided (DS), which indicates the number of surface areas that can hold information. Likewise, each side can have either a single data layer (SL) or double data layer (DL), which determines how much information can be stored on one side.

The data transfer rate is indicated by the X factor, however, the X factor in a DVD drive is different from the X factor in a CD-ROM drive. X1 in a DVD has a 1.3 MB/second data transfer rate as compared to the 150K/second data transfer rate of an X1 CD-ROM drive.

CD Writeable Drives

CD writeable drive is the general name given to CD-R and CD-RW drives. CD-R drives can be written to only once, while CD-RW drives can reuse a CD by writing and erasing data.

Both the CD-R and CD-RW drives have multiple strength lasers. One works at a higher power and is capable of burning pits into the CD. Another works at a lower power and is used to read information from a CD. The CD-RW drive has a third used to erase pits from a CD.

CDs used in a CD-R drive are manufactured with a spiral groove that helps guide the laser and maintain the proper rotation speed required to properly burn pits into the CD. Once the CD-R drive burns a pit, it cannot be removed.

There are two rates of speed used to describe a CD-R and CD-RW. These are the X rate found on CD-ROM drives, which indicates the data transfer rate, and a lower data transfer rate, which is the data transfer rate used to write data to the CD.

CDs created by a CD-R drive can be used in today's standard CD-ROM drives and in CD audio drives such as those in your stereo system. However, CD-RW are likely to only work in the CD-RW drive.

CD-RW drives work differently than a CD-R drive. CD-RW is made from material that can be pitted and erased. A high-power laser melts the crystals of the CD-RW into a pit. The pit is actually a reformed crystal that doesn't reflect light the same way as the unpitted crystal.

A medium-powered laser is used to heat the pitted crystal, which returns the crystal to its unpitted form. This has the same effect as erasing information from the CD-RW. However, the reflective quality of the pitted crystal is less than that of a pit used in a CD-ROM. This is why CD-RW is rarely readable on a non–CD-RW drive.

A CLOSER LOOK AT THE COLOR OF CDS

Blank CDs that are used for burning data into a CD come in various colors. Bluish-green, silver, gold, and yellow-green are the more common colors. Sometimes the colors indicate the quality of the material used to create the CD and other colors are camouflage.

Original blank CDs were gold—and actually contained a very small amount of gold. Gold was used because the metal is more stable than any other metal; however, stability came with a relatively expensive price tag.

Silver CDs replaced blank gold ones. Similar to the gold CD, the silver CD contains small amounts of silver, which provide a good reflective quality at a reasonable price. However unlike gold-colored CDs, silver-colored CDs can corrode because the nonwritable surface tends to experience microscopic cracks that permit particles in the air to enter the protective coating.

Other colors are used to disguise the underlying type of CD. The shades of gold and silver are typically part of a patent and cannot be used by other manufacturers without permission. A way around the patent is to use a different color for the CD.

MAGNETO-OPTICAL DISCS ....

A magneto-optical disc uses a combination of technology found in CDs and disk technology. The surface area of the magneto-optical disc is a permanent magnet similar to the iron oxide coating on a disk.

Data is encoded onto the magneto-optical disc by changing the polarity of a segment of the surface area similar to storing data on a disk. However, that's where the similarities between the magneto-optical disc and a disk ends.

Simply using a read/write head cannot change the polarity of a permanent magnet. This is because the polarity of the magnet is fixed—otherwise it wouldn't be called a permanent magnet.

Applying heat to the magnet can weaken its strength. Here's how this works. A permanent magnet loses its strength as the magnet's temperature rises close to the magnet's Curie temperature. Once the Curie temperature is reached, the magnet is no longer a permanent magnet. However, it regains strength as the magnet's temperature falls below the Curie temperature.

Tech Talk

Curie temperature: The temperature at which a permanent magnet loses its magnetism.

Engineers used this theory to change the polarity of the permanent magnet on the magneto-optical disc. A laser is used to heat the magnet just enough so that its polarity can be changed by the read/write head without losing all its magnetism. Once the laser is turned off, the magnet cools and is set in its new polarity.

The laser is once again used when reading information stored on a magneto-optical disc. Light from the laser is focused on the magnet. The light is reflected at different angles based on the polarity of the magnet. Detector circuits in the magneto-optical disc drive detect the angle of the reflected light to determine the polarity of the magnet, i.e., if the magnet contains a zero or a one.

The most important measurement of a magneto-optical disc drive is the drive's coercivity rating, which measures how difficult it is to change the polarity of the magnet. The higher the rating, the harder it is for information stored on a magneto-optical disc to become corrupted by nearby magnetic fields.

Magneto-optical disc drives are used whenever there is a need to permanently store important data such as security data. They are not economical for everyday business use because the drive is expensive and there are lower cost alternatives such as floppy disks and CDs.

THE PRACTICAL SIDE TO CD DRIVES ....

After reading about the various types of CD drives on the market, you're probably asking yourself what should you purchase. Here are guidelines I follow when evaluating a CD drive. I've also included a list of formats that these drives should be compatible with (see Table 5-1).

Let's begin with a CD-ROM drive. I find the 4X data transfer rate fine for most of my needs, which includes games and multimedia applications. However, my friend disagrees because she likes to play games from the CD, therefore she looks for the highest data transfer rate that she can afford to buy. She needs a fast data transfer rate so the software can keep pace with her game playing.

Many CD-ROM drives come with onboard memory called a buffer or cache. Find one with 64K. The larger the cache, the better the performance.

Average access time isn't very important to me because I don't use my CD-ROM drive to randomly access data stored on a CD. If you need to look up data on a CD, then look for a CD-ROM with an average access time of 80 milliseconds or lower.

Of course make sure that the CD-ROM drive is compatible with the interface you are using and that there is room inside the computer for the CD-ROM drive if it is attached internally to the computer.

If you're looking to burn your own CDs, then consider a CD-RW drive because you'll at least be able reuse CDs. Choose one that has a high data transfer rate for both reading and for writing data to the CD. The average access time for a CD burner is higher than for a CD-ROM because of the weight of the read/write laser mechanism.

As with a CD-ROM, the size of the cache is important. A large cache improves performance. The interface that you choose might impact your experience burning CDs. Some of my friends suggest that you use only a SCSI interface because it seems to give you fewer headaches, especially if you intend to burn CDs frequently.

My friends also strongly recommend using the SCSI interface if you purchase a DVD drive because SCSI seems to give them less trouble than other interfaces. I agree—even if the SCSI interface is the expensive route to take.

The DVD drive must have an MPEG-2 decoder. This enables you to decompress information that is compressed on the DVD disc. However, you might still experience a delay in performance because MPEG-2 decompression, called MPEG-2 processing, requires a lot of computer horsepower to give you a television-quality performance.

The MPEG-2 decoder is integrated into an expansion card circuitry called the MPEG-2 decoder card. The advantage of this card is to limit the use of the system bus for transfer video information because the monitor is plugged directly into the MPEG-2 decoder card rather than into the video adapter. The disadvantage is that the

video you see on the monitor does not take advantage of the high resolution produced by the video adapter.

Another type of expansion card used for DVD drives is the video port extension
(VPE), also known as an inlay card. Unlike the MPEG-2 decoder card, the VPE card
sends the DVD signal into the video adapter. This lets you capture screenshots and get
the higher resolution that is available from the video adapter. The chief disadvantage
is that the system bus processes all the video information. This means that it might be
impractical to use other applications while watching DVD video.

Table 5-1   Capability table

Read formats	CD formats
CD-DA	ISO 9660-HFS
CD-ROM Mode 1	Rockridge
CD-ROM XA Mode 2	CD-I Bridge
Form 1	CD-I
Form 2	CD-I Ready
Multisession	CD-Extra
CD UDF	CD-Plus
CD-R (orange book part II)	Enhanced CD
CD-RW (orange book part III)	CD-R
Video CD	CD-RW
CD bridge	CD+G
	CD-Midi
	CD-Text

ALL DUPLICATES ARE NOT DUPLICATES

Be careful of the mode you use to burn CDs because you might discover that the copy you make is not necessarily an exact duplicate of the original. Here's what happens. Each sector on the CD holds 2,352 bytes. The complete sector is used to store audio data such as your favorite song. However, the first 2,048 bytes are used to store data such as a game program if you are not copying audio data. The remaining bytes are used for error correction. And this is where a problem can occur whenever you duplicate a CD.

CDs are burned in raw or cooked mode. In raw mode, the entire sector, including the portion of the sector used to trap errors, is copied. This means that errors that occur during the transfer are not caught.

In contrast, only the data portion of the sector is copied in cooked mode, which also performs error checking. The result of the error-checking procedure is stored in the remaining bytes of the sector. Therefore, the cooked mode catches errors during copying.

Errors are common whenever you make a copy from a copy rather than from the original. So if you're copying an audio CD, you can use either mode because you won't notice the errors when you play back the CD. However, you must use the cook mode if you're copying data such as a backup copy of a program or database.

INSIDE RAM STORAGE DEVICES...........................

The speed at which information is retrieved from a hard disk or a CD is immaterial for most applications because most of us are willing to wait a fraction of a second to use the application.

There are other applications, however, that require a near instantaneous response such as an ATM machine and web-based applications. The only way to provide fast access is to use memory instead of a hard disk or CD.

Computer memory is basically a lot of electronic switches as described in Chapter 3. Each byte of memory is identified by a unique address, which is addressed by the processor whenever data is stored or read from memory.

As you learned in this chapter, data is stored in clusters on a hard disk. This is similar to computer memory in that each cluster has a unique number that is accessed each time the OS needs to store or retrieve data from the cluster. However, clusters and computer memory differ in size and organization.

The OS can organize computer memory to resemble a hard disk and store data into computer memory simulating the storage of data onto a hard disk. The disk is called a RAM disk or RAM drive.

Once the RAM disk is created, the OS treats it as another disk. That is, the RAM disk is assigned a drive letter and is used to store and retrieve data just as the OS would do accessing a hard disk. Of course the RAM disk exists only as long as the computer is powered up. All data stored in a RAM disk is lost once the computer is turned off.

Typically, a computer application loads a database or a portion of a database into a RAM disk from a database stored on a hard disk or CD. The RAM disk database is then accessed whenever a user requests data. The response is immediate because the search of the database occurs at nearly the speed of light. There is no meaningful data transfer time as is experienced when searching a database on a hard disk or CD.

Tech Talk
Database: An organization of data stored on a hard disk or CD.

Another common use of RAM as a storage device is with Personal Computer Memory Card International Association (PCMCIA) cards, commonly called PC cards. A PCMCIA card is an enclosed circuit board the size of a large business card that slips into a PCMCIA slot in a computer. The PCMCIA slot functions as an expansion slot linking the PCMCIA card to the motherboard.

PCMCIA cards use flash memory and are able to work at the speed of memory yet don't lose the contents of the main computer memory. There are three kinds of memory chips used in PCMCIA cards. These are the electrically erasable programmable read-only memory (EEPROM), DRAM, and ferror-magnetic random access memory (FRAM) chips.

EEPROM and FRAM don't lose their contents when power is removed from the PCMCIA card. DRAM maintains data by being powered by a small battery that is in the PCMCIA card.

PCMCIA cards are used for a variety of purposes that include operating as a type of RAM disk. They can also be used as modems, network adapter cards, and other devices that are not integrated into the motherboard.

Two other variations of the PCMCIA card are the SmartMedia card and the CompactFlash card. Both are memory cards that are used to store data for devices such as digital cameras.

One of the most recent storage devices to enter the market is IBM's Microdrive. The Microdrive is a hard disk less than 2 inches square and has the capacity to hold up to 1 GB of data. This makes it a perfect choice for data storage on devices that use CompactFlash cards because the Microdrive fits perfectly into a CompactFlash slot.

The Microdrive uses a disk and mechanisms commonly found in a hard disk although they are near microscopic in size. These mechanisms consume power much greater than CompactFlash and SmartMedia cards. Therefore, the Microdrive is not suited for continuous use such as listening to music stored on the Microdrive. It is well suited for storage of data such as a database.

INSIDE TAPE DRIVES ....

A tape drive is typically used to make a backup copy of all or a portion of a hard disk onto a magnetic tape similar to that used in a VCR. Data is written to a tape sequentially, which is different from the way data is stored on a disk.

This means that if you want data stored at the end of the disk, the tape drive must read all the data from the beginning of the disk before the tape drive can access data you need. This makes tape drives an unsuitable replacement for a hard disk drive where data can be accessed randomly.

Tape drives provide an economical solution for backing up data because it can hold over 1 GB of data on a relatively inexpensive tape. And restoring data from a tape drive is much faster than expensive alternatives as long as you are copying a block of sequential data such as the contents of a directory on a hard disk.

There are three types of tape drives: quarter inch cartridge (QIC), digital data storage (DDS), and advanced data recording (ADR). QIC is the granddaddy of tape drive technology and has been around since before the personal computer was born.

QIC uses the serpentine recording technique. The tape is divided into multiple tracks. Each track can hold data. Recording begins on the first track. Once the end of the track is reached, which is at the end of the tape, the tape drive begins recording the second track in the reverse direction.

This means the first track begins at the beginning of the tape and the second track begins at the end of the tape. The tape drive zigzags across the complete length of the tape until all the tracks are recorded, which could take many passes that increase the wear on the tape (see Figure 5-7).

The QIC tape drive has a time-saving read-while-writing feature. This enables the tape drive to read a track while writing to another track and thereby eliminating the need for another pass over the tape.

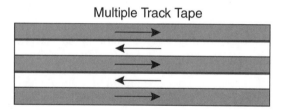

Multiple Track Tape

Figure 5-7
Data is written on multiple tracks of a QIC tape using a zigzagging
technique

DDS technology uses a helical scan recording method, which is also used in
VCR recordings. The helical scan technique angles the recording head across the
width of the tape to create diagonal tracks. All tracks are written in one pass of the
tape and minimize wear and tear on the tape. DDS technology also employs the read-
while-write feature (Figure 5-8).

ADR technology is a proprietary technology that records eight tracks with one
pass over the tape and therefore minimizes wear on the tape.

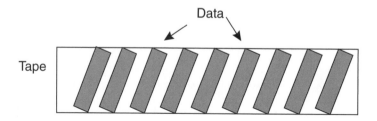

Data

Tape

Figure 5-8
Data is written on a DDS tape using an angular technique

THE PRACTICAL SIDE TO TAPE DRIVES ....

Technology used in tape drives is fairly straightforward especially when compared to hard disks and CD drives. A tape drive isn't necessary for most computers because other backup methods are more economical.

For example, I have two kinds of information on my hard disk. These are applications such as a word processor program and data files such as documents produced by the word processor program.

I'm only concerned about backing up my data files because I still have the original CDs that contain my applications. And most, if not all, of my data files can fit on a floppy disk. Therefore, a tape backup is more for convenience than a requirement.

Let's say my hard disk crashes. I can reinstall my applications from the CDs and the data files from the floppy disks. However, if I backed up the original hard disk to a tape backup, I need only to restore all the files from the tape backup without having to reinstall each application.

You need to weigh the cost of a tape drive against the inconvenience of restoring each application and data separately. Businesses don't have this option when mission-critical applications are in jeopardy. In that case, a tape drive is necessary to protect the business against a system malfunction.

Here are the guidelines I use when selecting a tape drive for one of my clients. First, I determine the capacity required to back up information. I basically make sure that the tape drive and tape have a larger capacity than the hard disk that is being backed up.

Next, I consider the backup and restore speed of the disk drive. This is the amount of time necessary to back up or restore all the files from the hard disk to the tape. Speed is measured in megabytes per second. The higher the rating, the faster the tape drive can work.

The technology used by the tape drive to write data to the tape is less of a concern because if I have the capacity and speed I required, I really don't care how the tape drive writes data to a tape.

A word of caution: Tapes are not necessarily compatible with other tape drives. This means a tape recorded on one drive may not be readable on another drive even if that other drive is the same make and model as the drive that created the original tape.

SUMMARY ··

There are many devices that can be used to store data. The most widely used device is the hard disk drive. A hard disk drive uses several disks that are coated with iron oxide. A magnetic read/write head is used to change the polarity of the iron oxide particles based on the binary value of data. A particle having one polarity is considered a zero and the other polarity a one.

The hard disk is organized physically and logically. The physical organization of a hard disk consists of concentric circles called tracks, which are divided into sections called sectors. The operating system logically organizes sectors into clusters. A cluster consists of several sectors that contain data.

The next most widely used storage device is a floppy disk drive. A floppy disk drive stores data on a disk similar to that used on a hard disk drive. However, a floppy disk is removable. Hard disks are not removable unless a removable hard disk drive is used in the computer. A removable hard disk drive uses removable disks called cartridges that have a capacity nearly that of a hard disk.

CD drives are challenging disk technology as the storage device of choice. Most computers have a CD-ROM drive, which enables the user to read large amounts of data such as a computer application from the CD.

CD-R and CR-RW drives are another type of CD drive that can read and write data from a CD. A CD-R drive writes data to a CD. Once written, the data cannot be erased or written over. In contrast a CD-RW drive can write, erase, and rewrite data to the CD.

A CD has a spiral circle called a track that is divided into sections called sectors. Sectors are further divided into small areas where a laser is used to burn a pit into the CD surface. Some areas within a sector have pits and others don't have pits depending on the binary value of the data stored in the area. A pit represents a one and the absence of a pit represents a zero.

A low power laser shines a light into each area within a sector. The light reflects one way if the area contains a pit and another way if the area doesn't contain a pit. The detector circuit in the CD drive interprets the reflection as a zero or one and passes the binary value to the operating system for processing.

Other storage devices include RAM disks, PCMCIA cards, SmartMedia cards, CompactFlash cards, Microdrive, and tape drives. All but a tape drive are based on using computer memory as the storage technology. Tape drives use technology similar to that use in video tape recordings.

Summary Questions

1. How does a CD-RW drive erase information from a CD?

2. What is the difference between QIC technology and DDS technology in a tape drive?

3. How does a magneto-optical disc drive save information to a disk?

4. What is the difference between the X rating of a CD drive and a DVD drive?

5. How does a TrueX drive read data from a disk?

6. What is the primary difference between an audio CD and a data CD?

7. What is the importance of having adequate wattage for a hard disk?

8. How is rotation of a hard disk drive and a CD drive different?

9. What is the purpose of MPEG-2 processing?

10. What is the serpentine recording technique?

6 Printers

In this chapter...

- Inside Printing
- Inside Inkjet Printers
- Inside Laser Printers
- Inside Impact Printers
- Inside Nontraditional Printers
- Inside Networked Printers
- The Practical Side to Printers

"The paperless society is only a myth."

Regardless of what you read and hear about a paperless society, take it from me that paper and printers will be with us for many decades to come. For some reason, most of us feel secure in knowing that we have a printed version of whatever we have stored in our computer.

Great strides have been made in printing technology over recent decades that has led to many households having a color printer with which to print letters, homework assignments, and quality photographs.

Likewise, industrial-strength laser printers give everyone in the office the ability to produce top-quality reports complete with graphics at the speed of a copy machine. In fact, a laser printer has reduced the number of copy machines required by a typical office.

Although most of us know how to print a document from our computer, few of us know what actually happens after we click Print. And this gap in knowledge makes us vulnerable whenever we are called upon to choose a new printer.

I'll help you fill this gap by telling you about the latest in printing technology and give you advice on selecting a new printer. Here's what you'll learn:

- Printing technology

- Hidden cost of printing

- Printer languages

- Measuring the quality of a printer

- Color printers

- How to choose the best printer for the job

REALITY CHECK ....

Printed information isn't as secure as you may think and can be dangerous at times. Let's face it, most of us believe that information generated by a computer in the form of a printed report is fairly reliable. For example, my bank statement is usually far more reliable than the register in my checkbook.

And yet a similar report produced for a manager at a Wall Street firm nearly cost the company hundreds of millions of dollars—and the career of an executive. Executives who ran profit centers for this Wall Street company received weekly status reports from the systems department. This is similar to receiving weekly bank statements.

The report told each executive the strength of his or her profit center. The executive in question had her assistant enter this information into a computer spreadsheet for her own tracking and reporting purpose. And this is where problems started.

The executive and her colleagues made business decisions based on reports generated by information on the spreadsheet rather than by data generated by the company's tracking system. The spreadsheet and the company's tracking system were assumed to contain the same information—and both did.

The problem: The printed copies of the spreadsheet reflected the current date but contained outdated information. The executive assumed her assistant had kept the spreadsheet up to date, which was a wrong assumption.

Her assistant had skipped a few weeks, and when the executive needed a printed copy of the spreadsheet for a meeting to decide whether or not to sign a multimillion-dollar agreement with a vendor, her assistant was absent so the executive printed the spreadsheet herself.

Nothing on the spreadsheet gave a clue that the numbers were outdated. And since the date on the spreadsheet was recent, the information on the spreadsheet was assumed to be reliable.

The executive didn't realized that her assistant had coded the spreadsheet program to automatically place the current date on every printed copy regardless of when the information was updated. A decision was made based on the spreadsheet—and it was the wrong decision.

INSIDE PRINTING...

Whenever I click Print, I expect my document to be printed perfectly within a few seconds. You probably have the same expectations, but if you're like me you probably haven't given much thought of what happens from the time you click Print to the time the page spits out of the printer.

Some very interesting processes occur when a page is printed. Let's become acquainted with the printer before exploring those processes. A printer is a device that places a tiny mark on paper. The mark is called a pel, sometimes known as a picture element or pixel. You may recall reading about picture elements in Chapter 4 when I talked about video displays.

All text and images that appear on paper are printed in nearly the same way as text and images are displayed on the screen. Pels generated by the electron gun are really glowing phosphor on the screen. Pels generated by a printer are tiny particles of ink.

The printer contains a print head, which places the pel at a particular location on the paper. The printer also has circuitry that moves the print head and the paper, enabling the print head to place pels anywhere on the page.

Tech Talk

Print head: The component inside a printer that produces text and images on paper.

The printer circuits know where to move the print head and the paper based on instructions received from the operating system (OS). Here's how this works. When you click Print, the program translates text and images on the page along with page layout information into instructions written in a language that the printer understands.

The program then tells the OS to send the instructions to the printer port, which is typically a parallel or serial port embedded into the motherboard (see Chapter 3). Sometimes the printer port is integrated into an expansion card.

Instructions are then passed by the OS to the printer where the printer's circuitry translates the page description language instructions into mechanical movements so the pel is placed on the page.

A lot of things must occur at the correct time to print a document. For example, the print head must be moved to the proper horizontal and vertical coordinates on the page. Next, the print head must place just the right amount of ink on the page. The ink must be fast drying, otherwise there is a likelihood that it will smear when either the print head or the paper is moved.

All these steps must occur many times per second. I use the term *ink* in a very general sense. As you'll learn later in this chapter, some printers place pels on a page without using ink.

Page Description Languages

A printer was a luxury in the early days of computers much like the Model-T was with automobiles. And just like the Model-T those early printers were no-frills simple because the frills that we expect today from a printer such as producing color graphic images weren't technologically feasible in those days.

Printers were capable of printing the standard ASCII character set (see Chapter 3) using character blocks. A character block (see Figure 6-1) consists of a fixed number of pels that can produce any character in the standard ASCII character set.

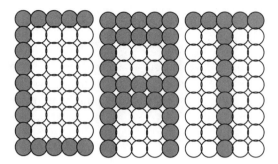

Figure 6-1
Early printers printed characters using a character block

For example, a typical character block contained a grid of 5 pels across and 9 pels down for a total of 45 pels. The printed page was divided into a fixed number of character blocks, usually 80-character blocks called columns on each line and 60 lines to a page.

A program that wanted to print a document supplied the printer with the column position and the ASCII value of the character to be printed. It was assumed that the character was to be printed on the current line because the printer lacked the capability to accurately move the paper up and down to a particular line on a page.

The next bold move in printer technology came with the introduction of the extended ASCII set of characters. This extension provided ASCII values for graphical components such as a line, a top left corner, a bottom right corner, and other similar shapes (see Figure 6-2). The extension enabled programmers to produce limited graphic images such as boxes.

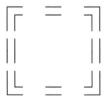

Figure 6-2
The extended ASCII character set consisted of graphical shapes

Printer manufacturers enhanced their products by recognizing the extended ASCII values. However, printers were still limited to character block printing, which dramatically limited the kinds of graphical images that could be printed.

The next revolution came with the development of a graphics printer. Today we assume all printers are capable of printing graphics, but that wasn't always the case. A special control character had to be sent to the printer telling the printer to move from text mode (character blocks) to graphics mode.

Tech Talk

Control character: One or more ASCII characters used to give directions to a device such as a printer.

Once the printer was in the graphics mode, a program could address every pel individually rather than addressing a block of pels as is the case in text mode. This enabled programmers to draw any image on the page. Furthermore, text characters could be printed using various fonts and sizes rather than the fixed font and size found in text mode.

The number of pels that could be addressed by the program was substantially higher than the number of character blocks that were previously addressed by the program. For example, a typical line had 80 character blocks and 400 pels.

Each pel is considered a column so there were now 400 columns rather than 80 columns in text mode. The programmer had to tell the printer the column number of the pel that is to be printed on the current line. As printer technology improved, printing devices were able to randomly scan the entire page, which enabled the print head to move to any line on the page. This required the programmer to specify both the column and line to print the pel.

A line in graphics mode is not the same as a line in text mode. There are 60 lines in text mode and 540 lines in graphics mode. This is because each character block typically contains 9 lines and there are 60 character-block lines on a page.

You can imagine the complexity involved in determining the column and line coordinates required to position a graphic image on a page. And the complexity became even more challenging as printer manufacturers increased the resolution of their printers.

The number of pels that fit on a page determines the resolution of a printer. By decreasing the size of each pel, printer manufacturers are able to produce higher resolution printers that are capable of printing sharp images.

The downside to increasing the resolution is that there are many more pels that must be addressed by the programmer to print an image. Instead of hundreds of pels, new printers had thousands of pels, each having its own column and line coordinate.

Hewlett Packard (HP) developed the first laser printer called the LaserJet and with this introduction, HP created the page description language call the Printer Control Language (PCL).

The objective of PCL was to make it easy for a programmer to describe to the printer how a document should be printed. PCL enabled programmers to specify the font, style, size, margins, and other measurements used to describe the layout of a page. The only drawback of PCL was graphics. PCL was primarily designed for text-based printing in graphics mode. Programmers still had to address each individual pel to print a graphic image.

Apple Computer's LaserWriter quickly challenged the HP LaserJet. The Laser-Writer introduced a new page description language called PostScript. PostScript had syntax that enabled programmers to completely describe every aspect of a page to the printer, and the printer—as long as it was a PostScript printer—responded by producing a typeset-quality printed page.

Most of today's printers are PostScript printers and the PostScript language has been enhanced many times since the introduction of the LaserWriter.

Raster and Vectors

There are two general ways—rastering and vectoring—in which text and images are printed on a page. Rastering is a process similar to that used to display images on a screen. As you'll recall from Chapter 4, an electron gun in the monitor zigzags across and down the inside of the monitor. An electron is shot whenever a piece of the image is to be displayed at that particular pel location on the screen.

Printers also use rastering as a way to place pels on paper (Figure 6-3). The rastering technique requires that the print head be initially positioned in the upper left corner of the page, then move across the first line of pels on the page. The print head then drops to the next line and prints pels moving right to left on the line. This pattern continues until the print head reaches the bottom right corner of the page, then the page is ejected from the printer.

Some printers that use the rastering technique print in one direction, so after completing the first pel line on the page the print head is moved to the beginning of the next line before its starts printing again.

Vectoring is a more direct approach to printing because the print head is instructed by the program to move to a particular coordinate and print a pel on the page. This means that the print head doesn't move to every pel position, as is the case with rastering. Instead, the print head goes directly to the position on the page where the pel is printed.

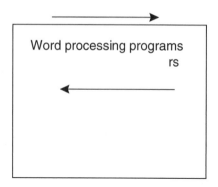

Figure 6-3
Some printers that use rastering print in both directions as the print head moves down the page

The vectoring technique combined with a page description language is used to draw complex images quickly on the page. Here's how this works. Let's say that the programmer wants to draw a circle on the page. The programmer could provide all the pel locations used to create the circle or simply tell the printer through the use of a page description language to draw a circle.

The page description language knows the commands required to draw a circle, but it doesn't know the size of the circle, the width of the line (called line weight) used for the circle, or the position of the circle on the page.

The programmer need only provide the pel coordinate (column and line) of the center of the circle and provide the radius of the circle and line width. Page description language instructions tell the printer to use the vectoring technique and to move the print head to the proper locations to draw the circle on the paper.

Printer Memory

I'm a rather impatient guy when it comes to printing. I expect the printer to generate the page just as quickly as a high-speed copier produces a document. However, my hope for speed is often dashed when printing a page that contains images. The printer seems to take forever to print the page.

Pages that contain graphical images or complex layouts require a lot of processing time because many instructions written in a page description language must be read, translated, and executed by the printer.

Many of today's printers are computers themselves since they have their own memory and processor. Page description instructions are sent from the motherboard into the printer's random access memory (RAM) where the instructions remain until the printer processes the instructions.

The speed at which the printer can print a page is dependent on a number of factors including the complexity of the image. For example, a full-page color photograph takes longer to print than a one-page letter, primarily because the photograph has many more pels that need to be addressed by the printer.

Another important factor is the amount of printer memory available. The more memory the printer has, the faster the page is printed. Likewise, the more expensive the printer, the more memory the printer has onboard.

Typically the lower-priced color printers that you and I have at home have little or no onboard memory; they use the memory in your computer to store the page as the page is being printed.

Fonts

A font is the shape of a character that is printed on the page such as scriptlike characters. If you have had any experience using a word processor you probably realize that there are hundreds of fonts to choose from when you write your document.

Each font is described by a unique name, size, and style. The designer names the font, which is distributed as either a component of a program such as a word processor, as a resource available to all programs within an operating system such as Windows, or is something extra you purchase for your computer.

The size of a font is defined as point sizes that can range from 1 point to beyond 96 points (see Figure 6-4). The higher the point size, the larger the font size. Some fonts come in a limited range of sizes while others use the full range. Style refers to whether the font is bold, italics, and/or underlined. Style also specifies if a character is printed as superscript or subscript. All styles are not available with every font.

Figure 6-4
Fonts range from small to enormous

Another characteristic of a font is the width of each character. Character widths are described as either proportional spacing or fixed spacing. Proportional spacing adjusts the width of the character according to the shape of each character. For example, the letter "I" has half the width of a typical character and the letter "w" has more than the width of a typical character.

In contrast to a proportional font, a fixed space font is one where every character has the same width, which is similar to type produced on a typewriter. A few fonts are fixed spaced fonts. Most fonts use proportional spacing because this makes texts appear professionally typeset.

Although you select a font by name and other characteristics (i.e., style, size), the page description language translates your selection into print specific pels that collectively produce the image of the character in the selected font.

Color Printing

Printing text and image in color is an interesting process that is similar to the process used to generate a color image on a computer screen. Using a mixture of four hues creates colors that are used on the printed page and on the screen. These four colors are called primitive colors and the set of those colors is called the color model.

For example, a typical monitor uses red, green, and blue as the color model (RGB). Color printers use cyan, magenta, yellow, and black as the color model (CMYK). The color model determines the range of colors that can be created, which is called the color gamut.

Images printed in color don't reflect all the colors of the real object. This means that if you look at the sunset and look at a color image of the sunset printed by a color printer, you'll see less color on the printed image than in the sunset. This is because the color model used in the printer cannot reproduce all the colors that you normally see.

The printed color image is probably fine for most of our needs, but the differences in colors are a problem for designers and artists who have to match colors accurately.

Let's say that you were photographing an automobile for an advertising brochure and for a web page. After you take the picture, you scan the picture and display the picture in a graphics program such as PhotoShop. You also print a color version of the picture. This sounds simple enough, but this is fraught with problems.

Tech Talk

Scan: The technique of using a scanner to convert an image into a digital image.

There is a wide color gamut when you look at the car on the street. The RGB color model used to display the picture of the car on the screen has a different color gamut. And the color printer uses still another color gamut because the printer uses the CMYK color model. Technically none of the color images truly represent the color of the car.

Printers who produce the automobile brochure use a color model that includes many primitive colors and are able to come closer to the actual color of the car than the colors that can be reproduced by a color printer and monitor.

The International Color Consortium (ICC) is a standards organization that has developed a set of color correction profiles for printers and monitors. A color correction profile is an internal reference table used by monitor drivers and printer drivers to determine the specific mixture of primitive colors to produce a standard set of colors.

Tech Talk

Driver: A program that translates OS instructions into instructions recognized by a device such as a printer that is connected to the motherboard.

This means that the color correction profile rectifies as much as possible differences in colors among monitors, printers, and other similar devices. The color management module in Windows 98 contains color correction profiles for popular devices.

As you'll learn later in this chapter, there are various ways in which text and an image can be printed on paper. Regardless of the method, all produce color basically the same way; each primitive color is stored as a separate ink, ribbon, or toner cartridge.

INSIDE INKJET PRINTERS ....

An inkjet printer is the most commonly used home printer primarily because of its initial price and because most inkjet printers print color. Contrary to popular belief, inkjet printers are not cost effective. Ink cartridges are very pricey. Four sets of ink cartridges equal the price of the printer. However, inkjet printers are desirable for occasional printing.

There are two ink cartridges in a typical inkjet printer. One contains black ink and the other contains the rest of the colors of the CMYK color model. Black is the most frequently printed color and that is why one cartridge is devoted to black ink.

Ink used in an inkjet printer is specially designed to dry quickly before the paper is ejected from the printer. However, I suggest that you give a few extra seconds before handling the paper, especially on important documents. Otherwise you might smear the ink.

The quality of paper is a factor on how well the ink adheres. Paper manufacturers have created a special blend of inkjet paper that absorbs the ink faster than standard paper or copier paper. This special blend reduces the likelihood that ink will smear once the page is ejected.

Inkjet printers are commonly used for reproducing near photo-quality images especially from photos taken with a digital camera. As you'll learn later in this book, all but very expensive professional digital cameras actually reproduce color at the same color gamut as a film camera, although the quality of the image printed by an inkjet printer is adequate for most home use.

You can improve upon the photographic image by using specially blended photographiclike paper and an ink cartridge that contains a glossy coating. The paper and cartridge are not economical if you plan to print many photos, but they are worth the expense for occasional printing.

One of the reasons that inkjet printers are less expensive is because they normally don't come with an onboard processor and RAM. The computer performs all the processing of the page descriptive language. This is why printing is slow.

INSIDE LASER PRINTERS

Anyone who likes the quality of the document that is produced from a laser printer should give a "well done" to Chester Carlson who invented the xerographic printing technique that became the copy machine in the late 1960s and the laser printer in the mid-1980s.

Laser printers are common in the office and some computer fanatics like myself have a small one at home. Mine is one of the first HP LaserJet printers built. Until the onset of inkjet printers, the laser printers were the only ones on the market that could reproduce quality images.

A laser printer uses xerographic printing technology to reproduce images. Here's how this works. A laser printer contains a rather odd shape box called a toner cartridge. The toner cartridge actually has the guts of the printer within the cartridge. This is a good thing because after the printer runs out of toner, you toss the toner cartridge and install a new one. It's like having a new laser printer each time you change the toner cartridge.

Tech Talk

Toner: A chemical compound that contains dry inklike material and a bonding agent.

Photoconductive material: A component within a laser printer's toner cartridge that is a metal cylinder covered with a photoconductor coating.

The toner cartridge contains a photoconductive material that receives an electrostatic charge by circuitry inside the laser printer before the image is transferred to the photoconductive material for reproduction. The laser is scanned across the photoconductive material similar to how the electron gun scans the rear of the monitor screen.

Unlike the electron gun, light from the laser is shined on areas that are not part of the image, leaving the electrostatic charge only on the area of the photoconductive material that contains the image. These areas contain pels of the image.

Particles of toner are then spread across the photoconductive material and adhere to only the electrostatically charged areas, which are the areas of the photoconductive material that contain the image.

The laser printer mechanism moves a sheet of paper from the tray and into the toner cartridge. The paper is then electrostatically charged with a charge that is opposite that of the area of the photoconductive material that contains the image.

As you probably remember from science class, opposites attract, so the toner particles adhere to the paper. The paper is then moved over a heating element that permanently bonds toner particles to the paper. This is why paper that has recently been ejected from a laser printer or a laser copy machine is warm to the touch. Toner particles are then removed from the photoconductive material and the process begins over again with a different image.

Laser printers are more expensive, yet they are one of the most economical because laser printers have a low cost per copy. You and I probably don't give much thought to the cost of printing a document because we only print occasionally. My wife prints directions to a friend's house, my daughters print their homework, and I print a copy of my manuscript.

In contrast, businesses use printers many times during the day so the business office is sensitive to the cost to print one page. Inkjet printers have a high cost per page because of the expensive ink cartridge. A toner cartridge costs three times that of a typical inkjet cartridge, but can print many more pages. See "The Practical Side to Printers" later in this chapter to determine the cost per copy for your printer.

INSIDE IMPACT PRINTERS ....

Impact printers, the first on the market, used typewriter technology to place an image on paper. Not too long after IBM introduced the IBM personal computer, a kit that connected the IBM personal computer to the IBM electric typewriter was released. This enabled the computer to use the IBM electric typewriter as an impact printer.

There was a drawback to this technology—the technology was too slow. Engineers came up with a better approach called a dot-matrix printer.

A dot-matrix printer used one print head as compared to the many die-cut print heads—one for every two characters—used by typewriter technology. Dot-matrix printer technology simulated the character block technology used in computer displays at that time (see Chapter 4).

The print head of a dot-matrix printer consists of a block of tiny metal rods sometimes called wires, each resembling a pel within a display's character block. The metal rods form a matrix and each rod can place a dot on a page, hence the term *dot matrix* (see Figure 6-5).

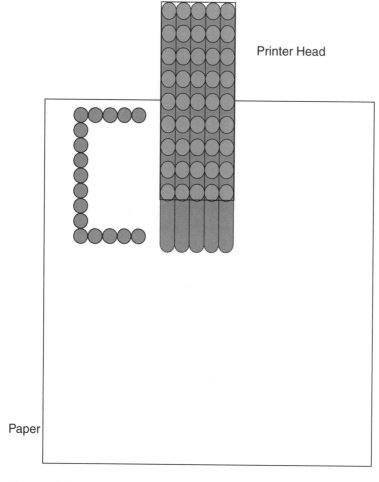

Figure 6-5
A dot-matrix printer uses metal rods in the print head to form characters on paper

The printer's circuitry used electronic energy to extend specific rods sufficiently out of the printer head block to strike an inked ribbon, similar to ribbons used in a typewriter. Each extended rod pressed the inked ribbon against the paper leaving a tiny dot on the paper.

Characters are formed by extending a specific set of rods based on the ASCII character value sent to the printer by the operating system. The dots produced by the extended rods were so small that collectively they blended into an image of an ASCII character.

The quality of characters produced by a dot-matrix printer increased when manufacturers expanded the number of rods in the printer head and refined the end of the rod that struck the inked ribbon.

Furthermore, the printer's circuitry was also enhanced to enable the operating system to address each rod. This broke the character block limitations of the printer and opened the door to reproduce graphic images.

Impact printers were used in offices and with home computers until the laser and inkjet printers were introduced. Impact printers had three major drawbacks, the most critical of which was noise.

Next, impact printers used inked ribbons, which were messy to replace and needed to be replaced frequently. The final straw was paper. Most impact printers used continuous paper instead of individual sheets. Holes on the sides of the paper had to be positioned over sprockets inside the printer. The paper was pulled into the printer behind the inked ribbon and print head as the printer mechanism turned the sprockets.

This limited the type of paper that could be used to print documents and caused a panic whenever the holes in the paper misaligned with the sprockets while a document was printed. Paper would jam but the printer kept on printing.

Impact printers are still used today, but typically in large printing rooms where mass mailings are printed. Most offices traded in their impact printers years ago in exchange for laser printers, and owners of home computers switched to inkjet printers.

INSIDE NONTRADITIONAL PRINTERS ....

Inkjet, laser, and impact printers are the more common printers, but they are not the only kinds. I call these other kinds of printers nontraditional because few of us ever heard of them. Two of these are dye printers and wax printers.

Dye printers are used to produce photographic quality printing in full color. A dye printer works much the same way as the technique developed by Polaroid in its instant cameras. A ribbon that contains dye in primitive colors sits above paper. The print head consists of a heating element that heats a specific color dye in the ribbon causing the dye to turn into a gas cloud. The cloud of colored gas, the size of a pel, strikes the paper, then returns to a solid state creating a pel on the paper. This is sometimes called a dye transfer process.

Dye printers are slower than traditional printers and require specialized paper. However, they produce top-notch images, and it is for this reason that companies in the graphics arts industry find dye printers a cost-effective way to reproduce graphic images in nontraditional sizes. Dye printers are not limited to letter and legal sizes.

Wax printers also use a ribbon, except instead of dye or ink, the ribbon contains wax colored in primitive colors. The ribbon lies very close to the paper. The printer head heats the wax, which is liquefied and adheres to the paper, creating a pel when the wax cools.

A number of technologies are used to heat the wax, however the most commonly used method is by wires that are heated using electricity provided by circuitry in the printer. Wax printers are the least used printers today. The images they produce on paper simply don't compare to images produced by inkjet and other printers. Furthermore, wax printers are more costly and less convenient than inkjet printers.

INSIDE NETWORKED PRINTERS ....

In the mid-1980s, when personal computers were found on every desk, the demand for printers skyrocketed. Up until then, most workers didn't require their own printer because most printed occasionally.

Engineers realized that it wasn't cost effective to attach a printer to every computer in an office, so they came up with a way to share printers. Their initial solution was to use a switch box. A switch box had three openings, two for printer cables from two computers and the other a printer cable to the printer. This meant the two computers could share one printer.

The front of the switch box contained a dial that pointed to one of two positions identified as A and B, which led to the switch box to be called an A/B box (see Figure 6-6). The A position activated the connection to one computer and the B position did the same for the other.

This worked fine until new designs in the switch box increased the number of computers that could share a printer to the point that a backlog developed. Simply stated, there were too many computers that needed to print at the same time. Eventually this condition lead to networking printers and computers.

A computer network is like an electronic highway that connects computers to network devices such as printers. Each device connected to the network is assigned a

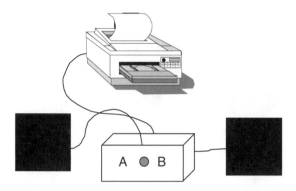

Figure 6-6
The original switch box enabled two computers to share a printer

unique address called an Internet Protocol (IP) address. This is similar to the address of your house.

Information such as the document that you want to print is divided into small pieces and placed into an electronic envelope called a packet (see Chapter 7). The electronic envelope contains the address of the destination device such as the printer and part of the document that is to be printed.

Most printers on a network are connected to a dedicated computer called a print server that manages printing for computers that are connected to the network. I like to think of the printer server as a personal computer that acts like a traffic cop controlling the order in which documents are sent to the printer.

Printing to a network printer is not the same as printing to your local printer because the network printer determines the order in which documents are printed. Here's a behind-the-scenes look at what occurs when you print to a network printer (see Figure 6-7).

The print server temporarily stores the incoming documents in memory called simultaneous peripheral operation online (SPOOL), also known as a spooler. Sometimes the print server is known as the print spooler.

During heavy demand, the print server can run out of memory. When this occurs, documents that can't fit on the spooler are temporality stored on the print server's hard disk, which is typically large enough to handle most printing demands.

The document that you print is called a print job and is logged in a queue in memory called a print queue. This is similar to the line at the grocery store and sometimes there is a long line of documents waiting to print.

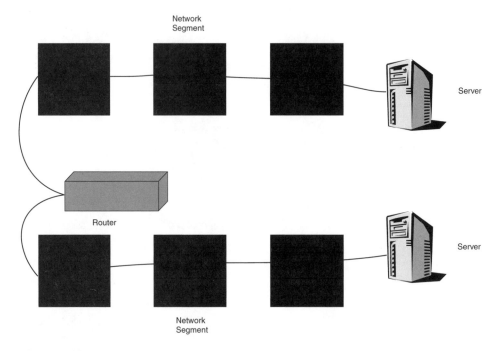

Figure 6-7
Each network segment contains clients and one or more servers

As a print job comes to the top of the print queue, the print server sends the document from the print spooler to the printer, then all the other jobs move up on the queue. This makes room in the print spooler for a job that is temporarily stored on the print server's hard disk.

A network printer can be directly connected to a print server using a printer cable or the network printer can be directly connected to the local area network (LAN) using hardware built into the printer, which requires the network printer to have its own IP address. A network printer connected directly to a print server doesn't require an IP address because documents from the print server flow to the printer over the printer cable and not over the LAN.

Tech Talk

Local area network: A network of computers, printers, and other devices that are within the same vicinity, such as on the same office floor or office building.

The network administrator grants access to a network printer. Access means not only the right to print a document, but the right to change jobs on the print queue. The permissions to manipulate the print queue depend on which network operating system is used. Most systems allow every user to review the print queue and delete his or her own print job from the print queue.

Typically, only the network administrator can delete or rearrange all print jobs on the print queue. However, the network administrator can assign these rights to any user.

THE PRACTICAL SIDE TO PRINTERS ....

How do I choose a printer that is cost effective? Selecting a printer isn't as complex as picking a computer because your options are fairly limited.

First, I determine if I'll be printing at my desk, over a network, or on the road. This helps me to focus on a particular category of printers. Next, I decide if I'm going to print occasionally or in high volume and whether or not I plan to print in color.

I suggest selecting an inkjet printer if you only need to print occasionally at your desk. Avoid printing multiple copies of the same document using an inkjet printer because you'll find this to be a costly way to copy a document. Instead, print one copy and use a photocopier to duplicate the document.

There is a strong tendency to print business reports in color. I have friends who have an inkjet color printer connected to their computer at work and have access to a networked printer. The networked printer is used for normal business and the inkjet color printer is used for fancy reports they show their bosses.

Color makes a report stand out but can cause problems. First, the boss may like your presentation so much that she makes your color printer the de facto report printer for the department. The only problem with that is the printer is directly attached to your computer so you spend most of your time printing reports for other managers.

Furthermore, reports are typically duplicated using a copy machine and distributed throughout the office. Some colors that make the original copy of the report attractive such as red become shades of gray and even black when photocopied. The pizzazz that color gave the original copy of the report can work against you when the report is photocopied.

Stick with one-color—black—laser printers for networked printing. You'll find that a networked laser printer is more cost effective than other kinds of printers. Avoid choosing color laser printers unless computers attached to the printer are used to produce graphics such as brochures.

You'll find that color laser printers are more costly than one-color laser printers and they can easily become abused. Once managers discover they can print in color, you'll find all reports contain color even when there is no benefit.

Don't use a color laser or inkjet printer to reproduce any quantity of documents. Instead, print one copy in color, then have a professional printer reproduce the document. This is the most cost-effective approach.

Printers are rated by the number of pages that can be printed per minute. The higher the number of pages, the better the printer—and higher the cost of the printer. Another important factor to consider is the cost of replacing the ink. Inkjet printers use ink cartridges, one for black ink and one for the other colors. Laser printers use toner cartridges. Impact printers use inked ribbons.

A typical toner cartridge can print 3,000 letter-sized pages. This rating isn't foolproof because it is based on printing one page of a typical document. So expect to print fewer pages if you plan to print a lot of full-page images such as photographs.

There are a few ways in which to save a few dollars on the price of cartridges. Buy in bulk if you find yourself using a lot of cartridges. Instead of buying one cartridge, buy a case. However, make sure you determine the shelf life of the cartridges. Make sure that all the cartridges are used before the shelf-life period expires.

Tech Talk

Shelf life: The time period after manufacturing when the quality of the product becomes unacceptable.

Another way to save money is to buy refill cartridges. Supply houses charge a lower price for a toner cartridge if you accept a recycled cartridge rather than a new one. A recycled cartridge is one that has been previously used then refurbished with new parts, if necessary, and new toner. Likewise, you can purchase kits to refill inkjet cartridges. A word of caution: Nozzles in inkjet cartridges can become clogged, so even after refilling the inkjet cartridge you may find that the cartridge doesn't work properly.

The cost per page rating is the most sobering way to measure a printer because this rating tells you how much you pay to print one sheet of letter paper. The cost includes the cost of the printer amortized over the life of the printer, the cost of any repairs, and the cost of replacing the cartridge or ribbon.

Tech Talk

Amortization: A technique of prorating (annual cost) the cost of a printer over the expected useful life of the printer.

SUMMARY ··

A printer is a device that places a tiny mark on paper. The mark is called a pel sometimes known as a picture element or pixel. The printer contains a print head, which places the pel at a particular location on the paper. The printer also has circuitry that moves the print head and the paper enabling the print head to place pels anywhere on the page.

The printer circuits know where to move the print head and the paper based on instructions received from the operating system. When you click Print on your program, the program translates text and images on the page along with page layout information into instructions written in a page description language that the printer understands.

The instructions are then passed by the OS to the printer where the printer's circuitry translates the page description language instructions into mechanical movements so the pel is placed on the page.

There are two general ways in which text and images are printed on a page. These are rastering and vectoring. Rastering is a process similar to that used to display images on a screen. Vectoring is a more direct approach to printing because the print head is instructed by the program to move to a particular coordinate and print a pel on the page. This means that the printer head doesn't move to every pel position, as is the case with rastering. Instead, the print head goes directly to the position where the pel is printed.

There are several kinds of printers. These are inkjet printers that place dots of ink on paper; laser printers that uses xerographic printing technique to place images on paper; impact printers that press against an inked ribbon to place a dot on a page; and nontraditional printers such as dye and wax printers.

Printers have a number of important characteristics. These include the number of pages per minute that can be printed; whether or not the printer is shared over a network; whether or not a printer prints in multiple colors other than black; and the cost of replacing the ink. Typically ink is stored in either a cartridge or on a ribbon.

The expense of operating a printer is measured as the cost per copy. The cost per copy is considered the initial cost of the printer and ink cartridge, which is divided by the number of copies the printer prints per cartridge.

Summary Questions

1. **What is a color model?**

2. **Why can't a color printer print all the colors that our eyes can see?**

3. **How does a printer work over a network?**

4. **What does character block printing mean?**

5. **What is the purpose of a printer control language?**

6. **Why is printer memory important to printing a document?**

7. **What is a color gamut and how does it influence color printing?**

8. **How is a color correction profile used in color printing?**

9. **How does a laser printer produce an image on paper?**

10. **How does a dye printer work?**

7 Modems and Networking

In this chapter...

- Inside Modems

- Inside the Telephone System

- Inside Networking

- Sending and Receiving Information Over a Network

- Inside Network Cards

"Everyone wants to have connections."

Anonymous

Noone has been connected as much as we are today, thanks to telephone lines, computers, and computer networks. Jot down a few thoughts in an email and with a click of a mouse your words are sent across oceans and continents at nearly the speed of light.

All you need is a telephone for your computer called a modem and a link into the Internet using an Internet service provider (ISP), and you can use your computer to exchange information from anywhere in the world, even from a ship in the middle of the ocean.

The same technology used to share information over the Internet is also used where you work to exchange email, data, and all kinds of information over your company's private Internet called the intranet. Instead of using a modem, a network card is used to connect your computer at work to your company's intranet.

Most of us know how to use the Internet and intranet because we've been taught the proper procedures to follow to communicate with others who are connected to these networks. However, few of us know what happens after we make that connection.

I'll give you an inside look at computer hardware devices that give you access to computer networks. You'll learn about:

- How modems work

- Available communication lines

- How a computer network works

- Network addresses

- Network devices

REALITY CHECK ....

Let the truth be known. I love email. Although some of my colleagues feel that they spend all day responding to emails, I think a lot of work gets done that would normally take days and weeks to accomplish, especially if you use email intimidation.

Email intimidation is when you send a courtesy copy (cc) to all the important managers on an email. Let's say the systems department is avoiding you when you ask for a report. With each request for a status report to the systems department you cc a higher level manager on the email. Eventually you discover which manager has the magic power over the systems department.

However, email intimidation can backfire if you click Reply All rather than Reply. That slight mistake has caused countless embarrassing moments for more than one manager, especially when businesslike email messages turn to "nastygrams."

One such case occurred at a major Wall Street firm that purchased software from a vendor to process international security trades. The software was less than what the sales representative had promised, but the vendor had an existing relationship with the Wall Street firm and the vendor provided payroll services. That service worked fine.

In an effort to maintain communications between the two firms on this project, the project manager created an email mailing list. There had to be 50 people on the mailing list, both employees of the vendor and of the Wall Street firm.

Nearly a year passed and the software still didn't work properly. Nastygrams flew, in which managers of the Wall Street firm questioned the competency of the vendor. However, those managers assumed that the email mailing list contained only their employees. It wasn't until a call from the Wall Street firm's chief administrative officer that proved the old adage about assuming. The vendor's managers received a copy of every email because they too were on the email mailing list.

INSIDE MODEMS ....

A modem is a telephone for your computer that dials a remote computer, then translates digital information to analog information so the zeros and ones that comprise information can be sent over the telephone lines.

The telephone system is designed to transmit voice, which is analog information (see "Inside the Telephone System" section later in this chapter). Before information from inside your computer can be sent over the telephone system, the information must be encoded into an analog signal. This technique is called modulations.

When the analog signal arrives at the receiving modem, the modulated signal must be decoded back to a digital signal, which is called demodulation (see Figure 7-1). A modem is responsible for both modulation and demodulation—and that's where the modem gets its name. MO is for modulation and DEM is for demodulation.

Information from inside your computer is sent to the modem over the internal bus if the modem is integrated onto the motherboard or over the serial port if the modem is external. Internal and external modems operate in the same fashion.

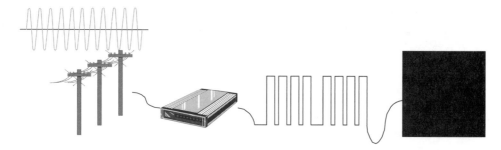

Figure 7-1
Modems modulate digital information before sending the information over the telephone lines and then demodulate the information when the signal is received

The speed at which a modem sends information over the telephone line is measured as the modem's baud rate, which was named after Jean-Maurice-Emile Baudot, who, in the 19th century, was one of the first to develop a transmission code.

A baud rate is the transmission of one symbol per second. The concept of using a symbol to transmit information is strange since we've been talking about sending bits. A symbol can represent any number of bits. The more bits that are represented by a symbol, the faster information is transmitted over the telephone lines.

When a connection is made between two modems, both go through a handshaking process and agree on the speed and method (protocol) for communication.

The agreed-upon baud rate is the highest that both modems are capable of transmitting. This means a 56 kilobits per second (Kbps) modem will transmit at 28.8 Kbps if the highest baud rate of the other modem is 28.8 Kbps.

As you can see, a modem's baud rate is different than the actual transmission speed because transmission speed depends on a number of factors, including the data transmission speed of the port to which the modem is connected. A modem can be connected to a USB or a standard serial port or integrated directly onto the motherboard.

Transmission speed measured in baud rate isn't the most important measurement of data communication. Throughput is. Throughput is the amount of information that is transmitted per second.

The key difference between baud rate and throughput is that throughput considers retransmissions due to transmission errors, something not factored into the baud rate. Here is how this works. Bits of information are sent along the internal bus on the motherboard to the serial port and into the modem.

The modem converts the digital data into analog data, which is sent over the telephone line. Sometimes stray signals enter the telephone line and interfere with the transmission. The receiving modem detects the problem and requests the sending modem to resend the information.

This means two transmissions are necessary before the information is successfully received by the other modem. Therefore, throughput in this example is double the baud rate used to transmit the information.

Types of Modems

Most modems are data or fax modems. A data modem is used to transmit and receive data over the telephone line such as when you connect to your ISP to surf the Internet.

A fax modem converts your computer into a fax machine enabling you to send and receive faxes using your computer. Of course the documents that you can fax are limited to information you have stored inside your computer.

For example, faxing a word processing document is as easy as printing. However, you'll need a scanner if you want to fax anything that does not originate from a computer, such as an insurance form. The scanner converts a document into a digitized file that can then be faxed using a fax modem. Fax modems also send data.

Newer modems are capable of sending voice along the same telephone line as data. These are called analog simultaneous voice and data (ASVD) and digital simultaneous voice and data (DSVD). Both voice and data are transmitted and received at the same time. Of course you will need to have a microphone and speakers connected to your computer before you can use an ASVD or DSVD modem.

Most modems that work with standard telephone lines are capable of transmitting and receiving up to 56 Kbps. However, all 56 Kbps modems can also transmit and receive information at lower speeds such as 33.6 Kbps, 28.8 Kbps, and 14.4 Kbps.

Four other kinds of modems that are available today are cable modems, satellite modems, ISDN modems, and digital subscriber line (DSL) modems. Cable modems are used to connect computers to cable television lines to access the Internet. Unlike telephone lines that transmit only analog signals, a cable television line is capable of transmitting digital information.

Information is transmitted at 10 Mbps, which is far faster than using a standard modem and telephone line. Not all cable television companies offer Internet connections because the cable television system is set up to handle one-way communication from the cable television company to television sets. Internet access requires two-way communications. This means that cable television companies must modify their systems before they can offer a modem link.

Satellite modems are used to link computers to a satellite network such as DirectPC (see Figure 7-2). A satellite modem connects your personal computer to a

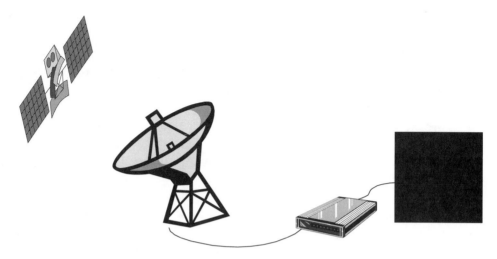

Figure 7-2
Satellite modems are used to receive information from satellites

small satellite dish, which is used to receive Internet access and television signals. Information is received at 400 Kbps. However, satellite is one-way transmission, that is, transmission from your computer to the satellite network is over telephone lines. Transmission from the satellite network to your computer is using the satellite.

ISDN modems and DSL modems are used with alternative telephone service available from local telephone companies. ISDN modems transmit at 512 Kbps and DSL at 8 Mbps. You'll learn more about these services later in this chapter.

The Practical Side to Modems

The type of telecommunication service that you subscribe to determines the choice of modem. Most of us use a standard telephone line, which requires us to use a standard modem. Nearly all the standard modems are 56 Kbps. Buying a modem with a lower baud rate doesn't make sense.

I find it immaterial whether an internal or external modem is used. Many new computers come with an internal modem so you don't have another device to connect to your computer. Also internal modems are powered by the computer's power supply.

A wall socket must power most external modems. I've found that external modems are pricier than internal modems; however, you can easily install an external modem on another computer, an advantage if you purchase a new computer. Instead of purchasing a new modem, disconnect the modem from the old computer and connect it to the new one.

You could do the same with an internal modem, but you'll need to pop open the computer case and stick your hands into its guts. Some of us would rather leave that to someone else.

Stick with a data/fax modem because that's the most useful on the market. Avoid a voice modem until the technology is widely accepted. It doesn't make sense why you need a voice modem unless you make a lot of long-distance telephone calls. Voice modems work over the Internet so you get to talk long distance at local telephone rates.

DSL modems, ISDN modems, cable modems, and satellite modems are nice to have, but can be expensive compared with a standard telephone line and standard modem.

INSIDE THE TELEPHONE SYSTEM ....

Alexander Graham Bell probably never appreciated his contribution to society. Can you imagine life today without the telephone? Bell and his long line of fellow inventors, scientists, and engineers have enabled all of us to talk with someone around the world just as if the person were sitting in the same room with us.

Telephone technology is also the keystone that enables our computers to talk with one another regardless of where they are located in the world—as long as the computer is connected to the telephone system. The signal that leaves our telephone or modem enters a complex system technically called the public switch telephone network. Think of it as the international superhighway.

Tech Talk

Public switch telephone network: A network of cables and switches that routes signals to any telephone on the network based on the telephone number dialed by the caller.

We know the public switch telephone network simply as the telephone system at the end of the wire leading from our telephone. While this is true, the telephone system is actually a network of networks connected by a sophisticated set of switches, which is where the name switch telephone network is derived. A key feature of the telephone system is the ability to connect to various networks nearly instantaneously. This is called real-time switching.

Tech Talk

Real-time switching: The ability of the telephone network to connect to any point in the telephone system when someone makes a call.

Let's jump on a telephone call and follow it through the telephone system. Regardless of whether we are telephoning a friend or connecting to our ISP, we are making a telephone call. The telephone system does not know if we are speaking, sending a fax, or sending a stream of computer data.

Our initial step is to dial a telephone number, which sounds like a series of strange tones played by the telephone. The sounds are called dual tone multi-frequency (DTMF). The telephone or modem generates two tones called frequencies for each number of the telephone number.

The tones are similar to those used by an electric keyboard, although I don't suggest trying to learn to "play" your telephone since this can become an expensive lesson. By dialing the telephone number, you are actually encoding the telephone number into DTMF, which is sent to the central office of your local telephone company where the numbers are decoded into an address signal of the telephone or modem that you are calling.

The central office is technically the other end of your telephone line. After the telephone number is deciphered, computers in the central office parse it. That is, the telephone number is broken down into components.

There can be three components: area code, exchange, and the number that identifies the telephone within the exchange. The area code isn't required and calls without the area code are assumed to be located within the caller's area. The caller's local area is shrinking because the telephone company is running out of telephone numbers within the older area codes. At one time, a state might have two area codes. Today, you might have to dial an area code when calling within the same city.

Here's one way to picture this relationship. My telephone is connected to a small network within the public telephone system. This is called an exchange, which is housed in the central office of my local telephone carrier. The first three digits that follow the area code identify the exchange.

When I call someone who is also attached to my exchange, my telephone call stays within the central office. You'll recognize this as a local call, one that doesn't require an area code and normally is included in your monthly telephone charge.

The area code groups together central offices within a metropolitan region of the country. Where one area code once was used for a northern part of a state, there is now one area code for a handful of municipalities.

Generally, we can say there are three networks. There is a network of telephones called the central office or exchange; the network of central offices called an area code; and a network of area codes.

The central office routes a call along the appropriate path on the network. If the first digit of the telephone number is one, then the computer in the central office assumes that the next three digits comprise the area code and forwards the call to the long-distance carrier (i.e., network of area codes) to process the call.

However, if the first digits represent a country code, then the central office forwards the call to the long-distance carrier that in turn passes the call to telephone service in that country.

If the first digit is not a one, then the computer in the central office assumes that the call is not a long-distance call and the call is destined for a telephone within the area code. However, a decision still must be made to determine if the telephone number is within the exchange or outside it. The first three digits answer this question. If these digits represent the exchange of the central office, then the call is routed to the telephone that is assigned to the next four digits; otherwise the call is routed to the central office of the exchange.

Switched and Dedicated Services

Calls that we dial ourselves use the switched service provided by the telephone company. The term *switched service* is the technical term used to describe something most of us do every day—make a telephone call.

The telephone company creates a temporary circuit between our telephone and the phone of the person we are calling, and in the case of computers, our modem and the modem of the remote computer.

The temporary circuit is called a virtual circuit. Intuitively we have some notion of what is meant by the term *circuit* and we usually conjure the image of a circuit board.

Tech Talk

Virtual circuit: A temporary connection between two points on the telephone network that disappears once the call is completed.

While the image is correct, we need to have a more formal definition to fully understand the concept of a virtual circuit. A circuit is a physical connection between at least two points, like a string that connects two paper cups to form a crude telephone circuit. You can touch a physical circuit because, as with the paper cup telephone circuit, you can hold the complete circuit in your hands.

However, the term *virtual* changes this concept since virtual implies that something appears real but is a figment of our imagination. Anything virtual is not physical therefore you can't touch it.

Virtual and circuit used together to describe something seems to be contradictory—a paradox. Yet virtual circuit actually describes the path of your telephone call. The telephone systems consist of a network of networks that are connected through a set of switches.

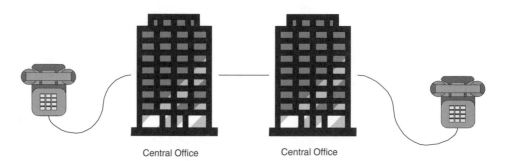

Central Office   Central Office

Figure 7-3
A temporary circuit exists for as long as the telephone call

Each switch connects one network to another and several switches are used to connect the network in your telephone company's central office to a central office located on the other side of the country.

These connections create a temporary circuit between your telephone or computer and the telephone or computer at the destination (see Figure 7-3). The circuit exists for the duration of the telephone call. Once the call is completed, the circuit disappears. That is, the direct connection between your site and the destination no longer exists and must be re-created when you make another call to that remote location. This is a virtual circuit, which is the keystone of a switched service provided to you by your telephone company.

Dedicated Service

The switch service is ideal for typical voice and remote computer access such as when you and I connect to the Internet. We pay for the duration of the call and the physical circuits and switches used to create our virtual circuit can be reused once our call is completed.

However, there are situations when dialing the telephone or modem becomes time consuming, especially when you are dialing the same telephone number frequently. I'm not talking about calling your friends. I am talking about a business calling another business, as in the case of two Wall Street trading partners where one partner picks up the telephone and the second partner is already on the other end. No dialing is necessary.

The telephone company makes a direct connection between both sites. This is called a dedicated service. The circuit isn't temporary and doesn't disappear when the receiver is placed back in its cradle.

Tech Talk

Dedicated service: A permanent connection between two points on the telephone network. The connection remains intact after each call is completed.

Dedicated service is sometimes referred to as having a dedicated or private line between sites. The telephone company charges a flat monthly fee for a service allowing an unlimited number of calls to be made between these sites. However, the dedicated line cannot be used to call anyone else since the dedicated service lacks the capability to receive, decode, and route telephone numbers to other locations. Companies frequently use the dedicated service to connect a computer to a remote site. This enables two locations to share information 24/7 (twenty-four hours a day, seven days a week).

Although the advantage of using a dedicated line is obvious, especially for remote computer access, there are drawbacks. The company that rents the private line must manage dedicated lines. The telephone company manages switched service.

This may seem to be a trivial cost of doing business, but it isn't if a company has private lines connecting multiple sites. A technical staff must be hired to track the inventory of lines and maintain and repair hardware needed to link to the dedicated service.

Dedicated lines are expensive, therefore they are typically used to handle communication that is critical to the operation of an organization. And this critical traffic adds to the complexity of using a dedicated service because multiple lines are commonly use to link two sites. One line is used as the primary link and the other as backup in case the primary fails. Telephone companies have seized this complexity as an opportunity to offer expanded services, which include the telephone company staff in place of a firm's technical staff managing dedicated lines.

The Layout of Private Lines

The layout of a network is called the network's topology, and since the telephone system is also a network, there is also a topology used to connect telephone cables. The topology of private (dedicated) lines plays an important role in the decision to use such lines to link to a remote computer because it affects costs and reliability of the connection.

Four private-line topologies are offered by many telephone companies: point-to-point, multipoint, star, and mesh. A point-to-point topology is one where both computers are connected to each other using a single line, much the way a string is used to connect two paper cups. Of course if something happens to the line, all communication between the two connections is lost—and the connection cannot be reestablished by redialing the telephone number of the remote computer. This is because a dedicated service rather than a switched-service is used.

The multipoint topology is designed to provide redundant connections between two sites. That is, more than one line is used to connect two locations. One line is designated as the primary line and the others are secondary or backup lines used in case the primary line fails.

The star topology (see Figure 7-4) is used to connect multiple remote sites to one central location called a hub. This is identical to the star topology described in the previous chapters only the telephone company configures the private line network, which is used to connect to locations outside of a building. Organizations favor a star topology private network whenever there is a need to poll remote computers.

Tech Talk

Polling: Describes the regular transfer of data between a series of computers located in remote locations. A central computer systematically calls (polls) each computer to initiate the exchange of data.

Central Office

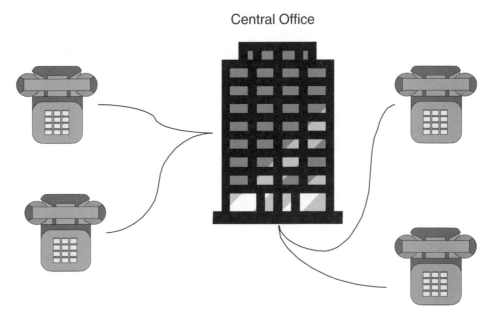

Figure 7-4
Multiple remote sites are connected to one central location called
a hub

Let's say that you owned a chain of supermarkets. Prices for every product in the store are entered into a central computer at the home office. Each evening when stores are closed, the home office computer connects to each store's computers and uploads the price list. This is referred to as polling, where the home office computer "asks" the store's computer if it is ready to receive the updated prices.

In a mesh topology, all nodes on the network are connected to each other to form a fault-tolerant network. If a private line becomes disabled, one of the other lines in the mesh topology goes into action and keeps the lines of communication open to that node. A mesh topology ensures the transmission will go through, but a high monthly cost is the price a firm pays for such service. This is because there is a larger number of private lines used in a mesh topology than with other topologies.

Signaling and Store and Forward Switching

You probably have a good idea what I mean when I mention that telephones provide two channels of communications. These two channels enable us to speak and hear the person we call at the same time, similar to how we hold a face-to-face conversation.

This contrasts to the way a police officer in the field must pause after transmitting a call and wait for a response. Police radios use a single communications channel to send and receive a call.

However, there is more to the telephone system than meets the eye. The telephone system has a third communications channel, called Signaling System 7 (SS7), that is used to manage the call. SS7 is like a stage mom who keeps a watchful eye over all her little children (telephone calls). SS7 is a signal that routes calls, provides a dial tone and a busy signal, Caller ID, and 800 and 900 number services. And I mustn't leave out the most important information carried over this channel—tracking information used to calculate our telephone bill.

Tech Talk
Signal System 7: A third communications channel in the telephone network used to manage telephone calls.

I think of SS7 as the telephone network's own telephone network, since this is the way central office "talks" to your telephone and to other carriers. For example, once the central office decodes the first digit of the number you dial as a 1, an SS7 signal is transmitted to the long-distance carrier that you selected to say, "Hey! Wake up! This call is for you." The call is then turned over to the long-distance carrier for further processing.

SS7 is used by telephone companies to provide advanced services such as voice mail that do not require the sender and receiver to be available at the same time. This is known as store switching, which means information is collected from the sender, then held until the receiver is online. Our normal telephone calls use forward switching, which sends our information to the receiver immediately.

Store switching offers a wide variety of ways to communicate over the telephone system. For example, one call can be automatically transmitted to many receivers and attempts to transmit can occur multiple times until the message is received. Likewise, information can be transmitted at off-peak times, which could reduce the cost of the call.

Private Branch Exchange (PBX)

Our telephones connect directly to the central office of the telephone company and for this privilege we pay a flat monthly charge plus another charge for other calls. Some calls are included in the monthly charge, while others such as long-distance calls are charged based on the call. Some telephone companies charge per local call. Cost of this service isn't too pricey unless we have a need to make and receive many calls simultaneously, such as in the case of a business.

Businesses are able to reduce the expense of telephone service by creating their own telephone network within their premises. This is called a private branch exchange (PBX).

Tech Talk

Private branch exchange: A privately owned telephone system that performs the function of an exchange on the telephone network.

A PBX is similar to the central office of the telephone company in that all the telephones within the business converge into a central hub. The central hub, a computer, routes telephone calls among telephones within the business and calls to a location outside of the PBX. That is, between the PBX and the telephone company.

The telephone company assigns the business a block of telephone numbers such as 555-7000. The telephone company routes any telephone number between 7000 and 7999 for the 555 exchange to the business's PBX system (see Figure 7-5). Computers in the PBX system decode the telephone number, then route the call to the proper telephone extension within the business.

PBX systems are economical because they reduce the need of telephone lines coming into the business. Let's say the business has 100 telephones. If you or I had 100 telephones, we'd require a telephone line for each one.

However, only a few telephones are used at the same time. This means that most of the 100 telephone lines sit idle, yet the company still pays the telephone company a monthly charge for those lines.

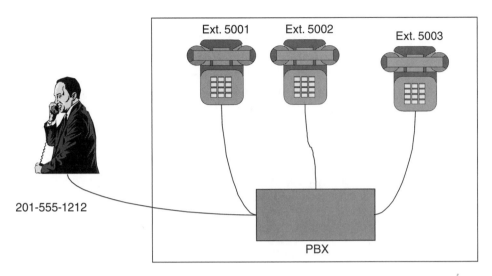

Figure 7-5
A PBX saves organizations money by creating its own telephone exchange

The PBX system interfaces with the telephone company through the use of special telephone lines, which are discussed later in this chapter. These telephone lines can handle many incoming and outgoing calls at the same time. The PBX computer assigns these lines to telephones within the PBX system when a caller needs them.

Based on experience, the business and the telephone company can estimate the number of telephone lines that are required. Typically, the number of telephone lines between the business and the telephone company are far fewer than telephones used in the business. In addition, the PBX system is used to route calls within the company without incurring charges from the telephone company.

Although a PBX system takes on the role of a telephone company's central office, there are differences that impede communications. For example, some PBX systems cannot be used with a modem to connect to a remote computer because the PBX system uses different technology than is used by the telephone company when transmitting through a modem.

Types of Lines and Services

Wide area networks (WAN) connect to the public telephone system using services and special lines that provide an efficient means to transmit and receive digital information over the telephone network.

Digital data service (DDS) was one of the first services offers by telephone companies to carry digital information. DDS used a special device called a channel service unit/digital service unit (CSU/DSU) to connect remote computers using a dedicated line. The CSU/DSU is like a modem.

DDS ensured a higher transmission quality than those offered by the telephone company's dedicated analog line service and was able to transmit information at 56 Kbps. A limitation of the DDS is that a dedicated line is required, which prohibits connections to other remote sites.

The telephone company overcame this limitation by offering Switched 56 service. Switched 56 service is also a digital service, however it uses circuit switching in place of the dedicated line. This enables a company to connect to one of many sites that also uses Switched 56 service by dialing a special telephone number. Switched 56 service has been replaced with the Integrated Services Digital Network (ISDN).

ISDN

ISDN is a term that you probably heard bantered around the office by the office gurus. I'm not sure that they're so cool unless they convince the company to pay for it because an ISDN line is overkill for most of us.

In 1984, the telephone company introduced ISDN as an alternative to the analog telephone network, which is designed for voice communication rather than data transmissions. ISDN divides the communications line into channels much like we have television channels. Each channel can handle a transmission at the same time.

There are two flavors of ISDN: Basic Rate Interface (BRI) and Primary Rate Interface (PRI). This is the standard consumer model.

BRI consists of three channels called B1, B2, and D. B1 and B2 are commonly called the B channels and each is used to transmit and receive either voice or data at 64 Kbps. The D channel is used to control the call. Think of the D channel as the telephone company's own private network to keep track of calls. Information is transmitted over the D channel at 16 Kbps. In some situations, the D channel can also be used to transmit data.

PRI contains 23 B channels and a D channel, which enables 23 phone calls to be made at the same time over the same line. Those calls can transmit voice or data. The D channel in PRI is also used to control the calls.

T1-T4 Lines

The telephone company offers data transmission services and other wide area communication services because high-speed communications lines are used in place of the telephone cable that you and I have in our homes.

The high-speed lines are called a T-carrier line, of which there are four categories, one through four. T1 and T3 lines are commonly found in data communications. Unlike our home telephone lines, T-carrier lines can be used to transmit on multiple communication channels. Each channel is capable of transmitting voice or data.

The category of a T-carrier line implies the number of channels that the line can transmit. T1 lines carry 24 channels; T2 lines, 96 channels; T3 lines, 672 channels; and T4 lines, 4,032 channels. As you can imagine, the increase in the number of channels a T-carrier line carries is represented in the higher price a customer pays for the service.

Multiple channels offer customers a way to transmit and receive a lot of data within a short time period. For example, a T1 line can transmit 1.544 megabits per second (Mbps); the T2 line, 6.312 Mbps; the T3 line, 44.736 Mbps; and the T4 line, 274.175 Mbps.

For you and me, using a T-carrier to connect to a remote computer such as we do when using the Internet is more than we need. This is like buying a tractor-trailer to pick up our groceries at the supermarket. However, T-carriers are a perfect way for businesses to economically transfer large amounts of information. Similar to how a tractor-trailer is used by the supermarket to receive its shipment of groceries.

T-carrier lines are slowly being retired as the cable of choice for data transfer and are being replaced with DS-carrier lines. A DS-carrier line uses fiber-optic cables instead of the copper cables used in T-carrier lines. DS-carrier lines are categorized similar to categories used for T-carriers. That is, DS1, DS2, DS3, and DS4. These categories are equivalent to the number of channels and speed of their counterpart T-carrier category.

DSL

You've probably heard of how someone set out to solve a problem and inadvertently made a great discovery? This happened at the 3M company when a research engineer who sought a new adhesive stumbled across one that didn't stick too well. Today we call it Post-it Notes.

Nearly a similar situation occurred at Bellcore, one of the spin-offs of AT&T. In 1989, long before anyone dreamt of the e-economy, engineers were looking for a way to transmit video over the telephone network. Video contains a lot of information that must be transmitted quickly at 30 frames of video per second, otherwise continuity is lost between frames.

Unfortunately, the telephone network is designed for voice transmissions and couldn't handle the demand of video. Bellcore engineers created the DSL. However, with the onset of cable television, the demand to provide video over the telephone line diminished. But DSL is fast becoming the service used to connect our computers to the Internet.

Here's how DSL works (see Figure 5-5). The telephone cable is similar to a highway where lanes are like communication channels. Communication channels are defined by a frequency. Voice transmissions used frequencies below 4 kilohertz (kHz) (4,000 cycles per second) although the telephone cable can handle a greater range of frequencies. And it's these unused frequencies that engineers use to provide DSL service.

A DSL service uses a special DSL modem to transmit data using frequencies above 4 kHz. You could think of this as using the shoulder of the road to increase the number of vehicles that can travel over the highway at the same time.

Frequencies above 4 kHz are divided into 256 subchannels, each of which can transmit data at 32 Kbps. Half the channels are used for transmission and the other half for receiving data. This technique is called discrete multitone modulation (DMT).

Engineers use a compression algorithm to reduce the number of bits needed to transmit information, which increases the transmission throughput. Compression is the technique of representing a sequence of identical characters by fewer characters.

Let's say we needed to transmit 111110000000000. We could rewrite this to say "5-1 10-0" using 8 characters to represent 15 characters. This is an example of a compression algorithm, although a less sophisticated one than used in data communication. When the transmission is received, software deciphers the compressed data into a full representation of the data.

DSL travels on the same telephone network as voice communication until the signal reaches the central office of the telephone company where the DSL signal is routed over the telephone company's data network. This relieves congestion caused by the convergence of voice and data that is transmitted by a standard modem. In contrast, data you send using a modem competes for the same frequencies as do voice transmissions.

There are several versions of DSL (see Table 7-1). These are Asymmetric Digital Subscriber line, DSL Lite, High-Data-Rate Digital Subscriber Line, Very High-Data-Rate Digital Subscriber Line, Rate Adaptive Digital Subscriber Line, Symmetric Digital Subscriber Line, and Integrated Services Digital Subscriber Line.

Table 7-1   Types of DSL services

Type of service	Description
Asymmetric digital subscriber line (ADSL)	This uses different transmission speeds to and from the customer. Typically 8 Mbps are sent to the customer and information from the customer to the remote computer travels at 1 Mbps.
DSL Lite	This is the type of DSL service the Information Services (IS) guru has at his or her home. DSL Lite does not split the voice and data transmissions, therefore this is much slower than ADSL yet faster than using the traditional modem. DSL Lite is sometimes called Universal DSL.
High-data-rate digital subscriber line (HDSL)	This is a premium service that is found more in businesses than with residential customers. Unlike ADSL, HDSL provides the same data transmission speed going to the customer that is sent from the customer.
Very high-data-rate digital subscriber line (VDSL)	This provides a very fast communication. VDSL service uses a combination of copper cabling and fiber-optic cables to provide a very high data transfer rate.
Rate adaptive digital subscriber line (RADS)	This has the same features of ADSL, however adjustments are made in the signal speed to compensate for the various cabling that is used between the sender and the telephone company's central office.
Symmetric digital subscriber line (SDSL)	This has the advantages of HDSL, but with its own twist. SDSL uses the same transmission speeds to send and receive data, however the speeds are slower than those provided for in HDSL.
Integrated services digital subscriber line (ISDS)	This is similar to the ISDN service (see ISDN previously in this chapter), however customers are charged a flat monthly fee, which is different from ISDN service. In addition, ISDS does not transmit voice, which is transmitted over the ISDN service.

Practical Side to Telephones

It is easy for you and me to overlook the importance of the telephone network because we see only a telephone set and a wire that goes into the wall. We realize that the wire is snaked through the wall and somehow makes its way to the telephone pole outside our house. Beyond that we probably haven't an inkling where the telephone wire goes from there.

And from a very practical aspect we shouldn't care. We should care about the cost of connecting our computer to another computer using the telephone network. We should also be concerned about the speed at which information can be transmitted over the telephone line because that impacts directly on our cost.

I've found that a standard telephone line works well for me whenever I connect to the Internet, send and receive emails, and exchange files with friends. Sometimes during peak periods I must wait while an image is downloaded, but that's more the exception than the rule.

The speed of my modem and the standard telephone line are just two of the factors that influence the delay. Equipment at my ISP, Internet devices such as routers, and the overall traffic on the telephone network can also slow transmissions.

Your choice of telephone service and telephone line is limited by the amount you want to spend for telephone service and the service offered by your local telephone company. For example, DSL service is more expensive than a standard telephone line, yet still within the reach of many households. However, you have to be located near your local telephone company's switch center to receive DSL service.

An ISDN line will provide better service than a DSL line, but you must pay for the telephone company to run a special line to your house or business. And some local telephone companies refuse to install an ISDN line in a house. The cost of an ISDN line is out of the reach of most households.

Therefore, the best approach is to use a standard telephone line and subscribe to an ISP that has a local access telephone number. In this way, you don't pay for local connection to the Internet unless your local telephone company charges for local telephone calls. In this case, a local call is less expensive than a long-distance call or a call placed over other kinds of telephone lines. If you want to learn more about the telephone system, then I suggest reading my book *The Essential Guide to Telecommuncations*.

INSIDE NETWORKING ································

Computer networks use technology perfected by the telegraph, telephone, radio, and television networks to transmit information in a digital format using binary math to process the information. Information is composed of alphabetical characters and symbols that are encoded into eight switches by using the ASCII code.

The setting of each switch is represented by a zero or a one, which is transmitted to computer devices such as the CPU, memory, disk and tape drives, a printer, and a monitor. These components were large during the early days of the mainframe computer and were linked by cables to form a network of computer devices.

Personal computers required the same components, however the size of these devices was greatly reduced to fit on a large circuit board within the personal computer cabinet. Instead of using a cable, these devices were connected using wires etched into the circuit board.

Demand grew in the late 1990s to share resources among personal computers. This brought about the forerunner of the first personal computer network where two or more personal computers shared a printer. The small printer network showed that information could be shared among computer devices and an all-out effort was made to devise a way for personal computers to share information.

The early solution came with the development of the modem, which linked two personal computers using the public telephone network. Information was easily exchanged between computers, however the modem link was costly since each personal computer required a private telephone number.

The business community demanded that a mechanism be developed that would enable a group of personal computers to share information over the same cable without the use of the public telephone network.

The LAN was born and met this demand. The early LAN linked personal computers, one of which was a file server. The file server acted as a depository for files that could be shared among personal computers on the network. This became the forerunner of today's LANs.

Transmitting Your Thoughts

As we write a message using a word processing program, our keystrokes are converted by the OS into switch settings in memory, which are echoed onto the computer monitor.

Switch settings can be saved to a disk and stored into a file, then reloaded back into memory anytime we need to access the information. The same characters can be sent over a cable to a distant computer.

Both digital and analog technology is used to move a signal from one computer to another. Each bit that represents information is encoded into an electrical signal that is generated by a network card located inside the computer. You'll learn more about those other things performed by the network card later in this chapter.

Tech Talk

Network card: A circuit board that, among other things, takes information from memory and encodes it into a signal that is transmitted over the network cable.

There are two methods used to transmit the network signal: baseband and broadband. The best way to understand these terms is to envision a highway. A single lane highway enables one car at a time to travel in the same direction. This is similar to baseband technology. However, a multilane highway enables more than one car to travel at the same time. This is similar to broadband technology.

Tech Talk

Baseband technology: One bit at a time is transmitted on a digital signal.

Broadband technology: Multiple bits are transmitted at a time on an analog signal.

Baseband transmission uses digital technology to distribute the information. There are two disadvantages of baseband transmission. First, a bit of information at a time can be transmitted over the cable, which could affect the time it takes to transmit information. There are many other variables involved with transmission speed other than the kind of transmission technology selected for communication.

The other problem is the distance over which a baseband signal can travel. Baseband technology transmits a shorter distance than broadband technology and must use repeaters to amplify the signal.

Tech Talk

Repeater: A device that receives a network signal, then retransmits the signal giving it a boost in power.

Broadband uses analog technology that is digitally encoded with information. Information is encoded into analog technology in the form of a sine wave. A sine wave begins on the baseline, then moves to a height determined by the electronic power used to transmit the wave. As the power is fluctuated, the sine wave returns to the baseline, then continues to a height below the baseline (see Figure 7-6).

A common way to encode a bit onto a sine wave is to adjust the fluctuation in the transmission signal. Power is measured in voltage or microvoltage depending on the size of the circuit. For example, a +5 voltage, which is the height of the wave above the baseline, might represent a binary one, and a −5 voltage, which is the height of the wave below the baseline, might represent a binary zero.

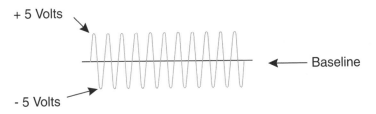

Figure 7-6
A sine wave travels above and below a baseline

Broadband technology enables multiple signals to flow over the network at the same time and for a greater distance than baseband technology. Each signal is transmitted on its own frequency, called a channel, so as not to interfere with other signals. This is similar to how radio and television signals are broadcast.

INTERFERENCE

We've all experienced the problem of having a stray radio signal interfere with our favorite radio station. This is frustrating to say the least and there is little you could do to remedy the situation. The same phenomenon occurs with broadband technology.

Like a radio receiver, the network card is also a receiver that is designed to receive a specific signal. The network cable can pick up stray signals and transmit them to network cards across the network, which can disrupt the success of the transmission.

Precautions are taken to insulate the network cable from stray signals. Furthermore, steps are taken to ensure that signals purposely transmitted over the network use frequencies different enough from other signals to avoid interference.

Measuring Transmission Speed

In the days before the telegraph, sending a message to the other coast required a week or so in the saddle by a series of Pony Express riders. The speed of transmitting the message was measured in days, which was acceptable until the telegraph became popular. Telegraph messages were received minutes after they were sent. The coded message actually arrived within seconds, but the telegraph operator had to decipher Morse code.

Today, seconds are even too long to wait to receive a message because we judge acceptability of communication by our experience and compare all forms of communications to the fastest form that we experience, which is surfing cable television.

I was preparing for a television appearance with the interviewer who said that we had about four minutes on the air. She pointed out that we needed to change the slant on the topic almost every 5 to 10 seconds if we were to attract the most audience. Apparently television producers found that 5 to 10 seconds is the length of a viewer's attention span before the viewer clicks to another channel.

Most of us inadvertently apply the cable television expectation to a computer network, that is, a response of less than about 10 seconds creates frustration. However, there isn't another channel to switch to, so we tend to speak in unpleasant terms to the computer.

Network engineers determined two critical factors that influence transmission. These are the size of the message being transmitted and the number of communication channels that can be used to transmit the information.

Tech Talk

Communications channel: A pathway used to transmit information.

The size of the message is one of the critical factors in transmission. For example, the number of pages that could be sent by Pony Express was limited by the space available in the mail pouch. In comparison, only a few words were transmitted by the telegraph because of the labor-intensive process needed to translate and decipher the telegraph signal.

The size of the message is also a factor in transmitting information over a computer network. The first computer networks were expected to transmit characters. Today's networks are expected to send and receive sound, pictures, and animation at the same speed as our words are transmitted. However, sound and graphics require more bits to be transmitted than words.

Engineers devised a method to reduce the number of bits that are necessary to represent information transmitted over the network. This technique is called compression.

Tech Talk

Compression: A technique for reducing the number of bits to represent information.

There are many compression techniques used, too many to list here. However, we'll explore one of the first compression techniques to illustrate the concept of compression. The objective of a compression technique is to shrink the number of bits that needs to be sent over the network and to remove repeating bits and indicate the number of times the bit is repeated. Instead of encoding five binary-1 values, the compression method encodes that the binary-1 value is repeated five times. The destination computer then decodes the information and expands the message back to its original number of bits.

The speed at which bits are transmitted is measured in a baud rate, as discussed earlier in this chapter. The other critical factor affecting transmission is the number of communication channels available to transmit a message. For example, a modem uses a telephone line, which is a single communication channel. That is, one bit at a time is transmitted.

The number of communication channels available for transmission is referred to as the network's bandwidth. Networks with larger bandwidth can transmit more bits at the same time across the network. The size of the bandwidth is limited by various hardware components that comprise a network.

Tech Talk

Bandwidth: The number of communication channels available to transmit information across the network.

SENDING AND RECEIVING INFORMATION OVER A NETWORK...

Moving information from inside the computer and across the network is a complex operation, especially when you consider the obstacles. Engineers needed to design a process that followed strict rules yet remained flexible to work with various applications and on different kinds of hardware such as computers, routers, and other network devices.

And to further complicate the situation, engineers needed to make each process independent yet able to communicate with each other. This made sure that network components could be enhanced without reengineering other components.

Sending information across a network begins when an application running on a computer makes a request for a network resource, such as a file server used to store a file. Practically any application, for example, a word processor can make such a request.

Tech Talk

Network resource: Any device or file available on a network. This includes file server, printers, modems, and other such devices.

Network software that runs on the computer makes network resources appear as if they are local to the computer. For example, a file server might appear as the 'I' drive similar to how the local 'C' drive appears.

A request for a network resource must be translated into a format that is recognized by the network operating system. Let's say that you want to save a word processing document to the file server. You select File/Save As from the menu bar, then choose the letter of the drive.

Your request causes network software on your computer to change the format of the document from a word processing document to a format required by the network operating system to send the document to the file server.

During this process, the documents might be compressed and encrypted for security. Next, a session must be established with the network. You can think of a session as the process of initiating the conversation and determining whether or not your computer has security rights to access the network resource. Assuming you pass security clearance, then your document is placed within one or multiple packets.

Tech Talk

Packet: An electronic envelope that contains the address of the destination network resource, the address of the computer making the request, and either all or a piece of the request along with information that controls the packet.

LOGICAL AND PHYSICAL ADDRESSES

Every computer and resource on the network are identified by two addresses similar to addresses you and I use to identify the location of a friend's house. These addresses are called the logical and physical addresses.

Let's say my wife asks me to stop by our friend Bob's house on the way home to pick up a package. All I need to know is that it's Bob's house, because I already know how to get there. So in this example, "Bob's house" is the logical address, which is a name we'd recognized that relates to a real address.

However, I might ask my father-in-law to pick up the package. He doesn't know where Bob lives, so I give him the address 121 Maple St. This is the physical address of Bob's house.

Each device on the network is assigned a physical address, which is encoded in the network interface card (sometimes referred to as the network card). This is the circuitry that physically connects a device to the network.

LOGICAL AND PHYSICAL ADDRESSES (CONTINUED)

As you will see later in this book, many networks enable the network administrator, who is the technician who runs the network, to assign logical addresses to a device. For example, a network printer might be identified as "NetPrinter 1."

A file contains both the logical and physical addresses. If a request contains a logical address, network software searches the file for the logical address, then assigns the corresponding physical address to the packet that contains the request.

Let's say you want to save a memo that contains 2,560 characters. Engineers could send all these characters plus the address and control characters to one packet, then transmit the packet across the network. However, unnecessary delays could occur if an error is detected in the transmission, in which case the packet must be retransmitted.

This is similar to having a busload of friends going on vacation and the bus driver leaves someone standing at the bus station. Everyone on the bus must return to pick up the missing person.

A much better approach is to divide the busload of friends into several cars. In that way, if someone is left behind, only one car has to return to pick up the person, while the others continue toward the destination. This is basically the technique used to transmit the memo over the network.

Instead of stuffing the entire memo into a single packet, engineers developed software that divides a document into smaller packets. In our example, five packets of 512 characters can be used to transport the memo. If an error is detected, only the packet that contains the error is retransmitted.

Additional information besides characters of the document is stored in each packet. These are the destination address, the originator's address, sequencing information, and error detection information (see Figure 7-7).

Each packet contains the physical address of the network resource (i.e., file server) that is to receive the information and the physical address of the network resource (i.e., computer) that sent the packet. This enables both resources to communicate with each other during the transmission process.

Since the information that is being transmitted is divided into more than one packet, engineers devised a way to track the order of the packet. This is referred to as sequencing.

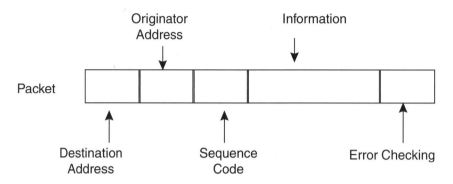

Figure 7-7
A packet is an electronic envelope containing data and information
needed to send the packet to its destination

Tech Talk

Sequencing: A method that tracks the order of packets.

Each packet has a sequencing number that enables the destination resource to reassemble information contained in the packets. You can think of this as numbering each car in the caravan of friends headed for vacation so that each automobile can be accounted for when they reach the destination.

Error checking is critical to successful network transmission. Although we tend to assume messages are reliably transmitted, this can be deceiving because we only see the results of successful transmissions. Retransmissions of packets are hidden from us.

Tech Talk

Retransmission: The process of resending a previously sent packet because the destination network resource suspects the data within the packet is corrupted.

Cyclical redundancy check (CRC): A method used to determine if errors occurred in transmission.

Engineers came up with a method to have network software determine the likelihood that an error has occurred in transmission. This method is called cyclical redundancy check (CRC). The name might sound imposing, but the concept is easy to understand.

Remember that packets contain only binary values that are encoded into an electronic signal. Therefore a packet contains a series of zeros and ones. It would be nice if network software could read the words in our information to determine if it was transmitted in its entirety, but that's not the case.

The next best thing is to perform a calculation using the binary values contained in the packet, then store the result in the packet. Software on the destination resource performs the same calculation and compares the result with the result stored in the packet. If the results are the same, then an assumption is made that the information was received intact. If the results are different, then an error is suspected and a request is made to retransmit the packet.

When packets are successfully received, the process reverses. Address and control information are stripped from each packet and pieces of information are reassembled into the complete document. The document is then expanded if it was compressed and deciphered if the document was encrypted. The original format of the document is restored and the document is ready to be read (i.e., by the word processor).

INSIDE NETWORK CARDS ....

The device inside your computer that continually listens to the network is called the network interface card (NIC) or simply the network card. The network card is an integral part of the computer just as if it were built into the motherboard.

Engineers designed PCs for expandability. That is, they realized technology evolves. Rather than redesign circuitry inside the computer each time someone devised a new device, they developed a way to add and remove circuitry directly to the motherboard. The method they developed was to create expansion slots. Personal computers contain expansion slots inside the computer and laptops use a PCI slot located on the side of the laptop computer.

The network card is an add-on circuit board that slips into an expansion slot and handles communications between the network cable and the computer. Each expansion slot is assigned an address on the computer's bus.

Each NIC is assigned a unique network address. This is similar to a house number on your street. Engineers are able to avoid assigning conflicting addresses by having a block of them assigned to each network card manufacturer. Manufacturers then assign a unique address within their block of addresses to each network card they manufacture. These addresses are stored inside a chip on the network card.

INSTRUCTIONS VS. DATA

An instruction is information that tells the CPU to do something and data is information that is manipulated by an instruction. Let's say the number 300 is stored at memory location 1 and the number 40 is stored at memory location 5. We want the computer to add these numbers and place the sum at memory location 7.

Here are the instructions necessary to complete this objective:

a. retrieve the value from address 1

b. retrieve the value from address 5

c. add the value from address 1 and address 5

d. store the sum in address 7

However, the data are:

a. 300

b. 40

c. 340

The role of a network card is to facilitate communication between devices on a network such as between a workstation and a file server. The process begins when network cards in both devices determine how to communicate with each other. This is called handshaking (see Figure 7-8). Instructions for handshaking are contained in a chip located on each network card. The chip contains software called firmware that manages the handshaking process.

Tech Talk

Handshaking: The process each network card uses to determine the data size that can be transmitted, transmission timing, data confirmation, and data transmission rate.

Handshaking can be different for each network card, even for cards produced by the same manufacturer. For example, an older version of a network card may lack features found in a new version. However, newer versions are frequently backward compatible. That is, the newer card contains both older and newer features and therefore can automatically use an older feature to communicate with an older network card.

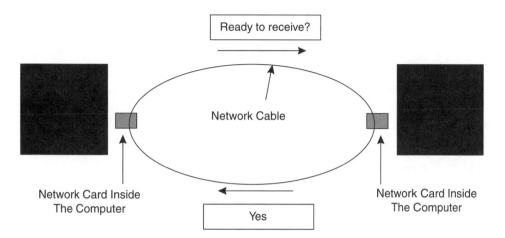

Ready to receive?

Network Cable

Network Card Inside
The Computer

Network Card Inside
The Computer

Yes

Figure 7-8
Handshaking is the process where a computer asks if the other computer is ready to receive data, and the other computer then replies

Settling on the data size before communication begins is a critical concern, otherwise data could be lost. If data size isn't agreed upon, then there will be memory overflow. Simply put, there is no room to store new incoming data.

Tech Talk
Data size: The amount of data that the destination network card can store in memory before the destination computer processes the data.

This is similar to the days you rushed home to tell your folks about how you scored the winning goal in your grammar school soccer game. You probably burst into the room recounting every moment of the game without taking a breath. No one understood you because you were talking faster than they could listen and process what you were saying. You were told to slow down and begin over. You informally agreed on a data size that was acceptable to both of you.

The timing factor, too, is a critical component of network communications since it determines the time that will elapse between each transmission. This is typically the time that is necessary for the destination network card to process the previous data.

After data is transmitted, the NIC that originated the transmission waits for a confirmation that the data was received without errors. However, this can be an endless wait if the destination network card malfunctions and is unable to send the confirmation message back to the originating network card.

Engineers anticipated this problem and made a confirmation factor part of the handshaking process. The confirmation factor sets the time delay before the destination network card will transmit a confirmation message. An error is suspected if the confirmation isn't received by this deadline.

The transmission rate is the speed at which communications will occur. The agreed-upon rate is the highest common rate that is possible for both the destination and origination network cards.

Choosing a Network Card

There are three factors that determine which network card is suited for a network device (i.e., computer). These are the kind of network device, the type of network, and the performance. Fortunately for most of us, technicians make this choice.

By now you realize that a network device is any device that connects directly to the network, which is typically a computer or server. These devices are further defined by the bus used to transport data and instructions inside the device. There are three commonly used buses: ISA, EISA, and PCI. Each bus type requires a specific kind of network card.

There are a variety of types of networks and each has specifications that must be met by the network card. For example, a network card designed for a fiber-optic network cannot be used to link a network device to a coaxial cable network. This is like trying to install a Ford fuel injection on a Chevy. It just doesn't fit.

You can also think of a network card like a toll stop on a highway. Every car exiting the highway must stop and be processed. Cars begin to back up if the toll stop cannot keep pace with incoming traffic. Before long a bottleneck occurs.

The same is true on a computer network. Any network device that cannot process data at the same speed as other devices on the network will slow down network traffic. This, too, is called a bottleneck. Therefore a network card is selected based on its capability to keep up with the rest of the devices on the network. There are two factors that influence the efficiency at which a network card can receive and process data. These are the use of memory and the use of the CPU.

Tech Talk

Bottleneck: Any network device that slows the transmission of packets over the network.

Ideally data received by the network card is immediately passed along to communications software on the network device where packets are stripped down and data is reassembled into information. No bottleneck occurs if the communications software keeps pace with incoming data.

This rarely occurs in the real world because the efficiency of the communications software is dependent upon other factors, such as the processing capabilities of the network device and other software running on the device while transmission is occurring.

Engineers increase the throughput of data communications by storing incoming data in memory rather than passing the data directly to the communications software.

Tech Talk

Throughput: A measurement of how many bits can be completely processed within a second.

Memory used to temporarily store incoming data is called a buffer or cache. You can think of it as a mailbox. For example, a mail carrier can ring your doorbell, then wait to give you your mail. This is similar to a network card passing data directly to the communications software. However, this doesn't happen, otherwise no one would receive mail. Instead, the mail carrier drops your mail in the mailbox, which is like a buffer or cache.

Memory must be allocated for use by the network card and the size of the allotted memory must be determined before the network card is ready to receive data. That is, someone must designate the box that will serve as the mailbox and decide the size of the box.

There are three areas in which memory can be reserved for use by the network card. These are memory on the network device exclusive to the network card called direct memory access (DMA); shared memory between the network device and the network card; and memory located on the network card called RAM buffering.

Tech Talk

Direct memory access: The ability of the network card to directly use the memory of the network device.

RAM buffering: A network card that contains its own memory used to temporarily store incoming packets.

In addition to having sufficient memory to store incoming data, engineers are also concerned about how the data is processed. The CPU is the component of the network device that processes incoming data by following instructions given by the communications software. Typically, data is moved from the buffer to another area of memory for processing, which doesn't seem time-consuming, but this is time that slows down throughput.

Another hindrance to throughput is the availability of the CPU to process incoming data. Although the destination and origination network cards are synchronized to communicate with each other, the CPU in the destination computer might be running other programs during transmission. For example, you might be using your word processor at the same time as you receive email. The problem is that the CPU cannot do two things at the same time.

Engineers devised two schemes to reduce the delay of moving data in memory and the contention for the CPU to process that data. The first is to make memory on the network card used to store incoming data available to the network device's CPU. This eliminates the need to move data from a buffer to memory that the CPU uses to process the data.

The other scheme is to incorporate a CPU into the network card. This gives the network card the hardware that is necessary to process incoming data without having to rely on the CPU in the network device. This is called bus mastering.

The Practical Side to Networking

Unlike modems, you probably won't have to choose a network card unless you are involved in running a computer network. The network administrator, who is the person responsible for the operations of the network, typically selects network cards.

First, the network administrator narrows the options to network cards that work with the topology used on the network. A topology describes the way network devices are connected to each other.

Next, the network card must be capable of keeping up traffic sent to the device that contains the network card such as your computer. A network device such as a print server that receives a lot of packets requires a network card that has an onboard processor, a large RAM buffer, and direct memory access. However, these aren't required for an average computer. Another consideration is the type of expansion slot available inside the device. I told you about expansion slots in Chapter 3.

Once the network card is installed in the device the network card needs to be configured, which is setting the parameters within which the network card will operate. Fortunately, the network administrator configures the network card for you so you don't need to become involved in details of making the card operational.

However, if I stirred your curiosity to learn more about computer networking, then I suggest that you pick up a copy of my book *The Essential Guide to Networking*.

SUMMARY ··

A computer can communicate with other computers by using the telephone network or a private network called a LAN. The telephone network consists of telephone lines that connect homes and businesses and are used traditionally for voice communication. Over the past few decades the telephone lines have begun carrying an increased amount of data traffic, such as computers accessing the Internet.

A computer connects to the telephone network using a modem. A modem receives digital information from the motherboard and encodes the digital information into an analog signal, which is sent over the telephone line. This process is called modulation.

The modem connected to the other end of the telephone line decodes the analog signal back to digital information, which is then sent to the motherboard of the receiving computer for processing.

Modems transmit information at a speed measured as a baud. One baud is equal to sending one transmission symbol per second over the telephone line. A symbol can contain one or more bits of information. Most modems can transmit at several rates although only the highest baud is quoted in advertisements.

Two modems agree on the highest baud both can handle during the handshaking process that occurs during the first few seconds after making the initial connection. This means that a modem may not transmit information at the advertised baud.

There are a variety of modems depending on a user's needs and the type of line that is used to transmit information. The more common modems are a data mode, fax modem, and voice modem. Other kinds include a cable modem, DSL modem, ISDN modem, and satellite modem.

Computers that are connected to a LAN use a network card rather than a modem. A network card is a device that listens to traffic over the network and intercepts packets of information destined for the network adapter card's computer. A packet is an electronic envelope that contains parts of information being transferred to another computer.

A network card must be capable of processing information from the network to the motherboard and from the motherboard to the network efficiently, otherwise a bottlenecks occurs. A bottleneck is similar to a five-lane highway merging into a three-lane tollbooth island. The tollbooth plaza can only process a maximum number of vehicles before traffic backs up on the highway.

Some network cards contain a small amount of memory used to store packets. An interrupt is sent to the processor on the motherboard whenever a packet is received from the network. The process then moves the packet from the network card into main memory where the packet is processed. However, a bottleneck develops if the processor is unable to move packets faster than the network card receives additional packets.

A better strategy used by other network adapter cards is for the card to have access to main memory on the motherboard. This is called direct memory access. The network card also has its own processor so when packets are received from the network, the network card automatically moves the packet into main memory without waiting for the main processor to respond to an interrupt.

Summary Questions

1. **What is the difference between a DSL and ISDN telephone line?**

2. **What does baud measure?**

3. **What is the difference between a satellite modem and a cable modem?**

4. **What is the difference between a data modem and a voice modem?**

5. **How does direct memory access improve performance of a network card?**

6. **What happens during the handshaking sequence with a modem?**

7. **What speed is used by two modems to transfer data?**

8. **What is the difference between a T1 line and a DSL line?**

9. **What is the difference between baseband technology and broadband technology?**

10. **What is the purpose of a repeater on a computer network?**

8 Input Devices

In this chapter...

- Inside Keyboards

- Inside a Mouse

- Inside Game Controllers

- Inside Graphics Tablets

- Inside Speech Recognition

"A good solution begins with good input."

Anonymous

Engineers who design and build computer programs are frequently compared to rocket scientists, probably because both work with abstract concepts that many of us find incomprehensible—and the results of their work are dramatic.

A computer program that performs seemingly impossible tasks at nearly the speed of light and a plumage of rainbow colors from a rocket headed into outer space are enough to get a wow from any casual bystander.

Yet none of that would happen if computer engineers and rocket scientists didn't subscribe to the KISS philosophy of design—keep it simple stupid. Computer programs and rocket ships have at least one thing in common. Both are operated by people who tend to make errors when presented with complex situations.

You and I and astronauts want to avoid creating mistakes by giving computers simple instructions on how we want the computer to run our business or how to get the rocket ship to dock with the space station.

The way we give instructions to a computer is called input, and the device we use to provide direction to a computer is called an input device. This chapter explores common input devices that are used with computer. You'll learn:

- How keyboards work

- The secrets of a mouse

- The gaming facts of game controllers

- How graphics tablets work

- The techniques used in speech recognition

REALITY CHECK ....

There is a deep, dark secret in the executive suite of many companies. No one speaks about it and executive assistants quickly raise an iron shield to protect their bosses if anyone comes close to uncovering the unmentionable.

However, I learned of the secret when I developed computer systems for some of Wall Street's most prestigious firms. And now, for the first time, I'm free to reveal what I learned. Many who reside on executive row resist using a computer—so what's new?

They resist not because using a computer is beneath them. They resist not because they are computer phobic. They resist because they don't want anyone to know that they cannot type. Yes, they are typing illiterates.

Many like myself who type for a living find it difficult to appreciate the fear and embarrassment that people who don't type face every day when they sit down in front of a computer.

Imagine being under pressure at work and knowing the keyboard stands between you and getting the work completed. You know what to say and do. You know how to respond to prompts displayed on the computer and yet you can't get the fingers to move in the proper direction.

The solution adopted by some executives is to put on a front, acting as if they're busy and asking an assistant to enter the necessary information into the computer program. And if the assistant isn't around, there is always the fallback strategy of going behind closed doors and hunt-and-peck your way through the program.

INSIDE KEYBOARDS ....

Chris Sholes probably has had more impact on computers than Bill Gates—and yet Sholes hasn't received the glory or the financial rewards that befit a person of his stature. You probably never heard of Sholes. Few of us have heard of him, but in 1860, Sholes revolutionized the business office with the invention of the typewriter keyboard.

Sholes is the guy who arranged characters on the keyboard in what seems to be an illogical order; however, there is a very good reason for the arrangement. A typewriter uses mechanical arms containing die-cut characters to make impressions on a page. Typists became so adept at pressing keys quickly that the arms would jam.

Typewriter jamming was a major headache for typists and cut down on productivity. Typists spent more time unlocking the mechanical arms then they did typing correspondence. Sholes had an idea to slow down typists by rearranging characters on the keyboard so that commonly used characters were far enough apart on the keyboard to reduce the likelihood of jamming. His invention is called the QWERTY keyboard, which are the six letters on the second row of the keyboard.

There have been countless attempts to develop a better keyboard design, including the natural keyboard design, also known as an ergonomic keyboard, that is built to reduce chance of repetitive stress injury. The natural keyboard divides the traditional keyboard into two sections that are positioned similar to the natural position of your hands.

And yet with all these attempts, Sholes typewriter keyboard layout has remained the choice of many computer users and keyboard manufacturers.

Keys Are Switches

A computer keyboard is really a set of switches; each key is a separate switch. When you press a key, a signal is transmitted to the computer where it is translated into ASCII characters. I'll show you how this works in the next section of this chapter. There are a number of different types of switches that are used in a keyboard.

The more common types are mechanical, membrane, and capacity switches. A mechanical switch keyboard operates like a light switch. When two metal connectors in the switch touch, the switch is closed and electricity flows through the switch. When two metal connectors are separated, the switch is opened and electricity stops flowing through the switch.

The keys on a mechanical keyboard, called dry-contact switches, are held in the open position by a spring. You overcome the resistance of the spring when you press the key. A metal post at the bottom of the key makes contact with the electrical connector on the keyboard, thereby closing the circuit until the key is released.

While mechanical switches are economical and efficient, they have a major drawback in that some do not provide feedback (such as a clicking sound) when the key is pressed. As you'll learn later in this chapter, feedback is a critical factor that increases a typist's productivity.

Probably the most commonly used keyboard switch is the membrane switch, also known as a domed elastomer key. I like to think of a membrane switch as a switch sandwich, where a sheet of artificial rubber is sandwiched between the switch and the circuit board.

Conductive material is contained on the circuit board side of the rubber layer. Each time you press a key, the bottom of the key causes the rubber layer to contact the circuit board, thereby completing the circuit. The rubber layer provides springlike resistance against the key and contains a conductive.

Membrane keyboards are exposed or enclosed. The exposed membrane keyboard is the kind that you find on many desktop and laptop computers. The enclosed membrane keyboard is used on appliances and is intended for single-character entry rather than rapid typing. For example, you'd use an enclosed membrane keyboard to select the wash cycle on a washing machine.

The capacity keyboard is used to change the state of a circuit rather than to allow electricity to flow to the circuit. The best way to understand how a capacity keyboard works is to imagine an electrical circuit that contains a red and green light and one switch.

The red light is turned on when the switch is set to one position and the green light is turned on when the switch is moved to the other position. The switch isn't turning electricity on and off to the circuit. Instead, the switch is redirecting the flow of electricity from one light to the other light.

How Keyboards Work

A keyboard is like a small computer unto itself with enough processing power to translate your keystrokes into signals to send to the operating system (OS). Your keystrokes are communicated to the operating system in two ways.

The keyboard tells the operating system when you press a key and when you release a key. Both pieces of information are critical if the OS is to recognize the key you selected.

Furthermore, the keyboard gives you an indication that you pressed and released a key. This is called feedback, which is indicated by a clicking sound and tactile clues whenever you successfully press a key on the keyboard.

You and I probably never give much thought to what happens when we press Shift or any other key on the keyboard as long as the computer responds accordingly. Yet a lot occurs behind the scenes.

Let's say that I want the letter q to appear on the screen. I press Q on the keyboard. However, before the letter appears on the screen, the operating system checks the state of the Caps Lock key.

Caps Lock is typically unlocked when the computer is powered up. Each time I select the Caps Lock key, the keyboard changes the state of the Caps Lock from off to on or from on to off. If the state of the Caps Lock is on, the OS in my example knows to display an uppercase Q.

If the state of the Caps Lock is off, then the OS performs the additional step to determine if another key is pressed—but not released. Holding down Shift while pressing Q causes the operating system to display an uppercase Q. However, if Shift is released before I press Q, then a lowercase q is displayed.

Nerds call this a key combination because two keys on the keyboard are used to produce one result, which is an uppercase Q. There is variation of this theme called a key chord. A key chord consists of three keys pressed at the same time such as the infamous CTRL+ALT+DEL chord. This is where the combination of three keys produces one result.

The Matrix

The keyboard is a small computer that runs a program to monitor all the keys and transmits a specific signal when one or several keys are pressed and/or released. Each key coincides to a position on a wired matrix inside the keyboard (see Figure 8-1).

The keyboard program scans the matrix many times a second to determine if a key is pressed. When a key is pressed, it closes a point on the matrix causing the keyboard program to either send information to the OS or to change the state of a key.

For example, pressing the Caps Lock key doesn't send a signal to the operating system. Instead, the keyboard program changes the state of the key and activates a light on the keyboard indicating that Caps Lock is on.

There is two-way communication between the keyboard program and the OS, which enables programs other than the keyboard program to change the state of the keys.

Let's say that you are using a math program that requires you to use the number pad to enter data. Sometimes the Num Lock state is off, which means keys on the number pad signal movement of the cursor rather than enter a numeric character.

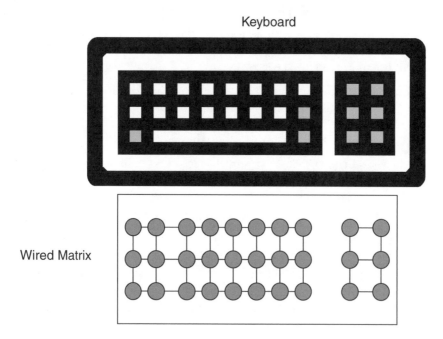

Figure 8-1
Each key on the keyboard is associated with a wired matrix located inside the keyboard

The math program can tell the OS to change the state of the Num Lock to on, which requires the OS to forward the request to the keyboard program. Only the keyboard program can change the state of any key.

The OS also tells the settings for the keyboard's typematic action such as the amount of time that elapses before the keyboard resends a signal when a key is held down. This is called time delay.

Tech Talk
Typematic action: Typing metrics such as time delay.

You'll notice that whenever you press the Spacebar. The cursor moves one space then pauses before moving rapidly across the screen. The time delay is the length of the pause, which is about a half of a second. The number of spaces entered while the Spacebar is held is called the repetition rate, which is about 10 characters per second.

The part of the OS that talks to the keyboard is called the keyboard controller. It receives a signal from the keyboard program called a key scan code. Each matrix point has a unique key scan code.

The keyboard controller stores key scan codes in the keyboard buffer, which is a portion of random access memory (RAM), then sends an interrupt to the processor. The interrupt tells the processor to stop whatever the processor is doing and run the interrupt service routine (see Chapter 2) that processes the key scan codes stored in the keyboard buffer.

Each key scan code represents one key that was pressed on the keyboard. Before the interrupt service routine finishes processing, the state of other keys must be evaluated, such as Shift, Caps Lock, and Num Lock. The state of these keys and the key scan code determine how the interrupt service routine interprets the key scan code.

The interrupt service routine interprets the key scan code into the equivalent ASCII value, then stores that value into main memory and erases the key scan code from the keyboard buffer.

Some keyboards have built-in custom keys called programmable keys. For example, there are keyboards custom made for use on the Internet and others for particular operating systems such as Windows or Linux.

These keyboards contain the standard set of keys and include extra keys for use with the customized program. The additional keys have their own key scan codes, but are not recognized by the keyboard controller that comes with most operating systems.

Therefore, a special keyboard driver must be installed to translate the special key scan codes into those recognized by the keyboard controller. Those key scan codes are meaningful only to the OS or a specific program running on the computer.

For example, next to the ALT key on some keyboards is a programmable key showing the Microsoft Windows logo. Pressing this key causes the Windows Start menu to be displayed. However, the key is useless if you are running a different OS.

The Practical Side to Keyboards

Selecting a keyboard is similar to selecting a monitor in that our personal preference outweighs an objective review of a keyboard specification. My preference is to keep things simple so I don't look for a keyboard that contains built-in features such as speakers, scanners, or customized keys.

Speakers built in to the keyboard never sound as good as speakers that hang from my monitor or sit on my desk. A keyboard with a scanner is overkill for most of us and I've found that I'm paying a premium for the keyboard.

Customized keys really don't help. In fact, they decrease my level of proficiency using a computer because I've become so accustomed to using the customized keys that I am lost without them.

Try a keyboard at your local computer store before you take it home. For example, the natural keyboard looks modern but you may feel uncomfortable using it. I prefer the standard keyboard style.

I also prefer a heavy keyboard to a light one because a heavy keyboard withstands inadvertent movement while I'm typing. However, my friend likes a light keyboard because she places it on her lap while typing.

....

WHEN YOUR KEYBOARD GOES FOR A SWIM...

A rule in the computer labs at Columbia University is not to eat or drink while using the computer. Although lab assistants vigilantly police the labs, a few students manage to skirt the rule and sneak a drink into the lab. And as you probably expect, many get caught—especially after spilling the drink on the keyboard.

After reading the riot act to the student and expelling him from the lab, the lab assistant then goes to work correcting the problem—with a sponge. Here's how they do it just in case you find yourself in a similar situation.

Turn the computer off and disconnect the keyboard. Place the keyboard upside down in a sink or someplace where you can let the liquid drain. After the excess fluid drains, reverse the keyboard and soak up as much as you can using the sponge. Let the keyboard sit in a dry place for a day or so. This will give the remaining liquid time to evaporate. Connect the keyboard to the computer, then power up the computer. The keyboard is working again in <u>most</u> cases.

INSIDE A MOUSE ....

Until the mid-1980s most of us ran for a trap and cheese at the mere mention of the word *mouse*, except if the word was prefaced with Mickey. However, Doug Englebart changed all that. Now most of us handle a mouse every day without giving it a second thought. Englebart is the Stanford Research Institute scientist who invented the mouse/pointing device back in the 1960s.

The need for a computer mouse came about when software and hardware manufacturers such as Microsoft and Apple Computer adopted a graphical user interface (GUI) for their operating systems. You know this better as Windows and the Macintosh OS.

A GUI uses a combination of words and graphics to run programs and interact with users through the use buttons, scrolling lists, and other features that we have come to expect from every software application.

Designers of GUIs needed an easy and intuitive way for a computer user to click buttons and make selections from scrolling lists. A sequence of keys could be used, but there were too many keystrokes. A simpler approach was required.

Designers needed a device that let the user easily move the cursor to a GUI object on the screen and make a selection. Englebart's computer mouse filled that need, which forced the dictionary publishers to expand the definition of the word *mouse*.

The computer mouse gave birth to a mutant mouse called a trackball. As you'll learn later in this chapter, a mouse and trackball use the same basic technology except the trackball is basically an inverted mouse.

How a Mouse Works

A GUI operating system such as Windows and the Macintosh OS has two cursors. These is the mouse or pointing device cursor and a cursor marking the position for data entry, which is usually with a GUI object on the screen such as an edit box.

The OS places the mouse cursor on the screen when an application is launched. Pel coordinates (see Chapter 4) identify the location of the mouse cursor. You can think of coordinates similar to the row and column number of a cell on a spreadsheet, except the pel is the cell (see Figure 8-2).

A mouse tells the OS to add or subtract rows or columns from the mouse cursor's current position. Let's say the OS places the mouse cursor in the upper left corner of the screen. We'll call the coordinate row 1, column 1.

As you move the mouse to the right, the mouse tells the OS to add values to the column coordinate. The more the mouse moves to the right, the higher the value is added to the existing mouse cursor column position.

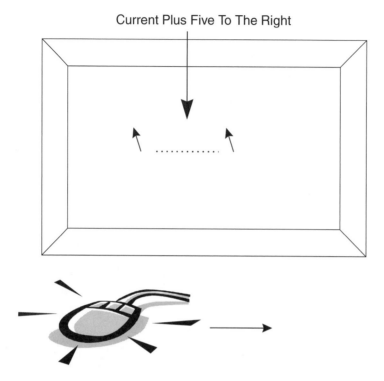

Figure 8-2

A mouse tells the operating system to move the mouse cursor a specific number of pels from the current position

Likewise, moving the mouse down causes the operating system to add values to the row position of the mouse cursor. Dragging the mouse at an angle toward the lower right corner causes the operating system to add values to both the column and row coordinate.

There are several kinds of mice, the most common of which is the mechanical mouse. Inside the mechanical mouse is a ball and two rollers—one roller detects side-to-side movement and the other forward and back movement. The mouse ball is in direct contact with the rollers so the movement of the mouse ball is translated to movement of one or both of the rollers (see Figure 8-3). Circuitry attached to the roller mechanism sends the appropriate signal to the operating system.

In an optical mouse two lights are used instead of a ball and rollers to detect the motion of the mouse. Each light is a different frequency (color). One light detects side-to-side movement and the other forward and back movement.

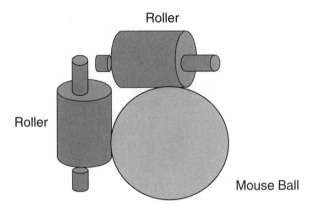

Roller

Roller

Mouse Ball

Figure 8-3
Two rollers inside the mouse detect movement of the mouse ball

The light shines on a special mouse pad which contains reflective material that is imbedded with a grid of lines. The mouse sends a signal to the OS each time one of the lights crosses a line on the mouse pad.

Another version is the opto-mechanical mouse. It has nearly all the components of a mechanical mouse, except a light-emitting diode and a sensor are used to detect movement in the rollers. Each roller has notches that allow light to pass through to the sensor. As the rollers rotate, the sensor picks up more light, which sends a signal to the OS to move the mouse cursor accordingly.

The latest mouse on the market uses a refined optical technology to detect the movement of the mouse. This works on any surface even without a mouse pad.

Buttons and Wheels

Microsoft and other OS manufacturers continue to simplify the way you and I interact with the computer and have included various buttons and wheels on the mouse. These features enable the mouse rather than the keyboard to be the most frequently used input device.

The number of buttons on a mouse varies depending on the manufacturer. Typically Apple uses a one button mouse, Microsoft a two-button mouse, and Sun Workstations a three-button mouse.

Buttons do the same thing regardless of the number. When a button is pressed or released, a signal is sent to the OS, which sends a message to all the programs that are running saying that a specific mouse button was pressed or released. The program displayed in the window beneath the mouse cursor is responsible for reacting to the message.

Let's say that you are saving a file in Word. You place the mouse cursor over File on the menu bar and left-click. The OS sends a message to all the programs that you made a selection.

Word receives the message and determines that the mouse cursor is over an object in one of its windows. Word is programmed to display a particular drop-down menu whenever the mouse cursor is placed over File and the mouse is left-clicked.

Some programs may ignore the click of a particular mouse button. Therefore, the number of buttons on a mouse is important only if programs that you run on your computer recognize those buttons.

The same is true with other features on the mouse such as a wheel. On some Microsoft mice there is a wheel between two buttons. The wheel is used to scroll up and down an application window such as a long Word document. However, the wheel is ignored on programs that don't recognize the wheel.

Many manufacturers that offer nonstandard features also provide a mouse driver that translates those features into standard key scan codes.

For example, the mouse drive probably sends a scroll-down message to the OS whenever the wheel is turned backward. This is the same message that is sent if the mouse cursor is over the down arrow on the vertical scroll bar while the left mouse is pressed. All GUI programs react to the vertical scroll bar message regardless of how the message was originated.

Non-Mouse Mice

A computer mouse requires desk space so you can move the mouse without bumping into something. This especially became evident when laptop computers entered the market. All laptops can use a mouse, but they also have other space-saving pointing devices. These include a trackball, the IBM stick, and the touch pad.

A trackball is an inverted mouse, where you use your fingers to move the ball rather than dragging the ball over a mouse pad. Otherwise, the same basic technology is used in a trackball as is used in a mouse.

IBM's solution to the space limitation problem is a pointing stick, called the TrackPoint, located in the center of the keyboard. The TrackPoint is similar to a joystick in that you push the stick in the direction you want the mouse cursor to move on the screen. Sensors translate the direction into a signal that is sent to the OS. The signal is similar to the signal sent by a mouse and trackball.

The touch pad is a dark square beneath the bottom row of keys on a laptop computer. Unlike the mouse, trackball, and pointing stick, there are no mechanical components in a touch pad. Instead, there are two sets of electrodes placed at right angles embedded into the touch pad.

Electricity flowing to the electrodes varies depending on the area of the touch pad where you place your finger. The variation in electricity is translated by circuitry in the touch pad as an adjustment to the mouse cursor's current position on the screen. Tapping the touch pad with your finger simulates the click of the left mouse button on some touch pads.

LET THE FORCE BE WITH YOU

An interesting innovation that has come along in computer mouse technology is the force feedback mouse from Logitech. It gives you a tactile response to each mouse movement based on the location of the mouse cursor.

Here's how it works. GUI applications such as those found in Windows and Macintosh divide the screen into objects such as windows. Those objects have shapes such as edges. The force feedback mouse adjusts the resistance of the mouse to give you a feel that you—actually the mouse cursor—have crossed over into another area of the screen.

You'll feel a bump whenever the mouse cursor crosses an edge of a window and you'll feel recoil after clicking on a button on the screen. This is similar to the feeling you get after pressing a key.

However, the force feedback that impressed me the most was the resistance I felt when I increased the size of a window. I actually felt as if I was pulling something. The force feedback mouse adds another dimension to the normal boring experience of using a mouse.

The Practical Side to a Mouse

All computer mice do the same thing. Each lets you move the mouse cursor and select an object by clicking the left mouse button. Therefore, I place a mouse in the same category as a keyboard when deciding the proper mouse for your computer.

The best mouse is the one that you feel comfortable using. A mechanical mouse works fine for me although I need to clean dust and other things from the mouse ball every so often. I'd stay away from the pure optical mouse unless the mouse came with my computer. Some workstations are only able to use an optical mouse.

Two buttons are a must if you are using Windows because many applications use the right mouse button to provide short cuts to long menu trees. The third button and the wheel might be nice to have if your applications or OS uses those features, but otherwise they are not necessary.

An important feature for me is the length of the mouse cord because I like to place my computer towers away from my desk. I simply run out of patience when I move the mouse only to find that I'm tugging on the mouse cord. A long mouse cord provides all the slack I need.

Avoid using smooth, fancy mouse pads such as those that have pictures or advertisements on them. You need a rough surface when using a mechanical mouse. Many mouse pads with pictures or advertisements tend to be smooth and lack traction for the mouse ball.

Trackballs, pointing sticks, and touch pads are convenient if you have space limitations, but it takes time getting used to them especially if you have been using a mouse. I've used all three and find them all worthwhile, although I plug a mouse into my laptop computer whenever I have the space to stretch out.

TAPE YOUR MOUSE CLEAN

Don't you hate it when your mouse seems to skip and you find yourself rolling the mouse with the same energy you use to rev-up a toy friction car. The problem is the mouse ball has picked up lint and other debris from your desk—and probably some bits of last week's lunch, too.

Every mouse user knows that you can twist the ring on the bottom of the mouse and pop out the ball. The real challenge is how to get the stuff off the ball. You can spend a few hours with a tweezers picking the ball clean or you can do it the smart way.

Here's what to do. Wrap a long piece of adhesive tape around your hand with the sticky side facing out. Next, roll the ball around in your hand making sure that all surfaces of the ball touch the tape. After a few minutes you'll notice that the ball is clean and the tape is filthy.

Place the ball back into the bottom of the mouse and lock the ball in place with the ring. You'll be good for another few months.

YOUR MOUSE IS AMBIDEXTROUS

Having written about computers for many years I thought I saw all the gimmicks. Then I walked into my friend's office one day and noticed a box on her desk. She had purchased a left-handed mouse.

I realize that we live in a right-handed world, which frustrates my friend and others who are left-handed. And although she moved the mouse to the left side of the keyboard, she still ran into problems since mouse buttons are designed for right-handed people.

Don't purchase a left-handed mouse if you're left-handed! Instead change the button settings using Windows. Here's how to do it. Select MyComputer, then the Control Panel. Next click on the Mouse icon to display the Mouse Properties Dialog Box. Select the Button tab where you'll see the right-hand and left-hand options. Click on left-hand, then click OK. You now have a mouse for left-handers.

INSIDE GAME CONTROLLERS...............................

There is a blur between computer games and sophisticated computer simulations that give the look and feel of real life. I discovered this fact when one of our editors at a computer magazine was given the weeklong task of testing the accuracy of Microsoft Flight Simulator.

The editor was chosen because of his naval aviation background. He flew F16s. We considered him our top gun, although he was no competition for Tom Cruise. He was behind closed doors for a week flying a variety of aircraft both in visual flight mode and in instrument mode.

He concluded that Microsoft Flight Simulator was very similar to flying a real aircraft except for the controls. All that was available at that time was a standard joystick. I'm sure if he revisited that test today he would find nearly a complete set of controls including foot pedals.

A joystick and other devices that attach to your computer to let you interact with a computer game are called game controllers. Game controllers come in a variety of shapes and sizes. Some resemble the controls of real-life objects such as the yoke of a plane or steering wheel of a car. Others are simpler in design, such as a joystick.

Game controllers are an important element in playing computer games or simulating a real-life experience on a computer. While images on the computer screen provide the look of real life, the game controller provides the feel of real life.

And this is becoming very true with the introduction of the force feedback game controllers. *Force feedback* is a term given to how well a game controller provides the tactile feel of the real-life experience.

For example, a force feedback steering wheel gives greater resistance to turning the wheel when you are driving a tractor-trailer and less resistance when driving a car. Game software sends information to the force feedback game controller that sets an appropriate amount of resistance based on the simulation appearing on the screen.

How Game Controllers Work

A game controller consists of two types of components: switches and servomotors. A switch can take on various forms, the most common of which is a button. A signal is sent from the game controller to the motherboard when a button is pressed and when it is released. The signal is then passed to the game program, which must be programmed to react to the button.

The number of buttons on a game controller varies based on the design and technology used in the game controller. Many game controllers are designed with at least two buttons; analog game controllers are limited to four buttons. Digital game controllers can be designed with an unlimited number of buttons.

Tech Talk

Analog game controller: A game controller that sends variable values to the motherboard such as a standard joystick although some joysticks are designed to send digital values.

Digital game controller: A game controller that sends one of two values to the motherboard such as a button.

The shape of a game controller button can vary depending on the purpose of the button. Many buttons are rounded and are positioned on the base of the game controller. Others are irregular shaped and positioned in more advantageous places on the game controller, such as on a joystick beneath your first finger. This is typically used as a trigger to fire a gun.

Another common position for a button is on the top of a joystick. This is called a hat switch. This, too, enables you to quickly fire a gun with your thumb. However, some hat switches are a toggle switch with multiple positions available. This is typically used to alter the viewpoint of a game such as looking out different windows of a plane.

Joysticks, steering wheels, and foot pedals are also switches. These are called variable switches because they have a range of positions. Typically, variable switches send to the game program a value that reflects the position of the switch within the range.

Let's say a foot pedal has a range from zero to 100 with the zero value sent when no pressure is placed on the foot pedal and 100 sent when you push the pedal to the metal. The game software associates the value sent by the foot pedal with visual and sometimes sound response, such as showing the speedometer moving to a higher speed as images move quicker on the screen and the engine noise revs up.

Servomotors are used in a game controller to provide force feedback. Based on values sent to the game software by the game controller, the game software sends the game controller a signal that causes the servomotor to increase or decrease the resistance in the switch.

Tech Talk

Servomotor: A motor that can be turned an incremental speed. A nonservomotor turns at one speed.

A characteristic of a variable switch is the number of axes that are controlled by the switch. An axis is a direction such as forward and back. There are three common axes used in a game controller and they are identified by the letters x, y, and z.

The x-axis is the left and right movements. The y-axis is the forward and back movements. And the z-axis is the up and down movements. A different signal is sent to the game software for each axis. The game software then translates the signal into movement on the screen.

Although a variable switch sends the game software a value within a range, some game software works better with set values. For example, instead of the foot pedal game controller sending all the values between zero and 100, the game controller may send values in increments of 5 such as 5, 10, 15, etc. The game software then must be prepared to react to 20 possible values instead of 100 values.

A game controller that sends incremental values is called a nonproportional game controller. In contrast, a game controller that sends all values is called proportional. Some game controllers can do either by changing modes.

Engineers who design game controllers are faced with a unique challenge of creating a game controller that has all the components that meet the needs of most game software. While some game software is similar in design, such as aiming and firing a gun, each has a unique flavor.

It is this difference that causes problems for game controller designers and for guys like me who enjoy playing computer games. In a perfect world, each computer game would have its own game controller.

However, we don't live in a perfect world, so game players need to find the best game controller for each game they play. For example, a force feedback steering wheel and foot pedals are a must for playing any driving game because other game controllers such as a joystick don't give you the tactile feeling of driving.

Likewise, there is always a problem with switch assignments. For example, a button on a game controller might fire a gun just fine, but the button is located in a disadvantaged position on the game controller.

A solution is to purchase a game controller that can be programmed and enables you to create a profile for all your game software. This is called a programmable game controller. Here's how this works. A programmable game controller comes with software that is used to associate switches on the game controller to specific functions in a game. You can also adjust the sensitivity of the variable switches using this software.

Those settings create a profile that can be stored in a file, giving you a different profile for each computer game. Simply load the proper profile before starting the game so features of the game controller are properly associated with functions in the game.

Game controllers connect to the motherboard using the game port or to the universal serial bus (USB) port. Although most computers have one game port, you can increase the number of game controllers that can be used on the game port in two ways.

First, you can use a special cable called a splitter that divides the game port into two connectors for a game controller. Some game controllers come with a splitter. Another approach is to daisy-chain game controllers by connecting one to another if there is a connector available in the game controller attached to your game port.

The Practical Side to Game Contollers

It should go without saying that the game controller that you select must compliment the game. Play the game for a while with the game controller before buying a specialized game controller such as a steering wheel and foot pedals. Otherwise you might lose interest in the game and your investment in the controller is wasted.

Consider purchasing a force feedback game controller if you enjoy playing computer games that offer a force feedback feature. Force feedback game controllers add another dimension to playing computer games.

Always purchase a programmable digital game controller. The programmable feature makes it convenient to switch among different computer games without first having to reconfigure the game controller—or the game. Digital game controllers provide a better response than an analog game controller provides.

And above all, test the game controller thoroughly at your local computer store before making the purchase. Make sure that you compare the specifications of the demo computer that is running the game at the computer store with your computer. Sometimes you'll find that your computer lacks the game port and the horsepower to run the game and the game controller.

INSIDE GRAPHICS TABLETS ....

A graphics tablet is probably the least common input device of the devices I discuss in this chapter because it is used more in design companies than in the home. A graphics tablet is similar to having an electronic pen and paper, except anything that you draw on the graphics tablet appears on the screen rather than on the tablet itself.

The graphics tablet is mapped to the screen. That is, if you place a dot in the upper left corner of the graphics tablet, the dot appears in the upper left corner of the screen. This is sometimes confusing for artists who are used to looking down at the paper when they draw instead of at a screen.

You don't use a pen with a graphics tablet. Instead you use a stylus or a puck. A stylus is an electronic pen that works in some ways similar to a mouse. The tip of the pen is like the left button on a mouse.

When the stylus is placed on the graphics tablet, the mouse cursor appears in the same position but on the screen. You draw a line on the screen by pressing and dragging the stylus on the graphics tablet similar to how you hold down the left mouse button while dragging the mouse.

With some graphics programs, you can change the width of the line on the screen by the amount of pressure used with the stylus. For example, lightly pressing the stylus against the graphics tablet creates a light line and pressing the stylus as hard as you can creates a dark line.

Circuitry is able to detect the amount of pressure used with the stylus and translates the pressure into one of a range of values that is sent to the graphics program. Of course, the graphics program must be designed to accept these values as line thickness, otherwise the width of the line will not change according to the pressure placed on the stylus.

A puck is a mouse-like device with crosshairs and several buttons and is used to digitize a printed image (see Figure 8-4). The image such as a photograph is placed on the top of the graphics tablet. The crosshairs of the puck is placed over a portion of the image, then a button on the puck is clicked, causing a dot to appear on the screen in the same position.

This process is repeated until dots on the screen form the image that appears on the graphics tablet. Dots are then connected by a graphics program to re-create the image on the screen.

The number of buttons on a puck varies depending on the amount of graphics information that can be captured by the puck. For example, some buttons are used to change the color of the dot that appears on the screen.

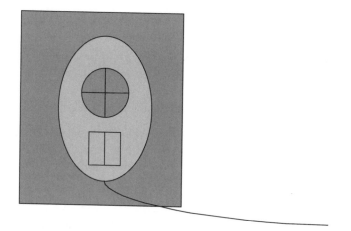

Figure 8-4
A puck is a device the size of a mouse that contains crosshairs used
to place a dot on the screen

The graphics tablet contains a grid of wires that transmits a constant signal. The stylus or the puck is a receiver. When the stylus or the puck receives the signal, the grid coordinate of the stylus or the puck is sent by the graphics tablet's circuitry to the motherboard, which is translated into a position on the screen.

Some graphics tablets use a technology that reverses this process. The stylus or the puck transmits the signal instead of the graphics tablet. The graphics tablet receives the signal, calculates the coordinate of the stylus or the puck, and forwards that information to the motherboard for processing.

The Practical Side to Graphics Tablets

Avoid purchasing a graphics tablet unless you cannot achieve the result that you are looking for using a scanner (see Chapter 10). Years ago designers used graphics tablets to digitize images so the image could be displayed on a computer. Scanners handle most of the digital imagery today.

Make sure that the graphics program you use accepts all the features provided by a graphics tablet. There is no need to purchase a feature-filled graphics tablet if your graphics program doesn't take advantage of those features.

Consider purchasing a graphics tablet that uses a cordless stylus if you intend to create freehand drawings. Otherwise you might find that the cable that connects the stylus to the graphics tablet limits movement.

Use a puck with a graphics tablet if most of your work involves plotting points on an image, because a puck doesn't lend itself to creating freehand drawings.

INSIDE SPEECH RECOGNITION ....

Speech recognition is one of the all-time paradoxes of computers because telling a computer what you want done is the easiest way to input information. And yet the technology required for the computer to understand what you are saying is the most challenging because computers lack the intelligence of a newborn baby.

A computer must be able to listen, then convert sound into zeros and ones and recognize the sequence of zeros and ones as a word. Next the computer must join words into a sentence and compare the sentence to recent sentences that were spoken to determine the context in which we are speaking.

And I probably left out one of the most important factors. The computer must distinguish between the sound of our voice and all the sound around us. Considering all these variables, it is amazing how computers are able to recognize what we are saying.

The initial approach to speech recognition was to associate a sound with a word or a series of words. The sound used in speech is called a phoneme, which we associate with one or more letters of the alphabet.

However, some words sound identical but have different meanings such as *to*, *two*, and *too*. Therefore, early attempts at speech recognition failed. The computer cannot simply associate sound with a word. Instead, the computer needs to analyze what has been previously said, then determine the correct word to associate with the sound.

How Speech Recognition Works

Computers don't have ears, so they can't hear anything we say unless we attach a microphone to the computer. A microphone detects vibrations and translates them into electrical waves.

Nerves around our vocal cords stimulate them to vibrate at various frequencies to produce sound waves. When we learn to understand and speak a language, we are associating sound with words and concepts. Our minds are able to send the right signal to our vocal cords to reproduce the sound that we recognize as words.

A cardboardlike element inside the microphone is connected to an electromagnet and circuitry. Electricity flows through the circuitry and beneath the electromagnet. The element in the microphone is set into motion by sound waves that push against the element with the same frequency of the device that produced the sound, which in this example are our vocal cords.

The element causes the electromagnet to fluctuate the electricity flowing in the circuit at the same rate as the fluctuation of the sound waves. This converts sound waves to an analog wave of electricity.

An analog wave contains a range of values depending on the words that we speak in this example. Computers store one of two digital values—zero or one. An analog-to-digital converter circuit board is used to translate analog values to digital values.

Once the conversion is completed, the computer must run speech recognition software that relates the digital values to words and expressions common to our language.

Speech recognition software uses two technologies to understand what we are saying: interrupted speech and natural speaking. Interrupted speech technology requires that you pause between every word spoken into the microphone. Natural speech technology does not require a pause between words.

Interrupted speech technology is older and uses the pause between words as a delimiter. That is, the pause tells the software where a word begins and ends. Digitized sound between the pauses is then matched against known words in the software's database of sound and words.

However, we don't speak using interrupted speech. Therefore, the novelty of using interrupted speech technology soon loses its shine after dictating a typical document into the computer. Natural speech technology does not have this limitation.

Software that uses natural speech technology is able to process our words at the same speed as we speak them because the software anticipates what we will say by using contextual clues in what we have already said.

Let's say that you said into the microphone, "Two cars are parked on the street. One of them is blue." The speech recognition software has a problem with both sentences. The first sentence has the word *two*. When you say this word into the microphone, you could mean *two*, *to*, or *too*.

The software analyzes other words in the sentence and realized you said *cars*, which is plural, and infers that the word "*two*" is the word you said. The other words *to* and *too* are grammatically incorrect if used in that sentence.

Likewise, the word *one* in the second sentence is a problem. Do did you say *one* or *won*? The answer lies with an analysis of other words in the sentence and the previous sentence. "Won of them is blue" is grammatically incorrect, so you probably didn't say *won*. Also, the previous sentence referred to two cars, so the next sentence probably is saying something about one of those cars.

The degree of complexity of using natural speaking technology is astronomical, which is why speech recognition software isn't perfected yet. The best speech recognition on the market has a 97 percent accuracy rate, which isn't bad when you consider the alternative of using the keyboard to type sentences into the computer.

Speech recognition software requires you to read a standard set of words and sentences, which is used to create a profile of your voice and the way you pronounce words. The profile is referenced when the software interprets what you say into the microphone.

Natural speaking technology has drawbacks, the most important of which is that it can only interpret one speaker at a time. This means the software cannot take down minutes of your meetings.

However, the software does accept multiple profiles so that more than one person can use the software, although not at the same time. Before speaking into the microphone you must be sure that your profile is the active profile.

The Practical Side to Speech Recognition

Speech recognition software is resource intensive. That is, you need plenty of RAM, hard disk space, and pure horsepower to run the software effectively. Read the minimum computer specifications before purchasing speech recognition software. Don't make the purchase if your computer falls below the minimum requirements because you'll be disappointed in the performance of the software.

I strongly recommend that you beef up your computer close to the ideal system specified by the manufacturer of speech recognition software rather than meeting the minimum requirements. I've heard many complaints from people who felt that speech recognition software didn't perform as well as was advertised. The reason for such poor performance had nothing to do with the manufacturer, but had to do with the fact that the system didn't meet the manufacturer's standards.

Take time to train the software. Reading standard text into the microphone is boring but necessary to reduce errors when you dictate a document into the microphone. Consider upgrading the microphone that comes with the speech recognition software. Some of my friends decreased the number of errors by buying a better microphone.

Speak clearly into the microphone whenever you speak and avoid breaking your speech pattern with "ahs" and other meaningless sounds. Especially be alert to misunderstandings if you use speech recognition software to give commands to your computer. Many speech recognition software can be placed in confirm mode, where the command is displayed on the screen and requires you to confirm that your command was interpreted correctly.

Realize that speech recognition software is not perfect and will definitely make errors. Some errors are highlighted in the document and others you must find yourself. ViaVoice by IBM and NaturalSpeaking by Dragon System are two of the popular natural speaking software on the market.

SUMMARY ....

There are various devices used to input information into your computer. These devices are generally called input devices and include keyboards, mouse, game controllers, graphics tablets, and speech recognition devices.

In 1860, Chris Sholes developed the typewriter keyboard that is used with today's computer keyboards. Keys are arranged on the keyboard so that the most frequently used keys are away from each other. This has little relevance today, but prevented typewriters from jamming.

A keyboard is a set of switches. The more common are mechanical, membrane, and capacity switches. The keyboard communicates your keystrokes two ways. First, the keyboard tells the operating system the key or keys that you selected. The keyboard also tells you that you successfully pressed the key.

The keyboard is a small computer that runs a program to monitor all the keys and transmits a specific signal when one or several keys are pressed and/or released. Each key on the keyboard coincides with a position on a wired matrix inside the keyboard. Each matrix point has a unique key scan code.

The interrupt service routine interprets the key scan code into the equivalent ASCII value, then stores the ASCII value into main memory and erases the key scan code from the keyboard buffer.

A mouse and its relative, the trackball, tell the OS to add or subtract rows or columns from the mouse cursor's current position. Let's say the operating system places the mouse cursor in the upper left corner of the screen. We'll call the coordinate row 1, column 1.

As you move the mouse, the mouse ball rotates rollers inside the mouse that signal the OS to move the mouse cursor a proportional distance on the screen. There are two other pointing devices that move the mouse cursor. These are the TrackPoint, which is a pointing stick, and a GlidePoint control commonly called a touch pad.

A game controller is an input device that is used to give direction to a computer game. Game controllers come in all shapes and sizes, from a simple joystick to a full-blown steering wheel and foot pedals.

Some game controllers use force feedback technology where servomotors provide tactile resistance to the game controller based on conditions in the game. For example, you can feel the runway in a joystick during take-off.

A graphics tablet is like having an electronic paper and pencil because images drawn on the graphics tablet are displayed on the screen. A stylus or a puck is used to draw the image. A stylus is like a pen in that the harder you press down, the wider the line appears on the screen.

A puck is similar in style to a mouse except the center of the puck contains crosshairs. Crosshairs are positioned over a portion of an image that you want to digitize. Clicking a button on the puck causes a dot to appear on the screen in proportionally the same location as the crosshairs on the graphics tablet. Graphics software is able to connect the dots and reproduce the image on the screen.

A speech recognition device is capable of translating the spoken word into text on the screen or a command that can be executed by the operating system. A speech recognition device consists of a microphone and speech recognition software.

There are two commonly used speech recognition technologies: interrupted speech technology and natural speaking technology. Interrupted speech technology requires you to pause between words. Natural speaking technology lets you speak naturally into the computer.

Speech recognition technology is not perfect. Even the best devices are 97 percent accurate. This means that you must carefully review documents produced by a speech recognition device and correct errors manually.

Summary Questions

1. **How does a graphics tablet work?**

2. **Why is it important for the keyboard controller to recognize a key press and a key release?**

3. **How can you convert a right-handed mouse to a left-handed mouse?**

4. **What is the relationship between a key scan code and the ASCII code?**

5. **What is the disadvantage of using a programmable keyboard?**

6. **What is the difference between an analog game controller and a digital game controller?**

7. **What problems prevent a speech recognition device from automatically taking minutes at a meeting?**

8. **How are your words converted into information that a speech recognition device can recognize?**

9. **How does an optical mouse work?**

10. **What is the purpose of an ergonomic keyboard?**

9 Audio Devices

In this chapter...

- Inside Sound
- Inside Sound Cards
- Inside Speakers and Headphones

*"The end of a day on a computer
is marked with fanfare."*

Anonymous

Ready for a test? What is the difference between a computer and a stereo? There was a time when this question would be easily answered because a computer crunched numbers and a stereo played music. But today the differences are blurred since both play CDs.

You could answer the question by saying that a stereo has a powerful amplifier and quality speakers—but you can purchase similar equipment for a computer. You could also say that a stereo has a built-in equalizer to filter unwanted frequencies—but so does a computer.

There is very little difference between a computer and a stereo because years ago engineers realized that the market place wanted computers to become a multimedia center capable of showing movie quality videos and reproducing theater-quality sound.

The sound quality generated by a computer is almost indistinguishable from that coming from a stereo and in some cases computer sounds resemble sounds that we hear in real life. I'll explore computer-generated sounds in this chapter, where you'll learn:

- How sound is generated in a computer

- The difference in sound cards

- Two-dimensional and three-dimensional sound

- How to choose a speaker

- How to find the best headphones

- About audio files such as MPG3 and MIDI

REALITY CHECK ....

There are some great sound snippets that you can download for your computer, but I'll warn you to be careful because certain sounds could get you into hot water especially if you play them at work.

A friend of mine was a computer technician for a major Wall Street firm. One of his assignments was to double-check installations of new computers around the firm. He had a habit of showing off by loading interesting software he found on the net and running them on newly installed computers.

A top executive had stepped out to lunch while my friend examined her computer. Afterward all hell broke loose. The executive kept hearing a bird chirping somewhere in her office. The chirping was intermittent so she was unable to pinpoint the source of the sound.

For hours she searched her office thinking a bird had somehow flown 23 stories into one of the air ducts. She found nothing, so she ordered the maintenance staff to pull down the ceiling and check every air duct near her office looking for the bird.

You can image the uproar the chirping bird caused—and the thousands of dollars in expense to rip down the ceiling and air duct. However, the bird could not be found no matter where they searched.

Then my friend stopped by to tell the executive that her computer checked out fine when he was told of the problem. Let's simply say that my friend was more than a little embarrassed when he told her the chirping was coming from her computer.

My friend had installed a screen saver that automatically darkened the computer screen and chirped to remind everyone that the computer was still turned on. The sound generated by the computer demonstrated the realistic quality of the sound card in the computer, but this didn't go over well with the executive.

My friend was sent packing and the systems department was sent the bill for dismantling and reinstalling the ceiling and air ducts.

INSIDE SOUND ....

You probably remember from your grammar school science class that sound and light are basically the same although they appear differently. Sound and light are waves of atoms moving within a range of frequencies.

Let's use a dishpan filled with water to illustrate this point. Fill the pan with water then wait a few minutes until the surface of the water is still. Gently place the point of a long knife into the water, then move the knife up and down.

You'll notice that your movement generated a wave in the water that is proportionate to the amount of energy that you used to move the knife. If you could remove the side of the pan, you would notice that the wave has a high point and a low point.

The distance between high points in a series of waves is called the wave's length. The number of waves that occur per second is called the wave's frequency. The length of the wave plays a critical role in radio transmission.

Radio transmission uses this basic science except you don't hear or see a transmitted radio signal. The length of the wave is used to design an antenna to receive a radio signal. For more information about radio transmissions, pick up a copy of my *Essentials of RF and Wireless Communication.*

The frequency of a wave determines the characteristics of the way we experience the wave. Some waves (like sound waves) we can hear, others we can see. Waves are organized into frequency ranges based on their characteristics in the electromagnetic spectrum (see Figure 9-1).

Tech Talk

Electromagnetic spectrum: The organization of frequencies into wave characteristics.

Visible light is a characteristic of a higher frequency than sound waves and produce waves that we can see. The waves in the dishpan have an even lower frequency than sound waves, but have the same basic characteristics as sound waves.

Producing Sound

Sound is generated any time something vibrates at a frequency with the sound range of the electromagnetic spectrum. This means that your squeaky brakes produce sound similar to your vocal cords because both vibrate at a frequency that you and I can hear.

Neurological signals are transmitted from our brain over the nervous system to cause our vocal cords, which are muscles like membranes, to form a specific shape. At the same time another neurological signal is sent to our lungs to exhale, forcing air through the vocal cords causing them to vibrate the surrounding air molecules.

Air molecules vibrate in sympathetic vibration with the vocal cords. This means that the vocal cords expand and contract at a specific frequency setting air molecules vibrating in the same frequency.

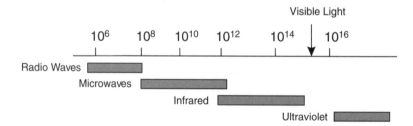

Figure 9-1

The electromagnetic spectrum organizes frequencies by wave characteristics

You've seen something like this happening with the knife in the dishpan. The knife is similar to your vocal cords and water molecules are similar to air molecules. Actually, air molecules around the knife are also placed in sympathetic vibration, but the frequency is so low that you don't see or hear it.

By tightening and loosening, the vocal cords change their shape frequencies, which are further modified by our larynx, lips, and cheeks.

Hearing Sound

Membranes in our ears vibrate at the frequency of surrounding air molecules. Those frequencies are translated into neurological signals that are transported to our brain where they are decoded into an image that we associate with those frequencies.

Each of us has developed a memory bank of images associated with sound based on our experience. Those images are actually formed by a combination of what we see and feel when we hear one or more frequencies.

Let's say that you witnessed a two-car collision. Chances are good that you heard the screeching of brakes before you saw the two cars collide. You also heard a loud bang and other noises as the metal was crunched. Afterward you probably saw passengers in the car dazed and possibly injured.

That experience associated with the frequencies that you heard during the crash is stored in your brain for future reference. The next time you hear brakes screeching, your brain anticipates the crunching of metal and dazed or injured passengers even if you don't see any cars.

It is this phenomenon that Hollywood filmmakers bank on when they enrich the soundtrack of their movies. Filmmakers know that they can conjure images of things that you've experienced by using sound combined with scenes that lead up to and follow those experiences. In this way they can save money by not filming expensive scenes.

For example, filmmakers could show a scene of a car speeding along a highway, then cut to a shot of the roadside scenery while broadcasting frequencies of brakes screeching followed by sounds of crunching metal. The next scene is two crumbled cars. You didn't see the accident, but got nearly the same feeling as if you had, thanks to the clever use of sound to misdirect you.

Loud and Soft

We recognize sound as a range of loudness that we describe as extremely loud, very loud, loud, soft, and very soft. Each of these terms is subjective, because I might think acid rock is extremely loud and you might disagree.

The loudness of sound reflects the amount of energy used to produce the sound and is measured by the height of the wave (see Figure 9-2). When you shout, you force air to move through your vocal cords within a short time period. The same frequency is produced by your vocal cords as if you moved a lower volume of air through them. Therefore the frequency of the sound is the same. However, the height of the wave is higher than if you spoke in a normal voice because you've used more energy to produce the sound.

We typically shout whenever we want the sound of our voice to travel a distance greater than the distance our voice travels in normal conversation. Actually our voice doesn't travel. Instead the force of air from our lungs is transferred to our vocal cords and then is transferred to air molecules.

This means that the height of the vibrations of our vocal cords causes the sympathetic vibrations of air molecules to have the same wave height as the frequencies produced by our vocal cords.

The membrane in our ears fluctuates a distance with each wave. The distance that the membrane fluctuates is determined by the height of the wave of surrounding air molecules. The greater the height of the wave, the wider the distance the membrane fluctuates.

The membrane in your ear can tolerate a maximum distance before sending a neurological signal to your brain indicating pain. This happens when sound is too loud for membranes in your ear to handle. If sound is extremely loud, the membrane in your ear could rupture, causing deafness. Our tolerance to loud sound varies depending on the condition of the membrane in our ear.

The amount of energy used to produce the original sound wave determines the distance sound can travel. Each air molecule is naturally resistant to being placed in motion. A portion of the energy in the sound wave must be used to set each air molecule in motion. Eventually the sound wave runs out of steam and doesn't have sufficient energy to continue. The height of the sound wave is so short that you can no longer hear the sound.

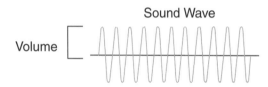

Figure 9-2
Volume is measured by the height of a sound wave

Two-Dimensional Sound

We hear sound as one-dimensional because the membrane in our ear detects one set of frequencies. The sound we hear is comprised of many frequencies that are produced by nearly everything around us. Our brain is able to differentiate important frequencies from those we can ignore.

As every parent has experienced, you can clearly hear a baby crying in a crowded room and yet you may not remember hearing the person next to you. This is because our brain is able to recognize the importance of a baby's cry compared with other sounds that we hear.

Our brain interprets sounds based on two dimensions because each ear detects sound and translates the sound into separate neurological signals that are sent to our brain. We use two-dimensional sound to determine the direction and distance of the sound.

Direction and distance of sound is influence by the delay in which the sound arrives at both ears. When someone is speaking to us on our left side, the sound of the person's voice is reaching our left ear sooner than our right ear because the person is closer to our left ear (see Figure 9-3).

The delay of the person's voice reaching our right ear is minimal, yet enough so that our brain can interpret it as a direction of the sound. Detecting the direction of sound becomes important whenever the sound is interpreted as threatening. Knowing the direction of a threat helps you prepare to react.

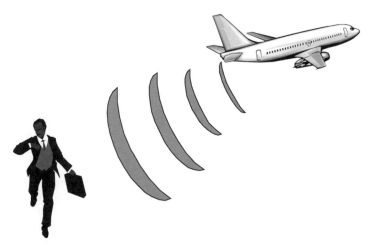

Figure 9-3
The delay in hearing a sound helps us determine the direction of the object that generated the sound

Likewise, two-dimensional sound helps us judge the distance of the source of the sound. Our brain interprets a loud sound as coming from a source close to us and a soft sound as coming from a distant source.

However, sound must come from either our left or right side for us to benefit from two-dimensional sound. We hear in one dimension if the source of the sound is above or below us or in front of us.

Feeling Sound

Our ears are the primary organ in our body that detects sound, but sound is also detected in other ways. For example, your skin can feel sound, which you probably experienced if you have ever sat near the speakers during a rock concert.

Sound is really the movement of air molecules at a specific frequency and at a specified wave height. Your skin detects pressure placed on the skin such as the pressure of a bedsheet lying on your legs.

Air molecules around your skin generate pressure. When your skin detects pressure, a neurological signal is sent to your brain, which either causes a reaction or is ignored. The normal pressure of air molecules is called atmospheric pressure and is basically ignored by your brain.

However, the pressure of a fly on your skin is interpreted as an abnormal pressure and typically causes the brain to execute a defensive reaction such as moving your arm or swatting the fly.

A sound that generates a large wave height transfers enough energy to air molecules to increase the normal pressure around the skin. This is the way you feel sound. Filmmakers, sound engineers, and musicians use this phenomenon to influence your experience seeing and listening to a film. I'm sure that you've watched a film in a movie theater and felt as if you were in the scene.

This is because the soundtrack contained many different sounds, especially those in the lower range of audible sound such as a contrabass that made every part of your body feel the sound.

Three-Dimensional Sound

Sound technology has advanced to the stage where sound has taken on a third dimension that gives us the feeling of real life. We usually are not aware that we hear the same sound coming from multiple directions, reaching us at different times.

Let's say that we hear a car driving along the street in front of our house. Various components in the car such as the engine, exhaust gases, and metal vibrate at a frequency that you can hear.

We hear the sound of the car directly from the car, which is a mixture of one-dimension and two-dimension sound. One-dimension sound is detected when the car is directly in front of us. Two-dimension sound is detected as the car approaches and leaves us. This is called the Doppler effect.

However, a third dimension is heard as sounds from the car bounce off objects outside and inside your house. Technically you still hear these sounds as one-dimensional and two-dimensional depending on whether the sound bounces directly in front of you or to your right or left. The delay in which the sound is detected by your ears gives the sound the third dimension (see Figure 9-4).

As you'll learn later in this book, engineers have designed circuits called sound cards to simulate three-dimensional sound generated by your computer. Technically, the sound card uses sound delay and other techniques to trick you into believing that you are hearing realistic sounds.

Recording Sounds Using a Computer

Waves that produce sound contain a sine wave that has continuous values from above and below zero to the height of the wave. A sine wave stores analog information. In contrast, a computer stores digital information, which you learned about throughout this book.

Figure 9-4
Sound reflected from objects around us causes a three-dimensional
sound effect

Sound waves are converted into electrical waves (see Chapter 8) using a microphone. The element in the microphone vibrates in sympathy with air molecules around the element similar to how the membrane in our ear detects sound.

The vibrating element in the microphone causes an electromagnet to fluctuate electrical current, thereby creating a wave equal in frequency and height to the sound detected by the microphone.

The wave created by a microphone is an analog wave and cannot be directly used by the computer. Instead the wave must be converted to a digital signal. The sound card is the device inside the computer that converts the analog signal to a digital signal. The digital signal is then stored to a file.

An analog sound wave has many values. These are the height of the wave and frequency of the wave, which must be converted to a series of zeros and ones. For example, the wave height ranges from zero to the height of the wave, then back down to zero. All the values between zero and the height of the wave must be converted into digital values. A sound card converts an analog sound wave to a digital sound wave by sampling the analog sound wave and representing each sample as a series of bits.

Let's say there was a large jar of jellybeans of all colors. You had to determine the number of each color jellybean in the jar. You could count each one, but you'll need a lot of space on the table to do this. A better way is to stick your hand into the jar and pull out a jellybean. This is called sampling. The more samples that you take, the closer your estimate will come to the actual count. This same principle is used when the sound card samples an analog sound wave.

Good sound reproduction by a computer begins with an audio file that contains sufficient information for the sound card and speakers to reproduce the sound. Engineers determined that a sample rate of 44,000 times per second stored as a 16-bit number provides the right amount of information that is necessary to reproduce quality sound.

When you hear a saxophone play a note, you are hearing more than one frequency played. There is a primary frequency, which is the musical note played by the instrument, and there are less noticeable frequencies called harmonics.

Tech Talk

Harmonics: Sound frequencies that give tone and color to an instrument or other sound-generating devices.

Unless you are a skilled musician, you probably don't realize that you are hearing harmonic frequencies when you hear a saxophone being played. Yet you would quickly notice the harmonics if they were missing because harmonics give a saxophone that rich sound that we enjoy hearing. Harmonics are present in all sounds we hear, not only in sound produced by musical instruments.

The quality of any sound reproduced is called fidelity. A high-fidelity recording contains more harmonics than a low-fidelity recording. A low-fidelity recording sounds tinny because the recording doesn't have the rich harmonic sounds heard in a real-life performance.

Engineers had to strike a balance between capturing the primary and all the harmonic frequencies in the sampling and the disk space required to store the sampled data. The higher the sampling rate, the more harmonics are recorded and the larger the disk space is used to store the information.

The 44,000 sampling rate records sufficient harmonics to reproduce high-fidelity sound, yet the sampling rate does not capture the entire range of harmonics of the sound. Harmonics at the higher frequencies are less likely to be heard and therefore are not captured.

Reproducing Sounds from a Computer

No recording system has been invented that records the primary frequency and all harmonics of every sound you hear in real life. Some frequencies are always lost when sound is recorded.

Engineers use technology to enhance a recorded sound and to minimize the impact of imperfect recordings. Dolby/AC3 is one of the more commonly used technologies for this purpose. Dolby/AC3 requires six speakers to play back the sound.

There are speakers for the left, right, and center of the listening area. Two speakers are placed behind the listening area for surround sound and another speaker called a subwoofer is placed in the front of the listening area (see Figure 9-5). A subwoofer generates low-frequency sounds such as the rumbling of a jet engine in a flight simulation game.

Figure 9-5
Speakers are placed strategically around the listening area to give the experience of live sound

Another version of Dolby is called Prologic, which reproduces sound with four speakers using a similar arrangement as Dolby/AC3, but without the center speaker and subwoofer. Dolby Prologic is just one of many technologies that try to give you a fidelity-rich audio experience with less than the ideal set of speakers. Other technologies simulate three-dimensional sound using two speakers or a headphone.

Sound is also reproduced in a computer by synthesizing sounds produced by musical instruments using the musical instrument digital interface (MIDI). The synthesized process begins with the sound card producing a pure frequency, which is a sound without harmonics. Next, the sound card synthesizes the harmonics based on the instrument selected by the program that is using the synthesized sound.

However a synthesized instrument lacks the high fidelity found when someone plays the same instrument in a live performance because the synthesizer is unable to reproduce all the harmonics that you hear in a live performance.

Dedicated computers that are used to professionally synthesize instruments such as keyboards played by your favorite rock group use a sampling technique of real instruments to reproduce sound.

For example, one or more saxophones are sampled then stored on a computer chip. Those samples are used and modified to reproduce the instrument rather than to create the sound electronically from a pure tone. See "More About MIDI" later in this chapter.

INSIDE SOUND CARDS

A sound card is the circuitry inside your computer that generates sound. Sometimes this circuitry is contained on an expansion card, which is why the sound card is called a card. Other times, such as with laptop computers, sound card circuits are imbedded into the motherboard.

Sound cards generate two types of sound: waveform audio and MIDI audio. Waveform audio is the reproduction of sound recorded using sampling and stored in a file. MIDI audio is the synthesized sounds generated by a sound card without any pre-recording of the sound.

In waveform audio, the sound card reads digital information that describes the sound and translates that information into an analog signal that is encoded into electrical current and sent to speakers or a headphone. Speakers or a headphone uses an electromagnet to vibrate a cardboard-like membrane similar to the membrane used in a microphone (see "Recording Sounds Using a Computer"). The membrane vibrates surrounding air molecules, which in turn vibrate air molecules around the membrane in our ears.

A sound card must be able to read the popular waveform audio format, otherwise the sound card limits the type of waveform audio files that you can use with your computer. There are five commonly used waveform audio file formats: audio format, audio interchange file, MPEG (acronym for Moving Pictures Experts Group), RealAudio, and Windows audio.

The difference among waveform audio file formats is with compression. Compression is the technique of reducing the size of digital information by removing repeating information. Let's say that I had 30 zeros in the uncompressed file. I could write the number 30 and one zero to imply that when I read the file I should assume there are 30 zeros. Of course compression techniques are more complicated than this although they follow the same basic concept.

Some waveform audio file formats use compression and others do not because compression can lose information and influence the fidelity of the reproduced sound. Waveform audio file formats that use compression employ various compression ratios.

A compression ratio is the ratio of bits from the uncompressed file to the compressed file. Generally, the higher the ratio, the lower the fidelity of reproduced sound. Some waveform audio file formats such as MPEG enable the person who is making the recording to decide which compression ratio to use from a set of options.

Table 9-1   Waveform audio file formats and file extensions

Waveform audio format	Waveform audio file extension
Audio Format	AU
Audio Interchange Format	AIF
MPEG	MP3
RealAudio	RA
Windows Audio	WAV

Sound Channels

Sound cards are used to record and play back sounds. An important characteristic of a sound card is the number of channels used to record sound. Generally, the more channels used, the more realistic the sound.

The music you listen to from a CD is recorded in a professional recording studio where many channels are used to record the music. Each instrument and each singer is assigned a channel. This enables the sound engineer to adjust the sound coming from each instrument or singer similar to how you use an equalizer when listening to a CD.

A recording studio that uses one channel lumps all the sound together. Not only can't the sound engineer adjust sound coming from each instrument or singer, but the recording can only be played back in monaural sound. This means there isn't a way to separate the sound so that lower-range instruments come from one speaker and the other instruments and singers come from the other speaker.

Nearly all recordings are made with multiple channels, sometimes called tracks, and are played back using two channels, which we called stereo sound (see Figure 9-6). This allows separation of sound during playback by sending some channels to one speaker and the remaining channels to the other speaker.

As you learned previously in this chapter, computers are capable of generating more realistic sounds than is reproduced using stereo sound. Realistic sound reproduction depends mainly on two factors.

The original sound must be recorded on multiple channels and the sound must be played back on multiple channels using several speakers strategically positioned around the listening area.

Therefore, you'll require a sound card that has multiple channels to record and play back sound. Nearly all sound cards have at least two channels. Some have up to five channels, which is necessary to take advantage of games that have realistic sound.

Digital Sampling

Sound cards are used for recording as well as for playing back sound. The quality of the recording made by a sound card is dependent on three factors: sampling method, sampling rate, and sampling size.

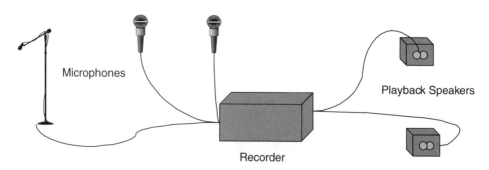

Figure 9-6
Recordings are made using multiple channels and played back in at least two channels

Sampling method is the method used by the sound card to sample the audio signal and convert the audio signal to digital information. There are three common sampling methods. These are adaptive delta pulse code modulation, linear encoding, and pulse code modulation.

Many sound professionals belief the linear encoding method is the best because each sampled valued is digitized and stored in the file. This results in large files. Other methods use various techniques to reduce the amount of information that must be stored in the file, thereby reducing the size of the file.

The sample size is the amount of information that is stored in each sample. The higher the sample size, the better the quality of the recording and the larger the file size. Sample size is measured in bits. The CD audio standard used to record CD music is 16 bits. This means if you want CD audio quality—both recording and playback—you'll need a sound card that supports a 16-bit sample size.

As I mentioned previously in this chapter, the sampling rate is the number of times per second that the sound card captures the audio signal. The higher the sampling rate, the better the quality of the sound recording and the larger the file. The highest sampling rate is the digital audio tape (DAT) standard, which is 48,000 times per second and is sometimes noted as 48,000 Hz. Hz is the abbreviation for the measurement hertz. One Hz is one cycle per second—one sample is taken per cycle.

More About MIDI

A sound card contains one or more chips that synthesize the sound of musical instruments and nonmusical sounds such as someone speaking or talking. This is strikingly different from waveform audio that records and plays back sound. Waveform audio can reproduce musical instruments and vocal sounds as long as those sounds are recorded.

The sound card contains instructions, called a standard, embedded in chips to synthesize sound by embellishing a pure frequency with harmonic frequencies produced by the real musical instrument or sound.

MIDI standards define the number of instruments that can be played simultaneously, the method used to organize a MIDI file, and the protocol used to connect the sound card to MIDI devices such as electronic keyboards.

There are three MIDI standards: general, basic, and extended. The general MIDI standard is the original standard developed in the 1980s and has 16 channels, each used to play back 16 of 128 possible instruments. Basic MIDI and extended MIDI are enhanced versions of the general MIDI standard and can offer more than 256 channels.

A MIDI file contains instructions that tell the sound card which instruments are playing what note for a specific duration and at a specific volume. In contrast, a waveform audio file contains the actual performance of an instrument. The MIDI file is like sheet music and describes how the music is to be played.

The quality of sound from a MIDI file is dependent on the MIDI standard used by the sound card and the method the sound card used to generate the sound. There are three methods used to generate sound: FM synthesis, wave-table synthesis, and wave-guide synthesis.

FM synthesis requires the sound card to produce a pure tone then add harmonic frequencies to create the sound of a real instrument. FM synthesis does not contain all the harmonics found in every instrument. Instead enough harmonics are used to create a plausible resemblance to the real instrument.

The wave table synthesis method greatly improved the quality of the MIDI sound generated by a sound card by incorporating actual samples of instruments. Each sample contains the primary frequency and harmonic frequencies of each instrument playing 12 notes. The sound card then synthetically changes each note to reflect the octave required by the MIDI file. Wave table synthesis produces a more realistic sounding instrument than FM synthesis because harmonic frequencies missing from the FM synthesis sound is present in the wave table synthesis sound.

Wave-guide synthesis improves upon the wave table synthesis method by creating a virtual musical instrument. A virtual musical instrument is a musical instrument that sounds like it is a real instrument but the instrument exists only in the computer.

Instead of relying on samples of musical instruments, wave-guide synthesis uses the relationships among pure tone and harmonics of a real instrument to calculate all the frequencies necessary to reproduce the instrument synthetically.

Parts of a Sound Card

A sound card contains chips, circuits, and connectors used to receive information from a sound source, process from the sound source or a file, and send information to speakers or a headphone.

The processor on the sound card is different from the processor on the motherboard in that the sound card processor is designed to generate sound rather than process information like the motherboard processor. It is the sound card processor that synthesizes MIDI instruments.

The sample rate generator is another component of a sound card. The sample rate generator is a circuit that determines when the sound card takes a sample of an analog sound wave. This is similar to the clock circuit on the motherboard that sets the pace for transporting information around components of the motherboard.

A sound card contains two converter chips. One is an analog-to-digital converter (ADC) and the other is a digital-to-analog converter (DAC). The ADC is used when sampling sound from an external source such as a microphone. The DAC is used when taking digital sound files and sending the signal to speakers or a headphone.

Connectors on the sound card are places where you plug in other devices such as speakers, a microphone, and a headphone. There are four connectors that are common to many sound cards: line-in, mic, line-out, and game port.

The line-in connection is used to connect external sound sources such as a CD player, VCR, and similar devices to the sound card. This enables you to copy sound from other sources and store them on your computer, with programs that enable you to add your own sounds to actions occurring in the program. For example, you can assign your own sound to events that occur in Windows, such as closing windows.

The mic connection is similar to the line-in connection in that you connect external sound-producing devices to the sound card, except the mic connection is reserved for a microphone. This means you can plug a microphone into the sound card and record your voice.

The line-out connection is used to send an analog signal from the sound card to external devices that do something with the signal. A speaker is plugged into the sound card using the line-out and is external recording equipment such as a tape recorder.

The analog signal that is sent out of the line-out connector is a relatively weak signal, which is strong enough to be used directly in headphones but too weak to be used in most other devices.

External devices that receive the signal usually use amplifiers that increase the strength of the signal before using it. For example, most computers have two speakers. One speaker connects to the sound card and to the other speaker. The speaker that connects to the sound card contains an amplifier.

The game port connection is used to connect to the sound card game controllers (see Chapter 8) and MIDI devices such as an electronic keyboard. A special adapter is used to connect a MIDI device to the game port. The adapter splits the game port connection into two segments.

One segment is called MIDI-in and the other MIDI-out. The MIDI-in segment is used to receive MIDI instructions from a MIDI instrument such as an electronic keyboard. This enables the sound card to capture a performance played using a MIDI instrument.

MIDI-out is used to send MIDI instructions to a MIDI instrument. Typically a MIDI instrument is a specialized computer that has its own sound processor and can interpret instructions in a MIDI file to generate the sound of musical instruments.

Some sound cards also contain other kinds of connections, such as for a subwoofer speaker and a line-out connection that delivers an amplified signal.

The Practical Side to Sound Cards

After reading about sound cards you probably realize that a quality sound card is important to have a good experience with your computer especially if you use the computer to play games. The MIDI feature of a sound card produces background music and other sounds that make a computer game enjoyable to play.

Here's what I tell my friends when they ask me which sound card they should buy. First, determine the features of a sound card that you'll need. If you play computer games, then look for a sound card that can produce three-dimensional sound and a sound card that is polyphony. Polyphony means that the sound card can generate multiple MIDI sounds at the same time. Most if not all sound cards have MIDI capability.

If you are going to record sound, then get a sound card that has a sampling rate of at least 44,000 samples per second. This gives you CD-quality sound recording. Keep in mind that the objective of a sound card is to reproduce sound close to the original performance. The sound card itself doesn't enhance the performance. Don't expect the sound card to make a bad sound better sounding.

Look for a sound card that has duplex mode. Duplex mode lets you record and play sound at the same time. Avoid sound cards that are half-duplex mode because you'll be able to either record or play sound but not both simultaneously.

Buy a sound card with a high signal-to-noise ratio (S/N). The sound that you hear is comprised of multiple frequencies. Although a sound card records those frequencies, unwanted frequencies are also recorded. These unwanted frequencies are called noise that you and I recognize as a hissing sound. Noise also is created when the sound card sends a signal to speakers and other devices.

Circuitry in a sound card attempts to minimize noise, and how well a sound card succeeds in minimizing noise is measured by the S/N, which is measured in decibels (dB). This tells you the amount of sound compared with noise that exists in a signal generated by the sound card. An S/N of 95 is acceptable. The higher the noise ratio, the better quality sound is generated by the sound card.

The last factor I tell my friends to consider is a sound card's frequency response. All sound cards record and produce sound within the frequency range that we can hear, which is 20 Hz to 20 kHz. However, the degree of accuracy is measured as a flat rate in decibels. The lower the flat rate, the better quality sound is produced by the sound card. One decibel is characteristic of a top-quality sound card.

INSIDE SPEAKERS AND HEADPHONES ....

A sound card doesn't reproduce sound although many sound card manufacturers make such claim. A sound card generates a signal that represents sound. Speakers and headphones actually reproduce the sound that you and I hear.

A speaker uses the sample technology as is used in a microphone to translate an electrical signal that is encoded with sound information into frequencies that can be detected by our ears.

The speaker contains a cardboardlike membrane that vibrates in sympathy with the movement of an electromagnet. When current flows to the electromagnet from the sound card, the electromagnet moves, causing the membrane to move. The electromagnet returns to its original position when current stops flowing and moves the membrane back to its original position.

The speed at which the electromagnet moves is determined by the frequency sent by the sound card, because the movement of the electromagnet is synchronized by the frequency carried by the signal. This is the same frequency that was generated by the original sound. The electromagnet and the membrane reproduce the frequency of the original sound.

There are three important factors of a speaker that determine how well we'll be able to hear sound: the size of the speaker, the number of speakers, and the power used to vibrate the membrane in the speaker.

Although a speaker receives the full range of frequencies that you and I can hear, the speaker may not be able to reproduce those frequencies because of the size of the membrane in it.

A small speaker has enough membrane area and power to reproduce frequencies in the higher audible range but not the lower range. Larger speakers with more membrane area are required to reproduce low frequencies.

Each frequency can reproduce sound within a specific frequency range, which is called the speaker's frequency response. Speakers are typically sold as a set rather than individually. This means that the entire set of speakers reproduces sound in the complete audible range of frequencies, which is 20 Hz to 20 kHz.

The quality of a speaker is measured by how well it reproduces the complete characteristic of the sound wave. This is called the flat rate, which is similar to the flat rate of a sound card.

The flat rate is quoted in decibels. The lower the decibel's value, the better reproduction of the sound by the speaker. Top-quality speakers have a 1-dB rating with the average computer speaker having a 3-dB rating.

The best sound reproduction is produced by a set of speakers that contain five speakers. These typically have two small speakers in front of the listening area, one subwoofer on the floor to reproduce low frequencies, and two other speakers behind the listening area for three-dimensional sound reproduction.

The amplifier connected to the set of speakers determines the amount of power that is used to reproduce the sound. Power is measured in watts. There are several power measurements that appear in advertisements for speakers. The one that is important is called the root mean square (RMS), which tells you the amount of power that is continually delivered to the speaker by the amplifier.

Generally, the higher the wattage rating of a speaker, the better the speaker can respond to quick changes to higher and lower frequencies and the stronger the sound is heard in the very high and very low frequency ranges.

Five watts is fine for a speaker system that does not include a subwoofer. Subwoofers require 40 watts to reproduce the best-quality low frequencies.

The Practical Side to Speakers and Headphones

Always buy a set of speakers that complement your sound card. Remember that the sound card and speakers work as a team. If you bought a sound card that reproduces three-dimensional sound, then you'll need more than two speakers to hear the third dimension.

Most speakers that come with your computer are adequate for all but the most sound-oriented games and musical CDs. Whenever my friends want to buy the latest speakers for their computer, I asked them why. If their reason is to listen to CDs, then I suggest they simply purchase a home stereo system. It'll be cheaper in the longer run than trying to make a computer a home stereo system.

Headphones are a good alternative to high-price speakers for your computer because headphones give you good quality sound without the expense of amplifiers and speakers. Headphones don't require amplification.

SUMMARY ....

You and I think of sound as the screeching of brakes right before a clash of metal. Yet sound is vibration of air molecules within a specific frequency range, which is 20 Hz to 20 kHz. Air molecules are set in motion by other things vibrating such as a musical instrument, metal, or our vocal cords. This is called sympathetic vibration.

Vibrating air molecules around the membrane in our ear cause the membrane to vibrate and send a signal to our brain that is interpreted as a specific sound. Associating a particular sound with other simulation such as seeing and feeling enables us to understand the implication of a particular sound.

Sound vibrations cause a wavelike form to occur. The number of waves that occur within a minute is called the sound's frequency. The height of the wave reflects the amount of energy that is powering the wave. You and I recognize the height of a wave as the loudness of the sound.

Sound is one-dimensional since each sound generates one sound wave. However, you and I hear sound in two dimensions because we have two ears. Typically a sound wave arrives at each ear at slightly different times, which gives us a feeling of listening to a two-dimensional sound.

We actually hear sound in three dimensions because a sound wave travels in many directions in addition to directly reaching our ears. Three-dimensional sound occurs when a sound wave reflects off objects such as walls, trees, and other items around us. The reflected sound wave also reaches our ears at a fraction of a second later than two-dimensional sound reaches are ears.

Engineers have designed sound cards to reproduce two-dimensional and three-dimensional sound that gives us the feeling that we are hearing realistic sound. However, a good quality sound card must be complimented with a set of multiple speakers that separate sound similar to the way sound is separated in real life.

A five-speaker set is perfect to hear three-dimensional sound. Two speakers are placed in front of the listening area. Another speaker called a subwoofer is placed on the floor. The other two speakers are placed behind the listening area to provide a full surround-sound experience.

There are two ways in which sound is generated by a sound card. These are as a waveform file or as a MIDI file. A waveform file contains digitized sound that is recorded by a sound card using the sampling method.

The sampling method requires the sound card to capture the analog signal generated by the sound source many times per second. A top-notch sound card samples at 44,000 times per second.

Analog samples are converted to digital values by the sound card and are stored into a waveform file on a hard disk. The sound card converts the digital values back to the analog signals whenever you play a waveform file. The analog signal is then sent to the speakers.

A MIDI file contains instructions for the processor on the sound card to generate sounds such as musical instruments. The processor first generates a pure sound, then enhances the pure sound with harmonic frequencies to create the sound of an instrument.

Instructions contained in a MIDI file simply tell the sound card processor the musical note to play, the instrument selection, the duration of the note, and the volume. The sound card processor then generates the sound of the instrument.

Summary Questions

1. How does a sound card record sound?

2. What is the difference between two-dimensional and three-dimensional sound?

3. What is the relationship between light and sound?

4. How is the volume of sound measured?

5. How can you feel sound?

6. How does a microphone work?

7. How does a speaker work?

8. What is a harmonic frequency?

9. What is the difference between a MIDI file and a waveform file?

10. What is the purpose of each converter in a sound card?

10 Digital Cameras and Scanners

In this chapter...

- Inside Digital Cameras

- Inside Webcam

- Inside Digital Video

- Inside Scanners

Don't you become agitated if you have to wait? I hate to admit it, but I do whether I'm rushing to go home or standing in the cafeteria line at work. There's just something about waiting that irritates me. I blame it on the television remote control after a television interview I gave to NBC a few years ago.

During the preinterview telephone conference the interviewer told me I had five seconds to attract viewers. If I didn't select sensational talking points I'd lose viewers to the next station on the remote. It would be another 10 minutes before they returned, and by that time I was history.

The same can be said about digital photography. No one wants to wait to have film developed. Instead they want to snap a few dozen pictures, load them into the computer, and email the best shots to friends located at the other end of the country.

And guys like me are thankful that digital photographic technology has kept pace with my rapidly depreciating patience. Only a few years ago, Polaroid produced the only camera that provided instant gratification when taking pictures. Of course, the price of Polaroid film brought a sense of economical reality that tempered my impulsive nature.

Today there isn't film. There is just the camera—and a computer, printer, software, photographic-like printer paper and ink. Most of us have computers that came with photographic software and a printer, so stepping up to digital photography is an economical move.

However, before purchasing digital photographic equipment, which includes a scanner, you should have a good understanding of the technology. I'll give you a walk-through of:

- How digital cameras work

- The advantages and disadvantages of digital photography

- How to create your own webcam

- Choosing the best scanner for your needs

- The techniques used for streaming video on the Internet

REALITY CHECK ....

Digital photography has had a dramatic impact on the news media. Late-breaking news was always an exciting time when I was a reporter for a daily newspaper. It wasn't the news story that got the city room buzzing. It was the chance to make a few dollars on the side by winning the ticket pool. The person who came closest to guessing the time the cops gave the news photographer a speeding ticket won the pool.

A news photographer had to capture the breaking news story on film, get back into the car, and rush to the newspaper office. Time worked against him because once he arrived at the office, the film hand to be unloaded, developed, and printed before the photo editor could select the picture for the morning paper. And all this took time. Once the deadline passed, the breaking news story became history and so did the photographs.

The newspaper hired off-duty cops as photographers so they could skirt the traffic regulations a little on their way back to the office. One of our photographers was noted for flashing a sign to any cop who was trying to pull him over. The sign said he was a police office on assignment. This all happened while traveling 70 miles an hour down a highway.

Time has changed for the better. Today some news photographers use professional digital cameras and a laptop with a wireless connection. Within seconds after taking the pictures, the photograph is on the photo editor's computer screen ready to be electronically placed into the newspaper.

INSIDE DIGITAL CAMERAS ....

When your friend tells you to look at the new car driving down the street, you're not seeing the car. Instead you are seeing light waves that are reflected from the car. Light waves are similar to sound waves, which you learned about in the previous chapter, in that a light wave is an atom that is vibrating within the frequency range of visible light. The atom that vibrates is called a photon.

All the frequencies of light are contained in a ray of sunlight. As the sun's rays strike objects like the passing new car, the object absorbs some light frequencies and other light frequencies are reflected away from the object. We see the reflected light waves (see Figure 10-1).

Sunlight appears white because sunlight contains all the visible light frequencies. An object that appears black absorbs all the visible light frequencies and therefore doesn't reflect any light. This is why you and I can't see anything in a dark room. We appear to see other colors when some light frequencies are reflected by an object. The actual color we see is dependent on which light frequencies are reflected.

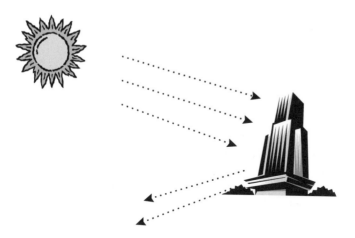

Figure 10-1
Objects absorb some or all of the light waves from white light

Reflective light is captured by the lens in our eyes and is focused on the retina. The retina, a membrane located in the back of the eye, is sensitive to light and converts light waves into neurological signals that conjure images in our brain.

A camera is very similar in that it has a lens and light-sensitive material that translates light waves into an image. The nature of the light-sensitive material and the method used to create the image is dependent on the type of camera that is being used.

A traditional camera uses acetate-based film to capture an image. Film is a sheet or roll of one or three layers of gelatin-like material that is coated with silver halide crystals, which are sensitive to light. One layer is used for black-and-white film and three layers for color film. Each layer contains dye used to give a color photograph its color (see Figure 10-2).

When light reaches the film, some silver halide crystals are exposed to light and others are not. The exposed silver halide crystals change color and remain attached to

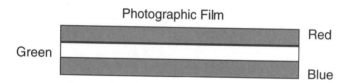

Figure 10-2
Photographic film consists of three gelatin layers each representing a primitive color

the film during processing. The unexposed silver halide crystals are washed away during processing.

A digital camera including scanners uses an electronic component instead of film as the light-sensitive material that captures an image. The component is called a charge-coupled device (CCD) and there are three CCDs used in a digital camera, one for each primitive color—red, green, and blue.

The CCDs divide the image being photographed into tiny elements called pixels, which you learned about in Chapter 4. Each pixel contains a subpel that records one of the primitive colors based on the light captured from that particular area of the image.

Tech Talk
Subpel: A portion of a pixel that contains a primitive color.

A pixel is represented by a series of bits. The number of bits used to represent a pixel determines the number of colors that can be stored by the digital camera, which is called the pixel depth. The more bits used to store a pixel, the wider the color range that can be captured by the digital camera.

F-Stop, Depth of Field, and Focal Length

No light passes through the lens of a camera until you press the shutter. The shutter opens for a time during which light in front of the lens is reflected into the camera. The longer the shutter is open, the more the CCD or film is exposed to the light waves.

Tech Talk
Shutter: A device that exposes light to the light-sensitive material in a camera.

The amount of time a shutter remains open is determined by the f-stop setting of the camera. In a room with little light, you need to adjust the f-stop to increase the length of time the shutter is open once you press the shutter button. This enables sufficient time to collect all the possible reflective light in the room. However, the camera must remain steady while the shutter is open, otherwise the image will become blurry, which you've probably experienced with a film camera.

The f-stop setting also changes the depth of field of the image. Depth of field determines how much of the image is in focus. The less light that is captured by the camera, the greater the depth of field.

A digital camera doesn't have a shutter and some digital cameras don't have f-stop settings. The purpose of a shutter is to expose the light-sensitive material to reflected light from the image.

A digital camera achieves the same effect by electronically activating each CCD for a particular time. Those digital cameras that have f-stop settings enable you to set the length of time CCDs are active.

Some digital cameras claim to have a shutter but it is used as protection for the CCD rather than exposing the CCD to light. The shutter speed of a digital camera does not affect the depth of field of the image that is being photographed.

Whether or not the foreground or background of an image is in focus when you take a picture is determined by the camera's focal length. The focal length is the distance from the center of the lens to the point where light waves from a distant object converge and is determined by the length of the camera lens. You set the focal length by turning the lens (see Figure 10-3).

However, digital cameras don't have a true focal length because regardless of how much the lens is turned, every focal length is in focus. This means that you won't be able to capture an artistic shot where the background is blurry and the foreground is sharply in focus unless you use a digital camera that has a portrait mode. Portrait mode electrically places the foreground or background out of focus.

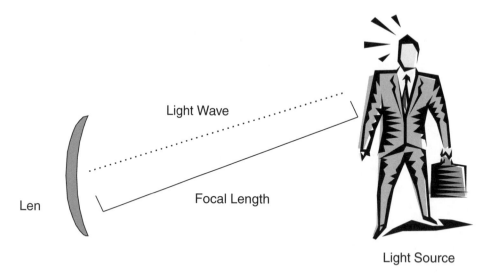

Figure 10-3
The distance from the center of the lens to the point where the source of the light wave is the focal length

Film Speed

An important factor that influences the quality of a photograph is the speed of the film used to capture an image. Film speed refers to the light necessary to properly expose the image and is measured as an International Standards Organization (ISO) number. Generally the higher the ISO number, the faster the shutter speed.

Digital cameras use gain instead of the ISO numbers for a similar purpose. Gain determines how sensitive the CDD is to light and is controlled by turning a knob, just like you use a dimmer switch to adjust the amount of light coming from a light fixture.

Increasing the gain is like using a faster film by introducing control degradation of the image. This is commonly referred to as electronic noise similar to the static sound you may hear on a poor telephone connection. You can control the amount of noise that appears in the image by adjusting the gain.

Tech Talk
Electronic noise: Degradation of an electrical signal.

Picture Resolution

The resolution of a photograph is determined by the quality of the film used to capture the image, which is the number of silver halide crystals contained in the film's coating. The resolution of a digital camera is measured in the number of pixels contained in the image and is quoted in advertisements as two numbers. These are the numbers of pixels used to display each row and column (see Figure 10-4).

A common resolution is 1280 x 1024 pixels. This means there are 1,310,720 pixels in each image taken by the digital camera. The higher the number of pixels, the higher the resolution of the photograph and the higher the price of the camera.

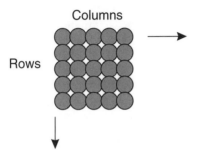

Figure 10-4
Resolution captured by a digital camera is measured in rows and columns of pixels used to re-create the original image

Resolution is one of the misunderstood areas of digital cameras. Everyone wants to take quality photographs and intuitively associates a quality photograph with a high-resolution photograph.

However, the definition of a high-resolution photograph is subjective unless we specify resolution in pixels. Most of us couldn't tell the difference in quality between a 2-mega-pixel photograph and a 3-mega-pixel photograph. Keep in mind that a 640 x 480 resolution digital picture is all you need if you want to display your photograph on the web.

The Practical Size to Digital Cameras

Is it time to toss the film camera and go digital? They answer is maybe, if you have a computer and printer and take mostly pictures of vacations and family events. I've found that the quality of the photos taken using a digital camera has the same resolution of a film camera for the average home photographer. Professional photographers will find it more economical to stay with film because of the high price of professional digital cameras.

Digital photography has challenges that you won't experience with a film camera, such as the power drain. A film camera uses battery power to advance the film and generate a flash. Digital cameras use battery power for nearly everything.

Electricity is needed to activate the three CCDs, store pixels in the camera's memory, run the autofocus lens, operate the LCD screen, and other internal components that adjust the quality of the image that is being captured. In addition, power is needed to download photographs to your computer. And to make matters worse, the CCD won't work unless the batteries are at nearly full charge.

Digital camera manufacturers advertise how long batteries will last when shooting pictures with a digital camera, but that's probably under ideal conditions. I normally halve that value and make sure that I use a digital camera that has rechargeable lithium-ion batteries. Otherwise, I'll have paid more for batteries than I would for film and developing using a traditional camera.

Now that you are aware of the power-hungry nature of digital cameras, I can tell you about other features that are important to consider. Make sure the digital camera that you buy has both a viewfinder and an LCD display.

Use the viewfinder to frame the photograph and the LCD display to review the picture. Make sure the image area is framed within the viewfinder, otherwise you'll be guessing which portion of the image is in the picture. Avoid using the LCD display as the viewfinder because the LCD display is a power-eating component that you can turn off when you're not in review mode.

Avoid buying a digital camera with a fixed focus lens because you'll be limited to the kind of photographs that you can capture. Instead, try a digital camera with both an optical and digital zoom lens. Digital zoom extends the reach of an optical zoom.

Buy a camera that has removable storage such as a memory stick, floppy disk, or a Microdrive because this saves on the cost of memory for the camera. Basically, you'll never run out of memory since you can simply insert another stick, disk, or drive into the camera and continue to shoot pictures.

Use a universal serial bus (USB) connection to download pictures from the digital camera to your computer. You'll find this is the fastest transfer method available. Avoid buying a digital camera that doesn't use a USB connection.

Digital cameras come with a variety of features that I categorize as "got to have, but never used." This is the same category that I place my surround sound for my television. The device has all the bells and whistles that you can imagine, but I never get around to using them.

Most digital cameras are used the way disposable cameras are—point and shoot. I don't know any one who shoots full-motion video. For that matter, I don't know anyone who watches home video shot with a camcorder. So my recommendation is that you find a digital camera that handles family affairs and vacations well and avoid fancy features that you won't use.

Once you've downloaded photos from your digital camera to your computer, you have to decide what you want to do with those photos. There are a number of software products on the market that enable you to create a digital photo album. However, you still need a convenient way to store the photos away from your hard disk, otherwise you'll soon run out of disk space.

Any storage device that I mention in Chapter 5 can be used to store digital photos. You could also print photos from your inkjet printer using matte or photo glossy paper. Both papers last for at least a decade before deterioration occurs. I normally store digital photos on a CD and print copies of important photos as a backup.

THE CHARGE OF THE BATTERY BRIGADE

The Achilles' heel of digital photography is power. Digital cameras eat batteries faster than a Walkman. You can't take digital photos without power and electrical cords don't stretch to every place where you want to shoot a picture. Therefore you must come up with a strategy for reducing power consumption. Here are my suggestions:

- Turn off the LCD viewfinder unless you are reviewing photos that you've taken.
- Don't turn off your camera between shots. Digital cameras go through a startup procedure similar to your computer. The startup procedure consumes power.
- Turn on the sleep mode. The sleep mode conserves power between shots.
- Set the sleep mode to maximum. The sleep mode is a timer that anticipates downtime between shots. Setting the camera to the maximum sleep mode reduces the number of times the camera "wakes up" and you're not ready to shoot.
- Avoid reviewing photos frequently. If possible, review photos only when you can plug the camera into a power outlet.
- Don't set the flash to forced-flash. Forced-flash requires the flash unit to be charged before each shot. The camera uses battery power to charge the flash. Some shots don't require a flash. Turn off the flash or set the flash to auto.
- Use the power outlet to download photos to your computer and whenever else a power outlet is available.
- Avoid placing batteries in extreme temperatures. Batteries maintain their best charge at room temperature, which is 68 degrees F.

INSIDE WEBCAM

My wife can easily check up on me when I'm on Columbia University's campus thanks to a webcam pointed directly at the commons. She simply logs on to Columbia University's web page that contains live pictures from the webcam. And if she looks carefully and I didn't get held up in traffic, she'll be able to see me walking up the stairs to my class.

Webcam technology has come a long way since the days of Quentin Stafford-Fraser's entrée into online photography. Stafford-Fraser and his colleagues at Cambridge, England, had a problem. They were big coffee drinkers and there was one coffeepot in their building. No one wanted to run down several flights of stairs only to discover the coffeepot was empty.

So Stafford-Fraser created one of the first webcams to solve the problem. He pointed a video camera toward the coffeepot and wired the camera to a computer running video-capturing software. Anyone on his or her local area network (LAN) could tap into the computer and see whether or not the pot was full or empty.

Today webcams are commonplace. Many heavily traveled intersections have webcams. You'll also find webcams at daycare centers enabling working parents to keep an eye on their child using the Internet while they are at work.

A webcam is relatively inexpensive and easy to build. All you need is a camera, a computer, webcam software, a connection to the Internet, a web site, and a web page.

You probably have a computer and are connected to the Internet. You can get your own web site for about $20 a month and many desktop office applications such as Word can be used to create a simple web site.

Here's how a webcam works. A camera such as a digital camera points to the image that you want to send over the Internet. This is like the commons area on the Columbia University campus.

The camera is connected to the computer typically using the USB connection similar to how you connect the camera to the computer to download photos. The camera is powered by a wall outlet rather than batteries because you'll quickly run the batteries dry.

Webcam software such as SpyCam runs on the computer and captures and downloads an image from the camera at regular intervals. You select the interval. The file containing the picture is transferred to the web site by the webcam software using the Internet File Transfer Protocol (FTP) utility each time a new picture arrives at the computer.

Tech Talk

FTP: Software used to copy files across the Internet.

The web page links to the picture each time someone visits or refreshes the page (see Figure 10-5). Web pages are written in Hypertext Markup Language (HTML). You don't really need to learn HTML to build a working webcam because desktop office software such as Word lets you build the page by selecting items from menus and typing the text that you want to appear on the page directly into a Word document. Word then translates the document into HTML, which you copy to the web site.

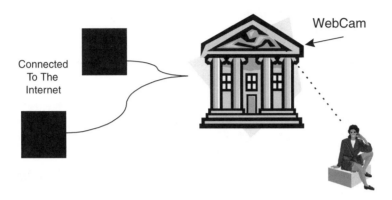

Figure 10-5
Each picture taken by a webcam is sent to a web server where
browsers all over the world can link to the picture

Some webcam software like SpyCam is available as shareware over the Internet. Shareware is downloadable free of charge. After you give the software a trial run and like it, then you send the author of the program a nominal fee, which is specified on the software. If you don't like the software, then uninstall it and you pay nothing.

You can also find on the Internet commercial webcam software that might have more bells and whistles than shareware webcam software. Visit *www.zdnet.com* and enter the word *webcam* into the search engine. At the site, you'll find a wealth of information about webcam software and you'll be able to download shareware webcam software.

INSIDE DIGITAL VIDEO ....

Nearly all digital cameras are capable of capturing a couple of minutes of digital video that can be played back using the camera or shown on the Internet. Digital video refers to the rapid recording of a series of digital photographs that when viewed in the same sequence and at the same speed tricks our brain into seeing movement.

Digital video is captured using the same basic technique that is used to capture images on film, videotape, and in animation. Images are captured on digital video a frame at a time. A frame is the same as a digital photograph. However unlike a digital photograph that is stored in a file, all the frames of a digital video are stored in the same file.

The amount of memory in the digital camera and the amount of hard disk space available on the computer used to download determine the limit of the digital video file size. A digital camera is designed to record single photographs that are not necessarily shown consecutively. Therefore, you shouldn't expect to use a digital camera to record video of your vacation or family gathering because there isn't sufficient memory to store all those frames.

Instead you can use an analog or digital video recorder. An analog video recorder stores images on a standard videocassette using the same format as videos that you rent for home viewing. A digital video recorder captures images the same way as a digital camera except those images are immediately transferred from memory to a videocassette using digital recording technology.

You can use a digital camera to record very short scenes such as a child blowing out birthday candles. Once you've captured the scene you can download the digital video to a computer, then place the file on the Internet or email the file to relatives so everyone can see.

Showing video on the Internet is not like showing your home videos on television because the video needs to be transported from the Internet web site used to store the video and copied to every computer that wants to see the video. Here's how this works.

There are two categories of Internet videos: nonstreaming and streaming. Nonstreaming videos require that the entire video file be copied to the computer that will display the video before the video is shown. This means that when someone comes to your web site and clicks on the video, the browser copies the entire video file to the computer that is running the browser.

The file transfer can be time-consuming depending on the size of the file, traffic on the Internet, and type of connection the browser has with the Internet. For example, a dial-up telephone connection to the Internet is slower than a digital subscriber line (DSL) connection. Pick up a copy of my *Essential Guide to Networking* and learn more about Internet connections.

Once the file transfer is completed, the browser runs the appropriate media player software such as QuickTime (see Figure 10-6). The media player must be able to read the video file format, otherwise the video cannot be shown.

Streaming technology, sometimes called streaming video, transfers and displays video before the entire file reaches the browser. When the user clicks on the web site's video link, the browser requests that the web site stream video to the browser.

As frames of the video arrive at the browser the frames are temporarily stored in memory called a buffer (see Figure 10-7). Simultaneously, the browser runs a media player that knows how to read and display the video file.

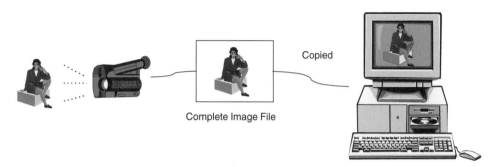

Figure 10-6
Nonstreaming video requires that the complete video file is copied
before the browser plays the video

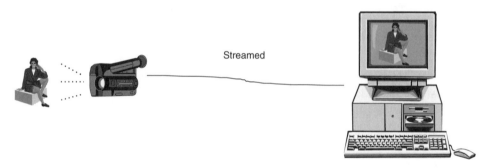

Figure 10-7
Streaming video is shown as the browser receives frames

Once the buffer is full, the media player reads frames from the buffer and displays them in the media player's window, which is like a small television. The browser and the media player work together to make sure that the buffer is always full with the next set of frames of the video.

As the frames are displayed, the browser requests more frames from the web site. Under ideal conditions, you would see an uninterrupted flow of frames displayed in the media player window, which is like watching a video at home.

However, ideal conditions rarely exist. Our brain links together frames to give us the impression of motion if those images are shown at 30 frames per second. Fewer frames result in jerky motion, which is unacceptable to most of us.

As you learned previously in this chapter, a frame of digital video consists of a fixed number of pixels. The actual number of pixels depends on the resolution used to capture the image. A typical image on the Internet has a resolution of 640 x 480, which is 307,200 pixels per frame. The higher resolution of 1280 x 1024 has 1,310,720 pixels per frame.

The number of pixels in each frame is a very important factor in streaming video—and nonstreaming video. For each second of video, the web site, the Internet, and the computer receiving the video must process 9,216,000 pixels (30 x 307,200). And that is at the lowest acceptable resolution. At the higher resolution of 1280 x 1024, 39,321,600 pixels must be processed per second.

Internet technology hasn't fully reached the processing speed required to transmit movie-quality videos over the Internet where you can see a full television-size screen movie. The viewing area of most media players is very small because of the number of pixels that must be processed in such a short time period.

Another limitation is the speed at which a typical Internet user connects to the Internet. Many times the media player has exhausted frames stored in the buffer before other frames are loaded from the web site. This means that you'd be watching the video for a couple of minutes before the media player blanks or freezes the image on the screen while the next frames are loaded into the buffer.

Video Formats

While everyone waits for the processing of the speed of the Internet to increase, engineers came up with a few ways to reduce the size of the video file, thereby increasing the number of bytes that can be transmitted over the Internet each second. Each of these methods is called a video file format, the more common of which are AVI, nonstreaming QuickTime, MPEG-1, RealMedia (RM), Windows media—streaming video (ASF), and streaming QuickTime.

AVI, nonstreaming QuickTime, and MPEG-1 are nonstreaming video formats. AVI and nonstreaming QuickTime are the granddaddies of digital video. Both formats use a data compression method to reduce the size of the video file.

However, files are still rather large because each frame is saved separately from the other frames. A 1-minute, low-resolution video running at half the acceptable frame per second rate requires about a 6 MB video file.

The advantage of AVI and nonstreaming QuickTime is that nearly all browsers, except for WebTV, can play back videos in these formats. The disadvantage is the size of the file required to store a lower resolution video.

Engineers designed MPEG-1 to overcome limitations of AVI and nonstreaming QuickTime. MPEG-1 gives you options that let you control the size of the video file and the display area of the video.

In contrast to AVI and nonstreaming QuickTime, MPEG-1 stores frames together as one image. This plus the variable compression methods help to reduce the size of a video file. For example, a minute of low-resolution video takes up about 2.3 MB of hard disk space.

There are three frame resolutions that you can choose from. These are 160 x 120, 320 x 240, and 352 x 240. MPEG-1 has the advantages of variable file sizes and videos can be viewed on WebTV. The disadvantage is that you'll need at least Windows 95 and a Pentium processor to view an MPEG-1 video file.

RM, Windows media-streaming video, and streaming QuickTime are streaming video file formats. Each of these formats requires two software components, one to serve the steaming file and the other to receive and play the file. This means the web site requires special software to distribute streaming video in either of these formats. And you need to have the proper viewer installed on your computer to watch the video.

The advantages of streaming video are its video file size, which is similar to MPEG-1, and not having to wait for the download to be completed before viewing the video. The disadvantage is the likelihood of interruptions in playing the video caused by delays in filling the buffer with new frames.

However, the disadvantage of streaming video is only realized if the video is viewed over the Internet. An alternative to this is to store the video on a CD, then stream the video from the CD to the media player on the computer. This technique works well if the viewer can wait until the CD arrives in the mail.

LEAVE BORING SHOTS ON THE CUTTING ROOM FLOOR

A 20-second video of your child blowing out birthday candles is short enough not to bore your relatives, but more lengthy events such as your child's soccer game and your vacation need to be trimmed down before being viewed by your public.

Editing your video is increasingly important if you want to transmit it over the Internet. You'll need to tell your story in the smallest possible file size. Today nearly professional-quality video editing software is available for personal computers.

Basically you download raw video to your computer, then drag and drop the clips into the sequence that you want them to appear in the final video. Expect to take a few hours of using the video editing software to get your feet wet. Once you get the knack of editing, you'll be able to dramatically reduce the size of the video file and improve the quality of the video by editing.

However, you'll need hefty horsepower in your computer before you'll be able to do any video editing. I suggest a 20 GB or larger hard disk and 128 MB or more RAM and a high-speed processor. You'll be disappointed in the performance if you use a computer with less power.

INSIDE SCANNERS ....

A scanner is similar to a digital camera in that a scanner captures images and converts them into a digital file format. And yet a scanner is different in that the focal length is fixed and you cannot adjust the f-stop as you would in a digital camera.

Here's how a scanner works. Let's say that you want to scan a photograph so you can send it to a friend. First, you place the photograph in the scanner. Some scanners are like a copy machine where you place the photograph under a lid. Others use a feeder, so you need to feed the photograph into the scanner like you do with a fax machine.

The scanner contains a light source that illuminates the photograph and reflects some light waves back to the light-sensing device where the reflected light waves, which are an analog signal, are converted to a digital signal.

The digital signal is forwarded to a file on your hard disk. You then can view the file with software such as PhotoShop, attach the file to an email, and post the file on the Internet so everyone can see your artistic work.

Two types of scanning technology are available to capture images. These are the CCD technology, which you learned about previously in this chapter. And there is contact image sensor (CIS) technology.

Both CCD and CIS perform basically the same task although in a slightly different way. CCD scanners contain a component that converts the analog light signal to a digital signal. CIS scanners use embedded logic that handles the conversion without having to use a separate component. Scanners that use CIS technology typically have a smaller footprint and cost less than CCD scanners because they do not need a converter.

Color, Optical Density, and Resolution

Three CCD or CIS devices are used to convert a color image into subpels of a pixel that represent three primitive colors red, green, and blue (RGB). As with a digital camera, the pixel depth of a scanner determines the number of colors a scanner can convert to an image file. The pixel depth is determined by the number of bits that the scanner uses to represent a pixel.

The higher the pixel depth, the more colors the scanner can capture. However, this doesn't mean that you'll see all those colors, because the device that displays the file must also have the same pixel depth.

Let's say that you used a scanner that has a pixel depth of 36 bits, which stores a decent range of colors in the file. And let's say you used a printer that has a pixel depth of 24 bits. The best quality that the printer can produce is 24 bits. This means that the printer reduced 36 bits down to 24 bits and some of the original color is lost, although most people probably couldn't tell the difference.

Simply stated, the extra money spent for a 36-bit scanner was wasted because the best quality you can get in this example is 24 bits. Typically highlights and shadows of an image are lost when a device reproduces an image of a higher pixel depth.

A scanner's optical density rating is used to measure a scanner's ability to capture a range of colors. Some people refer to this as the scanner's tonal value, which is the capability of the scanner to capture finer elements of an image.

The higher the optical density rating, the larger the range of colors that the scanner can capture. The optical density rating is very important for anyone doing professional quality imaging where it is critical that all the fine points of the image be captured.

A scanner's resolution defines how many pixels fill a square-inch area of the scanned image, and most scanners have two resolution ratings: optical resolution and interpolated resolution.

The optical resolution is the number of pixels per inch that are captured when an image is scanned. The interpolated resolution is the actual number of pixels that are stored in the image file using software to increase the optical resolution.

A high interpolated resolution value means that you can increase the size of the image beyond 100 percent without causing the image to lose detail. Here's what happens. When you scan an image at 100 percent, you have the same number of pixels in the image file as there are in the original image.

You can scan the original image to a larger size by using an option on the scanner. However, you'll have fewer pixels in the image file than there are in the original image. This means you have a larger image, but with less detail. Engineers fixed this problem by having software fill in the missing pixels by making an educated guess as to the colors of those pixels based on the surrounding pixels.

Let's say that there is an area of an image that has 4 pixels all colored blue. I enlarge the image to 200 percent, which results in the same area growing to 8 pixels. The original 4 pixels remained colored blue and the new 4 pixels are colored white (see Figure 10-8).

Software in the scanner interpolates the colors of the new 4 pixels by looking at the colors of the surrounding pixels, which are blue in this example. Therefore, the software sets the color of the new 4 pixels to blue.

The interpolated resolution identifies the highest number of pixels that can be stored in an image file when software is used to interpolate missing pixels. The interpolated resolution of a scanner is higher than a scanner's optical resolution.

However, the interpolated resolution does not give you any more information than is on the original image. Let's say that you have a picture of someone reading a newspaper and you see columns of text but can't read them. You decide to use the scanner to enlarge the photo so you can read the newspaper.

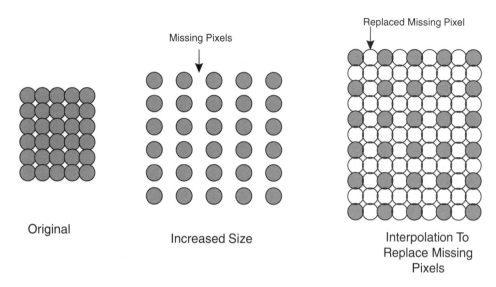

Figure 10-8
Missing pixels are replaced by using interpolation based on the existing pixels

The size of the newspaper in the scanned photo will be larger than the original image, but the enlarged image won't have the detail needed to read the newspaper. This is because the original photo lacked these details.

Scanner Options

Scanners come in various shapes and sizes, from a full flatbed scanner to a handheld, and either stripped down or with all the bells and whistles. Flatbed scanners are as long and wide as the largest size of the original image that can be scanned using the scanner. The original image remains stationary while the scanning sensors are moved down the length of the image.

There are also small footprint scanners, such as one built into the keyboard, that use a paper feed to move the image over the scanning sensors. Small footprint scanners are fine for single sheet images, but are useless if you need to scan an image from a book. A flatbed scanner is your best bet for scanning books.

Tech Talk
Footprint: The amount of space a device takes up.

You can also purchase a handheld scanner where you move the entire scanner over the image that you want to scan. There are two kinds of handheld scanners: those connected to a computer and those not connected to a computer. Instead, the scanner contains a built-in printer used to make a copy of whatever is being scanned.

Handheld scanners work well for scanning small sections of a page, but have serious drawbacks. First, the width of the scanner is typically smaller than the width of the image being scanned. This means that you have to make more than one pass, then attempt to use software to link together portions of the image to re-create the full image.

Furthermore, you must have a steady hand to move the scanner down the image. You're expected to simulate the steadiness and speed of either the scanning mechanism in a flatbed scanner or the paper feed in a small footprint scanner. If you don't, then you'll be disappointed with the quality of the scanned image—and you repeat scanning the same segment of the page over and over again until you get it correct.

A special adapter called a transparency adapter is required if you want to scan slides, photographic negatives, or transparencies. A transparency adapter alters the traditional way images are scanned. Here's how this works.

The scanner mechanism shines light on the original image at the same time the scanning sensors are activated. However, this technique doesn't work for slides, photographic negatives, or transparencies because these images must be lit before scanning sensors are activated. The transparency adapter does this.

Look for a scanner that comes with optical character recognition (OCR) software if you need to convert text from printed documents into ASCII text that you can read and modify using a word processing program.

However, be warned that OCR works well in theory, but has limited success in real life. Here's how OCR works. Once an image of text is scanned into a file, OCR software attempts to translate sequences of pixels into letters, numbers, and other characters that you find on your keyboard.

Success is dependent on the font used in the text and the quality of the OCR software. I've found that the OCR software I use is successful if the original image contains text in common fonts. I also learned that it is worth the extra dollars to purchase full-strength OCR software rather than using the limited versions that are distributed with many scanners.

Expect to experience errors in the translated text regardless of font or the version of the OCR software that you use. Translation of pixel positions into characters is still guesswork on the part of the programmers who created the OCR software. However, you'll find that those errors are easy to correct using a word processing program, especially when you consider the alternative—retyping the entire text.

You'll need an automatic document feeder if you frequently have stacks of images that must be scanned. An automatic document feeder function is similar to the automatic document feeders used on a copy machine.

The Practical Side to Scanners

You are faced with many decisions when thinking about buying a scanner: the size of the scanner, optical resolution, interpolated resolution, color depth, and options that I discussed in this chapter.

Answer these few questions before considering the purchase of a scanner. First, do you really need a scanner? Many of my friends plan to use a scanner to digitize photos of family events and vacations taken with a film camera.

I tell them not to purchase a scanner. Instead, pay a few extra dollars when the film is developed and have the developer create image files of your photos. Film developers typically use professional scanning equipment and deliver better-quality digital images for less money than you could produce using a scanner.

Consider purchasing a scanner if you plan to frequently scan images for other reasons such as for business presentations. Avoid buying a scanner for an occasional presentation because you'll find it more economical to use a service company to scan the images than doing it yourself.

The next question is, what kinds of images do you intend to scan? Look for a flatbed scanner if you need to scan bulky objects such as books. I'd stay with a flatbed scanner anyway as long as I have space near my computer to store the scanner. A sheet-feed scanner is fine if you don't have the space for a flatbed scanner and only scan images on single sheets. I don't recommend buying a handheld scanner. I've tried several and they can be frustrating to use.

Another question is, what resolution do you require? For most nonprofessional purposes, 24-bit pixel depth at 300 dots per inch (dpi) optical resolution is fine. OCR software requires a maximum of 400 dpi optical resolution. You'll need a 36-bit pixel depth and 1,200 dpi optical resolution for scanning professional-quality printed images.

Scanning slides, photographic negatives, and transparencies require 36-bit pixel depth and 2,400 dpi optical resolution. In addition, you'll require a transparency adapter. Keep in mind that scanners with a high pixel depth and optical resolution are pricy.

Balance the amount you spend for a scanner with how you plan to use the scanned image. Remember that the pixel depth and image resolution that you see is limited by the highest pixel depth and image resolution of the device that displays the image. So there is no need to spend a lot of money on a high-end scanner if you don't have an equivalent display device.

The speed of the scanner is also something to consider. Scanning speed is influenced by the amount of memory in your computer and the interface used to connect the scanner to your computer.

The more computer memory you have, the faster images can be scanned. You're probably about to ask, how much memory is enough? Here's what I do to answer this question. First, I estimate the size of the largest image that I'll scan. I do this by calculating the number of pixels contained in an image, then multiply this by the pixel depth.

Let's say the image is 1280 x 1024 pixels. I calculate the total number of pixels by multiplying these numbers to get 1,310,720 pixels. Let's say that I'm using a 24-bit pixel depth, which means I use 24 bits of memory for each pixel. I calculate the total bits of memory required to store the image by multiplying the total number of pixels by 24 to get 31,457,280 bits. And by dividing the total number of bits by 8, I determine the number of bytes needed to store the image (3,932,160 bytes). Multiply the number of bytes needed to store the largest image by 3 to determine the amount of free memory required to comfortably scan and work with the image.

There are three choices of scanner interfaces: parallel, USB, and SCSI. Avoid using a parallel interface with a scanner because this is the slowest on the market. Many older scanners are supplied with a SCSI interface, which includes an expansion card and cable. The SCSI interface is noticeably faster than a parallel interface. Newer scanners are designed to work with the USB port, which is a fast serial port found on many computers. You can install a USB port in your computer if your computer didn't come with one. USB ports are available as an expansion card.

SUMMARY ....

Nearly everything you see can be digitized using a digital camera or a scanner. Both digital cameras and scanners use similar technology to convert reflected light from an image into digital values.

A digital camera including scanners uses an electronic component instead of film as the light-sensitive material that captures an image. The component is called a charge-coupled device (CCD) and there are three CCDs used in a digital camera, one for each primitive color—red, green, and blue. The CCD divides the image into pixels.

Digital cameras function like film cameras in that both are used to capture images by exposing light-sensitive material to reflected light from the image. However, there are differences between the two.

A digital camera does not have a shutter, which is used to let reflected light into the camera. Instead, electronics within the camera are used to expose the CCD to the light for a specific amount of time.

A digital camera does not have a true focal length, which determines whether or not the foreground or background is in focus. This means that you won't be able to capture an artistic shot where the background is blurry and the foreground is sharply in focus unless you use a digital camera that has a portrait mode. Portrait mode electrically places the foreground or background out-of-focus.

A digital camera does not have a film speed, which refers to the light necessary to properly expose the image. Instead, gain control is used to set the camera to equivalent ISO film speed values.

The resolution of a digital camera is measured in rows and columns of pixels such as 1280 x 1024 pixels. Multiplying these two values tells you the number of pixels that are used to capture the original image. The more pixels that are used, the higher the resolution.

Two resolutions are used for scanners: optical and interpolated. The optical resolution is the number of pixels per inch that are captured when an image is scanned. The interpolated resolution is the actual number of pixels that are stored in the image file using software to increase the optical resolution.

The pixel depth determines the range of colors that can be captured by either a digital camera or a scanner. The higher the pixel depth, the wider the range of colors that can be stored in the image file. The pixel depth is measured in the number of bits used to store a pixel.

Resolution and pixel depth can be misleading. A digital camera and a scanner capture an image at a specific resolution and pixel depth. However, the device that displays that image must have a comparable resolution and pixel depth, otherwise you won't see the image with detail and color captured by the digital camera or scanner.

Summary Questions

1. What is the difference between the focal length used by both a film camera and a digital camera?

2. How can you minimize the battery drain on a digital camera?

3. What is the difference between digital video and photographs taken by a digital camera?

4. How is CCD technology different from CIS technology?

5. What is the difference between video streaming and nonvideo streaming?

6. Why must a transparency adapter be used to scan slides?

7. Why is OCR a viable option to capture text given OCR's limitations?

8. How does pixel depth determine the range of colors that can be captured from an image?

9. How does a camera capture an image both on film and in digital form?

10. How do you determine if you need to purchase a scanner?

11 Wireless and Mobile Devices

In this chapter...

- Inside Wireless

- Inside Cell Phones

- Inside Digital Wireless Services

- Inside Messaging

- Inside PDAs

- Inside Laptops and Notebooks

- Inside Mobile Power

"Beam me up Scotty" is a famous line from *Star Trek*. Captain Kirk made this request using a clamshell-shaped communicator. That was science fiction—or was it? There has yet to be anyone who has been transported on light waves, but many of us use a clamshell-shaped communicator every day. We call it a cell phone.

Wireless and mobile technology is taking the word *fiction* out of the expression science fiction. And we're just on the ground floor of this technology. We can speak with anyone, anywhere, and at anytime today.

Tomorrow promises that we'll be able to read any book, shop in any store, check up on our kids and our house, pay our bills, and do everything we do today using wireless mobile communication devices.

You've probably seen a glimpse of tomorrow in television commercials where travelers are buying or selling stock and rescheduling airline flights from their mobile device. How much of what you see is fact? You'll find out after reading this chapter, where you learn about:

- How wireless technology works

- PDAs

- Pagerlike messaging systems

- How cell phones work

- Laptop, notebook, and subnotebook computers

REALITY CHECK ....

There is a 60 percent decline in business travel according to a report by CNBC, although I'm more than a bit skeptical considering the crowds that jam into every airplane I get on. The reason for the decline is technology.

Today you don't have to be in the office to work. You can be practically anywhere including on the beach and be able to conduct business better than you could in a traditional office. For example, you might take a dip in the ocean between meetings—a much better situation than sitting in the office.

The publishing industry is a good illustration of how mobile we can be and yet still get our work accomplished. A friend of mind is responsible for building alliances among publishers and others in the communications business.

To this day very few people know where he physically works—and no one really cares. Anyone who needs his assistance either calls or emails. Calls are directed to his cell phone and roll over to voice mail in case he's not available. Emails are retrieved using a laptop that is sometimes connected to the email server through a traditional telephone line and other times linked using a wireless connection.

His office is where he is at the time a call or an email is received. You might think that this mobility is expensive for the company. Not necessarily, when you compare the cost of a good wireless connection with expenses for a traditional office facility.

There is a downside to becoming a mobile worker. You miss the opportunity to hear the office gossip at lunch.

INSIDE WIRELESS ....

The telegraph and telephone networks opened a new world of communications that enable communities and the nation's economy to grow beyond the distance they could see and the distance their voice could travel.

Yet there was still one major hurdle that hindered free flow of communication—a cable. A cable is the electronic pipeline that delivers words across vast lands. Telegraph sets, then later telephone sets, that were connected to the cable could tap into the words transmitted over the network. But without a cable there wouldn't be long-distance communications.

Economics played a crucial role in the expansion of the communications network. Telegraph and telephone companies were willing to lay cable in a community only if the firms economically benefited from the installation. That is, a community needed to be a center for business before any thought was given to bringing the network to a community.

Communities distant from commerce were left without access to the network and therefore without modern means of communication. Likewise, communities surrounded by natural barriers such as rivers and oceans that inhibited the installation cable also couldn't take advantage of the new media.

Those barriers were overcome with a new technology called radio developed by Guglielmo Marconi. Radio was able to transmit and receive sound without using a cable. It seemed miraculous at the time—and even today. Stop and think. Sound created from a far-off land is received by a radio in your home without any cable connection. I still find this amazing.

Radio isn't a miracle but is based on science and the wave phenomenon seen in telephone technology. Before trying to understand how radio is able to transmit and receive information over the air, you need to closely explore the wave phenomenon.

Waves are measured in height called the amplitude and the number of waves per second called the wave's frequency. Waves are also categorized by frequency in the electromagnetic spectrum.

Waves within each spectrum have similar characteristics. Sound waves can be heard over short distances that are not obstructed by solid objects. Radio waves cannot be heard but can be transmitted over longer distances and are not normally affected by solid objects such as a wall.

Marconi's challenge was fourfold: capture sound, encode the sound on radio waves, broadcast the radio waves over long distances, then translate the radio waves back to sound. If this could be accomplished, then no longer would communication be limited to the length of a cable.

The technology for converting sound to an electrical signal and an electrical signal back to sound was known and used in the telephone system. A microphone translates sound to electricity and a speaker translates electricity to sound. However, the frequency to transmit the signal over a cable wasn't in the radio spectrum. This meant the signal couldn't be transmitted over the air.

Radio transmission requires a signal be generated at a specific frequency within the radio spectrum and transmitted over the air to a radio receiver tuned to the same frequency. Marconi had to find a way to vibrate an object at a radio frequency. The solution was found in nature in the form of a crystal.

Tech Talk

Crystal: A chemical formation of molecules into a distinct pattern. Salt is a crystal that we come in contact with every day. When certain crystals are charged with electricity, the crystal vibrates at a consistent frequency and some crystals vibrate within the radio spectrum.

Air molecules around the crystal vibrate sympathetically similar to how our vocal cords vibrate the air. And similar to our voice, the distance over which the signal can travel is dependent on the energy used to generate the signal.

Our lungs provide the energy to our voice. The more air that is forced through our vocal cords, the further our voice travels. Electricity provides the power for radio waves. Therefore, the more electrical power used to cause the crystal to vibrate, the further the signal will travel through the air.

Radio transmission also requires an invisible cable over which information can travel. The invisible cable is called a carrier signal, which is the frequency generated by the crystal.

Tech Talk
Carrier signal: A radio signal that is transmitted at a consistent frequency used to establish a connection with a radio receiver.

Sound is transmitted over the carrier signal by circuitry that changes a characteristic of the carrier signal. This concept is difficult to appreciate, but imagine a still pond of water. There are no waves. You vibrate a stick in the water at a consistent frequency and you'll notice a steady frequency of waves in the water to correlate to the movement of the stick. This is similar to a carrier wave (see Figure 11-1).

A person at the other end of the pond notices the consistency of the waves. The height and frequency of the wave remain unchanged. Let's place information on the wave. Both of you agree that everything is fine with you as long as the height of the wave remains the same. However, help is required if the wave height increases. You can increase the height of the wave and still maintain the wave's frequency by using more power when vibrating the stick. The same number of waves per second occurs, but each wave is taller than the original.

The same basic concept used in the pond example occurs with radio transmission. Both the transmitter and the receiver are set to a specific frequency. The transmitter opens the communication channel by sending a carrier wave. Circuitry in the transmitter modifies the carrier wave based on the sound received by microphone.

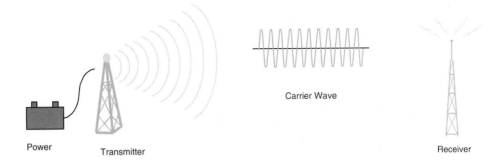

Power   Transmitter   Carrier Wave   Receiver

Figure 11-1
A carrier wave is a signal that maintains a communication link when information is transmitted

Circuitry in the receiver differentiates between the carrier wave and the modified carrier wave and translates the difference into the transmitted information. The signal containing the information is sent to the speaker so sound can be reproduced (see Figure 11-2).

Distance and terrain limit radio transmissions. Likewise there are practical limitations as to how far a message can be broadcast. For example, there is a limit to the amount of energy that can be used to transmit the radio signal. Technicians were able to overcome this problem by linking together radio stations to form a network of stations.

Cable and relay stations networked radio stations. A relay station is known as a repeater. The retransmission process strengthens the signal so the transmission can be received at a greater distance. This concept common in radio technology is also used in computer networks to transmit computer data a great distance over cables and over the air, as will be seen later in this book.

Tech Talk

Repeater: A device that receives a radio signal from a distant radio station, then retransmits the signal to other repeaters and radio stations. Retransmission introduces new energy to power the signal for longer distances.

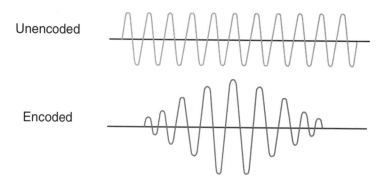

Unencoded

Encoded

Figure 11-2

Transmitted information is the difference between the carrier wave and the transmitted wave

Television

Shortly before World War II, scientists were able to use enhanced radio transmission technology to send pictures into living rooms around the world. We call this television. Television plays a critical role in the history of networks and computers since television technology is used in computer monitors.

Images on a television screen are composed of a series of tiny dots very similar to how photographs are printed in the newspaper. Hold a magnifying glass close to a newspaper photograph and you'll notice that the picture is really a group of dots. As you hold the picture further away from you, the dots seem to disappear and trick your mind into seeing an image.

Pixels are created by a stream of electrons fired from an electron gun located at the back of the monitor and hitting a coating on the back of the picture tube. When an electron connects with the coating, energy from the electron causes the coating to glow. This is similar to a dot that makes up a printed picture.

Electrons are tiny and cause only a tiny portion of the coating to glow, giving the appearance of a dot on the screen. As the electron gun zigzags across and down the screen, the glow remains visible until the electron gun retraces its path back to that position.

However, the glow isn't like a light bulb that remains lit until the power is turned off. Instead, the glow immediately begins to dissipate once the electron gun moves on, but the glow remains visible long enough for the electron gun to return to the position.

Scientists had the challenge of controlling when to fire the electron gun. If they could meet the challenge, then technology used to print pictures could be used to display pictures on the television screen.

Scientists turned to radio technology for the solution. Characteristics of a radio wave could be encoded to send a signal to a receiver to fire the electron gun. Once the electron gun was fired, a dot appeared on the television screen. Nothing would appear if the gun weren't fired. By properly encoding the transmission of the television signal, a scientist could broadcast a picture to distant receivers.

But how could an image be encoded into a radio wave? The answer came with the invention of the television camera. Circuitry in the television camera scanned an image in the same sequence as the electron gun in the monitor moved across and down the screen. The image captured by the camera is reproduced on the television screen by circuitry that controls the firing of the electron gun.

Radio waves provided the means to transmit the television signal and range in frequency from 10 kilohertz (kHz) to 300,000 megahertz (MHz). However, those signals could interfere with radio broadcast. The Federal Communications Commission

(FCC) assigned a new range of waves for television broadcast. This is called the television spectrum.

Tech Talk

Hertz: One complete cycle of a wave.

Kilohertz: 1,000 hertz.

Megahertz: A million hertz.

The television spectrum, like the radio spectrum, is limited by the distance the signal can be transmitted and by terrain. If you're located beyond the range of the television transmitter or a mountain range sits between your television set and the transmitter, then you are not able to receive the broadcast.

Technicians overcame these limitations by creating a television network. Although the term *television network* conjures images of NBC, ABC, and CBS, the term refers to a communication channel that transmits a signal over long distances.

Tech Talk

Communication channel: An electronic pathway over which a signal travels, very similar to a highway.

Television networks created a communication channel using repeater technology similar to that used to create a radio network. A television repeater is a receiver and transmitter that is placed at the fringe of the transmission range of the television broadcast signal. The repeater receives the broadcast signal then retransmits the signal, thereby increasing the range of the broadcast similar to technology used to form a radio network. This enables a broadcast signal to be transmitted across the country by using a series of repeaters to form the network.

By the late 1940s, corporations recognized the commercial viability of television technology. The federal government, through the FCC, regulated the industry by issuing broadcasters assigned frequencies within the television spectrum and areas of the country where they could broadcast their television signal. These regulations reduced the likelihood that signals interfere with each other.

Each broadcaster was responsible for creating television programs. As the industry matured, broadcasters such as NBC shared their programming with other television stations. In the first days of television, all broadcasts were live and were distributed to affiliated television stations using a repeater network to form their television network. Today's television networks still use repeaters along with other technology such as satellites and cable networks, which we'll explore later in this book.

Radio Technology

Probably the most common kind of wireless network uses radio technology to transmit packets encoded onto radio waves. A radio wave is a band of frequencies within the electromagnetic spectrum that can travel in 360 degrees over the air and through many physical obstructions.

While wireless radio networks seem to overcome limitations posed by infrared technology, there are drawbacks. Most radio frequencies are controlled by the FCC and require an FCC license before a wireless radio network can be established. Radio wireless is also vulnerable to eavesdropping and interference from stray signals.

There are three types of wireless radio networks (see Figure 11-3): low-power single frequency, high-power single frequency, and spread spectrum. Low- and high-power single frequency networks are similar except for the range the signal can travel.

Low-power single frequency covers an area of 30 meters, which is about the area of a small building. This is the least expensive wireless radio network. In contrast, a high-power single frequency wireless radio network can cover a metropolitan area.

Security is a concern when using low- or high-power single frequency technology because the signal can be received by anyone who has a device tuned to the radio frequency. Of course, packets can be encrypted to hinder the information from being reassembled by the cybersnoop.

A spread-spectrum wireless radio network is an alternative to the single frequency networks and uses multiple frequencies to transmit the signal using one of two methods: direct sequence modulation and frequency hopping. This makes it difficult for someone to electronically eavesdrop on the transmission.

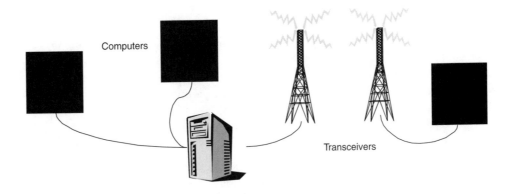

Figure 11-3
Wireless radio networks transmit information using radio waves

Direct sequence modulation: Bits of a packet are sent over multiple frequencies that the same time. The receiver reassembles the packet.

Frequency hopping: A packet is sent over a rotating set of frequencies.

Let's say there are 10 members of a track team. Each member is simultaneously running in his or her own lane on the track. In computer terms, each track team member is a bit, collectively the team is a packet, and the lanes are multiple transmission frequencies.

If you want to see all the members of the track team, you need to look at all the lanes at the same time. This is similar to if you wanted to receive the packet using direct sequence modulation (DSM) because each bit of the packet is transmitted on its own frequency. Therefore, if you want to see all the bits that comprise the packet, you must receive the frequencies used to transmit each packet.

Frequency hopping is like each member of a track team running behind each other in the same lane, then the coach signals to change to a specific lane in the middle of the run.

Both the transmitter and the receiver know which frequency is used to transmit the signal based on a set of rules established before the transmission occurs. A timing interval is used to determine when to change to another frequency. Packets are then reassembled in the order in which they arrive.

Microwave Technology

The term *microwave* is probably familiar to you since you probably use microwaves for cooking and maybe to receive direct television broadcasts. Microwave is a band of frequencies within the electromagnetic spectrum that travels in one direction.

There are two kinds of microwave networks: terrestrial and satellite (see Figure 11-4). Terrestrial networks use microwaves to transmit signals across a terrain such as between two buildings in an office complex. The signal can be received as long as there is an unobstructed view between the transmitter and the receiver. Since there are natural and manmade obstacles on earth, terrestrial networks must be carefully designed to avoid obstacles. Satellite networks also use microwaves for transmission, however it is less likely the transmission will be obstructed in space than on earth.

Satellite networks use microwaves to send and receive packets between a ground station and a satellite. The same technology is used between satellites to relay packets around the globe.

Although satellite transmissions can travel great distances relatively quickly, the speed may not be suitable for real-time communication.

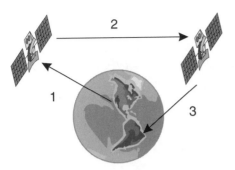

Figure 11-4
*Data is sent from an earth station to a satellite (1), then to another
satellite (2), and back to an earth station (3)*

<u>**Tech Talk**</u>
**Real-time communication: What we experience during a telephone call
when someone speaks then waits for the other person to respond.**

The transmission speed is slightly slower than terrestrial communication and
this delay causes an unnatural pause in the communication. You probably notice this
delay in a live international television broadcast where an anchor questions a field reporter who is located on the other side of the globe.

Wireless Networks

I tend to take for granted technology that has become commonplace. A few months
ago, a radio station in Missouri interviewed me by telephone. A listener called in from
his car and asked me a question. I had to stop for a moment. I'm in my attic in New
Jersey on the phone with a radio station halfway across the country answering a question from someone driving on the highway in Kansas.

Today we're starting to see a blur between cellular telephones and handheld
computers. You can purchase a cellular telephone that connects you to the Internet to
receive stock quotes, email, and browse your favorite website. And there's probably a
personal digital assistant (PDA) that can be used as a cellular telephone.

Engineers call these smart devices because they truly are intelligent mobile
communicators rather than a cellular phone or handheld computer. The Internet is the
driving force for the rapid development of smart devices because the Internet offers
the rich content demanded by people on the move.

The cellular network is the backbone of wireless connectivity to the Internet. Smart devices are able to receive information from the Internet through the use of the Wireless Application Protocol (WAP). WAP defines how information is to be transferred between the digital cellular network and the Internet. Other software is used on the smart device to modify the layout of web pages to fit on the smart device's small screens. For example, graphic images too large to fit on the screen are not displayed.

WIRELESS APPLICATION PROTOCOL (WAP)

The Internet is about to have its cable clipped by WAP, the wireless application protocol. WAP sets the rules for wireless communication with the Internet using mobile devices such as cellular telephones. Application developers used WAP to create microbrowsers, email applications, mobile handset messaging, and telefaxing among other types of software.

WAP was created in 1997 by the WAP Forum founded by Ericsson, Nokia, Motorola, and Unwired Planet. Over a hundred companies that include software developers and telecommunication carriers have since joined these companies.

WAP focuses on two particular areas: an application language used to create WAP-enabled applications and a transmission protocols used to communicate with the Internet.

The Wireless Markup Language (WML) is used to create WAP applications. WML is a subset of Extensible Markup Language (XML), which is used to develop web applications. XML uses tags to describe how a browser is to handle text within a web page. WML specifies the types of tags an application programmer is to use to enable the web page to work with WAP devices.

Transmission protocols represent layers of the ISO/OSI model and consist of the application, session, transaction, and transport layers. WAP also specifies a security protocol. WAP protocol functions similar to the transport protocol specified in the ISO/OSI model; however, the WAP protocol addresses the special requirements to exchange information using WAP devices.

WAP applications provide easy and secure access to banking, messaging, and entertainment available over the Internet using mobile devices. Furthermore, proprietary information that is normally found on an intranet such as data contained in corporate databases also can be accessed using a WAP device and WAP application.

You'll find more information about WAP in "WAP Essentials" and more information about the ISO/OSI model in The Essential Guide to Networking.

Bluetooth Technology, the Wireless Network

Bluetooth technology uses low-power radio transmission to connect network devices without the need for cables and can maintain the network connection even if the network device such as a computer is on the move.

Wireless networks have been around for years in the form of infrared light transmissions that required a clear line-of-sight between the infrared transmitter and the network device. However, offices typically have obstructions such as walls that inhibit widespread use of infrared wireless networks.

Bluetooth technology overcomes the line-of-sight limitation by using radio waves instead of light waves to transmit network information. Radio waves travel in all directions from the transmitter and can penetrate obstructions such as walls.

The key to Bluetooth technology is the low power used to broadcast the signal because the broadcast is limited to within an approximately 400-foot radius, which is expected to be extended to a nearly 4,000-foot radius. The current radius is perfect for a wireless network in an office. Eight devices can be linked together using Bluetooth.

Radio transmissions are vulnerable to interference and security breaches. Interference occurs from transmissions broadcast on frequencies close to the frequency used by Bluetooth technology. Security breaches are possible because any receiver tuned to the Bluetooth technology frequency can receive the signal.

Bluetooth overcomes both problems. Short data packets are used to maximize throughput and dramatically reduce the effects of interference. Packets that experience transmission errors are retransmitted, however the short size of the packet becomes advantageous because it shortens retransmission time. Bluetooth transmits at 1 megabit (Mb) per second.

Security is provided through the use of frequency hopping at 1,600 hops per second. This practically eliminates the exposure that the signal will be intercepted. Bluetooth technology also uses two additional security measures. Data is encrypted before being broadcast. Even if the signal is intercepted, the receiver still requires the key to decipher the data. Furthermore, Bluetooth permits only authorized devices to access network data.

Some see Bluetooth of great value to business travelers who currently need to carry an assortment of cables and connection devices to have their PCs link to networks outside their offices. The PC will have a Bluetooth technology transceiver that can communicate with networks in other offices and hotel rooms.

Signals broadcast using Bluetooth technology can simultaneously carry data and voice, redefining mobile computers, mobile phones, and similar devices. For example, a cellular phone using Bluetooth technology can easily become a mobile computer both inside and outside the office.

Pick up a copy of *Bluetooth Revealed* by Brent Miller for an in-depth look at Bluetooth technology.

Mobile Radio Networks

A forerunner of the cellular networks is the private radio network. Private radio networks are used by organizations such as government agencies, trucking companies, and service companies to communicate with employees in the field. You and I like to call them by their informal but more descriptive name—two-way radios.

The FCC set aside a range of frequencies for use by private radio networks. All transmissions on these frequencies are isolated from the cellular and standard telephone network, so there is no way for an employee in the field to use the private radio network to make a telephone call.

Early private radio networks transmitted only analog information, but this soon expanded to digital communication as the need for paging and messaging services materialized. Today, many delivery services such as FedEx use a private radio network to provide wireless package tracking. You've no doubt seen a driver scan package information into a mobile computer device, which is then transmitted over the private radio network to the company's computer.

Although an organization can purchase a private radio network, many find leasing time on another company's private radio network more economical. Telephone companies provide such a service called specialized mobile radio (SMR) network services.

Satellite Networks

Probably the most revolutionary wireless technology to come along is satellite networks. Just the sound of the name conjures images of Captain Kirk and the Enterprise.

We've heard about satellites being sent into space and how millions of dollars are spent to send work crews into orbit to perform electronic maintenance, yet most people know little about how satellites are used in communication.

Most satellites are repeaters that receive microwave signals from earth, then rebroadcast the signal to another satellite or to a receiver on earth. Repeaters are used in computer networks, too, as discussed in Chapters 3 and 4.

Although a satellite costs about $15 million to launch, this is far less expensive than placing a series of repeaters, called relay stations, around the globe. A satellite has a wide, unobstructed view of the earth, which enables it to retransmit the signal to a large area regardless of the terrain.

The first generation of satellites was used for military purposes and was stationed in an orbit that rotated at the same speed as the rotation of the earth. This is called geosynchronous and stationed the satellite at a fixed location 22,300 miles high.

It wasn't until satellites were used for commercial purposes that a characteristic of a geosynchronous satellite became a problem. The problem was a delay in communication. The time it took for a signal to be transmitted to the satellite and received by the earth station was too long for both commercial data and voice communication. Customers expected instantaneous transmission to which they were accustomed in wired communication.

The solution to this problem was to shorten the distance between the satellite and the earth from between 435 to 1,500 miles. This is called a low earth orbiting satellite (LEOS). Two other problems arose. First, LEOS covered a smaller area of the earth, which meant more satellites were required to give the same coverage area as covered by geosynchronous satellites.

The other problem was the location of LEOS. A change in the distance above the earth also changed the orbit speed. No longer are they in geosynchronous orbit. This means they travel faster than the rotation of the earth, which means ground stations have to locate a LEOS before beginning communication.

Another type of satellite is called the middle earth orbit (MEO), which orbits between 6,000 and 13,000 miles above the earth. Geosynchronous satellites, LEOS, and MEO all have something in common. Their life expectancy is between 7 and 15 years because the wear on solar cells that power the satellites and the technology used in the satellites are outdated.

Pick up a copy of *Fundamentals of Wireless Communication Applications* by Andy Dornan for more information about wireless communication.

INSIDE CELL PHONES ....

If you've seen the ads that try to talk you into signing up for a cellular telephone, you probably realize there are two types of cellular networks: analog and digital. An analog cellular network uses an analog technology to use variations in the signal to encode information. In a digital cellular network, digital technology is used to encode information as one of two values—a zero or a one.

The analog cellular network dates back to the 1970s when AT&T expanded its offerings to include mobile telephone service. It wasn't until mid-1995 that IBM developed the technology needed to digitize information over the cellular network. IBM's objective was to overcome the shortcomings of analog cellular transmissions when data instead of voice is transmitted.

Cellular networks are composed of transmitting and receiving towers strategically positioned around the country to link mobile telephones (see Figure 11-5). These are called base stations, each of which has a defined coverage area called a cell and links the cellular network to the telephone network. Cell phones communicate continuously with base stations as the cell phone moves through the network, as long as you turn on the telephone. When you place a call with your cell phone, the phone broadcasts a signal that is received by the base station nearest your location.

Your signal strength decreases as you move further away from the base station. Before your signal reaches the outer limits of the base station, the cellular network transfers your signal to a base station that is closer to your new location. This is called a hand off and causes the connection to be dropped for a fraction of a second before the signal is picked up by the next base station.

We rarely notice the hand off during the telephone call, but this split-second gap is very noticeable when data instead of voice is transmitted and is sufficient to cause errors in transmissions. The lack of capability to handle errors is a drawback to using the analog cellular network for sending data to a remote computer.

Data transmission errors occur regardless if the network is wired or wireless. However, data network protocols are designed to trap and correct errors and analog cellular network protocols are not designed for error control.

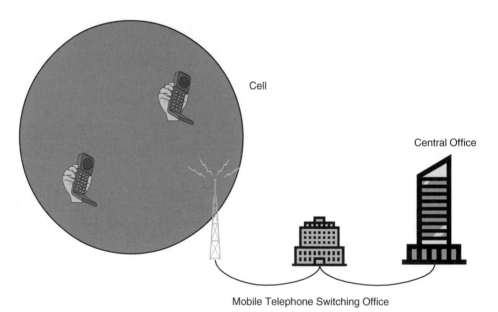

Figure 11-5
Cellular networks link mobile communication devices to telephone-based networks

The problem stems from the fact that analog cellular networks transmit one long burst of information compared to data communication networks that break up the information into small pieces called packets, frames, or cells.

And to compound the problem, an analog cellular network can either transmit or receive data, but it can't do both at the same time. This is called half-duplex. Duplex transmission is used by the wired-based telephone, which enables us to send and receive simultaneously. That is to say, analog cellular networks work much the same as how walkie-talkies work. Only one person can talk at the same time.

Let's say that you are sending a large message over an analog cellular network and an error occurs in the transmission because your call was handed off to another base station. Let's also assume the remote computer is smart enough to detect the error, similar to how a destination computer on a local area network (LAN) recognizes that an error has occurred.

The remote computer is unable to notify your mobile computer about the error because the remote computer cannot transmit the error message at the same time that your mobile computer is transmitting data.

IBM realized the power of the cellular network to free data communications from wired networks, so IBM engineers developed the Cellular Digital Packet Data (CDPD) protocol, commonly known as IP wireless.

Here's how CDPD works. Each mobile computing device is assigned an Internet Protocol (IP) address much like an IP address is assigned to computers on a TCP/IP network. A fixed IP address is important to reducing errors that occur when a call is handed off to another base station.

Your cellular telephone is assigned to a port in the cellular network. A port is an entry point into the network's base station and is identified by a unique port number. The port is reassigned each time your call is handed off to another base station.

Sometimes there are problems with the hand off and the cellular network is unable to re-establish the connection. For example, you are beyond the range of the first base station that has your original port assignment and the new port has not been assigned in the next base station.

A fixed IP address resolves this dilemma because your call is identified by your unique IP address, which cannot be lost by a hand off. If you are out of range of the first base station, the connection can always be re-established by using your IP address.

Tech Talk

IP address: The Internet Protocol address that uniquely identifies a communications device such as a cell phone or a computer that is connected to a network.

TCP/IP: A protocol that establishes communications rules for networks including the Internet.

A special modem called a CDPD modem is used to transmit small bursts of encrypted data over the existing analog cellular network. A burst frees the communication channel of transmission error messages by the receiver in between bursts.

Cellular networks promise to free your computer from being tied down to wires. However, new technology is required to fulfill those promises because cellular network transmission is slow compared with speeds required for data communications.

Analog transmissions have a throughput of 9,600 bits per second (bps) and CDPD improves throughput to 14,400 bps. These speeds are sufficient for remote entry of delivery information, inquiring about an order status, or providing remote access to email. However, they are not sufficient for full access to the Internet.

INSIDE DIGITAL WIRELESS SERVICES......................

Cellular networks provide the topology for data communications on the network. This is similar to how cables are connected together for a LAN. Digital wireless services use the IP wireless protocol to transmit data over the cellular network just as the TCP/IP protocol is used to transmit data over a LAN.

Tech Talk
LAN: A local area network.

The FCC reserved a set of frequencies within the radio frequencies of the electromagnetic spectrum for cellular communications. You can think of this as a fixed number of lanes on a highway.

Engineers developed multiplexing techniques that enabled each frequency to carry more than one call at a time. This is made possible because each call is divided into packets that contain control information. Control information includes the receiver's IP address, much how each car on the highway has a driver who knows the address of her destination.

There are three techniques used to multiplex transmission on a digital cellular network: code division multiple access (CDMA), time division multiple access (TDMA), and a third-generation wireless standard called 3G.

CDMA uses a spread-spectrum approach to transmission where the data is transmitted over more than one frequency. This increases the throughput of data over the network. CDMA also utilizes the soft hand off method when transferring a call to another base station. During the hand off, transmission from the mobile phone is held up until the connection is made with the next base station. The mobile phone temporarily stores the data in on-board memory as a way to keep transmission from the computer flowing into the transmitter.

In contrast, TDMA divides each frequency into time slots. Every call is assigned a time slot much like how computers share a network printer. Each waits its turn to use the frequency. The multiplexing technique 3G is still in development and uses both CDMA (called CDMA 3G) and TDMA (called TDMA 3G) to increase the throughput to 56 Kbps and beyond.

Text Input

The cell phone has most of the characteristics of a portable communications device and can be used for voice communications and to display a limited amount of text either from a messaging system or from the Internet. However, a characteristic that is missing is the ability to enter text similar to how you use a laptop to enter an email message.

Cell phones use a keypad that contains numbers and letters—at least in the United States. European telephones contain only numbers. Letters were originally used to identify a telephone exchange, which is the first three digits following the area code in a telephone number.

Each exchange was assigned a name, such as union, which implied the location of the local telephone switching office. In this example, union referred to Union City, NJ. The first two letters of the name—*UN*—were used in place of the first two numbers of the exchange. Today we use the number equivalent of these letters.

The telephone keypad contains all the letters of the alphabet except *Q* and *Z*. You could use these keys to spell a word so long as the word doesn't contain a *Q* or *Z*. However, there is a problem. Each key contains three letters. How is the telephone system going to know which of the three letters you want?

The problem was solved using one of two methods. The first method is for software in the cell phone to count the number of times a key on the keypad is pressed to determine which letter of the alphabet to display.

Let's say that I want to enter the word *Bob*. I'd press the number 2 key twice to enter the first letter *B*. The number 2 key has the letters *A*, *B*, and *C*. *B* is the second letter so by pressing the number 2 key twice I've told the software that I want the letter *B*. Likewise, I press the number 6 key three times to display the third letter of that key, which is *O*.

The other approach uses technology called T9 that helps disabled people communicate with the world. Some people with neurological injuries are able to move only their eyes and are unable to communicate otherwise.

T9 technology uses special glasses that track eye movement, enabling the person to type by moving their eyes in one of eight directions. Engineers assigned multiple letters to each of the eight directions. Today T9 technology is used with the keypad of the telephone.

Next, they developed an algorithm that predicted which one of the multiple letters the person wanted to type. They did this by analyzing the previous letters that were entered by the user. Here's how this works.

Let's say that I want to enter the world *men*. I'd press the number 6, then the number 3, followed by the number 6 again. There are three possible letters that I could want when I pressed the number 6. These are *MNO*. When I press the number 3, I could want *EDF*.

Table 11-1 contains the options the system has to consider when guessing the word I entered using the keypad. You'll notice that there are only two valid words listed in the third column. These are *men* and *neo*.

T9 technology will choose *men* as the default because *men* is used more frequently in sentences than *neo*. However, both words will be displayed on the cell phone screen requesting that we choose the correct word.

Table 11-1 Possible words that can be created using number 6 and number 3 on the keypad

Press number 6	Press number 3	Press number 6
m	md	mdm
n	me	mdn
o	mf	mdo
	nd	mem
	ne	men
	nd	meo
	od	mfm
	oe	mfn
	of	mfo
		ndm
		ndn
		ndo
		nem
		nen
		neo
		nfm
		nfn

Table 11-1 Possible words that can be created using number 6 and number 3 on the keypad (continued)

Press number 6	Press number 3	Press number 6
		nfo
		odm
		odn
		odo
		oem
		oen
		oeo
		ofm
		ofn
		ofo

INSIDE MESSAGING ....

One of the fastest growing areas of wireless and mobile communication is messaging, which has its roots in telephone pagers. You're probably very familiar with a telephone pager system. Yet, you probably didn't realize even older pagers received text messages. The text message consisted of numbers.

We assumed that the number on the pager referred to the telephone number of the person who beeped us and our assumption was correct. However, some clever people encoded messages into numbers sent to a pager

It was very common in the system support area of a corporation for a supervisor to send a telephone extension that ended in a triage category, the famous of which is 911. In this way, technicians who received the page would know the priority of the call.

A more notorious use of a pager was by drug dealers. Their clients placed orders by encoding the quantity of drug, the type of drug, and the location for the drug buy all in a set of numbers. For example, each location where drugs were sold was assigned a number, as was the type of drug. In this way police had a difficult time tracking down the dealer.

Pagers were later enhanced to accept a limited series of alphanumeric characters. Most users called a messaging service call center and gave their message to an operator who entered the message into a computer for transmission. Some corporations availed themselves of an advanced messaging service whereby they could use their own computers to generate and transmit the message.

Cell phones are a natural extension to messaging beepers since cell phone companies already had the technology and wireless devices to send and receive messages. Cell phone circuits had to be modified to accept text information in addition to voice.

However, what started out as an experiment has left cell phones in a difficult situation. Messaging was offered to cell phone customers on a limited basis to test messaging/cell phone technology. Cell phone companies didn't anticipate a heavy demand for this service since they were competing against existing messaging services and they offered voice mail.

They were wrong. Customers liked messaging on their cell phone. However, cell phone companies didn't have call services centers capable of keeping up with everyone who wanted to send a text message. As a compromise, cell phone companies adopted T9 technology that enabled customers to enter and send their own short message without the need for a call service center.

There are three kinds of messaging services used by cell phone companies. These are short message service (SMS), cell broadcast service (CBS), and unstructured supplementary services data (USSD).

SMS is widely used and has a character limit of 160 characters. Messages travel on the control channel, which is used by the cell phone company to control the telephone call. This means that messages can be sent and received simultaneously while sending or receiving a telephone call. Both phone call and the message use different communications channels.

Tech Talk

Control channel: A communications channel used by cell phone companies to manage telephone calls.

Messages may not be received immediately following their transmissions. Instead, messages are stored temporarily before they are forwarded to the receiver. This is called store and forward service, which is similar to voice mail and email.

CBS broadcasts messages instead of sending the message to a particular person. A total of 1,395 characters can be sent. These are divided into a maximum of 15 pages, each containing 93 characters. As you can image, CBS has not caught on simply because a typical message is addressed to one person and not everyone within the cell network.

USSD also uses the control channel and can transmit a message of a maximum of 182 characters. USSD does not use store and forwarding technology. Instead, a direct connection is made between the sender and the receiver very similar to a typical telephone call. This enables the receiver to respond immediately to any message received. This is the second widely accepted messaging method behind SMS.

INSIDE PDAS ....

Mobile computing power has become a necessity for anyone who is on the move, which is practically all of us. The ideal mobile computer is a device that is lightweight and small enough to fit into a pocket, runs the essential applications, and can operate constantly.

You're probably waiting for me to give you the name of a device that meets these requirements. Unfortunately, a device hasn't been built yet that meets all these requirements. However, personal digital assistant (PDA) comes very close to fitting the bill.

PDA is a broad term that describes many different devices from a simple digital telephone directory to a more elaborate device that contains a spreadsheet, word processor, email, and a variety of customized programs.

All PDAs are computers that contain an operating system, processor, memory, and a port similar to the components that you learned about in Chapter 3. There are three commonly used operating systems on a PDA. These are EPOC, Palm OS, and Windows CE. EPOC is used in the Psion product line, Palm OS in the Palm PDAs, and Window CE on various pocket PC devices.

There are a number of processors that are designed for the PDA market. These include the DragonBall processor built by Motorola and used in the Palm PDA. The DragonBall has 16 MHz clock speed.

The StrongARM processor manufactured by Intel is used in the Psion product line and some pocket PCs. StrongARM has a clocked speed of 200 MHz. Another competitor in the PDA processor market is the Crusoe processor manufactured by Transmeta, which also is found in some pocket PC PDAs.

As you can see, processing speeds can vary depending on the type of processor used in the PDA. However, you cannot equate a PDA's processing speed with that of a desktop or laptop computer because of the OS used by the PDA. Some operating systems such as Windows CE require more processing than a Palm OS PDA to perform a similar task. This means the extra horsepower required from a processor running under Windows CE does not necessarily perform a task any faster than a Palm.

Memory is very important in a PDA because it does not have any permanent storage device such as a disk drive. This means all the applications and data running in a PDA must reside in memory.

Every PDA uses two types of memory: read-only memory (ROM) and random access memory (RAM), which you learned about in Chapter 3. ROM is used to store bundled applications from the factory. These include a word processor, spreadsheet, diary, telephone directory, and other kinds of programs that you expect to find in a PDA.

Applications that are not bundled with the PDA and data for all applications including those that reside in ROM are stored in RAM. There are three types of RAM found in PDAs. These are dynamic RAM (DRAM), enhanced data output (EDO), and synchronous dynamic RAM (SDRAM). DRAM is the most commonly used RAM basically because DRAM is the least expensive RAM. EDO is found in some PDAs and SDRAM in very few.

Generally, the more RAM installed in a computer, the better the performance. However, PDAs are an exception to this rule. The amount of RAM that is necessary to adequately run a PDA is dependent on the OS running in the PDA. PDAs that run Windows CE require much more memory (i.e., 32 MB) to perform basic functions than a Palm (4 MB).

PDAs are rapidly evolving from an electronic data organizer. Many PDAs contain a USB port, which lets you connect many USB devices to the PDA. Others have keyboard and mouse ports and an infrared port used to transfer information between a PC and the PDA—and between another PDA.

Newer PDAs have an expansion slot for PC cards or for miniaturized PC cards called compact flash (CF+) cards. A card contains a component such as a modem, cell phone, network card, or additional memory that slips into an expansion slot on the PDA to enhance the PDA's functionality.

Tech Talk

Network card: A circuit board that connects a device to a computer network.

The feature that everyone looks for in a PDA doesn't exist yet, that is, a PDA that can run continuously during a business day without being connected to a power outlet. PDAs have the same problem as all mobile devices in that they need batteries to operate—and they drain batteries quickly. I'll tell you more about batteries later in this chapter in the section "Inside Mobile Power."

Inputting Data

While PDAs are light, slim, and contain commonly used applications, they all suffer from the same problem. They don't have a keyboard for data input. Although attempts have been made to create a tiny keyboard where you can use your thumbs to enter data or to include a collapsible keyboard, none have truly solved the problem of data input.

Some PDA manufactures tried to solve this problem by creating a virtual keyboard on a touch-sensitive screen. However, this requires you to hunt-and-peck your way, entering data using a stylus since you finger covers more than one key.

One of the most controversial methods used to input data into a PDA is handwriting recognition software. Software running in the PDA analyzes marks that you make on a touch-sensitive screen and guesses the character that you wrote.

Conceptually, handwriting recognition software sounds like a perfect solution. Engineers intuitively say this is wishful thinking because everyone's handwriting is different, that it would be nearly impossible for software, especially running on a PDA, to recognize handwritten letters.

The truth is that handwriting recognition works to an acceptable degree. Pocket PCs that run Windows CE can use an auto correct feature that minimizes errors. Palm uses its own brand of shorthand called Grafitti. Anyone who is willing to spend a few hours mastering Grafitti finds that taking notes on a Palm is almost as easy as writing with paper and pencil.

INSIDE LAPTOPS AND NOTEBOOKS ....

As soon as personal computers reached desktops, engineers were designing portable personal computers. One of the first was the Osborne portable computer, which was affectionately called a luggable computer.

The Osborne portable computer contained a 3-inch monitor, a floppy disk, and a processor built into a case that weighed 20 pounds. And back in the 1980s this was considered a luxury. The major problem with the Osborne, besides the weight, was that it was not IBM compatible and instead of running MS-DOS, it ran the CP/M operating system, which was a forerunner of DOS.

Panasonic soon came out with its own luggable computer that had a striking resemblance to the Osborne design. This, too, was in the 20-pound class and could withstand a 4-foot drop with damage only to the case (having dropped one when I was reviewing the Panasonic for a computer magazine).

It took nearly another decade before technology caught up with the demand for portable computing. This is the time when the laptop computer was introduced. Laptops are in the three-pound class and could be placed inside a briefcase.

Engineers shaved weight from laptops by using an LCD monitor (see Chapter 4), embedding common expansion circuits onto the motherboard, and used smaller and more efficient storage devices such as CD players and disk drives.

For example, you'll notice that a CD player in a laptop is stripped down compared with CD players for desktop computers. This is designed to save weight while maintaining functionality of the storage unit.

Engineers who design laptop computers expected users to adjust to the limitations of a laptop. These included the size and quality of the screen and the size of the keyboard. Screens on early laptop computers were small compared to a desktop monitor and had a limited viewing area. That is, the user had to look straight ahead to see the screen. They'd see a distorted image by looking at the screen from a side angle.

Laptop screens were improved to the point that the size of the screen is nearly the length and width of the laptop. Active matrix technology (see Chapter 4) made viewing possible at almost any angle.

The keyboard has always been a problem for engineers. The layout of the keyboard must be nearly the same as that of a standard size keyboard, otherwise touch-typists will have problems typing.

However, the keyboard still had to fit within the size of the laptop computer, which is narrower than the standard keyboard. Another issue was the size of each key. The key size must be at least the size of the average fingertip, otherwise users will be striking more than one key with each stroke.

IBM once tried to cleverly fold a standard-size keyboard into the laptop case. This was called the butterfly keyboard. IBM was successful, but the idea never caught on. Instead, IBM and the other laptop computer manufacturers settled on the largest keyboard that can fit within the dimensions of a laptop computer. This is functionally the same as a standard keyboard.

Three pounds was still too heavy for many users who demanded thin and light-weight portable computers. Manufacturers such as Sony met the demand with thinner laptop computers in the Vaio class.

The major difference between a laptop computer and an ultrathin computer are features. The ultrathin computers don't have built in many of the features that are found in a laptop computer.

For example, storage devices such as floppy disk drives and CD-ROM drives are not part of ultralight computers. Instead they are add-ons. This means that you need to attach these devices to the ultralight computer whenever you need them. Fortunately, you don't normally require them for everyday use since all ultralight computers come with a built-in hard disk.

Ultralight computers weigh less than a traditional laptop, but have approximately the same dimensions. Another category of portable computers is the notebook computers, which are smaller in dimension than the ultralight computers and laptops.

The category with the smallest computer is the subnotebook computer, such as the Libretto by Toshiba, which is 25 percent smaller than a notebook computer. They have a small screen and few of the features found on notebooks and ultralight computers.

The Practical Side to Mobile Computers

You have a wide choice of mobile computers from PDAs to laptop computers. The mobile computer that you select depends on your needs. All of these computers have a limited battery life, as you'll learn in the next section. This means regardless of your choice, the computer will run out of power when in consent use.

Define your mobile computing needs before considering any mobile computer. For some, mobile computing is limited to moving the computer around the house. In this case a standard laptop computer is the economical choice.

Laptops are less expensive than smaller computers that have the same features. And most of us have no trouble moving three pounds a few feet. Plus you can always connect a full-size monitor, keyboard, and mouse to the laptop.

My friend has the monitor and keyboard set up on a small computer table and connected to the laptop. He disconnects the monitor whenever he wants to move to another room to work on his computer where he sets up the laptop and the standard-size keyboard.

If mobile to you means traveling outside the house, then consider buying an ultralight computer or a notebook computer. I've found these to have all the features I need—at the weight I'm willing to carry for any appreciable distance.

A word of caution: Avoid bringing attachments with you when you travel. You probably don't need a CD-ROM player or a floppy disk drive because the software you need is probably loaded onto the ultralight or notebook computer's hard disk.

Most of these computers also come with a modem embedded into the motherboard or on a PC card. Therefore you could always email yourself copies of any files you create while on the road as a backup to copies of those files that you have on the mobile computer's hard disk.

I used to tease a colleague of mine whenever he went on a trip. He had purchased an ultralight computer to lighten the load when he traveled. Then he loaded his computer bag with the external floppy disk drive, external CD-ROM drive, and the battery recharger. The recharger is needed, but he never used the other external devices.

Think twice about purchasing a subnotebook computer. I've found them to be irresistible, but not very practical, especially when you consider improvements made with PDAs. I prefer using an ultralight or notebook computer and a PDA rather than purchasing a subnotebook.

The PDA contains all the information I need to keep handy, such as a telephone directory, financial records, meeting schedules, and general notes. I use the ultralight or notebook—or my desktop—to store the rest of my information, such as bank records and manuscripts.

Another word of caution: Not everyone needs a PDA. Here's a simple test I tell my friends to take before buying a PDA. Keep a Post-it note in your pocket and note each time you need to look up a telephone number or a particular set of data.

Most of my friends find the Post-it is blank after a month. This is because they either memorized frequently called telephone numbers or used other means to look up the information.

For example, I have a list of my colleagues and their telephone numbers next to my computer at work and a copy in my desk at home. I'm normally in either place whenever I need to call them. And I never call them unless I'm either at the office or at my home. Therefore, I don't need a PDA to store those telephone numbers.

However, if you find the note filled with telephone numbers and data, then a PDA might help—although some of my friends simply use a Post-it instead of buying a PDA.

There are many PDAs on the market each touting the latest-and-greatest technology. Before falling for the bait, determine if you'll really use that technology. For example, do you really intend to use the PDA to take notes? How many times in the past did you take notes? Most of us do so at meetings—and then used paper and pen.

Do you really intend to use a PDA for word processing or working on a spreadsheet? These are nice to have, but are not very practical because of the size of a PDA and the limited data input capability available with a PDA.

And the latest craze is a wireless PDA that lets you connect to the Internet. Do you really want to surf the net using a small-screen PDA that cannot display graphics? Before buying into a wireless PDA, calculate the cost. Although wireless access technology is changing and prices are declining, expect to pay a premium to surf the Internet using your PDA.

You can receive and send email using a wireless PDA and certain cell phones. However, compare the expense against the value of the email. Also consider that you're not receiving or sending email today by PDA or cell phone—and you're surviving. So your impulse to buy a wireless PDA should be tempered with the economic sense of reality.

INSIDE MOBILE POWER......................................

Mobile computing comes down to one thing—power. Everything in a PDA, cell phone, laptop, and other portable computing devices consume power. Although engineers have removed power hungry components from these devices and imposed power saving techniques, mobile computing devices have limited power.

For example, a cell phone battery will last 10 hours of talking while a laptop computer's battery is good for about 2 hours of steady work. The battery in a PDA has a maximum charge of 20 hours.

Power is measured in watt-hour, which means the number of hours the battery can supply one watt of power. A cell phone battery is rated at 10 watt-hour. This means the battery can supply one watt of power for 10 hours. Likewise, a laptop battery has a rating of 50 watt-hour and a PDA battery of 2 watt-hour.

The amount of watts used by a mobile computing device varies depending on the circuitry and power hungry components that are built into the device. In addition, power consumption is also dependent on the state of the device.

Mobile computing devices typically have three states: active, standby, and off. The active state is when the device is being used, such as when you are talking on the cell phone or writing a document. The standby state, sometimes called the sleep mode, is when all but the necessary components are turned off to minimize the drain on the battery.

The off state is when you turn off the device. Intuitively you may think this means no power is drained from the battery. However, this isn't true. Some power is used to maintain information in memory such as in a PDA and cell phone. Laptops and similar computers use a smaller battery other than the main battery for this purpose.

Types of Batteries

Batteries fall into two general classes: nonrechargeable and rechargeable. Two commonly used nonrechargeable batteries, alkaline and zinc-carbon, are used in PDAs and as an emergency backup for cell phones. Always choose alkaline batteries because they have a higher capacity than zinc-carbon batteries.

There are four types of rechargeable batteries. These are lead acid batteries, nickel cadmium (NiCad) batteries, nickel metal hydride (NiMH) batteries, and lithium ion batteries.

The original cell phones used lead acid batteries, which can be recharged many times. However, components of the lead acid batteries contain a dangerous ingredient. Therefore, mobile computing manufacturers moved to the safe NiCad battery.

The NiCad battery can be recharged 1,000 times before losing its ability to hold a charge. However, NiCad batteries must be fully discharged before they can be recharged otherwise the battery cannot be fully recharged. This is called the memory effect and is the reason mobile computer manufactures have moved to either the NiMH battery or the lithium ion battery.

The NiMH battery does not experience the memory effect. This means that you don't have to fully discharge the battery before you can fully recharge it. This battery has about a quarter more charging capacity than a similar NiCad battery.

My cell phone and laptop came with a NiMH battery. However, I decided to replace them with lithium ion batteries because they have a longer life and more charging capacity. They are also more expensive.

Both the NiMH and the lithium ion battery are considered smart batteries because each has a power meter to signal the battery charger when the battery is fully recharged.

SUMMARY ....

Technology is moving toward the day when all computing devices will be severed from their power and communication umbilical cord. However, before fully mobile computing devices become reality, they must be able to communicate over the airwaves.

Radio waves are used by wireless devices to communicate with each other using the same technology that is found in radio and television. Radio waves are similar to sound and light waves that you learned about throughout this book. Radio waves consist of atoms that are vibrating within the radio frequency.

A crystal inside a transmitter creates the initial frequency, which is amplified until the frequency is able to travel a distance to the receiver. The radio signal is transmitted using an antenna that beams the radio signal in a 360-degree direction. Antennas that are the length of the wavelength of the transmitted frequency pick up the signal and forward it to the circuitry within the mobile device.

A transmitter sends a carrier wave to receivers. A carrier wave contains a steady frequency that acts like a dial tone on your telephone. It basically tells the receiver that the connection is alive.

The frequency of the carrier wave is modified whenever information is transmitted. The modification depends on the information that is being transmitted. Receivers separate the modified frequency from the carrier frequency, then translate the modified frequency back into information.

The most commonly used wireless device is the cell phone. A cell phone converts voice to a signal that is transmitted and picked up by strategically placed antennas within an area called a cell. Antennas then forward the call to the telephone system. A cell phone receives a frequency from an antenna located within the cell and translates the signal into voice.

Cell phones can receive short textual information, which is displayed on the cell phone screen. Likewise, text messages can be sent using the telephone keypad to enter text. There are two ways in which text can be entered.

Most keys on the keypad are labeled with three letters. Pressing the key once then pausing causes the first letter to be sent. Pressing the key twice then pausing causes the second letter to be sent. And pressing the key three times then pausing causes the third letter to be sent.

Some cell phones use T9 technology to enter letters using the keypad. This technology requires that software in the cell phone guess at the word that you are typing. If there is more than one possible word based on the key strokes you enter, then the cell phone lists those words and prompts you to choose the correct one.

By displaying and sending text, cell phones have entered the arena of messaging devices such as pagers. Both pagers and cell phones receive text and some pagers are capable of sending text.

However, most text sent to a pager is entered into a computer in the messaging call center. Anyone wishing to send a text message and who does not have access to a pager that transmits messages must call the messaging call center and dictate the message to an operator. The operator then sends the message. Cell phone companies do not have call centers and therefore find it difficult to compete with pager services.

Cell phones and pagers are two of the common mobile computing devices. A PDA and a laptop computer are also popular mobile computing devices. A PDA is a pocket-size computer that stores information and runs various applications, and can be converted into a cell phone by inserting a special adapter. PDAs lack a convenient method to input information. Many PDAs recognize handwriting and some require you to learn their own shorthand before you can input data by writing.

Laptops and their younger cousins the notebook and subnotebook computers, are fully functional computers that use a keyboard and mouse or other pointing device to enter information into the computer. Notebook and subnotebook computers are smaller and lighter than laptops, but also have fewer built-in features. For example, a floppy disk drive and CD-ROM drive are not part of these computers. Instead, these are external devices.

All mobile devices have the same weakness. They run on battery power, which can be exhausted within a few hours depending on how the device is used. A device that is in constant use because frequent cell phone or laptop activity drains the battery faster than if the device is in sleep mode.

Summary Questions

1. How does a cellular telephone system work?

2. How is information encoded onto a radio wave?

3. What is the purpose of Bluetooth technology?

4. Why are satellites in geosynchronous orbit?

5. How did engineers solve the delay problem in geosynchronous satellites?

6. How does T9 technology work?

7. Why is memory important to a PDA?

8. What is a communication channel?

9. What is the purpose of the control channel in short message service?

10. Why is it beneficial to upgrade to a lithium ion battery?

Part 2 ▪ Computer Hardware Components

PUTTING IT ALL TOGETHER ....

Computers are amazing devices that can take two numbers—zero and one—and perform feats that baffle the mind. Yet when you look into the guts of a computer you soon realize that computers apply basic scientific principles that you and I learned in grammar school to manipulate information.

When you pop open the computer case, you'll see a city of components on a larger circuit board called the motherboard. The motherboard is like a small city where components such as memory and the processor are houses and the streets are etched wires called a bus.

The processor is the brains of the city and is responsible for manipulating information, and the clock is the heart of the city, setting a tempo for information moving among components. Computer memory is a temporary storage place where information and applications are stored until called upon by the processor.

Each component on the motherboard is assigned a unique address similar to a building address in a city. Whenever a component such as the keyboard or an application needs to have the processor process information, it sends the processor an interrupt. An interrupt is a number that tells the processor to stop whatever it is doing and execute an interrupt service routine.

An interrupt service routine is a program that is loaded into memory when the computer is powered up. Upon receiving an interrupt the processor looks up the address of the interrupt service routine in the interrupt table. The interrupt table contains the interrupt value and the address of the corresponding interrupt service routine.

Once the processor obtains the address, it copies the instruction that is stored at that address into the processor for processing. Each kind of processor recognizes its own set of instructions, which is called the processor's instruction set.

Programmers write groups of instructions called a program using an English-like language such as Java and C++, which is then converted into a processor instruction set by a program called a compiler. Instructions are then in machine-readable form commonly referred to as machine language.

The speed at which information is processed is determined by the internal and external clock speed, the amount of information that the processor can read at one time, and the size of the bus.

Clock speed is measured in MHz. The higher the MHz value the faster information can flow over the bus and inside the processor. The internal clock speed is the speed at which the processor can process information. The external clock speed is the speed at which information can flow over the bus.

The process can read a specific number of bits for each clock cycle. The more bits a processor can read for each cycle the faster information can be processed. A processor uses either the complex instruction set computing (CISC) or the reduced instruction set computing (RISC).

CISC instructions can require two or more clock cycles before the processor reads them. In comparison, RISC instructions are typically read in one clock cycle, meaning RISC processors generally perform the same task faster than a CISC processor.

The number of bits of information that can flow over the bus in one clock cycle is referred to the size of the bus. The larger the bus size the more information can flow into the processor for processing.

Displaying Information

Information is displayed on the screen as picture elements called pixels or pels. Each pel has three components called a subpel, one for each of the primitive colors (red, green, and blue). Each color is represented by a set of bits called the color depth. The larger the set of bits, the more colors that can be represented on the screen. Bits representing subpels are stored in video memory.

An application program sends instructions to the main processor whenever the application wants to display information on the screen. The main processor immediately sends the instruction to the video adapter. The video display adapter is like a little computer in that the video processor contains a video coprocessor, bus, clock, and video memory.

The instruction to display information is sent to video random access memory (RAM) by the main processor, which then sends an interrupt to the video coprocessor telling it that new information has arrived and must be displayed.

The video driver translates the main processor instructions into instructions that the video coprocessor understands. The video coprocessor uses a special instruction set that contains instructions specifically designed to draw pieces of images on the screen.

Bits that are used to represent the image are copied into a frame buffer. A frame buffer is the video memory image of the monitor's screen. Several bits in the frame buffer represent each pel on the screen. The actual number of bits used to define a pel is dependent on the color depth. That is, the number of bits used to define the color of a pel.

The video display adapter output circuit scans the frame buffer at the same speed as the electron gun in the monitor scans the screen. The movement of the electron gun is controlled by the horizontal and vertical signals generated by the video display adapter output circuit.

Electrons are given off as the cathode tube in the monitor is heated by electricity. Electromagnetics called a yoke direct the electron beam from the electron gun to the phosphor coating on the back of the screen.

A glow is emitted from the portion of the phosphor that is hit by the electron beam. The brightness of the glow is determined by the strength of the beam. The more electrons that hit the phosphor, the brighter the glow.

The phosphor glows for a short time, called the decay time, after which it turns dark. The electron gun must continue to refresh the phosphor to maintain a stable image on the screen. The length of time it takes the electron gun to reach every pel of the screen is called the refresh rate. The higher the refresh rate, the more stable the image on the screen.

Storing Information

Two of the more commonly used storage devices are a hard disk drive and a CD drive. The hard disk is organized physically and logically. The physical organization of a hard disk consists of concentric circles called tracks, which are divided into sections called sectors. The operating system logically organizes sectors into clusters. A cluster consists of several sectors that contain data.

CD drives are challenging disk technology as the storage device of choice. Most computers have a CD-ROM drive, which enables the user to read large amounts of data such as a computer application from the CD.

CD-R and CR-RW drives are another type of CD drive that can read and write data from a CD. A CD-R drive writes data to a CD. Once written, the data cannot be erased or written over. In contrast, a CD-RW drive can write, erase, and rewrite data to the CD.

A CD has a spiral circle called a track that is divided into sections called sectors. Sectors are further divided into small areas where a laser is used to burn a pit into the CD surface. Some areas within a sector have pits and others don't, depending on the binary value of the data stored in the area. A pit represents a one and the absence of a pit represents a zero.

A low power laser shines a light into each area within a sector. The light reflects one way if the area contains a pit and another way if it doesn't. The detector circuit in the CD drive interprets the reflection as a zero or one and passes the binary value to the operating system for processing.

Printing Information

When you click Print on your program, the program translates text and images on the page along with page layout information into instructions written in a page description language that the printer understands.

The instructions are then passed along by the operating system (OS) to the printer where the printer's circuitry translates the page description language instructions into mechanical movements so the pel is placed on the page.

There are two general ways in which text and images are printed on a page: rastering and vectoring. Rastering is a process similar to that used to display images on a screen. Vectoring is a more direct approach to printing because the print head is instructed by the program to move to a particular coordinate and print a pel on the page. This means that the printer head doesn't move to every pel position, as is the case with rastering. Instead, the print head goes directly to the position where the pel is printed.

Networks

Computers talk to one another through the use of a computer network or directly over the telephone using a modem. Computer networks are like private telephone systems only that computers and computing devices instead of people talk over the system.

Computers that are connected to a local area network (LAN) use a network card rather than a modem. A network card is a device that listens to traffic over the network and intercepts packets of information destined for the network adapter card's computer. A packet is an electronic envelope that contains parts of information that are being transferred to another computer.

A network card must be capable of processing information from the network to the motherboard and from the motherboard to the network efficiently, otherwise a bottlenecks occurs. A bottleneck is similar to a five-lane highway merging into a three-lane tollbooth island. The tollbooth plaza can process only a maximum number of vehicles before traffic backs up on the highway.

Some network cards contain a small amount of memory used to store packets. An interrupt is sent to the processor on the motherboard whenever a packet is received from the network. The process then moves the packet from the network card into main memory where the packet is processed. However, a bottleneck develops if the processor is unable to move packets faster than the network card receives additional packets.

A better strategy used by other network adapter cards is for the card to have access to main memory on the motherboard. This is called direct memory access. The network card also has its own processor so when packets are received from the network, the network card automatically moves the packet into main memory without waiting for the main processor to respond to an interrupt.

A computer connects to the telephone network using a modem. A modem receives digital information from the motherboard and encodes the digital information into an analog signal, which is sent over the telephone line. This process is called modulation.

The modem connected to the other end of the telephone line decodes the analog signal back to digital information, which is then sent to the motherboard of the receiving computer for processing.

Modems transmit information at a speed measured as baud. One baud is equal to sending one transmission symbol per second over the telephone line. A symbol can contain one or more bits of information. Most modems can transmit at several rates although only the highest baud is quoted in advertisements.

Two modems agree on the highest baud both can handle during the handshaking process that occurs during the first few seconds after making the initial connection. This means that a modem may not transmit information at the advertised baud.

Input Devices

An input device is any device used to enter information into a computer such as keyboards, mouse, game controllers, graphics tablets, and speech recognition devices.

The keyboard is a small computer that runs a program to monitor all the keys and transmits a specific signal when one or several keys are pressed and/or released. Each key coincides to a position on a wired matrix inside the keyboard. Each matrix point has a unique key scan code.

The interrupt service routine interprets the key scan code into the equivalent ASCII value, then stores the ASCII value into main memory and erases the key scan code from the keyboard buffer. A mouse and its relative, the trackball, tell the operating system to either add or subtract rows or columns from the mouse cursor's current position.

A game controller is used to give direction to a computer game. Game controllers come in all shapes and sizes from a simple joystick to a full-blown steering wheel and foot pedals. A graphics tablet is like having an electronic paper and pencil because images drawn on it are displayed on the screen. A stylus or a puck is used to draw the image. A stylus is like a pen in that the harder you press down, the wider the line appears on the screen.

A speech recognition device is capable of translating the spoken word into text on the screen or a command that can be executed by the operating system. A speech recognition device consists of a microphone and speech recognition software.

There are two commonly used speech recognition technologies: interrupted speech and natural speaking. Interrupted speech technology requires you to pause between words. Natural speaking technology lets you speak naturally into the computer.

Audio Devices

Audio devices such as sound cards, speakers, and headphones are used to enhance our experience using a computer, especially when playing computer games. Sound makes us feel as if we are having a real-life experience.

Sound is one-dimensional since each sound generates one sound wave. However, you and I hear sound in two dimensions because we have two ears. Typically a sound wave arrives at each ear at slightly different times, which gives us a feeling of listening to a two-dimensional sound.

We actually hear sound in three dimensions because a sound wave travels in many directions in addition to directly reaching our ears. Three-dimensional sound occurs when a sound wave reflects off objects such as walls, trees, and other things around us. The reflected sound wave also reaches our ears at a fraction of a second later than two-dimensional sound reaches our ears.

Engineers have designed sound cards to reproduce two-dimensional and three-dimensional sound that gives us the feeling that we are hearing realistic sound. However, a good quality sound card must be complimented with a set of multiple speakers that separate sound similar to the way sound is separated in real life.

A five-speaker set is perfect to hear three-dimensional sound. Two speakers are placed in front of the listening area. Another speaker called a subwoofer is placed on the floor. The other two speakers are placed behind the listening area to provide a full surround-sound experience.

A sound card is capable of generating the sound of musical instructions by using a MIDI file. A MIDI file contains instructions for the processor on the sound card to generate sounds such as musical instruments. The processor first generates a pure sound, then enhances the purse sound with harmonic frequencies to create the sound of an instrument.

Instructions contained in a MIDI file simply tell the sound card processor the musical note to play, the instrument selection, the duration of the note, and the volume. The sound card processor then generates the sound of the instrument.

Digital Cameras and Scanners

Digital cameras and scanners use a charge-coupled device (CCD). There are three CCD used in a digital camera, one for each primitive color—red, green, and blue. The CCD divides the image into pixels.

A digital camera does not have a shutter, which is used to let reflected light into the camera. Instead, electronics within the camera are used to expose the CCD to the light for a specific amount of time.

The resolution of a digital camera is measured in rows and columns of pixels such as 1280 x 1024 pixels. Multiplying these two values tells you the number of pixels that are used to capture the original image. The more pixels that are used, the higher the resolution.

Two resolutions are used for scanners: optical and interpolated. The optical resolution is the number of pixels per inch that are captured when an image is scanned. The interpolated resolution is the actual number of pixels that are stored in the image file using software to increase the optical resolution.

The pixel depth determines the range of colors that can be captured by either a digital camera or a scanner. The higher the pixel depth, the wider the range of colors that can be stored in the image file. The pixel depth is measured in the number of bits used to store a pixel.

A scanner uses the same basic technology as is used in a digital camera except a scanner uses a fixed focal length. That is, you are unable to adjust the lens of the camera since the lens is set to capture images at a fixed distance from the lens.

Wireless and Mobile Devices

Wireless devices such as cell phones and pagers use basic radio technology to transmit and receive information over the airwaves. A crystal inside a transmitter creates the initial frequency, which is amplified until the frequency is able to travel a distance to the receiver. The radio signal is transmitted using an antenna that beams the radio signal in a 360-degree direction. Antennas that are the length of the wavelength of the transmitted frequency pick up the signal and forward it to the circuitry within the mobile device.

A transmitter sends a carrier wave to receivers. A carrier wave contains a steady frequency that acts like a dial tone on your telephone. It basically tells the receiver that the connection is alive.

The frequency of the carrier wave is modified whenever information is transmitted. The modification depends on the information that is being transmitted. Receivers separate the modified frequency from the carrier frequency, then translate the modified frequency back into information.

Mobile computing devices such as PDAs and laptop computers have various degrees of functionality depending on the processor and memory used in the device. PDAs run the gamut from a simple telephone directory to a miniature computer complete with a word processor and spreadsheet application. Laptop computers are smaller versions of desktop computers with most, if not all, of the features found on a laptop.

Nearly all mobile computers connect to other computers using an infrared connection, USB connection, modem, or a device that functions like a cell phone modem.

All mobile devices have the same weakness. They run on battery power, which can be exhausted within a few hours depending on how the device is used. A device that is in constant use because frequent cell phone or laptop activity drains the battery faster than if the device is in sleep mode.

Part 3

Industry Overview

You probably have a good idea of how computer hardware operates having read the first two parts of this book. However, your exploration of computer hardware isn't complete until you learn about the businesses that develop, manufacture, and market computer hardware that enables you and me to work efficiently with a computer.

In writing this book I discovered that the industry that brings us computer hardware technologies is just as complex as the largest computer network. I also noticed that the industry is composed of many companies that are not household names because they provide the technology and infrastructure used by companies you and I read about.

Instead of creating large corporations with strong research, development, and marketing departments, businesses in the new economy create strategic alliances where each company does at least one thing better than the other. Collectively they work toward the same goal of improving technology— and making a profit.

In the next three chapters I take you on a tour of these businesses and discuss strategic alliances that form the cornerstone of the industry. The tour begins with Chapter 12 with an overview of how the industry is organized today.

From there we'll take a look into the future. The publisher asked me to look into my tea leaves and project how computer hardware technology will change in the foreseeable future. Our tour ends with a look at the leading companies in the industry.

12 Computer Hardware: The Industry

In this chapter...

- A Road Map of the Industry
- The Assembly Line
- Pricing and Profit
- Creating Demand
- Competition
- The Players

*"Rebooting doesn't always make
your troubles go away."*

Anonymous

Every driver wishes a car were like a computer, then whenever the car acted up, all a driver would have to do is turn off the engine, wait two minutes, then restart and all the problems would be gone. However, automobiles are not computers, although computers have made inroads into the engine compartment.

You've probably heard and read a lot about the technical industry and how a handful of computer makers seems to be driving the economy. Some of what is reported is true about the technical industry and other things are more hype than factual.

I'll take you on a walk through the industry in this chapter and give you a good foundation so you can better understand the impact—or lack there of—of stories you will read or hear. You'll learn:

- The segments of the industry

- How the industry works

- Common technical myths

- How to cut through the hype

REALITY CHECK ....

Companies that are out to capitalize on technology can easily mislead the press. I learned this lesson years ago when I was an editor for *Personal Computing* magazine, which was the leading technical publication in its day.

We were forever being pitched ideas for stories about new technical products and every manufacturer claimed his or her widget was going to change the industry. It is safe to say that very few products lived up to its claims.

Some pitches were comical. One company rushed to our offices to demonstrate a mobile computer that could connect to a company's mainframe computer while being driven in a car.

This wouldn't be revolutionary today. However, in those days only the wealthy few or top business executives could afford cell phones and a mobile computer was the size of a suitcase. This was also the time before the Internet became a consumer product.

A wireless connection for a mobile computer would be a breakthrough—if it worked. The head of the company demonstrated his device in our parking lot. I've never seen anyone squirm as much as he did that day. Hours after we assembled, he was still trying to get his gizmo to work.

He had a lot riding on the demo. The company needed a round of financing from Wall Street to survive and he needed a good review in a reputable computer magazine to convince Wall Street that his gizmo was a gem in the rough.

There was a flaw in his gizmo that happened to make its appearance in our parking lot. The cellular network wasn't as fully developed as it is today and there were many dead spots, one of which was in our parking lot.

The wireless computer worked fine next to a cell base station, but was useless in a dead spot. Furthermore, the link between the computer and the office broke each time the computer moved to a new cell, but that fact wasn't mentioned to us.

If conditions were slightly different, the company most likely would have received the good review that they were seeking. That is, if our parking lot weren't in a dead spot, then the connection would have worked. And if we were close to deadline, our editors would not have thoroughly tested the product under real-life conditions and would have announced the wireless computer long before the technology was fully developed.

A ROAD MAP OF THE INDUSTRY............................

The computer hardware industry is divided into segments, the success of which is dependent on the success of other segments of the industry. I group the industry into six segments, some of which overlap each other, and many have important subsegments. The segments are:

- Chip, circuit board, and computing device manufacturers

- Storage device manufacturers

- Input device manufacturers

- Video and sound device manufacturers

- Printing device manufactures

- Communication device manufacturers

Chip and circuit board manufacturers are at the center of the computer hardware industry because nearly all computer devices use computer chips that are assembled with other components on a circuit board.

A chip contains the logic to perform a specific process. For example, there are chips especially designed to process 3D graphics and others to produce 3D sound. Until those chips were manufactured, 3D graphics and 3D sound could not be used in any game.

In the healthcare industry, the news media and Wall Street stock analysts look toward the research labs of drug companies to find the next revolutionary cure. Likewise, they look to the research labs of chipmakers to discover the next exciting development in computer hardware technology.

A chip design determines the type and number of other components necessary for a circuit board and determines how much power is needed to operate the hardware device. Simply said, if chipmakers don't build in a particular feature into the chip design, then you and I don't see that feature in our computer.

How do chipmakers decide the features to include? The answer lies with the needs of customers, which are the circuit board manufacturers and manufacturers of devices in the other segments of the industry.

There are three fundamental factors that determine which features are included in a chip: market demand, price, and the state of technology. Here's how this works. Technology is evolutionary regardless of how revolutionary an idea might sound. Therefore, computer hardware makers look to build tomorrow's product a step or two ahead of today's product.

Take computer game hardware as an example. Programmers who first built computer games designed the games around existing technology. The games were initially boring by today's standards, but gradually became more challenging as programmers reached the limits of the hardware.

Game programmers needed faster chips to process graphics, sufficient memory to store the game's complex graphics, and monitors that could reproduce quality graphics. Furthermore, they needed to replicate complex sounds in sync with action taking place in the game.

Chipmakers had to assess the market needs and depth. Were consumers willing to buy sophisticated graphics cards and sound cards so they could play more challenging computer games?

Chipmakers needed to compare the cost of design and manufacturing graphics and sound processors with the expected revenue flow generated by the segment of the computer market that played computer games.

Until chipmakers identified sophisticated graphics and sound cards as a profitable product, they refused to design and manufacture chips that met the needs of game programmers. However, once the depth of the game market reached what chipmakers believed to be a profitable threshold, they manufactured the chips.

When sophisticated graphics and sound chips were available to graphics and sound card manufacturers, then the market was saturated with new and improved products. However, most if not all the graphics and sound cards and game software use the same basic technology that is designed into computer chips.

Computer chips are expensive to design although relatively economical to manufacture. Therefore, there isn't a lot of competition in the chip segment of the industry. It is very common for most devices to use the same set of chips made by one or two chip manufacturers.

THE ASSEMBLY LINE ....

Some of the most recognizable names in the computer hardware industry are assemblers and marketers rather than manufacturers. The assembly process begins with a chip set, which is purchased from the chip supplier.

Circuit board manufacturers design products around the requirements of a particular chip set. Circuit boards are designed for a particular purpose such as the motherboard for a computer, a circuit board for a modem, and a circuit board for a video graphics adapter. Simply said, the circuit board is the computer.

Assemblers typically purchase a chip set/circuit board package for use in their computer hardware device. Likewise, they purchase power supplies, cables, and the case to house those components each from separate manufacturers.

Components are then secured in place and sold to consumers as a complete computer device such as a computer or modem. It is not too uncommon for consumers to believe that one computer is better than another when in reality they contain the same circuit board.

Since assemblers buy components in vast quantity, they can influence the specifications of each component. In theory, this means that an assembler could require greater tolerance from a component manufacturer than another assembler does. In reality, most components are manufactured to an industry acceptable tolerance.

Tolerance is measured as a value that falls within a specific plus or minus range. Let's use an example from the automotive industry to illustrate this point. Sheet metal is fed into a machine that uses stamp die to push the metal into the shape of a car door.

The thickness of the metal and the condition of the stamp die determine how well the door will fit with the body during the assembly process. You and I look for a perfectly fitted door whenever we buy a car. However, "perfectly fitted" is subjective. That is, you know it when you see it.

Engineers have determined that a perfectly fitted door is one that is no closer than a specific number of inches from the body of the car and no further than a specific number of inches from the body of the car.

These measurements are determined by making mechanical tests, which indicate the distances when the door did not work properly. Engineers also showed consumers doors fitted at different distances and asked them, "Is this door fitted perfectly?" They were then able to associate specific values that are acceptable and unacceptable by their customers.

The consumer and the mechanical value ranges were used to set the specification for the door and the acceptable deviation from that specification. The highest and lowest values for both ranges were used to define the acceptable range—the tolerance.

The price of a part such as door or a chip is determined by the cost of manufacturing parts divided by the number of acceptable parts. Let's say that a chip costs $10 to manufacture (this is not the cost of a chip). However, only one chip in 10 that is manufactured is within tolerance. Therefore, the manufacturing cost of the acceptable chip is $100.

Each assembler must decide on a tolerance balanced by the price paid for the chip and the quality expected by customers. An assembler might be willing to accept a lower than normal tolerance for a device targeted at a specific market.

Let's say that an assembler is building an Internet appliance used as an inexpensive way to surf the net. It is unlikely that the customer will ever need the use of a math coprocessor (see Chapter 3). Therefore, the assembler is willing to purchase a chip that doesn't have a working math coprocessor as long as all the other features are operational. Yet this wouldn't be acceptable to another assembler who require a math coprocessor.

The chip in this example is considered a second and is typically sold in a secondary market to those assemblers who are willing to use parts unacceptable to other assemblers.

Anyone who has ever looked inside a computer soon realizes that there are few parts, especially when you consider that the circuit board is purchased completely assembled and includes the most popular features embedded in it.

For example, a typical computer has a power supply, motherboard, hard disk drive, floppy disk drive, drive controller circuit board (sometimes embedded on the motherboard), and case. A monitor, keyboard, and mouse round out the components.

You, too, could become an assembler by purchasing and assembling the components yourself. While this is an excellent experience, you'll find assembling your own computer more expensive than purchasing a brand-name computer because you'll be paying more for parts than a brand-name assembler.

PRICING AND PROFIT ....

It goes without saying that the purpose of every player in the technical industry is profit. Profit is achieved by supplying the market with a product it needs or perceives to need. And to maintain a profitable level, the market must continue to need your product.

Companies and investors rushed to play in the tech industry because they saw a heavy demand for products, which translates into high unit price. This means that a computing device with a $3,000 retail price included a $200 chip and the market absorbed every computer manufactured.

Market demand was driven by the efficiency of the computing device and the increase in productivity—and saved cost—for nearly every business in the country. Computing device makers, including personal computer assemblers and component manufacturers, knew that every desktop required a personal computer.

And as office software demanded more computing power, businesses needed to upgrade or replace every personal computer. This drove the technical industry for nearly a decade until the market became saturated. Even software makers realized that most businesses didn't require enhancements to their products and therefore didn't always upgrade or replace existing personal computers.

With the commercialization of the Internet and the concept of distributive software, market demands shifted from personal computers to servers and networking devices. This shift altered the strategy of many players in the technical industry to less volume and higher priced products.

For example, major corporations were willing to pay more than 10 times the price of an average personal computer for network servers and devices. These products, such as parallel processors and memory, require more chips (see Chapter 3). This meant that instead of a chip manufacturer receiving $100 per unit, it received $1,000 or more per unit. While the personal computer market stagnates, the network server and network device markets are growing.

Products are priced based on demand and perceived value. The higher the perceived value by consumers, the more they are willing to pay for the product as long as the need for it remains.

Need also influences price. As the need for a product drops, so does the product's price. Players drop out of the market when the market demand shrinks, usually leaving one player standing who can then increase prices because he or she is the only game in town.

This is what is happening to the personal computer industry. The market for personal computers is saturated. Assemblers are heavily discounting their products as a way to attract those few buyers who are left. While dropping prices attracts buyers, the reduced price shrinks profit margins on each unit. Companies find that they must sell more units than in previous years to achieve the same level of profit.

Assemblers try to maintain profits by reducing costs, which typically results in layoffs. Companies who forecast the saturation in the industry usually redirect their companies into new growth markets.

This is why you see leading personal computer makers offering Internet services and networking devices. Companies that are inflexible and attempt to focus on their existing dwindling markets find themselves in financial straits.

CREATING DEMAND ....

Technology has a long history of creating a need then fulfilling the need until a real need for a computer device comes about. This began with home computing. For a decade since personal computers entered the marketplace, personal computer markers had their eyes on the home computer market.

They touted the personal computer as a tool for keeping track of home finances, helping to educate children, and even keeping recipes handy. Personal computers became the craze and personal computer marketers had hoped that peer pressure rather than real need would drive the market.

Personal computers were very pricey and required special knowledge to use them. They weren't consumer products like radio and television. And there wasn't an overwhelming need for the average consumer to learn about computers.

As personal computers became widely used in business, consumers gradually overcame their computerphobia. However, consumers still had difficulty justifying the expense for a home computer—and all the extras such as printers and software.

It wasn't until the commercialization of the Internet that consumers were motivated into buying personal computers. By that time, personal computers were priced within the reach of the average household and a graphical user interface (GUI) such as Windows made personal computers relatively easy to use.

The same strategy is being used today with the growth areas of computer devices. These are cell phones, personal digital assistants (PDAs), Internet appliances, and wireless appliances. Cell phones provide an easy sell to consumers by using the safety factor. No matter where you are located you'll be able to call for help.

That fact wasn't truthful in the early days of cell phones because cell phone networks weren't as established as they are today. There were plenty of dead spots where the cell phone wouldn't work—and still are in remote, rural areas.

However, consumers who adopted cell phones early on were able to communicate on the road sufficiently to provide a steady revenue stream to cell phone companies. The price structure slowly changed to the point where using a cell phone is at times less costly than using the telephone in your home.

The initial claims that consumers should buy a cell phone for safety reasons created a demand that didn't exist. The reality was that very few consumers were ever placed in a situation where they needed to call for help. And even in those few instances there was usually a public telephone within walking distance.

However, the perception of risk was sufficient to kick start the cell phone industry until quality of service and prices reached a level that made cell phones a competitive alternative to traditional telephones.

A similar strategy is happening with PDAs. The PDA segment of the computer device industry sprung from calculators into electronic personal telephone books. I'd bet that not many consumers need an electronic personal telephone book because many of us tend to memorize or jot down frequently called telephone numbers. The electronic personal telephone book became a status symbol around the office and showed that you were in tune with the latest technology.

Electronic personal telephone books have grown into PDAs that run some of the same software that you find on a personal computer such as Word and Excel. The question I still raise is whether or not PDAs are useful. Most consumers who have PDAs also have access to mobile computers and desktop computers.

PDAs are trying to become the mobile computer of choice, although the supporting technology isn't there—at least not today. PDAs are pushing subnotebook computers from the market, but still have a way to go before attacking notebook computers.

A blur between PDAs and cell phones is recently developing. A PDA is a product looking for a market and PDA marketers are seeking to make a PDA the wireless communicator of choice that provides both voice and messaging information. Likewise, cell phone manufacturers are trying to stretch the capabilities—and market—for cell phones by making a cell phone a voice and messaging device.

Both PDAs and cell phones are stretching their technology and have yet to find a real need for such multipurpose devices. There is a demand for voice communication and a demand for mobile messaging. However, is a PDA or cell phone well suited to send messages? The answer is no, not until they have a better input device, which could happen with voice recognition and translating voice to text.

The wireless appliance is poised to enter the technology stage. Early reports claim that we'll be seeing computerized refrigerators, toasters, microwaves, and practically every other appliance found in the home.

Bluetooth (see Chapter 11) provides the technology foundation to make this a reality, and I'm sure appliance manufacturers are ready to jump on board. However, this, too, is technology looking for a consumer. Companies in the wireless appliance segment of the industry are coming up with a marketing line to build a perceived need for their products. This strategy has worked for personal computers and cell phones, so given enough time it should succeed, although I can't image why I would need a computerized refrigerator. But I said the same thing about a home computer years ago.

COMPETITION ....

Competition is keen in the technology industry especially once companies are tooled to produce products as was seen early on between Intel and Advanced Micro Devices. Intel created the processor adopted by IBM for its personal computers and therefore anointed Intel owner of 90 percent of the computer processing market.

Rather than rush to lay claim to the market, Intel hedged its risk by licensing its design technology to Advanced Micro Devices. In this way, Intel could meet demand without having to risk capital to rapidly expand operations—just in case personal computers didn't catch on in the business community.

The alliance between Intel and Advanced Micro Devices went well until the mid-1980s when it was obvious to everyone that the computer processor market was solid and could support expanded operations by Intel. It was at that point that Intel rescinded the alliance with Advanced Micro Devices.

Advanced Micro Devices won a lawsuit that reinstated the licenses to manufacture and sell Intel 386 processors, which Advanced Micro Devices was doing under the license agreement with Intel. But the company was prohibited from manufacturing future versions of Intel processors.

By that time, Advanced Micro Devices already had the facilities and the technical skills to create clones of Intel processors and compete directly with Intel for a segment of the processor market.

It was also at that time when Intel realized another problem—no one can trademark numbers. This meant that any company could call its chip a 386 or 486. Therefore, Advanced Micro Devices could create its own processor design to run the same software as Intel's processors and identify the processors with the same number as Intel's. This forced Intel to switch to using names such as the Pentium. Advanced Micro Devices holds about 15 percent of the personal computer processor market. Intel has about 80 percent and other processor manufacturers have the remainder.

Cyrix, a division of National Semiconductor, joined Advanced Micro Devices to compete against Intel. Both companies made processors that were compatible with Intel's. Cyrix is basically a concept firm that has strong design skills and formed an alliance with Texas Instruments and IBM to manufacture its processors.

Other chip makers also noticed a chink in Intel's armor and have targeted the processor market for expansion. Integrated Device Technology is one of the key players in the memory chip market, so it, too, has the technology to create a processor. Integrated Device Technology's Centaur Technology created a line of processors to compete directly with Intel.

The IBM Blunder

The benefit from competition has forced evolution of technology. Each competitor is quick to take technology to the next step in order to capture a greater market share and in doing so forces the entire industry to advance quicker than if there were no competition.

Until IBM made one of the biggest blunders in computer history, it owned the computer market. Businesses could buy any computer device they wanted as long as it was compatible with IBM equipment. The problem was that IBM computers were a closed system. That meant that few if any non–IBM-affiliated companies had the technology to make their device IBM-compatible.

Without competition, IBM could dictate prices and when to develop and introduce technological advances. It wasn't unheard of for IBM engineers to take years to develop specifications for new technology even before a prototype was built. There wasn't any competitive pressure, so IBM engineers could take as long as was acceptable to management to introduce new technology.

All this changed when IBM introduced its personal computer. Instead of continuing its closed-system policy, IBM opened its personal computer technology to the industry. This allowed circuit board manufacturers and component manufacturers to build IBM personal computer compatible products.

In addition, technology companies quickly realized that they, too, could purchase components and create their own IBM personal computer clones. Microsoft provided the MS-DOS operating system, which was for all purposes the same as PC-DOS used on the IBM. Intel sold its processor to IBM and to clone manufacturers.

IBM quickly found itself losing the personal computer market that it had created by standardizing a processor, motherboard architecture, and operating system. Clone manufacturers, however, didn't have the overhead that was found in IBM nor the layers of management approval that was necessary to introduce new technology. This placed IBM at a disadvantage that eventually caused it to lose the default ownership of the computer market.

Companies such as Motorola and Digital Equipment Company are also processor makers, although their processors are not compatible with Intel's. Motorola's processors are used in Apple computers and Digital Equipment Company processors are designed for computers running a version of Windows NT.

THE PLAYERS..

While some might disagree, I prefer to place players in the computer technology industry into six groups, which I listed earlier in this chapter. And in doing so, I'll admit that there is a blur among some categories; a number of players belong in multiple segments of the industry because they assemble or manufacture a number of computing devices.

In this section, I'll introduce you to the players by name, and I'll give you a brief profile of each company in Chapter 14. You'll also find each company's web site listed in that chapter. You can visit a web site and find practically every piece of information about a company including a list of officers and financial records.

Chip, Circuit Board, and Computing Device Manufacturers

Chips and circuit boards define every computing device, as you learned in this chapter. Many makers of chips also manufacture circuit boards. The major players in this segment of the market are Advanced Micro Devices, Cyrix, Digital Equipment Company, IBM, Intel, Integrated Device Technology, Motorola, National Semiconductor, and Texas Instruments.

Many of these companies also outsource manufacturing. Outsourcing is a business strategy where independent manufacturing facilities such as those in Asia make all or some components of chips and circuit boards on a contract basis. That is, the company identified as the chip or circuit board manufacturer designs the product, sets specification and tolerances, then contracts another firm to manufacture the product.

Outsourcing is typically used when a company's own manufacturing facilities are inadequate to meet current demand or when is it more economical to manufacture the product elsewhere. Outsourcing encourages competition among independent manufacturing plants, which results in lower costs. The outsourcing strategy is also used in other segments of the industry.

Companies such as Intel are called original equipment manufacturers (OEM), which means the company sells a component to an assembler at high volume and at specifications established by the assembler. Simply stated, OEM companies don't sell components directly to us. Instead we either buy assembled products such as a computer or purchase upgrade components from retailers and wholesalers.

Another group of companies that I place in this category are computer assemblers. These are companies that purchase personal computer, workstation, and PDA components from OEMs and assemble them into products that you and I purchase.

The list of assemblers is very long so I'll mention those who I think are major players in this segment of the industry: Acer, Apple Computer, Compaq Computer, Dell Computer, Gateway Computer, Handspring, Hewlett-Packard, IBM, Micron, Palm, Sony, and Sun Microsystems.

A number of assemblers such as IBM are also OEMs. And a number of them also manufacture multiple products. For example, IBM makes personal computers and workstations. Compaq, Sony, and Hewlett-Packard make PDAs.

Storage Device Manufacturers

Storage devices include floppy disk drives, hard disk drives, removable hard disk drives, and CD drives. Here are the major players in this segment: Acentia, Acer, CMS, Compaq Computer, Fujitsu, Hitachi, Hewlett-Packard, IBM, Iomega, La Cie, Maxtor, MicroNet, Panasonic, Plextor, QPS, Ricoh, Sony, Teac, Toshiba, Trek, and Yamaha.

You'll notice that some of these are the same names that appear in the previous segment. This is because many of those firms have divisions that specialize in manufacturing and assembling, or both, storage devices.

The market for storage devices is divided into two segments: the OEM market and the retail market. The OEM market, as you learned in the previous section are assemblers. The retail market consists of end consumers who are either replacing faulty storage devices or upgrading devices.

The importance of each of these markets to players in this segment depends on a number of factors, of which the most important is the nature of the storage device. Every computer contains a floppy disk drive, one hard disk drive, and one CD-ROM drive. Therefore, these products are primarily sold as OEM with a smaller portion going to the retail market.

However, CD-R drives, CD-RW drives, removable hard disk drives, and other types of storage devices that you learned about in this book are primarily sold in the retail market. This is because consumers have yet to demand that these devices be included in their computer. Of course, this is likely to change in the future, as CD-RW technology becomes the standard.

Input Device Manufacturers

Input devices are keyboards, mice, game pads, tablets, and any other device that is used to enter information into a computing device. As with storage devices, input devices are designed for the OEM market or for the retail market.

OEM market input devices are typically keyboards and mice because those are the primary devices used to input information into a computer. Although every computer comes with a keyboard and mouse, some consumers replace them with devices that contain additional features such as the ergonomic keyboard.

However, the retail market for keyboards and mice is small when compared to the OEM market. The opposite is true for game pads and graphics tablets because very few computers are sold with those devices as standard equipment. Therefore, consumers wanting to purchase game pads and graphics tablets must do so from retail outlets.

The major players in the input device segment of the market are: Acer, CalComp Technology, Inc., CH Products, Cross Pen Computing Group, DEXXA, KB Gear Interactive, Key Tronic Corp., Kensington Microware, Logitech, Micro Connectors, Microsoft, Mulitimedia America, Inc., Recoton, and Wacom Technology Corp.

As with other segments, a number of these firms such as Logitech manufacture more than one type of input device, and some such as Acer manufacture products in various segments of the market besides the input segment.

Video and Sound Device Manufacturers

The segment of the market that manufactures video and sound devices—monitors, video cards, digital cameras, scanners, and sound cards—find themselves in a changing segment. It wasn't too long ago when it was common for consumers to upgrade the video and sound card that came with their computer.

In fact, personal computer assemblers such as Dell were noted for including a minimally acceptable video and sound card with many of their computers. Consumers were then offered to upgrade those cards for $100 each. What's an extra hundred dollars when you're buying a $1,500 computer? Many consumers opted for the upgrade.

However, the market has changed since those days. Today many quality video and sound cards are embedded into the motherboard. This means there is less of an opportunity for consumers to require an upgrade.

There is still an OEM market for video and sound cards, although many motherboard manufacturers license the latest video and sound card technology from others so the most up-to-date can be embedded into their motherboards. The retail market is primarily targeted at consumers who are adventure-game players and who are willing to spend a few hundred dollars to see 3D video and hear 3D sound.

Most monitors are sold in the OEM market since every computer must be sold with a monitor. Consumers commonly upgrade the monitor at the time of purchase. This is because of a selling strategy by computer retailers who package lower-quality monitors with computers.

However, few consumers upgrade their monitors once the computer is purchased, because it is a hassle to purchase a new monitor and get rid of the old monitor especially when the old monitor is doing an adequate job.

Scanners and digital cameras are devices that are primarily targeted for the retail market because they are not typically packaged with a computer. The only exception is for computers that are dedicated to a job such as an artist workstation. Then an assembler might purchase a scanner and possibly a digital camera in the OEM market to be packed with a specially configured computer.

Here are the major players in the video and sound device market: 3DFX, Agfa, Apple Computer, ATI, ASUS, Canon, Compaq, Cornerstone Peripherals Technology, Creative Labs, Hewlett-Packard, Hitachi, IBM, Kodak, NEC, Microtek, Nikon, Olympus, Samsung, Sony, Sound Blaster, Umax, ViewSonic, and Visioneer.

Printing Device Manufacturers

The printer market segment is made up of two types of companies: firms that evolved their nonprinter products into printers and those that didn't. For example, Brother originally manufactured typewriters, and Canon and Xerox manufactured copy machines. Today all three manufacture printers. In contrast, Epson was one of the first companies to make impact printers and Hewlett-Packard did the same for laser printers. Today most manufacturers have a full line of printers that include laser and inkjet printers.

Printers are primarily sold in the retail market rather than in the OEM market since consumers consider a printer an option and not a necessity. However, some computer assemblers bundle a printer with a computer and therefore purchase printers in the OEM market.

Household consumers are targeted with nonlaser printers because of the initial price-point. Nonlaser printers such as an inkjet printer have a low entry price but high maintenance cost. This is because ink cartridges are pricey.

Business consumers seek more economical printers and therefore typically settle on laser printers. Laser printers have a relatively high initial price-point, but a low maintenance cost because thousands of pages can be printed using a single cartridge.

Here are the major players in the printer market: Brother, Canon, Epson, Hewlett-Packard, Lexmark, NEC, and Xerox.

Communication Device Manufacturers

The communication device segment of the market consists of network cards, modems, and cell phones. Practically every computer is connected or will be connected to either a LAN or to the Internet. Those connected to a LAN require a network card. A modem is required to link to the Internet.

Modems have become an OEM market item because consumers expect computers to come equipped with one. Many modems are embedded into the computer's motherboard. Business consumers purchase specialty modems such as those used for DSL connections (see Chapter 7) in the retail market. This is because businesses don't use dialup networks to connect to the Internet. Instead they use dedicated lines such as T1 lines that are shared among computers in the office.

It is expected that household consumers will have similar connectivity to the Internet such as using cable television. When this occurs, dialup modems will be upgraded to specialty modems. However, those specialty modems will likely be sold in the OEM market to companies such as cable television companies that offer the advanced connectivity to household and business consumers.

The other growth area is with cell phones. As you learned in Chapter 12, cell phones are expected to become the major communication device for everyone. Although cell phones seem to have recently taken over the consumer market in the United States, the cell phone industry is widely established in Europe. And if the United States follows Europe's lead, expectations will become reality.

Here are the leaders in the communication device market: 3Com, Audiovox, Boca, Diamond Multimedia, Ericsson, Hayes, Kyocera, LG, Motorola, Nokia, Nextel, Samsung, Sanyo, Sprint, and Zoom.

SUMMARY ....

The computer hardware industry is comprised of various segments that are interdependent. These segments are chip, circuit board, and computing device manufacturers; storage device manufactureres; input device manufacturers; video and sound device manufacturers; printing device manufacturers; and communication device manufacturers.

Chip, circuit board, and computing devices include processors, memory chips, coprocessors, and circuit boards for various components such as motherboards, modems, sound cards, and video cards. Also included in this segment are companies that assemble computing devices such as personal computers, laptop computers, notebook computers, and PDAs.

The storage device segment of the industry includes manufacturers of devices such as floppy disk drives, hard disk drives, removable disk drives, and all flavors of CD drives. The input device segment includes devices like keyboards, mice, graphics tablets, and game pads. Practically any device used to enter information into a computing device falls into this segment of the industry.

The video and sound devices segment includes monitors, scanners, digital cameras, video cards, sound cards, speakers, headphones, and microphones. The printing device portion of the industry centers on printers. The communication device segment includes devices such as cell phones and all flavors of modems.

There is a blur among segments because some devices such as a microphones could be placed into more than one segment. A microphone is a sound device but is also an input device. Likewise, a touch-screen monitor is a video device and an input device. Therefore, you must be flexible when slotting products into industry categories.

You'll find a similar blur when trying to associate manufacturers with product segments because some manufacturers play in multiple segments while others focus on one segment of the industry.

The best way to understand the industry is not to compartmentalize products and companies but to focus on products and how products relate to other products. For example, the focal point of every computing device is the processing chip—and therefore companies such as Intel, which makes processing chips.

The processing chip defines the processing that can be performed by a computing device. That is, no computing device can offer features that aren't built into the processing chip. This is why you see a flood of new and improved devices hit the market several months after Intel or one of its competitors introduces a new processor. It was the processor manufacturer that caused the next step in the technological evolution to occur and not the device manufacturer.

I use the term *manufacturer* in a very broad sense because most companies that you and I consider as manufacturers are actually assemblers. An assembler is a company that buys components from OEMs and assembles components into products that are sold to consumers.

For example, Dell Computer might purchase motherboards from Intel, a monitor from Sony, a keyboard from Key Tronics, a mouse from Microsoft, a modem from Hayes, a sound card from Sound Blaster, a video card from Creative Labs, memory chips from National Semiconductor, and a power supply, cables, and a computer case from other manufacturers.

Dell Computer then assembles these parts into a desktop computer for sale in the consumer market. The consumer market consists of households, businesses, and government agencies.

An assembler makes bulk purchases of components and therefore can negotiate better terms with OEMs than you and I could buy similar products on the retail market. For example, Dell Computer requires that its name appear on all or most of the components. This means you might be typing on a "Dell" branded keyboard, but the keyboard might actually be manufactured by Key Tronics.

Some products such as keyboards are mainly sold through the OEM market because those products are a necessary part of a computing device. Other products such as printers are focused on the consumer market since only a few computers are packaged with a printer.

And still other products such as Sound Blaster sound cards are sold in the OEM market but are rarely branded with the assembler's name. This is because Sound Blaster and similarly recognized products have established a brand name in the consumer market. Therefore, consumers don't want just any sound card. Instead they want a Sound Blaster sound card. Private labeling such devices with an assembler's brand name would actually hurt sales.

Summary Questions

1. **How did Intel open the processor market to competitors?**

2. **What is the difference between the OEM market and the consumer market?**

3. **How does the household consumer market differ from the business consumer market?**

4. **Why are some devices sold more to the OEM market than to the consumer market?**

5. **How does tolerance affect the quality of a product?**

6. **What blunders did IBM make to open the personal computer market to competitors?**

7. **Why are services and routers more profitable for chipmakers than personal computers?**

8. **What does the term *create demand* mean?**

9. **How does creating demand help to build the computing industry?**

10. **Which segments of the computing market are growing and which are shrinking?**

13 Computer Hardware:
The Future of the Industry

In this chapter...

- The Common Sense Method of Prediction

- Chips, Circuit Boards, and Computing Devices

- Storage Devices

- Input Devices

- Video and Sound Devices

- Printing Devices

- Communication Devices

This is the point in the book when the publisher asks me to read tea leaves and predict the future of the computer hardware industry. Actually I don't use tea leaves, I read dust particles that I collect from my computer. These are just as accurate as tea leaves.

Predicting the future of the computer hardware industry is as difficult as weather forecasting. Most of us can predict the weather for the next week—by listening to the nightly weather reports. These are fairly accurate. However, long-term forecasting is a combination of wishful thinking and an educated guess.

In this chapter, I'll share with you my educated guesses as to where the industry as a whole is going and where I think each industry segment is headed. I'll look at:

- Chip, circuit board, and computing devices

- Storage devices

- Input devices

- Video and sound devices

- Printing devices

- Communication devices

REALITY CHECK ....

Back in the late 1970s and early 1980s, the term *computer* was synonymous with IBM. IBM owned the computer industry although there were a few competitors such as Sperry Rand. If you were a teenager or an adult during that period, you knew that a computer was a complex, large, delicate electronic device stored in a climate-controlled building.

Suppose someone told you then that in about 10 years that IBM would no longer be king of the computers. And suppose someone told you that a group of teenagers in a garage in California was going to topple IBM.

You won't give those predictions any credence and you'd be right—and wrong. No logical person, even engineers, in the industry would have disagreed with you. Yet that's what happened. Admittedly IBM made blunders (see Chapter 12) that lead to its downfall, but the fact remains that IBM lost its technology edge to a group of teenagers.

In the late 1980s, while the computer market was touting how every household will have a computer, I said that was crazy because households didn't need a computer.

At the time my prediction was based on fact. However, conditions changed. And while I knew about the Internet long before the Internet was commercialized, I couldn't foresee how well household consumers wanted to connect to the Internet. And of course they need a computer to connect to the Internet.

In the early 1970s, the cable industry was telling everyone that cable television will offer hundreds of channels, each one dedicated to a particular type of broadcast. No could believe there would be 24 hours of weather shows, 24 hours of news shows, and 24 hours of cooking shows. And yet today these are some of the most widely watched cable channels.

Therefore, view any prediction with skepticism because no one can predict the future. Even the money and brainpower of IBM failed to predict the personal computer revolution.

THE COMMON SENSE METHOD OF PREDICTION ...

The approach I used in predicting the next few years of the computer hardware industry is to assume that technology will progress along today's path. So with that, here are my predictions.

We'll continue to become less dependent on paper. I'm not sure there will ever be a paperless society, but the signs are fairly clear today that the amount of paper will decline. For example, 80 percent of the households and nearly 100 percent of businesses have computers that are connected to the Internet—and use email for most correspondence.

Email has had a dramatic impact on the postal service. And the next round of technological improvements will have a devastating blow on the postal service. Most of the postal service's business is delivering bills and bill payments. Today some companies and consumers pay bills through electronic wire transfer using the Internet to initiate the transfer.

My first prediction is that businesses and consumers will increasingly use computer hardware to settle transactions. And to make the future blacker for the postal service, the greeting card business is going to be completely electronic. This is happening today as it is gradually becoming acceptable to send someone an Internet greeting card instead of a paper greeting card.

Communication Central

You won't need telephone directories in the future because everyone will be assigned one telephone number, which will be maintained in a computerized directory. You simply speak the person's name into a portable communicator and the communicator will access the directory.

Notice that I refrained from using the term *cell phone* because cell phones as we know them today won't exist. I'll tell you why I believe this to be true in the "Communication Devices" section of this chapter.

The communicator will recognize you by your voice and dial the person's number. For example, you might say, "Get me Bob Farrell;" and the communicator looks up the "Bob Farrell" that you've called before. If there is more than one "Bob Farrell," the communicator will speak back to you and describe the different "Bob Farrells" you've previously called. The communicator might reply, "Do you want your brother-in-law or your lawyer?" assuming both have the same name. You'd respond by saying, "My lawyer."

Far fetched? Cell phones already have voice-activated calling. Computer generated speech has been around for decades. So you could see this feature available in only a few years rather than "some time in the future."

The Virtual Office

You'll always be at work and always at home in the future because you'll be working in a virtual office. The trend is to permit us to work from home as an employee benefit. However, I believe this trend will continue to the point where most workers work from home because this will benefit employers.

Computer hardware enables everyone to perform most—not all—work from a desk in his or her home. Many jobs involve communicating with colleagues and clients using the telephone or email, both of which are accessible from the home.

Business decisions are made based on analysis of data stored in the company's computers. This information can be accessed from home over telephone lines with practically the same security as it can from the office. Groups meetings can be—and are today—held online using video conferencing. And will be available from home.

The technology to work at home for all but manufacturing and service jobs is available today. I believe this will become the norm rather than the exception in the future for one reason—energy.

The energy crisis in California has shed light on our demand for energy and our ability to meet this demand. This includes electrical energy, gas, and oil. Home workers reduce the demand for overall energy because workers no longer need to drive to work. The need for electrical energy will transfer from the office to the home.

No Need to Pay Taxes

Complex number crunching and common decisions will be automatically made by software running on computer hardware. This will free us from routine matters.

I predict that in the future you won't have to file a tax return or pay taxes. Before you think that I've lost touch with reality, let me explain my logic. Most of us receive income from our employer and from interest on money we have in the bank. Some of us earn dividends from stocks, receive payment from bonds, and have capital gains from stocks we sell—and sometimes capital losses from those stocks.

Our income is already reported to the IRS. Employers send the IRS W-2 forms, the bank and brokerage companies send the IRS 1099 forms. In fact, many of these forms are sent electronically to the IRS, so the IRS computers already have our income on record.

Many taxpayers have only the standard deductions, the value of which the IRS already knows. Therefore, the IRS computers have all the information for most taxpayers to compute the taxpayer's taxes.

Some taxpayers have other than standard deductions such as property taxes and mortgage insurance. If the local taxing agency and mortgage companies electronically send taxpayer information to the IRS, the IRS computers could also compute those taxpayers' taxes.

Let's assume that I'm correct in that in the future computer hardware will have sufficient power to process information and that information providers will send information to the IRS. This means that the IRS computers have all the information necessary to calculate everyone's taxes.

How can I predict that you don't have to pay taxes? The IRS computers can easily tell the information providers (i.e., employers, banks, and brokerages) to withhold more of your income or simply transfer money from your bank or brokerage account.

You may say that this is Big Brother, but it is here today. The IRS has sufficient information about most taxpayers already. Their problem is that Congress won't give them money to upgrade the computers to the point where they can calculate everyone's taxes. I think that's likely to change.

Less Guesswork by Physicians

Whenever you visit your physician you probably see rows upon rows of medical folders. Take a close look because you won't see them in the future. In fact, you might not even visit your physician for routine illnesses.

A physician briefly sits with you, asks you a few questions, makes a few observations, then diagnoses you and typically writes a prescription. Sometimes additional tests are required and consultations with a specialist are necessary.

I predict that computer hardware will have medical accessories attached to the computer that will diagnose you. Here's how I think this might work. Based on your symptoms, a physician searches his or her brain and sometimes medical reference manuals for common causes.

Today medical computers associate symptoms with common causes. Furthermore, these computers in emergency room settings walk emergency room staff through procedures. Basically, the computer tells them what questions to ask, what observations to make, and what tests to request.

The answers to those questions and the results of observations and tests are entered into the medical computer, which either suggests a diagnosis and treatment or asks for further information.

Let's take technology further and say that medical accessories could be built that make observations and are able to conduct medical tests right in your home. Software running on the computer hard drive would use computerized speech to ask you questions and a voice response system to translate your response into information that is used to determine the cause of your problems.

Far fetched? Maybe not, because the "physician in the computer," as I like to call it, is here today. There are computers that take your blood pressure and pulse. There is a blood analyzer that tests blood samples and prints out the results of the test. The results indicate which aspect of the blood is beyond the acceptable range—and list the causes with the most common ones first. This is available today, too.

Entertainment at Your Finger Tips

You've probably seen the commercial where a seedy-motel operator tells a customer that he has every movie in every language available anytime day or night. This will happen in the future and you won't have to go to a motel because you'll have access to every available form of entertainment from your living room.

Here's how this is going to work. All existing movies, television shows, and other performances will be digitized and stored on a storage device. The storage device is likely to be memory chips because memory is much faster than disk or CD storage.

You'll use a computer device to request the show. The device will send a signal to a satellite, which is then bounced back to the company that owns the right to distribute the show. The show will be streamed to the satellite then back to your computer device at home where you'll watch the show.

Some first-run movies are being distributed today using a satellite to theaters around the country. Shows are already beamed into homes using satellite television.

CHIPS, CIRCUIT BOARDS, AND COMPUTING DEVICES ....

I've lumped together chips and circuit boards into computing devices because chips and circuit boards define the computing device. Today we have standalone computers such as the personal computer that you have at home and in the office. This will likely change dramatically as other devices acquires the functionality of computers.

Computer chips and circuit boards will be embedded into appliances such as refrigerators, stoves, toasters, televisions, telephones, and even walls. I predict that homes will have a computer closet similar to but smaller than computer closets found today in businesses. The computer closet will contain a central computing device probably similar to a desktop computer minus the screen and keyboard.

Intelligent appliances such as refrigerators and televisions will connect to the central computing device using a wireless network. This means that intelligent appliances will act as input and display devices and the central computing device will be used for software and data storage.

For example, many families write notes and place them on to the refrigerator using a magnet. In the future, refrigerators will have flat screens to display notes and messages. In addition, the flat screen will have a personal mailbox for each family member.

Family members will be able to dictate the message to the flat screen then store the message into a family member's mailbox. Family members receive the message by opening the mailbox using any intelligent appliance including the flat screen on the refrigerator, telephone, cell phone, television, or any number of devices that may or may not be connected to the household computer closet via a wireless connection.

Far fetched? Bluetooth technology (see Chapter 11) exists today and can link up to eight appliances. The central computing device also exists today in the form of a personal computer. There is already voice-input technology that converts the spoken voice into printed characters. And many of us already have email boxes.

Engineers have begun to think out of the box and the box I'm speaking of is the computer. If you've ever opened the case of a computer recently you realize that the motherboard isn't very large.

In fact, I recently attended a conference where one of the exhibitors showed a working personal computer that could fit in the palm of my hand—and this wasn't a personal digital assistant (PDA). This device had the full power of a desktop computer. The device is designed to be embedded into appliances.

Chipmakers will continue their efforts to build a complete computer onto a single chip. They still have technological obstacles to overcome but they are likely to achieve their goal in the future. Once they do, then the personal computer you have on your desktop will become the size of a postage stamp.

STORAGE DEVICES ....

Storage devices have been shrinking and will continue to shrink in the future as manufacturers try to address the storage requirements of intelligent appliances. The future will see more information stored on a smaller area of medium and access time dramatically decrease over what we have today.

Every appliance will be able to store more than 20 terabytes (TB) of information, which will be used as temporary storage, especially to process streaming video and forward store video. Forward store video is similar to voice mail where a caller leaves you a message that is digitized and stored on a disk. However, forward store video will enable a person to leave both video and audio messages.

I also foresee new kinds of storage devices used for mobile devices such as PDAs, cell phones, and communication devices that still haven't been invented. These storage devices will require very little power compared with today's power-hungry storage devices.

Storage devices will blend laser technology and memory technology to create a hybrid that enables permanent storage without requiring the device to be under constant power such as today's devices that require battery backup power.

It is difficult to comprehend how engineers can shrink the size of storage devices because you and I tend to associate the term *storage device* with a hard disk or CD. Yet IBM recently introduced the microdrive, which places permanent storage devices on the same size as RAM-based storage devices such as memory sticks.

INPUT DEVICES ....

I'll give some investment advice. Don't throw away your keyboard and mouse! They'll become valuable antiques in the future because you will no longer use those devices to input information into a computer.

Instead you'll speak to your computer or maybe point to objects on the screen using your eyes. Anyone who isn't a touch or hunt-and-peck typist can't wait for that day to come. Both these technologies are here today except improvements still must be made before they replace the keyboard and mouse in everyday applications.

Keep in mind that I predict that we'll be using computerized appliances rather than what we know of as computers. For example, you might use the telephone to dictate a memo. As you speak into the telephone, your words appear on a flat screen that is stationed on a nearby wall.

Once you're finished dictating and editing your document, you simply tell the telephone to save the document in a specific electronic file folder. And you might also find that the telephone would read back to you the document, just in case you left your eyeglasses at home.

You might be wondering who in their right mind would want to hold a telephone handset while dictating a long document. You won't have to hold the handset because you'll be using a high-quality speakerphone.

I also believe that graphic artists will benefit from using voice input instead of a keyboard, mouse, or graphics tablet. Many commercial artists such as those who design book covers, brochures, and ads build their works of art from pieces of existing art called clip art.

For example, I used clip art throughout this book. However, it was time consuming to sift through the hundreds of choices to find artwork that can be used in an illustration. And then I had to compromise by accepting artwork that was less than what I originally had in mind.

The future changes all this because graphic artists can tell the computer the type of clip art they want and the computer either searches existing artwork or creates the art from scratch. The computer won't come up with a perfect match; however, the artists can give the computer directions to alter the artwork to fit the artist's needs.

Let's say that I wanted a drawing of an office building. I could tell the computer to find or draw a picture of a structure with a specific number of floors or an office building that is like a specific office building such as the World Trade Center.

Furthermore, I could describe the building by the style of architecture, the period in which it was built, the type of façade, and the number and type of stores on the ground floor. And the computer modifies the original artwork to conform to my description.

VIDEO AND SOUND DEVICES ....

Stereos and television will be history in the future when a new computer appliance will be sold that gives you movie theater quality pictures and sound at the sound of your voice. Likewise, you'll hear concert hall sound quality from every performance by your favorite musical artists.

As I predicted earlier in this chapter, entertainment will be on demand, so you won't need to visit the video store or the music store to stock up on videos and CDs. Instead, you'll pay a monthly fee to have unlimited access to every movie, television show, and music recording that was ever produced.

And if you don't want to make your own selections, you'll be able to select groups of performances such as oldies, jazz, or chick flicks and men's action movies—all delivered to your new computerized entertainment center at the speed of light from a satellite.

There will no longer be film cameras. Every camera will be a digital camera with a power supply that will last for years. You'll be able to take single shots or hours of continuous shooting all with one camera.

Images are stored in the camera and on memory strips as backup in case the camera is lost or damaged. And when you get home, all you'll need to do is place the camera or the memory strip on a table and tell your entertainment center to copy the images into your home central computing device. Actually, you'll be able to place the camera or strip anywhere in the house because both of these devices connect wirelessly to your home central computing device.

There will also be new video devices that today are having trouble making inroads in the market. These are e-book readers, which displays a book in an electronic form. This means that you would no longer visit a bookstore. Instead, you'd browse books online similar to today, then purchase and download the book to your home central computing device.

From there, you can copy the e-book to your portable e-book reader by simply saying the book you want from your own personal library. The e-book will automatically be copied to the e-book reader regardless of where it is in your house.

Problems seen with today's e-book readers will not exist because of improved imaging technology that is currently being developed by companies such as Microsoft. Of course this also means that Microsoft will receive a percent of every e-book sale. I like to call that the Bill Gates tax, which already exists on all but Apple computers.

All monitors will be flat and nearly flushed with the wall. There won't be any video cable to connect the monitor to the computer device because all components including the monitor will be wirelessly connected.

PRINTING DEVICES ....

This is a difficult segment to predict because if half of what I predicted in the previous segments comes true, then we may not need to print anything on paper. Nearly every document that is produced in a typical office, with a few exceptions, doesn't have to be printed on paper today.

For example, a wide spreadsheet is still difficult to read on screen and lawyers like to have contracts printed to make it difficult for anyone to change text once the contracts are signed. However, these limitations may be lifted in the future when technology increases the size of the screen and the legal profession accepts digital signatures.

Otherwise, most documents are printed today for the convenience of workers. For some reason some people just like the feel of paper. I think it's an insecurity issue because there is a perception that a printed document is more secure than a document stored in and displayed by a computer. This is not true.

Paper can easily become lost and is difficult to modify, and you need a copy machine to reproduce it. In contrast, you press a button on the keyboard—or in the future simply say Print—and as many copies as you want are printed.

But in the future you won't need printed copies because everyone will have wireless devices to receive and share documents wherever anyone is located. I predict that we'll have 9 × 12-inch thin, lightweight tablets that we can take to meetings and on the road.

The tablet connects to a central computing device where documents are stored. You can electronically distribute documents required at a meeting. Attendees can call up those documents on their tablet.

During the meeting, you'll be able to point to portions of the document on your tablet and your references will automatically position an arrow on the attendees' tablets so they can follow along with your discussion.

Therefore, there will not be a need to print any documents in the office in the future. Even in the home there will be little need to do the same because various computing appliances will display documents.

Typically a household printer is used to print reports for school, resumes, and maybe a digitized photograph. However, this will be unnecessary because homework will be submitted electronically. Resumes are currently sent to prospective employers over the Internet and various computerized appliances will be used to view photographs.

So I predict that your printer will become one of those items that you'll find shown on the futuristic *Antiques Road Show*. You might discover that the printer is worth money decades from now.

COMMUNICATION DEVICES.................................

My prediction is there will not be any cell phones in the future. Instead we'll have less intrusive communications devices that can be worn as a watch, pin, necklace, belt buckle, or even a shoe. No, I don't envision someone holding a shoe up to his or her ear to make a telephone call.

The communicator will be the size of a computer chip and be able to be embedded in a variety of objects that we wear. In fact, we could be wearing many such communicators. Here's how I predict this will work.

The first piece of clothes or jewelry that we put on that contains a communicator chip becomes the primary communicator for that session. As we place other communicator chips on, they send a wireless message searching for an existing communicator chip. When they find one, they go to sleep until the primary communicator chip is no longer available.

There will no longer be a speaker for the communicator. Instead the communicator chip will send a strong, narrow beam of sound to our ears similar to how you roll a sheet of paper into a megaphone shape and speak through it. The narrow beam will prevent anyone else from hearing messages that you receive from the communicator chip.

Likewise, the communicator chip will have a unidirectional microphone that picks up sound waves from a very, narrow direction, which is from your mouth. In this way, you can listen and talk as if the person who sent you the message was standing alongside you.

Communicator chips will receive and transmit voice messages and will store information that is important to you, such as your medical records and frequently used telephone numbers. The communicator chip will also remind you of meetings and your spouse's birthday.

Let's say that after you dress for work you ask the communicator chip for your schedule for the day. The communicator chip tells you that it's your wedding anniversary tomorrow. You tell the communicator to order a dozen roses and have them delivered to your wife's office.

The communicator chip knows the telephone number of the florist that you use, knows your credit card number, and knows your wife's office address. The order is then sent electronically to the florist who has the roses delivered.

Having read about wireless and mobile devices in Chapter 11, you are probably wondering how I think engineers will solve the power problem that is currently facing today's devices.

The answer lies with the redesign of devices. First, Sun Microsystems is developing a clockless computer. As you learned in Chapter 3, information is transported within a computer using a pulsating clock. The clock uses power and by eliminating the clock, engineers are able to save power. We'll still have to see if this technology is successful.

However, an important way of reducing power is to reduce the number of components in the computing device. Notice that the communicator that I project will be available in the future is built into a single chip. This means that the power drain is miniscule and in fact could be recharged by either the sun or the movement of the chip as we walk.

SUMMARY ....

Computers that you and I use today are primitive compared with computing devices that we'll be using in the future. Notice that I say computing devices and not computers because computers will be embedded into devices that we don't think of as computers.

A computing device might be a thin, flat screen that is hung on the wall and is connected to a central computing device using a wireless connection. The central computing device will resemble a computer tower or desktop computer.

There will not be any keyboard or mouse. Instead, you'll speak to the computing device and the computing device will speak back or display a message on the screen depending on your desires.

There will be computing devices throughout the office and your home. Some will be freestanding devices such as a screen hung on the wall. Others will be embedded into appliances such as the refrigerator door or what you know today as a telephone. In the future there will not be telephones because the functionality of a telephone will be included in a computing device.

Each member of the family will have a personal communicator in the form of a chip. The chip will be embedded into clothes and jewelry. The communicator will send and receive messages that are currently being handled by a cell phone and pagers.

Personal communicators will also contain schedules and important information that can be retrieved by asking the communicator for the information. Likewise the communicator can remind you of important meetings and dates.

Nearly all segments of the technology will change and grow. There will be increasingly more components stored on one chip, which shrinks the size of computing devices and reduces dependency on power.

The printer device segment will be dramatically affected by change because there will be less demand for printing documents. As wireless communicators are built for the office, managers will be less likely to print documents. Instead, documents will be distributed and read using a wireless communicator.

Of course, these are my predictions. I based them on guessing at the next steps in the technological evolution. I believe most of these predictions will come true because the basic technology is already in place. It's a matter of time when engineers will be able to introduce these products to the market.

Summary Questions

1. How could computers do away with your paying federal taxes?

2. What is a clockless computer?

3. How could wireless technology change the way we use computers?

4. How will advances in technology affect the U.S. Postal Service?

5. How could a communicator know which person you are speaking about when you say a person's name?

6. Why does it make sense that all computer input will be made by using your voice?

7. How could technology change the way you receive medical treatment?

8. Do you think you would ever have the opportunity to select any movie in any language anytime day or night?

9. How do you think engineers will solve the power drain problem in mobile computing devices?

10. What roles will satellites play in the future of computer technology?

14 Computer Hardware: Profiles of the Major Players

As the saying goes, you can't tell the players without a scorecard. So I decided to provide you with your own scorecard in this chapter. I've listed many of the important players in the computer hardware industry and have given you a very brief introduction. You'll find the web sites next to each company's name, which you can use to learn more in-depth information about the company.

The list is far from complete. To find a web site for a company not listed, use a search engine such as Google (www.google.com).

You'll find the list in alphabetical order rather than organized by market segment, which I did in Chapter 12. I expect that you will use this chapter to reference some of the companies I mentioned in Chapter 12.

3Com www.3com.com

3Com practically invented the local area network (LAN) decades ago with the introduction of its network card commonly known as an Ethernet card. Every computer connected to a network must have a network card, although not necessarily an Ethernet card.

Ethernet is a network protocol like a set of rules for exchanging information over the network. More than 500 million computers use a network card manufactured by 3Com, although the market has become competitive in the past few years.

Acer America Corporation www.acer.com

Admittedly, Acer isn't a household name unless someone in your family works for the company, but many people have an Acer computer product on their desk at work or in their company's computer room. Although as well known as Dell Computer, Acer is not a newcomer to the business. It has been manufacturing computing hardware since 1977.

Acer has a broad line of products including desktop personal computers, notebook computers, network servers, and networking components. It has recently targeted the Internet market with a new line of Internet appliances.

Advanced Micro Devices www.adm.com

You've probably heard about a group of guys who had a great idea for a business. They scraped together a few bucks and opened their business from their living room. Then one day the business took off. Well, that's what happened to Jerry Sanders who started Advanced Micro Devices back in 1969.

Sanders worked at Fairchild Semiconductor, a major component manufacturer in those days. He and his friend John Carey quickly took on the king of microprocessors—Intel. The rest is history. They began making chips for Intel and now they're making and selling their own chips in head-to-head competition with Intel.

ASUS www.asus.com

Back in 1989, ASUS decided to capitalize on a crack in the motherboard marketplace and went into business to challenge the likes of Intel, which manufactured motherboards in addition to processors. Today more than a million computers contain an ASUS motherboard.

Since those early days, ASUS has branched into other areas of the computing hardware market including notebook computers and peripherals such as CD-ROM drives. It also makes network servers, SCSI cards, graphics cards, sound cards, and other circuit boards used in a computer.

ATI www.ati.com

ATI is a key player in the computer memory market by manufacturing memory chips such as SDRAM. It also plays in the expansion card arena. Some of its products include true-color 3D graphics cards, all-in-one TV, video and graphics cards, and an advanced graphics accelerator card used in workstations.

In recent years, ATI has expanded its product line to include a 128-bit graphics and DVD video acceleration card, which has attracted the attention of gamers and anyone who requires high-power graphics at lightning speed.

AT&T www.att.com

AT&T is the granddaddy of long-distance telecommunications companies that had its empire divided and opened to competition by an act of Congress. AT&T has managed to rebuild and fight off competition by developing new technologies at its AT&T Labs research and development arm.

Although AT&T has a strong position in telecommunications, 80 percent of revenues are from voice communications. Competitors are either concentrating on data communications or a combination of voice and data communications.

AT&T is the largest digital wireless network in North America and is one of the leading direct Internet access services for customers. Through acquisitions, AT&T is enhancing its network capabilities and is able to offer broadband video, voice, and data services throughout the United States. On the international front, AT&T has joined European partners to offer seamless domestic and international telecommunication services to corporate clients.

Brother www.brother.com

What is the relationship between a sewing machine and a printer? Nothing, except they are manufactured by the same company, Brother. Brother started out at the beginning of the 20th century making sewing machines in Japan.

The company was called the Yasui Sewing Machine Company. And by the mid-1980s, the company began making electric typewriters. Two years later in 1987, it introduced a laser printer. Today it manufactures inkjet printers, an electronic labeling system, and, of course, sewing machines.

Broadcom www.broadcom.com

Broadcom is a chipmaker whose products are used in cable modems and high-speed networking circuits that are used to connect locations to the Internet. Broadcom's products enable the high-speed transmission of data over existing communications infrastructures, most of which were not originally intended for digital data transmission.

You'll find Broadcom's chips in cable set-top boxes, cable modems, high-speed office networks, home networking, direct broadcast satellite and terrestrial digital broadcast, and digital subscriber lines (DSL). Broadcom has strategic customer relationships with 3Com, Nortel-Bay, Cisco Systems, General Instrument, Motorola, Panasonic, and Scientific-Atlanta.

At the heart of Broadcom's success is its ability to develop advanced digital signal processing hardware architectures, new communications systems algorithms and protocols, and high-performance analog and mixed-signal circuit design using industry standard complementary metal-oxide semiconductor (CMOS) processes.

Canon www.usa.canon.com

Canon has become a household word with its long line of consumer goods. The company is well known in the office for copiers, image filing systems, and fax machines. Canon was able to capitalize on its engineering skills by making printers for computers.

Its line of printers covers practically every niche in the market from personal printers to printers that are shared over networks. Canon is also in the semiconductor business and manufactures various printer components and components used in other electronic devices.

CH Products www.chproducts.com

Ask your computer buddy if she has every heard of CH Products. She may not have, but there's an excellent chance that she uses a product made by CH Products if she plays computer games. CH Products is a leading manufacturer of game controllers.

Its products include trackballs, state-of-the-art joysticks, and specialty game controllers that you love to test whenever you visit your local computer store. These include steering wheels, foot pedals, yokes, and practically any high-quality game controller used in simulation games.

Cisco Systems www.cisco.com

Anyone who listens to the nightly business report or reads the business section of the newspaper will recognize the name Cisco Systems. This is because Cisco Systems is the darling of Wall Street and owning its stock has made many an investor a millionaire.

Cisco Systems manufactures networking devices such as routers and switches, which are used to make sure information traveling over the Internet reaches its destination in the shortest possible time. Cisco Systems products are used by practically every medium- and larger-size business, educational institution, and government agency.

Compaq Computer www.compaq.com

Compaq Computer was one of the original assemblers of personal computers and one of the first companies to challenge IBM's right to claim the personal computer market for itself. Compaq Computer provided a viable, quality alternative to an IBM PC back in the days when corporations were on the hunt for millions of personal computers.

Today, as the personal computer market is reaching a saturation point, Compaq Computer has reinvented itself into a broad-range manufacturer of computing devices. It acquired the pioneer Digital Computer and is manufacturing computer components as well as its traditional line of personal computers and servers.

Creative Labs www.creativelabs.com

You may not have heard of Creative Labs, but there's a good chance you've heard of its marquee product, the Sound Blaster card. Creative Labs envisioned the time when a personal computer would be more than a device used to crunch numbers in a spreadsheet and an alternative to a typewriter. Its designers knew that personal computers would become the toy for gamers.

And with that vision, Creative Labs, founded in 1981 in Singapore, revolutionized computer sound by introducing what has become a personal computer sound standard for the entire industry. Creative Labs has turned a rather dull personal computer into a multimedia machine. Today Creative Labs manufactures DVD drives, graphics cards, videoconferencing hardware, and computer telephony integration equipment.

Cyrix www.cytrix.com

Very few companies saw an opportunity to build a business in the processor market dominated by Intel. Cyrix was one of those companies that trained itself to be a contender—and succeeded in wresting a segment of the processor market away from Intel.

Cyrix became a hot commodity that was initially acquired by National Semiconductor and later sold to VIA Technologies, Inc. VIA was founded in 1987 and manufactures core logic chip sets for the personal computer market and today is a prime player in the memory chip and motherboard segments of the industry.

Dell Computer www.dell.com

Dell Computer manufactures computers and network servers that are offered over the Internet and through telephone orders. Michael Dell, the founder of Dell Computer, was one of the first e-merchants to master the art of selling merchandise on the Internet. IBM followed his lead when deciding that IBM PCs would no longer be sold in stores.

Although Dell Computer is known for providing consumers with desktop and laptop computers, the company also manufactures a line of network servers, some of which run the company's e-commerce web site.

EMC www.emc.com

EMC is a key player in the market for intelligent enterprise storage systems, software, and services that are essential data-storage systems used to make the Internet efficient. The company's products store, retrieve, manage, protect, and share information from all major computing environments, including UNIX, Windows NT, Linux, and main-frame platforms.

Major customers include the world's largest banks and financial services firms, telecommunications providers, airlines, retailers and manufacturers, as well as governments, universities, and scientific institutions. These industry leaders rely on EMC's storage solutions for such applications as online reservation systems, transaction processing, customer billing, the Internet and corporate intranets, data mining, and data warehousing.

EMC became the first company to provide intelligent storage systems based on arrays of small, commodity hard disk drives for the mainframe market, which had developed in today's RAID (redundant array of inexpensive disks) technology. Its unique mirroring software made EMC the world's leading storage-based solution for business continuity and disaster recovery.

Epson www.epson.com

You probably recognize the name Epson as a world leader in computing hardware, but you probably didn't know that Epson is a great timekeeper, too. In 1881, K. Hattori & Co. was formed in Japan to manufacture timepieces. You know this company today as Seiko, the manufacturer of watches. The Seiko company later changed its name to Epson.

Until 1980, the company was considered the world's leading watch manufacturer, which dabbled in the printing business. Epson introduced the world's first mini-printer in 1968 long before the personal computer market took off. However, that experience was sufficient for the company to introduce one of the first personal computer printers in 1980 to gain control of the printer market. Today the company makes a full line of computer hardware including desktop personal computers.

Ericsson www.ericsson.com

One of the first names that come to mind when you think about a cell phone is Ericsson. Ericsson is the premier manufacturer of mobile telephones and other communications tools. The company provides cell phone and communication equipment to the world's top 10 mobile phone operators.

Ericsson has kept with its tradition since 1976 as a global technical business operator. Today Ericsson provides mobile infrastructure and mobile Internet to more than 140 companies and can make the claim that 4 out of every 10 mobile calls are handled by Ericsson equipment.

Gateway, Inc. www.gateway.com

Did you hear the story about these two guys in an Iowa farmhouse who built a computer business that challenged the industry's superstars? If so, then you probably know the story about Gateway. Back in 1985, Gateway began assembling personal computers and gave Michael Dell a run for his money.

Today as one of the top Fortune 250 companies, Gateway still assembles personal computers, but also is a proprietary Internet service provider (ISP) and manufactures a broad selection of peripherals and software.

Global Crossing www.globalcrossing.com

Global Crossing is playing a key role in making the Internet worldwide by laying undersea cables and providing the media to transfer international data. Its digital fiber-optic cables handle transmission of voice telecommunications as well as broadband applications such as the Internet, intranets, and video conferencing.

A concern of many corporations that seek to link local networks internationally is to deal with one vendor that offers a complete service and can increase or decrease telecommunications services as needed for business. Global Crossing is a global telecommunications carrier that provides one-stop shopping for international telecommunications services.

Although telecommunications companies are gradually replacing copper cables with fiber-optic cables, most of these upgrades take place on land. Few upgrade initiatives are in undersea fiber-optic cables. This is where Global Crossing is making inroads with 97,200 miles of fiber-optic cables connecting 5 continents, 24 countries, and 200 major cities.

Handspring www.handspring.com

Did you know that Handspring and the Palm both make personal digital assistants (PDAs) and they're related? Both the Palm and Handspring have the same father, you could say. Jeff Hawkins invented the original PalmPilot and was the founder of Palm Computing. Then after selling Palm Computing to 3Com, he set out to reinvent the PDA market with Handspring.

Handspring capitalized on the growing PDA market by enhancing the features of a PDA, transforming it into a cell phone and wireless Internet accessing device. PDAs are selling faster than cell phones, VCRs, and color TVs when they were first introduced to the public.

Hewlett Packard www.hp.com

Hewlett Packard began as a manufacturer of electronic measuring instruments targeted to the engineering and scientific community. Success in those fields caused HP to expand into the medical equipment arena and eventually into the computer hardware business.

HP became a major player in the laser printer segment of the industry decades ago and basically cornered the market for business-quality laser printers. Today the company has branched out to all areas of the computer hardware industry including personal computers and related peripherals.

IBM www.ibm.com

IBM is known as the mainframe computer king that was overtaken by PC manufacturers. However, IBM is one of the leading e-business solution providers.

The company's mainframe business also found new interest from larger corporations entering e-commerce. Consumers who purchase goods on the Internet require quick responses from e-merchants. The volume of visits and transactions place a strain on many servers. However, IBM's retooled mainframe computers easily handle this demand.

As e-commerce grows, so will the need for high-performance servers used to manage massive databases. IBM's mainframes are the likely choice to handle this job.

Integrated Device Technology www.idt.com

Integrated Device Technology is one of the pioneers in computer memory and introduced the first lower-power, high-speed static random access memory (SRAM) chip back in 1981. This was a year after the company was founded as a designer and manufacturer of industry standard integrated circuits.

Today IDT is a rival to Intel in the processor market and is focused on specialized memory for the networking and the wireless communications industry. Products include FIFO (first-in/first-out) and dual-port memories.

Intel www.intel.com

Intel manufactures computer microprocessors and circuit boards used in the majority of computers used to connect to networks and to the Internet and run about 60 percent of the web servers. Its products include the Pentium III Xeon processor used in mid- to high-end network services, the Pentium II processor designed for use in entry-level services, the Celeron processor used in value PC desktop systems, and the Mobile Pentium II processor for use in mobile PC systems.

In addition, Intel manufactures motherboards, which are the main circuit board in computers and servers. Intel also makes flash memory. Flash memory is reprogrammable memory that retains data when the device such as a mobile phone is turned off.

Another aspect of Intel's business is the manufacture of embedded control chips. These are chips specifically designed for use in automobile engine and braking systems, hard disk drives, laser printers, input/output control modules, cellular phones, and home appliances.

Iomega www.iomega.com

Iomega is the king of the removable hard disk drive market. The company began in 1980 and set its sights on building personal storage devices to help people manage information regardless of where they were located. In those days, floppy disk drives were the common device used storage information.

Today Iomega's Zip drives are used by millions of people to back up critical information and to exchange large amounts of information with others. For example, many creative companies and book publishers use Zip drives to store and transport art and manuscripts throughout the production process.

Juniper Networks www.juniper.net

Juniper Networks manufactures high-performance Internet routers that enable service providers to meet growing demands. Its family of routers delivers performance that is easily scalable and gives technicians manageable control over traffic while maintaining optimal bandwidth efficiency.

It has targeted its routers to transmit IP packets across the Internet backbone by combining a blend of a new class of integrated chip with software-based routing systems.

KB Gear Interactive www.KBGear.com

KB Gear Interactive isn't one of those companies that you hear about in business reports, but you will likely see kids rushing toward their displays in Kmart, Target, and leading computer stores. KB Gear Interactive manufactures attractive and clever computer input devices that are especially designed for the children's market.

The company began in 1994 and soon realized that it could simplify using a computer for children by redesigning the keyboard and by making the keyboard color-coded. Its initial success has led to graphics toolkits that include graphics tablets, a sound studio, and computer cameras.

Key Tronic Corporation   www.keytronic.com

It all started in 1969, when Key Tronic Corporation realized that improvements were needed to the keyboard. The company's designers set out to create a keyboard that was easy to use yet tough enough to withstand the pounding of the fastest touch-typist.

The company was well positioned once the personal computer revolution got underway. It became the first independent supplier of personal computer keyboards and quickly became the industry standard. Today the company has leveraged its OEM market to include laser printers, thermal printers, multimedia touch panels, and an assortment of computer components.

Kodak   www.kodak.com

George Eastman had an idea in 1888 to place a simple camera in the hands of every person in the world. His theory was "you push the button, we do the rest"—and it worked. Eastman is the founder of Kodak, one of the leaders in film cameras and photography.

With digital cameras nipping at its heels, Kodak has decided to become a joiner rather than a fighter by coming out with its own line of digital cameras. Kodak introduced one of the first full-featured digital cameras selling at below $1,000.

And in recent years, Kodak has branched out into the scanner market with the Kodak Digital Science Scanner. It also built a photo CD imaging workstation that allows commercial laboratories and photofinishers to offer customers copyright infringement protection for their digital images.

Kyocera Wireless Corp.   www.kyocera.com

Kyocera Wireless Corp. is a major player in the wireless phone market. The company acquired QUALCOMM, which is the company that developed Code Division Multiple Access (CDMA) technology. CDMA technology gives Kyocera cutting-edge features that aren't found in many competing mobile phones.

The company is poised to capitalize on the growing cell phone market and cell phone accessories market, which is expected to rapidly expand this decade. This is mainly driven by industry's practices of selling a new phone each time a customer's service contract expires.

Lexmark www.lexmark.com

When you think of color inkjet printers, you should also be thinking about Lexmark because it is one of the major players in this segment of the industry. Lexmark was the first company to introduce high-quality (1200 × 1200 dpi color printers to the under-$100 market.

Today Lexmark is focused on photo-quality printing and has joined with Kodak in the personal picture market, which is a photo-quality jetprinter that allows printing directly from a digital camera card without the need of a personal computer.

Logitech www.logitech.com

Logitech is the premier manufacture of computer input devices. The company specializes in keyboards, trackballs, mice, game controllers, and pointing devices. Logitech manufactures practically any input device you can think of.

The company is a very strong player in the retail and OEM market. In fact, you are probably using a Logitech keyboard every day without knowing it because Logitech private labels products for computer assemblers. The company has expanded into other computer hardware such as computer cameras and speakers.

Lucent Technologies www.lucent.com

Lucent Technologies is the forerunner of Bell Labs, which is the company that invented the transistor, among other technologies. Today, Lucent Technologies has its sights on bridging old telephone technology with tomorrow's Internet networks.

The company has 126 years of networking experience and created the existing telephone network. Lucent Technologies is developing ways to transmit digital transformation that blends voice, data, and video into a seamlessly networked flow of information over public and private networks.

Wireless systems, messaging systems, call centers, optical networking, semiconductors, data networking, and communications software are all Lucent strengths. Lucent Technologies is leading the way for the ultra high-speed optical transmission of voice and data.

Maxtor Corporation www.maxtor.com

Maxtor Corporation is one of the pioneers of the hard disk drive industry. The company was organized in 1982 with the task of manufacturing hard disk drives for the then-growing personal computer market.

The market has since slowed, but Maxtor remains one the leading suppliers of hard disk drives for desktop personal computers. Maxtor makes the Diamond Max line of hard disk drives including the high-performance DiamondMax Plus.

MCI WorldCom www.wcom.com

MCI WorldCom is a telecommunications company that offers fully integrated local, long-distance, international (65 countries), and Internet services to homes and commercial customers. Although MCI WorldCom handles voice communications, its primary objective is to transmit data-intensive telecommunications.

The goal of MCI WorldCom is to provide local-to-global-to-local telecommunication services throughout North America, Latin America, Europe, and the Asia-Pacific region without relying on local telecommunications companies. Its system will be fully integrated and self-owned.

In addition to offering a seamless, complete telecommunications package, MCI WorldCom offers customers virtual private networks, web hosting, and e-commerce services.

Micro Connectors www.microconnectors.com

When you come down to it, computer cabling must be a boring business. However, Micro Connectors has made the cabling business a booming industry. This is because every computing device manufactured anywhere around the world requires cables and connectors.

Micro Connector set out to corner the market and become the only name in the game. It is not the only company in the business, but it has turned out to be a dominant factor in the industry especially in the growing USB and networking market.

Micron www.micron.com

Micron Technology, Inc., has established itself as one of the leading worldwide providers of semiconductor memory solutions. Micron's quality memory solutions serve customers in a variety of industries including computer and computer-peripheral manufacturing, consumer electronics, CAD/CAM, telecommunications, office automation, network and data processing, and graphics display.

Micron's mission is to be the most efficient and innovative global provider of semiconductor memory solutions and is exemplified in its short cycle times, high yields, low production costs, and die sizes that are some of the smallest in the industry.

Microsoft www.microsoft.com

Microsoft provides the operating system used by most personal computers and many servers including servers used to host Internet applications and e-commerce. The company offers a wide range of products that include SQL Server, used to store and retrieve data, a communications server, WebTV, the Microsoft Network, and the commerce server.

Others products include operating systems for personal computers and networks, server applications for client/server environments, business and consumer productivity applications, interactive media programs, and Internet platform and development tools. Microsoft also offers online services, personal computer books and input devices, and it researches and develops advanced technology software products.

Microsoft products, available in more than 30 languages and more than 50 countries, are available for most PCs, including Intel microprocessor-based computers and Apple computers.

Microtek www.microtek.com

Microtek and scanner go together like apple and pie. That's because Microtek has taken ownership of the scanner industry and set out to make advancements in digital imaging technologies. And it has succeeded with over 100 patents, most of which are in the digital imaging field.

Microtek is also closely associated with the word *first*. It was the first company to introduce the color slide scanner in 1991, the first professional film scanner in 1992, and the first 600-dot-per-inch, 36-bit color scanner in 1994. And not to be outdone, Microtek introduced the first USB and SCSI scanner in 1999.

Motorola www.motorola.com

The Galvin Manufacturing Corporation working out of Chicago introduced the first battery eliminator that enabled radios to be operated from household current instead of batteries. That was back in 1928. By the 1980s, the Galvin Manufacturing Corporation changed its name and focus. It was called Motorola and manufactured one of the first microprocessors used in personal computers.

Around the same time, Motorola branched out into a new field called mobile telephone. It was one of the first companies to manufacture cell phones and introduced the first lightweight (3 ounces), pocket-size cell phone in 1996.

Network Appliance www.netapp.com

Network Appliances makes cache systems that retain frequently viewed information over the Internet. Prior to Network Appliances, data was stored on the application server, which slowed the response time to deliver data over the Internet.

The Network Appliances' solution is to move the data to a special service called a special network appliance that is responsible for serving data at high speeds. It was the first to devise this high-performance network appliance concept.

The network file servers and web caching solutions deliver fast, simple, reliable, and cost-effective access to data stored on the network or across the Internet, which is an extension of the industry trend toward dedicated, specialized products.

Network Appliances' data access solutions are used by businesses across a variety of industries and applications including the Internet and e-commerce, computer-aided design, engineering and manufacturing, electronic design automation, software development, and financial services.

Its products are used by corporations and ISPs, including 3Com, Adobe Systems, Tripod, John Deere, NationsBanc, and GTE to reduce the cost and complexity of managing their mission-critical data.

Nokia www.nokia.com

Look down at your cell phone and you'll probably see Nokia printed somewhere on the case. Nokia is one of, if not *the* major player in the cell phone industry. The company began as a manufacturer of paper then moved to becoming a rubber manufacturing company in the 19th century. The company was known as the Finnish Rubber Works.

The company capitalized on the new technological revolution at that time—the telegraph—and manufactured telegraph cables that later turned into telephone cables. This placed the company in the position to become the world leader in mobile communications today.

Palm, Inc. www.palm.com

Practically everyone has heard of Palm's PalmPilot PDA since it has been one of the most successful consumer electronics products of all times. Palm defined the standards for the PDA and holds a 75 percent share of the market worldwide.

Today, Palm is feeling the pressure from competitors such as Handspring, which was developed by the founder of Palm (see "Handspring" in this chapter). Palm is now part of the 3Com family after U.S. Robotics, the company that originally bought Palm, was acquired by 3Com.

Panasonic www.panasonic.com

When you think of Panasonic, you probably think about televisions, radios, and other consumer products. However, did you know that Panasonic, owned by Matsushita Electric, was a pioneer in portable computing?

Back in the 1980s following the launch of the IBM personal computer, Panasonic manufactured one of the first IBM-compatible portable computers, although in those days they were called luggable computers because the computer weighed nearly 20 pounds. Today, Panasonic manufactures a full line of computing hardware that includes laser printers.

Plextor Corporation www.plextor.com

The Plextor Corporation is a leading player in the high-performance CD drive market and has manufactured 12 generations of CD-ROM drives. It also makes a complete line of CD products including CD-R drives and CD-RW drives.

You may not recongize the company, but you are probably using one of its products if you purchased a CD-ROM drive with your computer. This is because the Plextor Corporation is one of the major companies in the CD drive OEM market. Plextor is owned by Shinano Kenshi of Japan.

Qualcomm www.qualcomm.com

Qualcomm manufactures the next generation of Internet-enabled cell phones and is the pioneer of CDMA, the technology of choice for next-generation wireless communications.

Over 65 leading communications manufacturers have licensed CDMA technology because it has unsurpassed voice quality, system capacity, privacy, and flexibility through the use of digital wireless communications products.

Qualcomm has various satellite businesses, placing it in a strategic position to benefit from global wireless Internet access that is expected to be available through most cell phones.

Qwest Communications www.qwest.com

Qwest is an Internet communications company that uses fiber optics to carry voice, data, and images. In the U.S. it covers 18,815 miles and connects to 150 cities across the country and 1,400 miles into Mexico.

The Dutch Telecommunications Company, KPN, joined with Qwest to create a 9,100-mile fiber-optic network that connects 40 European cities. Qwest is also a member of a consortium that is building a 13,125-mile cable from California to Japan and other Pacific Rim countries.

In addition to long-distance fiber-optic networks, Qwest has created its own local networks in 19 cities in the United States, where it offers homes and businesses fast access to the Internet through its DSL services.

Qwest also offers services besides providing a fast connection to the Internet and intranets. These services include web-based paging, Internet calling, and online faxing. For businesses, Qwest offers dedicated internet access, web hosting with high bandwidth connections, outsourcing resources for corporation Internet services, and virtual private networks.

Samsung Electronics www.samsung.com

When you hear Samsung, you probably think about televisions and other consumer electronic products. However, it is unlikely that you think about computer memory. Samsung Electronics is the world's leading manufacturer of memory devices.

The company designed and manufactures the 256-megabit dynamic random access memory (DRAM) chip and the 1-gigabit DRAM chip. Samsung Electronics also manufactures other products for the semiconductor industry.

Sanyo www.sanyo.com

In the 1950s, Sanyo was known in Japan for three products: a bicycle generator lamp, a plastic cabinet radio, and the whirlpool action washing machine. Nearly half a decade later, Sanyo is known for a complete line of consumer electronics and appliances.

Today, Sanyo is also a leader in cell phone manufacturing, LCD computer screen panels, digital cameras, and rechargeable batteries. As the company's name implies, Sanyo is in practically every market around the world. Sanyo in Japanese means "three oceans."

Sony Corporation www.sony.com

Sony is an another Japanese conglomerate that has become a global leader in technology. The company manufactures audio, video, and communications products and is also in the music, motion picture, and television production segments of the entertainment business.

The company is also pushing the envelope when it comes to computer design. Sony introduced a new, thin, lightweight line of computers called the Vaio that has raise the standard in the portable computer segment of the industry.

Sun Microsystems   www.sun.com

Sun Microsystems manufactures services that are used to host web sites. The company first made a name for itself building high-powered workstations that were quickly adopted by major Wall Street firms. As the Internet and e-commerce began to grow, Sun Microsystems retooled their products to meet the needs of Internet companies.

Web performance is up 400 percent and performance of Java applications, a language developed by Sun and used to develop Internet and intranet applications, is up 1,400 percent with the redesign of Sun's Solaris operating environment.

Sun has made its products scalable, which enables e-commerce companies to easily grow in synchronization with the e-commerce market.

Part 3   • The Industry

PUTTING IT ALL TOGETHER ....

There are hundreds of companies working toward the same common goal—to use computer technology to make our lives more interesting and productive. The previous three chapters gave you a brief tour of the computer hardware industry. I provided you with the web sites in Chapter 14 of important players in the industry, which you can use to continue your industry tour.

The computer hardware industry falls into six major categories: chip, circuit board, and computing devices; storage devices; input devices; video and sound devices; printing devices; and communication devices.

Chip, circuit board, and computing devices are the meat of the industry because collectively this segment defines what we called a computer. Storage devices are hard disk drives, CD drives, and other similar kinds of devices that are used to permanently store information.

Input devices include keyboards, mice, trackballs, game pads, and other devices used to input information into a computing device. Video and sound devices include monitors, digital cameras, scanners, speakers, headphones, sound cards, and video cards. Printing devices consist of any device used to print, such as a laser printer, ink-jet printer, and plotter. Communication devices are cell phones and wireless devices that let us transfer information among computers.

Computer hardware technology is dramatically changing and will change the way you and I use a computer in the future. Most if not all input will be made by using your voice. Simply stated, you'll tell the computer what you want and the computer will respond verbally and/or by displaying messages on the screen depending on your desire.

All computer screens will be flat panels, which will be embedded into communication devices instead of attached to a computer. And in many instances the flat panel will be the communication device.

You'll see communication devices built into what we know of as telephones today and in appliances such as the refrigerator door, which is a focal point for posting family information. Likewise, there will not be cell phones. Instead, we'll be using communicators on a chip embedded into clothes, watches, and even shoes.

There won't be speakers either. Instead, sound technology will develop into direct sound. This is where the communicator directs a narrow, strong beam of sound directly into you ear. You alone can hear it.

And there won't be microphones, at least the way you know them today. The communicator will have a built-in microphone-like device that will recognize only your voice and won't be distracted by outside sounds.

Communicators will be the personal assistant who can anticipate your every move. For example, the communicator will know when you're leaving work and warn you of traffic tie-ups as well as tell you how to avoid them.

I like to think of the new computer hardware technology as a disruptive technology. This isn't the first time that the world has seen a disruptive technology. Electricity, the internal combustion engine, the airplane are just a few technological inventions that have influenced every aspect of life.

If you think that my predictions are far-fetched, think again. Most of the technology that I speak of either exists today at some level of development or is only a few evolutionary steps away from becoming a reality.

Glossary

A/B switch box
A switch box that lets more than one computer share a printer.

Abacus
The first computer. Used rows of beads to assist in adding and subtracting numbers.

Accelerated graphics port
An expansion slot designed for video expansion circuit boards.

Active matrix LCD
A liquid crystal display that uses tiny transistorized circuits to display an image.

A-D converter
A connector on the motherboard that converts an analog signal to a digital signal.

Additive color model
A color model that adds together primitive colors to create other colors.

AGP
See Accelerated graphics port

Amortization
A technique of pro rating (annual cost) the cost of a printer over the expected useful life of the printer.

Amplifier
A circuit that increases power to a weak signal.

Amplitude
Height of a wave.

Analog
Representing information as a series of values.

Analog game controller
A game controller that sends variable values to the motherboard, such as a stand-alone joystick, although some joysticks are designed to send digital values.

Analog simultaneous voice and data
A voice modem

Analog-to-digital converter
A device that converts an analog signal to a digital signal.

Aperture grill
A type of mask made of thin vertical strips.

ASCII
A standard that associates letters and symbols with numbers.

ASVD

See Analog simultaneous voice and data

Asynchronous motherboard

The chip set on the motherboard that does not adjust the speed of a bus based on the speed of other buses on the motherboard.

Atmospheric pressure

The normal pressure of air molecules in the atmosphere.

AVI

A nonstreaming video file format.

Backup power supply

A battery-powered device that automatically provides power to a computer for a short time period during a power failure.

Bandwidth

The number of communication channels available to transmit information across the network.

Baseband technology

One bit at a time is transmitted on a digital signal.

Base-10 numbering system

A system of numbers that uses 10 digits from zero to nine. This is commonly called the decimal system and is the prevalent system used in everyday counting.

Basic input/output system

A set of instructions that provide minimum input and output capabilities to a computer.

Baud

The transmission of one symbol per second.

BIOS

See Basic input/output system

Bit

A binary digit that has the value of zero or one.

Bluetooth

Technology using low-power radio transmission to connect network devices without the need for cables, which can maintain the network connection even if the network device such as a computer is on the move.

Boot record

The first bytes of data read by the BIOS when a computer is started.

Bottleneck

Any network device that slows the transmission of packets over the network.

BPS

See Baud

Broadband technology

Multiple bits are transmitted at a time on an analog signal.

Bus

A set of etched wires on the motherboard that is used to transport information among components and is a characteristic of a motherboard.

Bus interface unit

The circuitry in the processor that connects the processor to the bus on the motherboard.

Bus mastering DMA

A technique that gives all devices access to main memory and the ability to communicate with other devices that are connected to the computer's bus called the DMA channels.

Byte

A set of eight binary digits.

Cable modem
A modem used to transmit and receive data over cable television lines

Cache
Computer memory set aside for a special purpose such as storing frequently used data.

Capacity keyboard
A keyboard where keys change the flow of electricity rather than stop and start the flow of electricity.

Carrier signal
A radio signal that is transmitted at a consistent frequency used to establish a connection with a radio receiver.

Cathode
A component of an electron gun that is heated to generate a flow of electrons.

Cathode ray tube
An electronic device that uses a stream of electrons to display an image on a screen.

CAV
See Constant angular velocity.

CCD
See Charge-coupled device.

CD-DA
A digital audio CD.

CD-R
A device that reads and writes CDs.

CD-ROM
A device that only reads CDs.

CD-RW
A device the reads, writes, and erases CDs.

Central processing unit
See Processor.

Channel
A recording or playback connection that contains one or more sources of sound.

Character block
A defined block of pels used to display a character.

Charge-coupled device
An electronic component in a digital camera or scanner that is light-sensitive material and used to capture an image.

Chip
A large-scale integrated circuit that contain the logic to store, retrieve, transmit, and process information.

Chip set
A group of integrated circuits that control the flow of information on the motherboard.

Circuit protection
A feature that cuts power to the motherboard if voltage and current exceed the maximum value that can be handled by the motherboard.

CIS
See Contact image sensor

Clock
A chip on the motherboard that synchronizes information flow on the motherboard.

Cluster
A group of sectors where the operating system stores data.

CLV
See Constant linear velocity

CMYK color model
A method of combining cyan, magenta, yellow, and black to create other colors. Called a subtractive color model.

Color

A light wave that vibrates at a specific frequency within the visible light range of the electromagnetic spectrum.

Color correction profile

An internal reference table used by monitor drivers and printer drivers to determine the specific mixture of primitive colors to produce a standard set of colors.

Color depth

Maximum number of individual colors that can be used to display a pel, sometimes referred to as the amount of data needed to display each pel.

Color gamut

The range of colors that is produced by a color model.

Color model

Defines the way in which a monitor generates colors.

COM

See Serial port

Communication channel

An electronic pathway over which a signal travels, very similar to a highway.

Compiler

A program that converts a program written in a higher language (i.e., C, C++, Java) to machine language.

Compression

A technique for reducing the number of bits to represent information.

Concentric tracks

Circular tracks that don't touch.

Conductive material

Material that has little or no resistance to the flow of electricity.

Constant angular velocity

The technique of maintaining a constant rotation speed of a CD.

Constant linear velocity

The technique of increasing the rotation speed of a CD as the laser moves closer to the center of the CD.

Contact image sensor

Scanner technology that uses embedded logic that handles the conversion without having to use a separate component.

Control character

A character embedded in a document that has special meaning to a device such as indicating that a page must be ejected from a printer.

Coppermine core

A design that uses copper-interconnect technology where copper instead of aluminum is used to connect components.

Cost per page rating

A measurement used to determine which printer is cost effective.

CPU

See Processor.

CRC

See Cyclical redundancy check.

CRT

See Cathode ray tube.

Crystal

A chemical formation of molecules into a distinct pattern. Salt is a crystal that we come in contact with every day. When certain crystals are charged with electricity, the crystal vibrates at a consistent frequency, and some crystals vibrate within the radio spectrum.

Current
The speed of electricity flowing over a wire.

Cyclical redundancy check
A way to check for errors on network transmissions.

Cylinder
Tracks on the same position on multiple platters in a hard disk drive.

Data
Information necessary to complete the task.

Data modem
A modem that transmits and receives data.

Data size
The amount of data that the destination network card can store in memory before the destination computer processes the data.

Decay factor
The time required for a pel to lose its glow after being struck by the electron beam.

Dedicated service
A permanent connection between two points on the telephone network. The connection remains intact after each call is completed

Deflection yoke
A component of an electron gun that uses electromagnetism to alter the path of the electron beam.

Defragger program
A program that copies clusters of a file into sequential clusters.

Depth of field
Determines how much of the image is in focus.

Desktop board
A term used to refer to a motherboard.

Difference Engine and the Analytical Engine
The first mechanical computer that was designed to add, subtract, multiply and divide, but was never commercially built. Principals used in this computer are still found in modern electronic computers.

Digital
Representing information as one of two discrete values (zero or one).

Digital game controller
A game controller that sends one of two values to the motherboard.

Digital sampling
See Sampling.

Digital simultaneous voice and data
A voice modem.

Digital-to-analog converter
A device that converts a digital signal to an analog signal.

Digital video
The rapid recording of a series of digital photographs that when viewed in the same sequence and at the same speed tricks our brain into seeing movement.

Direct memory access
A technique that gives a device's processor, such as the network adapter card, direct access to main memory without using the computer's CPU.

Direct sequence modulation
Where bits of a packet are sent over multiple frequencies at the same time. The receiver reassembles the packet.

Disk
A component on which data is stored.

Disk drive

A device that accesses data stored on a disk.

Dolby/AC3

A technology used to enhance a recorded sound to minimize the impact of imperfect recordings.

Domed elastomer key

A membrane keyboard.

Doppler effect

The soft-loud-soft sound as an object passes from side to side.

Dot-matrix printer

A printer that creates images on paper using a block of metal rods that strikes an inked ribbon.

Dot pitch

The distance between the same color subpel of two pels.

DRAM

See Dynamic RAM.

Driver

A program that translates operating system instructions into instructions recognized by a device such as a printer that is connected to the motherboard.

Dry contact switches

Switches used in a mechanical keyboard.

DSL modem

A modem used to transmit and receive information over a DSL line

DSM

See Direct sequence modulation.

DSVD

See Digital simultaneous voice and data.

Dye printer

A printer that uses a burst of color dye to create an image on paper.

Dynamic RAM

RAM that is refreshed frequently when the computer is powered up.

EBSDIC

A standard used on mainframe computers that associates letters and symbols with numbers.

EDO DRAM

See Extended data out DRAM.

Electromagnet

A piece of metal that is magnetized when electricity is passed around the metal.

Electron

An element of an atom that surrounds the atom's nucleus.

Electron beam

A stream of electrons flowing at a consistent rate from an electron gun.

Electron gun

An electronic device containing a cathode that is heated to generate a flow of electrons.

Electronic noise

Degradation of an electrical signal such as an image captured by a digital camera.

End of file (EOF) marker

A value that tells the operating system that there are no more clusters for the file.

Ergonomic keyboard

A keyboard arranged in a natural position built to reduce chance of repetitive stress injury.

Etch

The technique of removing the nonconductive material outer coating and exposing the inner conductive material.

Expansion circuit board

A circuit board that is inserted in an expansion slot on the motherboard.

Expansion slots

A receptacle on the motherboard where expansion circuit boards can be inserted to connect to the circuitry on the motherboard.

Extended data out DRAM

A type of video image RAM.

Factorial

A mathematical formula used to determine the number of unique combinations of a set of objects such as letters of the alphabet.

FAT12

A file allocation table standard that uses 12-bit cluster addresses.

FAT16

A file allocation table standard that uses 16-bit cluster addresses.

FAT32

A file allocation table standard that uses 32-bit cluster addresses.

Fax modem

A modem that transmits and receives data and faxes.

Fidelity

The quality of sound reproduction.

File allocation table

A directory of all clusters on a disk.

Film

A sheet or roll of one or three layers of gelatin-like material that is coated with silver halide crystals, which is sensitive to light.

Film speed

The light necessary to properly expose an image; it is measured in an International Standards Organization (ISO) number.

Firmware

Instructions encoded into a read-only memory chip that configures computer hardware.

Fixed space font

A technique that uses the width of the character for each character regardless of the shape of the character.

Flash memory

Retains its contents when the computer is powered down. A program can change information stored in flash memory.

Flat rate

A measurement of how well a speaker or a sound card reproduces the complete characteristics of the sound wave.

Floating-point

A method used to represent the separator (i.e., decimal point) between the whole number and the fraction.

FM synthesis

A technique used by a sound card to produce a pure tone with added harmonic frequencies to create the sound of a real instrument.

Focal length

The distance from the center of the lens to the point where light waves from a distant object converge.

Font

The shape of a character that is printed on a page or displayed on the screen.

Footprint

The amount of space a device takes up.

Force feedback

A technology that increases resistance in a pointing device or game controller depending on the object pointed to on the screen.

Form factor

The size and shape of a motherboard.

Formatting

The process undertaken by the operating system to prepare a disk for writing and reading data

Fragmentation

A file that is not stored in sequential clusters

Frame buffer

A portion of video image RAM that contains one screen full of information.

Frequency

Fluctuation of an object a specific number of times per second.

Frequency hopping

Sends a packet over a rotating set of frequencies.

Frequency response

The range of frequencies that can be reproduced by a speaker.

F-stop

A camera setting that determines the length of time a shutter is opened.

ftp

Software used to copy files across the Internet.

Gain

Determines how sensitive the CDD in a digital camera is to light and is similar to film speed in a film camera.

Game controller

An input device used to interact with game software.

General MIDI

A MIDI standard that has 16 channels.

Geosynchronous satellite

A satellite stationed at a fixed location 22,300 miles above the surface of the earth.

Gigaflop

A billion floating-point calculations per second.

GlidePoint control

A touch pad pointing device.

Graphics accelerator

A coprocessor specifically designed to display graphical information quickly on the screen.

Graphics tablet

An electronic paper and pencil used to draw or plot images on the computer screen.

Graphical user interface (GUI)

A method of enabling users to interact with the computer using small graphic images called icons rather than typing commands at a prompt.

Graphics mode

A mode in which a printer enables the operating system to address all the pels rather than a block of pels.

Handshaking

The process each network card uses to determine the data size that can be transmitted, transmission timing, data confirmation, and data transmission rate.

Harmonics

Sound frequencies that give tone and color to an instrument or other sound-generating device.

Header

The first few bytes of a sector.

Hertz

One cycle of an electronic wave per second.

Hold up time

A characteristic of how well a power supply maintains power during a power failure.

Horizontal scanning frequency

The length of time taken to display one line across the monitor.

Host bus

Transfers information between the processor and the chip set.

HSB color model

A method of changing the hue, saturation, and brightness of image to create various colors.

ICC

See International Color Consortium.

Immediate data item

Data contained within an instruction.

Industryl Standard Architecture (ISO)

An expansion slot found on older computers and on some new computers that want to maintain backward capability with existing expansion circuit boards.

Information

One or more words that are used to describe something.

Inkjet printer

A printer that uses a droplet of ink to create images on paper.

Instruction handler

Circuitry within the processor that is responsible for getting an instruction and interpreting the instruction.

Instruction set

Commands that are recognized by the processor.

Instructions

Statements of a program written by a programmer that tell the processor to perform a specific task.

Integrated circuit

A computer chip that contains many microscopic transistors connected together with the wires etched into the chip.

International Color Consortium

A standards organization that has developed a set of color correction profiles for printers and monitors.

Internet Protocol (IP) address

A unique address assigned to devices that are connected to a computer network.

Interpolated resolution

The actual number of pixels that are stored in the image file using software to increase the optical resolution.

Interrupt message

A message telling the processor to stop the current processing and run the program that is associated with interrupt message.

Interrupt request line

An etched wire on the motherboard that is used to transmit an interrupt message from a device to the processor.

Interrupt service routine
A program that is associated with an interrupt message.

Interrupt type
The contents of an interrupt message.

Interrupt vector table
A two-column table in memory that associates an interrupt message type with the address of an interrupt service routine.

Interrupted speech technology
A speech recognition technology that requires the speaker to pause between words.

Invar
A metal alloy that retains it shape under extreme heat and is used to create a mask.

IP
See Internet Protocol address.

IP address
An Internet Protocol address that uniquely identifies a communications device such as a cell phone or a computer that is connected to a network.

ISA
See Industrial Standard Architecture.

ISDN modem
A modem used to transmit and receive data over an ISDN line.

Java
The first universal software language designed for use on the Internet and corporate intranets. Enables programmers to write an application once that can be run without modification on any computer.

Key scan code
The code for each keyboard matrix intersect.

Keyboard
An input device that uses a set of switches to represents characters.

Keyboard buffer
Memory allocated to store key scan codes.

Keyboard matrix
A wired matrix inside the keyboard used to identify which key was pressed.

Large-scale integrated circuits
A chip that contains many integrated circuits.

Laser printer
A printer that uses a xerographic printing technique to create images on paper.

LCD
See Liquid crystal display.

Light emitting diodes
An electronic component that generates light when electricity flows through the component. Also known as LED.

Light wave
A series of photons vibrating within the visible light range of the electromagnetic spectrum.

Line regulation
Monitors and adjusts if necessary voltage coming from the power cord

Liquid crystal display
A monitor that uses electrodes or transistor circuits to adjust the liquid crystal fluid to allow a specific amount of light to pass through the liquid crystal fluid to display an image.

Load regulation
Monitors and adjusts if necessary voltage within the computer.

Local area network (LAN)

A network of computers, printers, and other devices that are within the same vicinity such as on the same office floor or office building.

Logical disk

When the operating system treats divisions of a physical disk as individual disks.

Machine language

A computer language understood by a processor.

Magnetic random access memory

Memory that uses magnetic settings rather than electrical charges to store information on the chip.

Mask

A grid of metal that sits between the electron gun and the phosphor-coated screen used to let some electrons hit the phosphor and let the grid absorb other electrons.

Mechanical keyboard

A keyboard that uses mechanical switches as keys.

Mechanical mouse

A mouse that uses a ball and rollers to move the mouse cursor.

Media player

Software run by a browser to play video and audio files.

Megahertz

A million cycles of an electronic wave per second.

Membrane keyboard

A keyboard that uses a membrane of artificial rubber between the keys and the circuit board.

Memory access method

The way in which the processor transfers information to and from memory.

Memory bank

The logical grouping of memory.

Memory bus

Transfers information between the processor and memory.

Memory cache

Fast-working memory located inside the processor.

Memory chips

Integrated circuits used to store information.

Memory mapping

A way in which memory locations are identified inside the computer.

Memory package

The physical grouping of memory.

Microinstruction

A special circuit within the processor that performs unique processing such as a math coprocessor.

Microprocessor

See Processor.

Microstore

A listing of special circuits, called microinstructions, within the processor that perform unique processing such as a math coprocessor.

MIDI

See Musical instrument digital interface.

MIDI File

A file that contains instructions for a MIDI processor.

Mission-critical database applications

Computer programs that manage data that is important to a business. The business would stop running if a mission-critical database application stopped running.

Modem

A device that modulates a digital signal to an analog signal for transmission over telephone lines and demodulates an analog signal to a digital signal for use by a computer.

Monitor

A device that displays information.

Motherboard

The main circuit board inside the computer that contains components such as the central processing unit, clock, and computer memory.

Mouse

A pointing device that contains one or more buttons and fits in the palm of your hand.

MPEG-1

A nonstreaming video file format.

MRAM

See Magnetic random access memory.

Multiplier lock

The speed of a processor is determined by the speed of a bus.

Musical instrument digital interface

A method of synthesizing sounds produced by musical instruments.

Natural speaking technology

A speech-recognition technology that requires the speaker to speak naturally.

Network adapter card

A device either integrated on the motherboard or inserted into an expansion slot that connects the motherboard to a LAN.

Network card

A circuit board that, among other things, takes information from memory and encodes it into a signal that is transmitted over the network cable.

Network resource

Any device or file available on a network. This includes file server, printers, modems, and other such devices.

Networked printer

A printer that is connected to a computer network.

Nonconductive material

Material that resists the flow of electricity.

Nonproportional game controller

A game controller that sends incremental values instead of a continuous value to the operating system.

Nonstreaming video

Requires that the entire video file be copied to the computer that will display the video before the video is shown.

NTFS

A file allocation table standard used on Windows NT.

One-dimensional sound

A single sound wave.

Operating system (OS)

A set of programs that operates the computer hardware and interfaces between the computer user and the computer hardware.

Optical character recognition

Software that convert a scanned image of text to ASCII characters.

Optical density rate

The capability of a scanner to capture finer elements of an image.

Optical mouse

A mouse that uses light waves and a reflective grid to move the mouse cursor.

Optical resolution

The number of pixels per inch that are captured when an image is scanned.

Opto-mechanical mouse

A mouse that uses a combination of light waves, ball, and rollers to move the mouse cursor.

OCR

See Optical character recognition..

Packet

An electronic envelope that contains the address of the destination network resource, the address of the computer making the request, and either all or a piece of the request along with information that controls the packet.

Parallel port

A connector on the motherboard that sends and receives information multiple bits at a time to and from external devices such as a printer.

Partial CAV

The technique of maintaining two rotation speeds of a CD, one speed toward the center and another toward the outer side of the CD.

Partition

A division of a hard disk into logical disks.

Pascaline

The first working mechanical computer that could add and subtract and was designed by Blaise Pascal.

Passive matrix LCD

A liquid crystal display that uses electrodes to display an image.

P-CAV

See Partial CAV.

PCI

See Peripheral component interconnect.

PCL

See Printer control language.

Pel

A picture element displayed on a screen.

Peripheral component interconnect

A type of bus that transfers information quickly between the motherboard and external devices.

Phosphor

A compound of chemicals that glows when struck by electrons.

Photo-conductive material

A component within a laser printer's toner cartridge that is a metal cylinder covered with a photo-conductor coating.

Photon

A molecule that generates light; an atom of light.

Pipelining

A way in which a processor gives each processing step its own path within processor.

Pixel

A picture element of an image.

Planar

A term used to refer to a motherboard.

Platters

Multiple disks in a hard disk drive.

Point size

A measurement of the size of a character.

Polarity

A positively or negatively charged particle of iron.

Polling

Describes the regular transfer of data between a series of computers located in remote locations. A central computer systematically calls (polls) each computer to initiate the exchange of data.

Port

An integrated circuit on the motherboard that enables external devices to be connected to the motherboard's circuitry.

Portrait mode

Electrically placing the foreground or background out-of-focus in a digital camera.

PostScript

A common page description language used to print text and graphics.

Print head

The component inside a printer that produces text and images on paper.

Print job

A document sent to a printer server to be printed on a networked printer.

Print queue

The order in which documents are printed on a networked printer.

Printer control language

A language developed by Hewlett Packard to control printing text on the HP LaserJet printer.

Printer server

A computer connected to the network that manages printing documents to a networked printer.

Private branch exchange (PBX)

A private telephone system used by businesses.

Processor

The large-scale integrated circuit that executes instructions written by programmers to process information.

Processor bus

See Host bus.

Program

A set of instructions that tells a computer how to process information.

Programmable game controller

A game controller where components such as buttons can be assigned to functions in game software.

Programming language

A set of words recognized by a computer and used to instruct a computer to perform specific tasks.

Proportional game controller

A game controller that sends a continuous value to the operating system.

Proportional spacing

A technique that adjusts the width of the character according to the shape of each character.

Proprietary operating system

A computer operating system that was specifically designed for a particular computer and not made available for use with other computers.

Protected mode

A mode of operation for a personal computer that enables multiple programs to run at the same time. Each program is restricted to a region of memory.

Public switch telephone network

A network of cables and switches that routes signals to any telephone on the network based on the telephone number dialed by the caller.

Puck

A mouselike device with crosshairs used with a graphics tablet to plot dots on the computer screen.

RAM

See Random access memory.

RAM buffering

A network card that contains its own memory used to temporarily store incoming packets

RAMDAC

See Random access memory digital-to-analog converter circuit.

Random access memory

A memory chip that contains information that can be changed.

Random access memory digital-to-analog converter circuit

A component of the video display adapter that converts a digital signal to an analog signal.

Rastering

A printing technique used to zigzag the print head across and down a page.

Read-only memory

A memory chip that contains information that cannot be changed.

Read/write head

The mechanism in a hard disk that reads data from a disk and writes data to a disk

Real mode

A mode of operation for a personal computer that enables one program at a time to run. That program has full access to main memory.

Real-time communication

What we experience during a telephone call when someone speaks then waits for the other person to respond.

RealMedia

A streaming video file format.

Real-time switching

The ability of the telephone network to connect to any point in the telephone system when someone makes a call.

Reflective light

Light waves that are not absorbed by an object struck by white light.

Refresh frequency

See Refresh rate.

Refresh rate

The time necessary for the electron gun to scan the screen.

Register

A small amount of memory located in the processor and used to temporarily store instructions and data.

Relay

A switch that is turned on and off electrically.

Removable disk drive

A drive where disks can be removed and replaced with another disk.

Repeater

A device that receives a signal then retransmits the signal to other repeaters or devices. Retransmission introduces new energy to power the signal for longer distances.

Reported capacity
The number that appears on the screen indicating the maximum number of bytes that can be stored on a disk.

Reset switch
A switch on the computer case that refreshes the computer hardware without going through the full startup procedure.

Resolution
The distance between subpels of the same color; the number of pels per line and the number of lines that can be produced on a monitor.

Retransmission
The process of resending a previously sent packet because the destination network resource suspects the data within the packet is corrupted.

RGB color model
The method of blending red, green, and blue to create various colors. Called an additive color model.

RM
See RealMedia.

RMS
See Root mean square.

ROM
See Read-only memory.

Root mean square
A measurement of the amount of power that is continually delivered to the speaker by the amplifier.

RS-232
See Serial port.

Sample rate generator
A component of a sound card that determines the sample rate.

Sampling
A method used by a sound card to capture most of an analog sound.

Sampling method
The technique used to sample a sound wave by a sound card.

Sampling rate
The number of times per second a sample of a sound wave is taken by the sound card.

Sampling size
The amount of information taken during each sample taken by the sound card.

Satellite modem
A modem used to receive information from a satellite.

Scan
The technique of using a scanner to convert an image into a digital image.

Scanner
A digital cameralike device that converts printed images into a graphic file.

Scanning
The method of zigzaging a CRT screen.

SCSI
See Small Computer System Interface.

SDRAM
See Synchronous DRAM.

Sector
A segment of a track where data is stored

Self-monitoring and reporting technology
A hard disk drive that continually examines its components in an effort to detect a potential problem.

Sequencing
A method that tracks the order of packets.

Serial port
A connector on the motherboard that sends and receives information a bit at a time to and from external devices such as a modem.

Servomotor
A motor whose rotation can be controlled incrementally.

SGRAM
See Synchronous graphics RAM.

Shadow mask
A mask made of triangular shaped holes.

Shareware
Software downloadable from the Internet that is available for a nominal charge.

Shelf life
The time period after manufacturing when the quality of the product becomes unacceptable.

Shutter
A device that exposes light to the light-sensitive material in a camera.

Signal System 7
A third communications channel in the telephone network used to manage telephone calls.

Silver halide crystals
A coating on film that change colors when exposed to light.

Simultaneous peripheral operation online
A term used to describe a printer server.

Slack space
Unfilled space in a cluster.

Slot
A receptacle attached to the motherboard that accepts the edge of the circuit board that contains the processor very similar to an expansion slot.

Slotted mask
A mask made of large rectangular slots.

Small Computer System Interface
A connector on the motherboard that sends and receives at fast speeds information and enables multiple external devices such as a scanner to be connected to the same port.

Socket
A receptacle attached to the motherboard that contains several holds, each of which is designed to match a pin in the processor.

Soldered
The technique of using heated metal to connect together two pieces of conductive material such as pins on a chip and etched wires on a circuit board.

Sound
Vibrations within the audible frequency range.

Sound card
A circuit that records, generates, and reproduces sound.

Spike
A sudden surge of electricity.

SPOOL
See Simultaneous peripheral operation online.

Spot size
The diameter of the electron beam.

Spread-Spectrum
A wireless radio network is an alternative to the single frequency networks and uses multiple frequencies to transmit the signal using one of two methods.

SRAM
See Static RAM.

Startup procedure
A process that occurs when a computer is powered up that prepares the computer for operation. Also called booting the computer.

Static RAM
RAM that is not refreshed frequently when the computer is powered up.

Streaming video
Transfers and displays video before the entire file reaches the browser.

Stripe pitch
The distance between stripes on a monitor.

Stylus
A pencillike device used with a graphics tablet to draw images on the computer screen.

Subpel
A segment of a pel that generates a specific color.

Subtractive color model
A color model that removes degrees of primitive colors to create other colors.

Subwoofer
A speaker designed to reproduce low frequency sound.

Superscalar architecture
A design that provides multiple pipelining in a processor enabling multiple instructions to be processed at the same time; *see* Pipelining

Synchronization range
A characteristic of a monitor that specifies the bandwidth of the monitor.

Synchronous DRAM
Video image RAM that has an 8-nanosecond access time.

Synchronous graphics RAM
Video image RAM that has a 6-nanosecond access time.

Synchronous motherboard
The chip set on the motherboard adjusts the speed of a bus based on the speed of other buses on the motherboard.

System board
A term used to refer to a motherboard.

TCP/IP
A protocol that establishes communications rules for networks including the Internet.

Three-dimensional sound
A single sound wave heard directly by two ears and the same sound wave reflected from other objects such as walls and trees.

Throughput
A measurement of the number of instructions that can be processed by the processor per second.

Time delay
The length of the pause between the time a key is pressed and when the keyboard sends repeating keys to the keyboard controller.

Tonal value
See Optical density rate.

Toner
A chemical compound that contains dry-ink-like material and a bonding agent.

Touch pad
A pointing device where a finger is used to move the mouse cursor; commonly found on laptop computers.

Track

A circular-like area of a disk or CD where data is stored.

Trackball

A pointing device that is an inverted mouse.

TrackPoint

A pointing stick introduced by IBM and commonly found on laptop computers.

Trailer

The last few bytes of a sector.

Transistor

A silicon-based device that performs the function as an electronic switch.

Transparency adapter

A device connected to a scanner to scan slides, photographic negatives, and transparencies.

Two-dimensional sound

A single sound wave heard by two ears.

Typemantic action

Typing metrics such as time delay.

Unicode

A standard that associates letters and symbols with a 16-bit or 32-bit number.

Universal serial bus

A connector on the motherboard that sends and receives at fast speeds information a bit at a time to and from external devices.

Universal serial bus hub

A device connected to the USB that accepts multiple USB devices.

UNIX

A computer operating system that can manage multiple users and multiple applications using the computer at the same time.

USB hub

See Universal serial bus hub.

USB port

See Universal serial bus.

Vacuum tube

An electronic switch that uses a charged plate to change the flow of electricity in a circuit.

Vectoring

A printing technique used to move the print head to a particular coordinate and print a pel on the page.

Vertical scanning frequency

The length of time taken to refresh the screen. Same as the refresh rate.

VFAT

A file allocation table standard that uses extended file names

Video cable

A cable that connects the video display adapter and the monitor.

Video display adapter

Circuitry that controls information sent to the monitor.

Video glasses

A monitor built into eyeglasses.

Video image RAM

Memory used to store video information.

Virtual 86 mode

A mode of operation for a personal computer that operates in protected mode, but simulates running in real mode using an 8086 family processor. This is used to run old DOS programs on new computers.

Virtual circuit

A temporary connection between two points on the telephone network that disappears once the call is completed.

Virtual memory

Memory that seems to exist but doesn't physically exist. An operating system combines physical memory with hard disk space to create virtual memory.

Voice modem

A modem that transmits and receives data, faxes, and voice.

Volt

The amount of electricity flowing over a wire.

Voltage regulator

Circuitry on the motherboard that maintains a steady voltage flow to components.

WAP

See Wireless Application Protocol.

Watt

The multiplication of volts and amperes, a measurement of current, to define a measurement of electrical work.

Wave height

A measurement of the energy of a wave.

Wave length

The distance between the height of two waves.

Wave table synthesis

A technique used by a sound card to produce the sound of a real instrument by using samplings of real instruments.

Waveform audio file

A file that contains a digitized recording.

Wave-guide synthesis

A technique used to create a virtual instrument with all the harmonics found in the real instrument.

Wax printer

A printer that uses melted wax to create an image on paper.

Webcam

A camera that connects to the Internet and provides regular images from one location.

Windows RAM

A type of video image RAM

Wireless Application Protocol

Defines how information is to be transferred between the digital cellular network and the Internet.

Wireless Markup Language

Used to create WAP applications.

WML

See Wireless Markup Language.

WRAM

See Windows RAM.

X-Axis

Left and right movement.

Z-Axis

Up and down movement.

Y-Axis

Forward and back movement.

Index

J

K

U

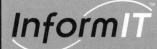

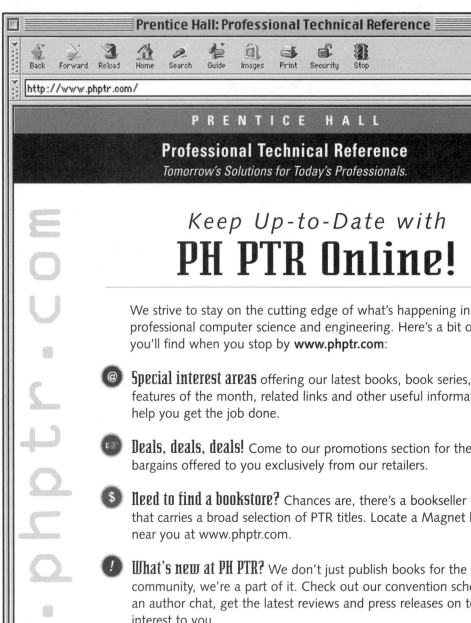